Legal Writing and Analysis

p 23-28

Second Edition

ASPEN PUBLISHERS

Legal Writing and Analysis

Second Edition

Linda H. Edwards
Mercer University

Wolters Kluwer
Law & Business

AUSTIN   BOSTON   CHICAGO   NEW YORK   THE NETHERLANDS

Aspen Publishers
Attn: Permissions Department
76 Ninth Avenue, 7th Floor
New York, NY 10011-5201

To contact Customer Care, e-mail customer.care@aspenpublishers.com, call 1-800-234-1660, fax 1-800-901-9075, or mail correspondence to:

Aspen Publishers
Attn: Order Department
PO Box 990
Frederick, MD 21705

Printed in the United States of America.

2 3 4 5 6 7 8 9 0

ISBN 978-0-7355-6229-5

Library of Congress Cataloging-in-Publication Data

Edwards, Linda Holdeman, 1948-
    Legal writing and analysis / Linda H. Edwards. – 2nd ed.
        p. cm.
    Includes bibliographical references and index.
    ISBN 978-0-7355-6229-5
    1. Legal composition. 2. Briefs–United States. I. Title.

    KF250.E378 2007
    808'.06634–dc22

                                                            2006101316

About Wolters Kluwer Law & Business

Wolters Kluwer Law & Business is a leading provider of research information and workflow solutions in key specialty areas. The strengths of the individual brands of Aspen Publishers, CCH, Kluwer Law International and Loislaw are aligned within Wolters Kluwer Law & Business to provide comprehensive, in-depth solutions and expert-authored content for the legal, professional and education markets.

CCH was founded in 1913 and has served more than four generations of business professionals and their clients. The CCH products in the Wolters Kluwer Law & Business group are highly regarded electronic and print resources for legal, securities, antitrust and trade regulation, government contracting, banking, pension, payroll, employment and labor, and healthcare reimbursement and compliance professionals.

Aspen Publishers is a leading information provider for attorneys, business professionals and law students. Written by preeminent authorities, Aspen products offer analytical and practical information in a range of specialty practice areas from securities law and intellectual property to mergers and acquisitions and pension/benefits. Aspen's trusted legal education resources provide professors and students with high-quality, up-to-date and effective resources for successful instruction and study in all areas of the law.

Kluwer Law International supplies the global business community with comprehensive English-language international legal information. Legal practitioners, corporate counsel and business executives around the world rely on the Kluwer Law International journals, loose-leafs, books and electronic products for authoritative information in many areas of international legal practice.

Loislaw is a premier provider of digitized legal content to small law firm practitioners of various specializations. Loislaw provides attorneys with the ability to quickly and efficiently find the necessary legal information they need, when and where they need it, by facilitating access to primary law as well as state-specific law, records, forms and treatises.

Wolters Kluwer Law & Business, a unit of Wolters Kluwer, is headquartered in New York and Riverwoods, Illinois. Wolters Kluwer is a leading multinational publisher and information services company.

To Frances,
for her unfailing support,

and to Emilie and Katherine,
for the inspiration of their courage

Summary of Contents

Contents

Part Three: Writing the Discussion of a Legal Question   63

Part Four: Predictive Writing   **125**

Part Five: The Shift to Advocacy   **157**

Appendices   **299**

Preface

This book is a concise text that tracks the traditional legal writing course syllabus. It groups relevant material together instead of scattering it in different stages of the writing process. It includes numerous examples and uses frequent short exercises to encourage students to apply new material. It provides students with the necessary structure for organizing a legal discussion. Finally, it includes discrete materials that offer students the opportunity to explore a deeper level of understanding than its small size would imply.

The Book's Organization: Part One explains the legal system and introduces lawyers' roles within that system. Part Two explains how to work with the raw material for analysis. It covers briefing and synthesizing cases, analogizing and distinguishing case law, and interpreting statutes. Part Three presents the traditional organizational formats for communicating the analysis of a legal question (the basic IRAC or CRAC structures). Parts Four and Five cover the components of office memos, letters, trial-level briefs, and appellate briefs. Part Six presents material on citation and style and Part Seven introduces oral argument.

How This Book Differs: The primary difference between this book and my earlier text, *Legal Writing: Process, Analysis, and Organization*, is the way the material is grouped. This book is not so unrelenting in its process approach, though it still recognizes writing as a process. The first book presents its material in stages defined entirely by a writer's progress toward completing a particular assignment. While that approach offers real advantages, course time and resources do not always permit its use and *Process, Analysis, and Organization* is less flexible pedagogically. In contrast, this book groups relevant material together in a more efficient manner while still providing guidance about the writing process. That guidance is identified throughout the book by the recurring symbol shown in the margin.

Examples and Exercises: Another characteristic of this book is its frequent use of examples and exercises. For instance, Chapter 1 succinctly describes the writing roles of planning and prevention, prediction, and persuasion, and then describes several hypothetical situations asking students to decide which kind of writing each situation would require. Later in that chapter, after an introduction to plagiarism and the purposes of citation, students see examples of when to cite and then read a short legal discussion and identify the ideas that need citations. This pattern of examples and exercises continues throughout the book.

Organizing a Legal Discussion: The book explains the standard IRAC and CRAC paradigms and explains how to use those paradigms in discussions of multiple issues. The book introduces the structures inherent in rules and shows students how to use those rule structures to identify issues and to organize their written discussions.

Flexible Levels: Each major section presents its material at a basic introductory level so all the core information is concisely grouped. Courses that have time for a more advanced treatment can also cover optional chapters that take students deeper into the material. For instance, the core chapters of Part Two explain briefing and synthesizing cases and interpreting statutes. This material is presented at a level appropriate for all students. Then, Part Two concludes with an optional more advanced chapter explaining the major forms of reasoning lawyers use and providing examples and simple exercises for that material.

Similarly, in Part Three, the core chapters explain how to organize and write a legal analysis, including how to analogize and distinguish cases. This material is presented at a level appropriate for all students. Then Part Three ends with an optional chapter showing students how to broaden and deepen their analysis in each part of their IRAC or CRAC structure. This chapter can be assigned as required reading, assigned as optional reading, or omitted entirely.

Finally, in Part Five, the core chapters explain how to write a trial-level and appellate brief. These chapters present everything a first-year student needs to know to write her first brief. Then Part Five ends with an optional and completely free-standing chapter explaining how a lawyer can use her awareness of a judge's legal philosophy to target her argument more effectively. Again, this supplemental chapter can be assigned as required reading, assigned as optional reading, or omitted entirely.

The goal of this book is to provide a pedagogically flexible text for basic legal writing, readily adaptable to fit the needs of any traditional legal writing course. It presents the fundamentals in a concise, lucid style for first year students. It also offers discrete sections of more advanced material that can be included or omitted at the discretion of the professor. The book includes ample examples and exercises, which relieve the professor of the burden of generating such material, but that may nonetheless be supplemented at any point. It is, in short, a basic text, adaptable to a wide variety of legal writing programs.

In the Second Edition, Chapter 12 ("Writing an Office Memo") now contains an additional format option for drafting a Question Presented. Otherwise, most of the changes pertain to re-ordering some of the material in Part Five ("The Shift To Advocacy"). The coverage has been reorganized to facilitate assigning the material in a useful order. In this edition, Chapter 14 is streamlined to include only the necessary introductory material and the standard components of both trial-level and appellate briefs. Chapter 15 then explains how to draft both questions presented and point headings. Chapter 16 covers writing the argument section and now includes the material on different kinds of legal issues (formerly found in Chapter 14). Chapter 17 now covers the standards of review, so that free-standing material can be assigned when and where appropriate. Chapter 18 covers fact statements (formerly Chapter 16). Finally, the citation and quotation material (Chapter 20) has been revised to match the current editions of the *ALWD Citation Manual* and the *Bluebook*.

Linda H. Edwards

December 2006

Acknowledgments

This book has benefited immeasurably from the assistance and support of many people. First and foremost, I am grateful to all of my Mercer colleagues. Their belief in the importance of legal writing has been manifested again and again through the years and has been the foundation on which this project, among many others, is built. Special thanks go to Susan Bay, Ted Blumoff, Jim Hunt, Mark Jones, Hal Lewis, Adam Milani, Jack Sammons, and Michael Smith for reading and commenting on parts of the book. Two Mercer Deans, Larry Dessem and Mike Sabbath, have assisted in innumerable ways. Billie Blaine and Carrie Murray provided careful research assistance, and Sandy Studdard provided ready administrative support. Finally, I am grateful to my students, whose hard work and probing questions have kept me learning.

I am privileged to be part of a remarkable national legal writing community. Space does not permit listing all of the colleagues who have shared generously of their vision, enthusiasm, wisdom, and experience. I hope they each know how thankful I am for their friendship and for their many contributions to our discipline. Two names cannot be omitted, however: Mary Lawrence, who has mentored generations of legal writing colleagues, and Tom Blackwell, whose memory will continue to guide us for years to come.

The chapters of this book dealing with the grounding of analysis and argument in underlying theories of jurisprudence would not have been possible without the friendship, advice, and encouragement of doctrinal law colleagues, especially Scott Brewer, Martha Minow, and Joseph Singer. Errors, of course, are my own. I owe a debt of gratitude to Darby Dickerson for her invaluable assistance with Chapter 20. Thanks are due also to the wonderful people at Aspen Publishers, especially Carol McGeehan, Melody Davies, Richard Mixter, Betsy Kenny, and Peggy Rehberger. I am especially grateful to the anonymous Aspen reviewers whose comments contributed so significantly to the book.

I would also like to thank the following copyright holder for permission to reprint the map of the federal judicial circuits:

Summer Judicial Staff Directory 935 (CQ Press 2006). Copyright © 2006 by Congressional Quarterly, Inc. Phone (202) 729-1817; URL: *http://jsd.cq.com*.

And finally, my deepest thanks to Dan Edwards. Yet again, words fail.

Legal Writing and Analysis

Second Edition

PART ONE

Lawyers and the Legal Landscape

CHAPTER 1

Overview of the Lawyer's Role

Most students entering law school would not call themselves writers; nor would they expect that in three years they will be professional writers, earning a significant part of their income by writing for publication. Yet that is precisely what lawyers do. Most lawyers write and publish more pages than do novelists, and with greater consequences hanging in the balance.

This book introduces the critical skill of legal writing. In this chapter, we begin with an exploration of the kinds of writing lawyers do, both in litigation and in other kinds of law practice. Understanding this legal landscape will help you understand the legal issues of the cases you read and the various research and writing tasks you will be asked to perform.

I. WRITING AND A LAWYER'S ROLES

Lawyers write many kinds of documents—court papers, letters, legal instruments, and internal working documents for the law firm. As different as these documents are from each other, they all fall into one of three categories defined by the lawyer's primary role when writing them: (1) planning and preventive writing; (2) predictive writing; and (3) persuasive writing. A lawyer's writing differs significantly depending on which of these three roles the lawyer is performing.

A LAWYER'S WRITING ROLES
- Planning and Preventive Writing
- Predictive Writing
- Persuasive Writing

Planning and Preventive Writing. Lawyers engage in planning and preventive writing when they draft transactional documents such as wills, trusts, leases, mortgages, partnership agreements, and contracts. Planning documents define the rights of the parties and the limits of their conduct, much as case law and statutes do for society at large. Thus, planning documents create what is, in effect, the "law" of the transaction. In some ways, planning and preventive writing is the most satisfying of the lawyering roles. Through planning and preventive writing, the lawyer creates and structures some of the most important transactions and relationships in an individual client's life or in the commercial world. Also, with careful planning, the lawyer can forestall future disputes, and most lawyers would rather help clients prevent injury than recover for injury.

Predictive Writing. Predictive writing is part of another satisfying task—client counseling. Clients often seek a lawyer's advice when they must make an important decision. When that decision has legal implications, the lawyer must research the law and predict the legal result of the contemplated action.

Lawyers engage in predictive writing in both transactional and litigation settings. In transactional settings, the lawyer must predict legal outcomes in order to analyze and prevent possible problems. In litigation, the client and the lawyer must decide many questions, ranging from relatively routine matters of litigation management (such as which motions to file) to such fundamental matters as whether to settle the case. To resolve any of these questions, the lawyer must predict the legal outcomes of the possible courses of action and must communicate those predictions to the client or to another lawyer working on the case.

In predictive writing, the lawyer must analyze the relevant law *objectively,* as a judge would do. The most common documents for communicating predictive analysis are the *office memo* (addressed to another lawyer who has requested the analysis) or the *opinion letter* (addressed to the client). The lawyer's role is to predict a legal result as accurately as possible, objectively weighing the strengths and weaknesses of the possible arguments. The answer may not be the answer the client or the requesting lawyer wants to hear, but it is the answer they need in order to make a good decision.

Persuasive Writing. Legal problems cannot always be prevented, and some of them inevitably result in litigation or a proceeding before some other decision-maker. When that happens, the lawyer takes on a persuasive role. No matter what result the lawyer may have *predicted*, the lawyer now must try to persuade the decision-maker to reach the result most favorable to the client. The lawyer must marshal the strongest arguments in her client's favor and refute opposing arguments. The most common persuasive document is the *brief* (also called a *memorandum of law*).

Although the goals of prediction and persuasion differ, on a fundamental level predictive (objective) analysis and persuasive analysis cannot be separated. To predict a result, a writer must understand the arguments each side would present. To persuade, a writer must understand how the argument will strike a neutral reader. Thus, as you improve your predictive analysis, you will be improving your persuasive analysis as well, and vice versa.

Before you go on, turn to Appendix A, which contains a sample office memo, and to Appendices B and C, which contain sample briefs. We will study the parts of each document in more detail later. Your goal at this point is simply to understand the function of each kind of document and to see what the end products will look like before beginning the process of creating them.

EXERCISE 1-1

Identify the primary lawyering role called for in each of the following situations:

1. A client (a widower) has been diagnosed with a fatal form of cancer.
   a. The client asks a lawyer to draft a will and trust to protect his assets for his children. *planning/preventative*
   b. The client asks whether there is a procedure by which he can designate a foster family to care for his children after his death and whether it would be wise for him to do so. *predictive*
   c. The client asks the lawyer to file a lawsuit seeking recovery against his employer for exposure to carcinogens in the workplace. *persuasive*
2. A client has located a piece of real property she wishes to buy and lease to a commercial tenant. The title registry lists an easement allowing the owner of the property next door to use the driveway along the back of the property. The client wishes to expand the existing structure on the property and eliminate the driveway.
   a. The client asks the lawyer whether the easement can be challenged legally. *predictive*
   b. The client asks the lawyer to approach the owner of the property next door and seek the release of the easement. *persuasive*
   c. The client asks the lawyer to draft the release of the easement and also to draft a lease for the new commercial tenant to sign. *planning/preventative*

II. OVERVIEW OF A CIVIL CASE

Since most of your first-year courses focus on reading appellate opinions, your understanding of those cases will be improved if you have an overview of how a civil case proceeds through the litigation process. This section summarizes the course of a fairly simple personal injury law suit with only one legal claim against only one defendant and raising no ancillary issues. As you read it, notice how many litigation stages require legal research and the writing of a legal document (identified by italics), even in a relatively simple case.

Initial Research. A civil case begins when a client consults a lawyer about a legal problem. Usually the client has been injured and believes that his injury was caused by the wrongful conduct of someone else. The client wants to know whether he has any legal recourse and, if so, whether he should pursue it.

To decide these questions, the lawyer must gather all the relevant facts and research the relevant legal issues. Rarely will the lawyer already know all the law that will be required to answer these initial questions, and the lawyer may not have time to research all of them herself. She may ask an associate to research some of them for her. The requesting lawyer will write *file memos* to the associate, providing the necessary information and setting out exactly what she needs to know. After finishing the requested research, the associate will write an *office memo* to the requesting lawyer, communicating the results of the research.

The first lawyer will review the research, analyze the client's possible claims, and provide that analysis to the client. The lawyer and client are likely to discuss the analysis face to face, but often the lawyer also writes an *opinion letter* memorializing the results of the research and her advice to the client. Together the client and the lawyer decide whether to proceed with the claim.

Initial Negotiation Process. The next step is writing a *demand letter* to the party whose conduct appears to have caused the injury (the defendant). Typically, the demand letter will explain the legal basis for believing that the defendant's conduct was wrongful; the legal and factual basis for believing that the conduct caused the plaintiff's injury; and the kinds of damages the law permits in such a case. The lawyer for the defendant will write a *response to the demand letter* explaining the legal and factual bases for the defendant's defenses. The negotiation process may continue for some time, with settlement offers and counter-offers communicated by additional *settlement letters* between the lawyers and *client letters* conveying settlement offers.

Filing a Lawsuit and Resolving Initial Defenses. If the case does not settle, the plaintiff's lawyer chooses the appropriate court and files a *complaint*, a document that sets out the facts of the case and the legal basis for the claim. Once the defendant's lawyer receives the complaint, he has only a few weeks to draft and file a response. His research may have shown that the defendant has one or more defenses that can be raised immediately. If so, the lawyer will raise these defenses in documents called *motions*, which state the defense and ask the court for some kind of action, such as dismissal of the case. Each motion will be supported by a *brief* (also called a *memorandum of law*), explaining the legal and factual basis for the defense. The motions may also be accompanied by other supporting documents, such as *affidavits* from witnesses and copies of evidentiary documents bearing on the defense.

Each time one party files a motion asking the court to take some action, the other party must file a *responsive brief*, usually explaining the legal and factual basis for the argument that the court should deny the motion. The responsive brief may be accompanied by other supporting documents such as *affidavits*. The party who filed the motion (the moving party) will file a *reply brief* addressing the arguments raised in the responsive brief, and there may be a hearing on the motion, after which the court will decide the issue.

Assuming that the court declines to dismiss the case, the defendant's lawyer must file an *answer*, a document that admits or denies all the facts alleged in the complaint and may raise additional defenses as well. The defendant's lawyer also may file a *counterclaim*, a document that alleges some wrongful and injurious conduct on the part of the plaintiff. The plaintiff will then file an *answer* to the defendant's counterclaim. The answer admits or denies all the facts alleged in the counterclaim and raises all possible remaining defenses against the counterclaim.

Factual Discovery. Now the case is ready for the discovery phase. In this phase, the parties gather all the available evidence in an effort to prepare for trial. During discovery, both parties draft and file *interrogatories* (questions directed to each other) and *responses to interrogatories* (answers to the questions). They draft and file *requests for production of documents, requests for admissions*, and *notices of depositions* (occasions for oral questioning of witnesses under oath). Parties can file *requests for entry on land* (to inspect the premises) or *requests for medical examination* (to subject a person to a physical or psychiatric examination). During the discovery phase, disputes may arise over how much or what kind of information can be sought. These disputes can become the subject of *motions to compel* (filed by the party seeking discovery) or *motions for a protective order* (filed by the party seeking to prevent discovery). Like other motions, discovery motions and *responses* to them are accompanied by supporting *briefs* and *affidavits*.

Motions for Summary Judgment. After the discovery phase, the parties often draft and file *motions for summary judgment.* A party seeking summary judgment is asking the court to rule on some or all of the claims or defenses without the necessity of a trial. Summary judgment motions are supported by *briefs*, by *statements of uncontested facts*, and by *affidavits*, excerpts from depositions, evidentiary documents, and excerpts from written discovery. The opposing party files a *responsive brief, affidavits*, and other supporting documents resisting the motion, to which the moving party files a *reply brief*. Oral argument is often held. The court might resolve the entire case at the summary judgment stage, or it might resolve some of the claims or defenses, thus narrowing the issues remaining for trial.

Trial. If the parties do not reach a settlement, they continue with trial preparations. If the case will be tried to a jury, both parties draft and file a set of proposed *jury instructions*. Jury instructions are statements to be read to the jury to help them understand the law governing the case and their role in the process. Each party also drafts and files a *trial brief,* a document that summarizes the evidence expected to be introduced, raises and argues any evidentiary issues the party anticipates, and argues for the adoption of that party's version of the jury instructions.

Trial begins with jury selection (if the case will be tried to a jury) and opening statements by each party's lawyer. Then the parties call their witnesses and offer their evidence. The trial concludes with closing statements from each lawyer, the reading of the jury instructions (if the case is tried to a jury), and a decision by the judge or the jury. Some *post-trial motions* may be decided, and then a final *judgment* will be entered.

Appeal(s). A party who is dissatisfied with the result of the trial court proceedings usually can file a *notice of appeal* to a higher court. This party is called the appellant. The other party (the appellee) may file a *notice of appeal* as well, raising other objections to the trial court result. A series of documents identify the issues to be argued in the appeal and designate the record of the trial court proceedings that will be sent to the appellate court.

After the record has been prepared and filed, the parties each file *briefs, responsive briefs*, and *reply briefs* arguing the issues raised in the appeal. Oral argument is often held, after which the appellate court issues an opinion. In some circumstances, either or both parties may seek to appeal the appellate court's decision to an even higher court. If so, the procedure described in this paragraph is repeated there. When all appeals are completed, the losing party either complies with the judgment (if applicable) or enforcement proceedings begin. After the judgment has been paid, a *satisfaction of judgment* is filed, and the case is closed.

III. ETHICAL DUTIES

Your legal practice, including your legal writing, will be governed by the ethical standards your jurisdiction has adopted for lawyers. Most jurisdictions have adopted a version of either the American Bar Association's Model Rules of Professional Conduct or the earlier Model Code of Professional Responsibility. Sanctions for violation of these rules range from private censure to disbarment. No matter what your jurisdiction's ethical rules or your lawyering role, your legal writing must meet at least the following professional obligations:

1. *Competency.* A lawyer must provide competent representation, including legal knowledge, skill, thoroughness, and preparation.[1]
2. *Diligence.* A lawyer's representation must be diligent.[2]
3. *Promptness.* A lawyer must do the client's work promptly.[3]
4. *Confidentiality.* Generally, a lawyer must not reveal a client's confidences except with the client's permission.[4]
5. *All lawyers are bound by the rules of ethics.* Every lawyer is bound by the rules of professional conduct, no matter whether that lawyer is in charge of the case or working under the direction of another lawyer.[5]
6. *Loyalty.* A lawyer's advice must be candid and unbiased. The advice must not be adversely influenced by conflicting loyalties to another client, to a third party, or to the lawyer's own interests.[6]

In addition to these general standards, your predictive legal writing must meet at least the following ethical standards dealing with giving advice:

7. *Moral, economic, and political factors.* While a lawyer's advice must provide an accurate assessment of the law, it may refer also to moral, economic, social, and political factors relevant to the client's situation.[7] However, the lawyer's representation of a client does not constitute a personal endorsement of the client's activities or views.[8]
8. *Criminal or fraudulent activity.* A lawyer must not advise or assist a client to commit a crime or a fraud.[9] When the client expects unethical

---

1. Model R. Prof. Conduct 1.1.
2. Model R. Prof. Conduct 1.3.
3. Model R. Prof. Conduct 1.3.
4. Model R. Prof. Conduct 1.6.
5. Model R. Prof. Conduct 5.2.
6. Model R. Prof. Conduct 1.7 and 2.1.
7. Model R. Prof. Conduct 2.1.
8. Model R. Prof. Conduct 1.2(b).
9. Model R. Prof. Conduct 1.2(d).

assistance, the lawyer must explain to the client the ethical limitations on the lawyer's conduct.[10]

Finally, your persuasive legal writing must meet at least the following ethical standards:

9. A brief-writer must not knowingly make a false statement of law.[11]
10. A brief-writer must not knowingly fail to disclose to the court directly adverse legal authority in the controlling jurisdiction.[12]
11. A brief-writer must not knowingly make a false statement of fact or fail to disclose a material fact when disclosure is necessary to avoid assisting a criminal or fraudulent act by the client.[13]
12. A brief-writer must not assert a legal argument unless there is a nonfrivolous basis for doing so.[14]
13. A brief-writer must not communicate ex parte[15] with a judge about the merits of a pending case, unless the particular ex parte communication is specifically permitted by law.[16]
14. A brief-writer must not intentionally disregard filing requirements or other obligations imposed by court rules.[17]

These ethical standards will apply to your legal writing after you are a lawyer. They will also apply, directly or indirectly, to the legal writing you do as a law clerk before you are admitted to the bar. They will be among the standards by which your legal writing teacher evaluates your law school writing. Be sure that every document you write meets these standards of professional responsibility.

IV. LEGAL CITATION

A. Plagiarism

Plagiarism is the act of presenting as one's own, words or ideas taken from another source. Most of us first encountered the concept of plagiarism in an academic environment. In academe, plagiarism occurs primarily in one or both of these two situations: (1) failure to attribute an idea to the source from which it was drawn; or (2) failure to use quotation marks to show that the words themselves, not just the idea, came from another source. In an academic setting, authoring a document constitutes a representation that the author is the source of all ideas and words not otherwise attributed. Thus, in an

---

10. Model R. Prof. Conduct 1.4(a)(5).
11. ABA Model R. Prof. Conduct 3.3(a)(1).
12. Model R. Prof. Conduct 3.3(a)(3).
13. Model R. Prof. Conduct 3.3(a)(1) and (2).
14. Model R. Prof. Conduct 3.1.
15. *Ex parte*, in this context, means without notice to other parties in the litigation.
16. Model R. Prof. Conduct 3.5(b).
17. Model R. Prof. Conduct 3.4(c) and 3.2.

academic setting, failure to attribute borrowed words or ideas constitutes plagiarism. It is both a lie and a theft.

In law practice, the concept of plagiarism can be confusing. Lawyers and judges often adapt and use, without attribution or quotation marks, language and ideas drawn from other lawyers' work. Firms keep form files and brief banks so documents prepared by one lawyer can be "recycled" by another. Law clerks write opinions to be signed by their judges. Judges incorporate into their opinions sections of briefs filed by the parties' lawyers. Associates write briefs to be signed by partners. Law publishers publish books of pleadings and other forms designed to be used nearly verbatim.

Some question whether the concept of plagiarism applies at all in a law practice setting. They argue that writing in law practice does not carry a representation that the author is the source of all unattributed ideas and words, especially not when the document is asserting a legal point. In legal practice, the writer's goal is not to take personal credit for originating everything in the document, but rather to serve the client efficiently and well. The identity of the writer is irrelevant. Proponents of this position argue that service to a client requires presenting the most effective material in the most effective manner for the least cost. Thus, they assert, a lawyer's signature on a document constitutes only the lawyer's representation that the document is not being presented for any improper purpose, including the purpose of causing needless increase in the cost of litigation; that the legal contentions are not frivolous; and that any factual contentions or denials are reasonably supported by the evidence.[18]

The application of the concept of plagiarism to law practice is currently a topic of debate. No matter what standards may apply to *law practice,* however, remember that your law school writing is being done in an academic environment where the writing assignment has pedagogical goals rather than goals of efficiency and economy. The law school project focuses on enabling the writer *to learn* and the teacher *to evaluate* that learning. You must generate ideas and text on your own so you can learn that skill, and your teacher must be able to identify your ideas and text to be able to evaluate them.

Your school's honor code probably prohibits plagiarism, which it may define to include conduct resulting either from an intent to deceive or from "mere" carelessness. Being charged with an honor code violation is serious business for any student, but especially serious for law students. Soon, you will be applying for admission to the bar, and most Bar Character and Fitness Committees ask questions designed to discover whether you have violated your school's honor code. Any honor code charge brings a risk that the proceeding will have to be reported to the Character and Fitness Committee, that you will have to appear personally to explain the charge, and that your bar admission will be delayed or denied as a result.

So carefully follow your teacher's instructions about using material from another source or working with another student. Be precise in your note-taking so you can remember where you found the ideas you will use and so you can distinguish between paraphrases and quotes. *Unless you have explicit*

---

18. Fed. R. Civ. P. 11(b).

instructions to the contrary, do not use the words or ideas of another without proper attribution and, where appropriate, quotation marks.[19]

B. When to Cite

Citation to authority has twin purposes. First, citations provide your reader with the authority that supports your assertions about the law. Providing your reader with supporting authority is essential to legal analysis and persuasive argument. Your citations should prove that the law is what you say it is and that it means what you say it means.

Second, citations attribute the words and ideas of another author to that author. Because a reader will attribute uncited material to you, a citation is your way of disclaiming credit for the words and ideas you did not create. Therefore, you should cite when you quote and when you paraphrase (that is, when you use your own words to express the authority's idea).

WHEN TO USE CITATIONS
1. When you assert a legal principle.

Example:
To recover under an implied warranty of habitability, a tenant must show that she gave the landlord notice of the defect and allowed time for its correction. *King v. Moorehead,* 495 S.W.2d 65 (Mo. App. 1973).

2. When you refer to or describe the content of an authority.

Example:
In a leading case, the leased premises had faulty sewer pipes, defective wiring, and crumbling ceilings. *Hilder v. St. Peter,* 478 A.2d 202 (Vt. 1984).

3. When you quote.

Example:
An earlier court had observed that today's tenants "seek a well known package of goods and services—a package which includes not merely walls and ceilings, but also adequate heat, light and ventilation, serviceable plumbing facilities, secure windows and doors, proper sanitation, and proper maintenance." *Javins v. First Nat'l Realty Corp.,* 428 F.2d 1071, 1074 (D.C. Cir. 1970).

---

19. *See* Chapter 20 for a discussion of when quotation marks are appropriate.

EXERCISE 1-2
Recognizing Ideas That Need Citations

Read the following passage[20] and identify the statements for which a citation is either necessary or desirable. Be prepared to explain your answers.

1   A lawyer has a fiduciary relationship with his or her client. The fiduciary aspect
2   of the relationship is said to arise after the formation of the attorney-client
3   relationship, and it applies to a fee agreement reached after the attorney-client
4   relationship has been entered.

5   At least three reasons support the imposition of fiduciary obligations on a
6   lawyer. First, once the relationship is established, the client likely will have
7   begun to depend on the attorney's integrity, fairness, and judgment. Second, the
8   attorney may have acquired information about the client that gives the attorney
9   an unfair advantage in negotiations between them. Finally, the client generally
10 will not be able to change attorneys easily, but rather will be economically or
11 personally dependent on the attorney's continued representation.

12 Several cases illustrate the contours of the attorney's fiduciary duty. In *Benson v.*
13 *State Bar,* the attorney borrowed money from a current client. The attorney "was
14 heavily in debt, and insolvent, at the time he approached [the client] for these
15 loans." In return for the loans, the attorney gave the client unsecured promissory
16 notes. In disbarring the lawyer, the court described the client's trust in the lawyer's
17 judgment and wrote:

18   The gravamen of the charge is abuse of that trust, and regardless of petitioner's
19   contention that he never specifically recommended the unsecured loans to
20   [the client], it is undisputed that in soliciting them he failed to reveal the
21   extent of his preexisting indebtedness and financial distress.

22 In *People v. Smith,* an attorney was under investigation for drug use, and he
23 offered to cooperate with Colorado police as an undercover informant. He secretly
24 recorded a telephone conversation with a former client in which he asked the
25 former client to sell him cocaine. He then met with the former client wearing a
26 body microphone. The recorded conversations ultimately were used to convict the
27 former client of three felony charges. The Colorado Supreme Court held that
28 although the attorney

29   no longer represented the [former client], the conduct in all probability would
30   not have occurred had [the attorney] not relied upon the trust and confidence
31   placed in him by the [former client] as a result of the recently completed
32   attorney-client relationship between the two. The undisclosed use of a record-
33   ing device necessarily involves elements of deception and trickery which do
34   not comport with the high standards of candor and fairness to which all
        attorneys are bound.

35 For these and other offenses, Smith was suspended from the practice of law.

---

20. Modified from Stephen Gillers, *Regulation of Lawyers: Problems of Law and Ethics* 61-62 (4th ed. Aspen 1995).

CHAPTER 2

The Legal System, the Common Law Process, and Kinds of Authority

The two most important sources of law other than constitutional provisions are case law (common law) and statutes. In this chapter, we begin our study of case law, including the structures and functions of courts and the concepts of precedent, stare decisis, and case holdings. Chapter 3 covers case briefing, the basic analytical tool for reading and understanding cases. Chapter 3 also explores the ways in which individual cases relate to each other. Then in Chapter 4, we will turn our attention specifically to statutes, exploring methods of interpretation and application of these increasingly important sources of law.

I. THE STRUCTURE OF COURT SYSTEMS

Each state has its own court system, and each state also participates in the federal court system. Federal courts have jurisdiction (authority) over cases entrusted to them by the constitution or by federal statutes. For the most part, these are cases raising issues of federal law[1] and cases involving parties from different states when the damages exceed $75,000.[2] State courts also have subject-matter jurisdiction over many of the same cases, so a plaintiff may be able to choose the court system he or she prefers. We will begin with an overview of the federal court system since it operates in the same way in each state.

A. The Federal Court System

The federal court system has three levels. Litigation usually begins in the United States District Court, which is the trial court of general jurisdiction[3]

---

1. 28 U.S.C. §1331 (2001).
2. 28 U.S.C. §1332(a) (2001).
3. A court of general jurisdiction is a court whose jurisdiction is not limited to certain kinds of cases. A court whose jurisdiction is limited is called, not surprisingly, a court of limited jurisdiction. An example of a federal court of limited jurisdiction is the United States Tax Court, which may hear only federal tax cases.

in the federal system. A federal district court may have a number of judges, but normally a proceeding is heard by only one judge. Other judges of that court are busy in other courtrooms hearing other cases.

Each state has at least one federal district, and many have two or more. For instance, California has four districts: the Southern District, the Northern District, the Eastern District, and the Central District. The full name for the federal trial-level court located in Los Angeles is the United States District Court for the Central District of California. The first four words of that long title identify the court as the trial-level federal court. The remaining words identify the court's particular district.

A district court's decision may be appealed to the intermediate appellate court, the United States Court of Appeals. Normally, an appeal is heard by a panel of three judges, but occasionally a case may be heard by all of the judges of that court. In such a case, we say that the court heard the case *en banc*.

For purposes of this intermediate appellate level, the country is divided into thirteen circuits. The First through the Eleventh Circuits cover multistate areas.[4] For instance, decisions appealed from the federal district court in Los Angeles would be heard by the United States Court of Appeals for the Ninth Circuit. Decisions appealed from the federal district court in New York City would be heard by the United States Court of Appeals for the Second Circuit. The first five words of this long title identify the court as the intermediate federal appellate court. The remaining words identify the court's particular circuit.

Figure 2-1 shows the geographic jurisdictions of the federal circuit courts of appeal.

Some federal cases ultimately are appealed to the United States Supreme Court, the highest appellate court in the federal system.[5] The United States Supreme Court reviews only a fraction of the cases decided by the federal circuit courts each year. At the level of the Supreme Court, some preliminary matters are decided by one justice or a panel of justices, but cases receiving full review are heard by all the justices of the Court.

B. State Court Systems

State court systems resemble the federal court system in many respects. Litigation usually begins in a trial court of general jurisdiction.[6] The names of these trial courts vary from state to state, but common names for them are district courts, circuit courts, courts of common pleas, or superior courts.

Most states have at least one intermediate appellate court. Larger states have several, whose jurisdiction is defined geographically, much as in the federal system. At the intermediate level, most appellate cases are decided by

---

4. The other two circuits are the United States Court of Appeals for the District of Columbia, which hears appeals from the District of Columbia, and the United States Court of Appeals for the Federal Circuit, which hears appeals from certain specialized federal courts.

5. The United States Supreme Court can also hear cases from a state's highest appellate court, but only when the state court's ruling was based on federal law.

6. Specialized courts (courts of limited jurisdiction) exist for hearing such matters as juvenile cases, probates of estates, cases alleging small damage amounts, and housing issues.

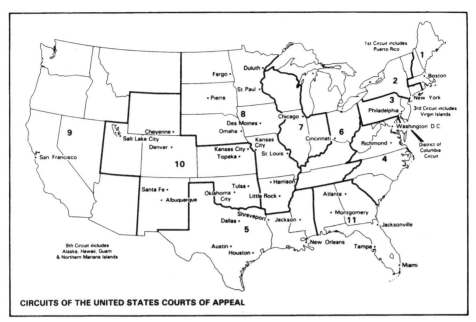

The federal judicial circuits, as shown in *2006 Summer Judicial Staff Directory* 935 (C.Q. Press 2006).

panels of an odd number of judges, often three. Some cases, however, are heard en banc, either initially or after a decision by a panel.

Finally, all states have an appellate court of last resort, the highest appellate court in the state. In most states, this court is called the Supreme Court.[7] Most cases are decided by all justices sitting together. This court is the last and highest forum for deciding matters of state law.

II. THE FUNCTIONS OF TRIAL AND APPELLATE COURTS

The functions of trial courts and appellate courts differ in important ways. Understanding these differences will help you understand the cases you will read and the arguments you can make on behalf of clients.

A. The Functions of Trial Courts

A trial court has two primary functions: deciding what law applies to the case and deciding who did what to whom. In other words, a trial court decides questions of law and questions of fact.

---

7. New York is a notable exception. There, the trial court is called the Supreme Court. The intermediate appellate court is called the Supreme Court, Appellate Division. The highest appellate court in New York is called the Court of Appeals.

A court decides *a question of law* when it decides what the law of that jurisdiction says about a legal question. Does the law allow relief for what the defendant is alleged to have done? What kind of evidence does the law permit the court to consider? What kind of relief is the court permitted to grant? These are pure questions of law. They can be answered solely by doing legal research in the law library. To decide them, the court need not decide anything about what actually happened to these parties. The court need only decide what the law will require *if a particular set of facts turns out to be true.*

A court decides *a question of fact* when it decides what actually happened in this case. Did Smith strike Jones? Did Kerry sign the document? Did Newman pull into the right lane? These are pure questions of fact. They cannot be answered by doing research in the law library. To decide them, the court must listen to the testimony, examine the documents and other exhibits, and decide what happened to these parties.

Questions of fact can be decided by a judge or by a jury. If the case is tried to a jury, decisions on questions of fact are made by the jury and not by the judge.[8] If the case is a bench trial (that is, a case tried to the judge without a jury), decisions on questions of fact are made by the trial judge. Either way, however, questions of law are decided by the trial judge, not a jury.[9]

B. The Functions of Appellate Courts

A trial court's decision usually can be appealed to a higher court. The party who appeals (the appellant) cannot simply argue that the result was wrong and ask the appellate court to decide the entire case again. Rather the appellant must identify the particular question(s) to be reviewed by the appellate court. Generally, a party seeks appellate review of a question of law or a question of fact.[10]

 Since the trial court had the opportunity to observe the witnesses first hand, the trial court's decision on pure questions of fact will not be disturbed by an appellate court unless the decision is clearly erroneous. In essence, to reverse a trial court's factual finding, the appellate court must believe that no reasonable interpretation of the evidence would support the trial court's decision. Thus, questions of fact are peculiarly within the purview of the trial court. Reversals on pure questions of fact are unusual.

The situation is reversed, however, for questions of law. On a question of law, the appellate court is free to decide that the trial judge's understanding of the law was wrong. The appellate court need not defer to the trial judge's understanding of the law. Because it is a higher court, an appellate court's decision on questions of law supersedes the trial judge's opinion. Most reversals involve questions of law.

---

8. A trial judge can, however, change a jury's factual findings if no reasonable understanding of the evidence could have resulted in the jury's findings. Thus the judge acts as a safety net protecting against a jury that has disregarded the evidence.

9. A third category exists: a mixed question of law and fact. We will explore this category in Chapter 17. For our purposes here, it is enough to understand the distinction between pure questions of law and pure questions of fact.

10. We will explore this subject in more detail in Chapter 17's discussion of standards of review.

EXERCISE 2-1

Decide whether an appellate court would have to give any deference to the following statements in a trial court's decision.

1. "The defendant cultivated a garden on the property each year between 1994 and 2002."
2. "To establish a claim to property by adverse possession, a party must prove that his or her use of the property was open and notorious for the entire statutory period."
3. "Abandonment occurs when a person in possession of real property leaves the property with no intention to return."
4. "When the defendant left the property to attend school in another state, her improvements and her household furnishings remained on the property."

III. THE COMMON LAW PROCESS

The American legal system is a direct descendant of the English legal system that began to develop in 1066, with the Norman invasion of Britain. The most significant characteristic of this Anglo-American legal system is its reliance on the common law process, that is, the process by which judges "make" law and then adhere to this judge-made law. To understand how the common law process functions, we must examine four closely related concepts: the doctrine of stare decisis, an opinion's holding, the breadth of a holding, and the distinction between a holding and dicta.

A. Stare Decisis

At the heart of the common law system is the doctrine of stare decisis. According to this doctrine, when a court has decided a case in a particular way, future cases should be decided the same way if the facts are substantially similar to the prior case. Although the doctrine sounds simple and straightforward, in operation it is more complex and interesting than it might appear.

First, the doctrine applies only when the pending case is similar enough to the prior case to justify the application. Since all pending cases differ somewhat from prior cases, the question of whether the cases are similar enough will almost always be subject to argument. Second, if there is good reason, a lower court can decline to follow the precedent of a higher court in that jurisdiction. The most common reason for this occurrence is a significant change in circumstances since the precedent was issued. Conceptually, the primary justification for such a decision is the belief that the higher court probably would not adhere to the prior decision if the question were now before it. Finally, a court can overrule its own prior decision when the court decides that the law should change. A court might decide that the prior decision was ill-reasoned originally, or that its application has produced unanticipated and undesirable results, or that modern conditions now call for a different approach.

A court usually overrules its own decision explicitly, by identifying in its new opinion the case to be overruled and directly stating the intention not to rely on it in the future. A court also can overrule a case implicitly, not mentioning the case at all but applying a different legal standard to the pending case.

B. Holdings

def: holding

In the common law process, the part of the precedent case that binds a future court is the holding. A case holding is a statement of the court's decision about the issues actually before it. No doubt you have already heard the term "holding." You may have seen the term defined in materials about how to brief cases, and your professors are probably asking you to state the holdings of the cases you read. A word of clarification is appropriate here.

The term "holding" is used in a number of different ways, varying according to the context, the task at hand, and one's particular legal philosophy. For instance, your contracts professor may want you to state the holding in terms specific to the parties in the case, while your torts professor may want you to state the holding as a general principle ready to be applied to future cases. Your civil procedure professor may not care particularly about whether you personalize the statement but may want you to include a rule statement in the holding. Your property professor may not want you to include a rule statement but may want instead a fairly complete statement of the important facts leading to the case's outcome.

Rest assured that each of these professors has a pedagogical purpose in mind, and you should follow each professor's preference in his or her class. You need not, however, be concerned that any of these preferences is wrong, even if some seem inconsistent with others. The purpose of stating holdings in a law school class is to teach you the basics of case reading, and each professor's approach emphasizes particular parts of that important skill.

In your legal writing class and in law practice, however, you will be identifying holdings for a different purpose—to decide whether and how that precedent case might apply to your client's situation. When you write statements of holdings in preparation for a contracts or torts class, you have only the precedent case before you. You rarely have a set of new facts to which the precedent may apply. In your legal writing class and in law practice, you will be reading the case for the purpose of relating it to a particular new set of facts. You will find that when you state holdings for this purpose, you will not need to worry about most of the differences you may have noticed among professors and among books and other materials discussing the term.

For our purposes, you can think of the holding as the court's decision on the particular legal issue plus the important facts—the facts that seemed to make a difference to the result. For instance, consider *Cantwell v. Denton*, a hypothetical case about assumption of the risk in a torts case. In *Cantwell*, faulty wiring in an apartment house caused a fire. A resident of one of the apartments arrived at the scene, observed the fire, entered the building anyway, and sustained injuries in the process. The resident sued the building owner to recover for those injuries, and the defendant raised the defense of assumption of the risk, a doctrine that, in various forms, prevents or limits recovery for damages caused in part by a voluntary assumption of the risk of injury.

Assume that the court in *Cantwell* decided that the doctrine of voluntary assumption of the risk did not apply to this plaintiff because he had entered the building believing his young daughter to be inside. You might state the holding as follows:

> *Holding*   Assumption of the risk applies only to voluntary conduct, and a father's choice to enter a burning building is not voluntary if he must choose between entering the building and failing to save his child's life.

No doubt you have already observed great variety in holding statements, even without regard for different preferences among professors. Differences are normal. The next sections will explain more about why you should not be surprised to find these differences and how you will use them in representing your clients.

C. The Breadth of Holdings

One of the ways holding statements can differ is in breadth. Consider again our hypothetical torts case, *Cantwell v. Denton*. The holding statement above is stated narrowly. It describes the holding as applying to fathers who are choosing between a burning building and the lives of their children. It does not tell us whether the rule would apply to persons other than fathers, to situations other than burning buildings, or to saving people other than children. It certainly tells us nothing about whether the rule would include saving property rather than lives.

But you may need to argue on behalf of a client in one of those situations. For instance, assume that your firm is representing Mr. and Mrs. Gregory in litigation against Jerico Autoworks, an auto repair business. Jerico advertised oil changes completed in twenty minutes "while you wait." One Saturday, the Gregorys put a turkey in their oven, set the temperature for 325 degrees, and left for town to have Jerico change the oil in their car. Jerico completed the job and turned the car back over to the Gregorys. The Gregorys paid Jerico and began driving the rural road toward their home.

They were only halfway home when they noticed the internal engine heat beginning to climb. They realized that they were running low on oil and surmised, correctly as it turned out, that Jerico had not sufficiently tightened the oil plug. But they also realized that the turkey in their oven was nearly done. They knew that this rural road was traveled so infrequently that the odds were small that they would be able to flag another driver and get home before the burning turkey might cause a fire in their kitchen.

They decided to drive on in the hope that they could get home before their kitchen (and perhaps their house) burned. The Gregorys got close enough to walk the rest of the way and so saved their kitchen, but at the cost of serious engine damage. Your firm has sued Jerico on behalf of the Gregorys, and Jerico has raised the defense of assumption of the risk based on the Gregorys' decision to continue driving.

An attorney in your firm has asked you to write a brief arguing that the decision to continue driving should not be considered an assumption of the risk. Assume that your only authority is *Cantwell v. Denton*. Suppose you stated the holding of *Cantwell* as we did above, that is:

> *Holding*   Assumption of the risk applies only to voluntary conduct, and a father's choice to enter a burning building is not voluntary if he must choose between entering the building and failing to save his child.

This holding statement would not tell a court much about whether the Gregorys' decision would constitute assumption of the risk. Can you state the holding more broadly? Whether you will be able to formulate a broader holding statement will depend largely on the court's language in *Cantwell*. Most opinions will contain at least several paragraphs explaining the court's decision, and this language may help you formulate a broader holding. Assume you find these paragraphs in the *Cantwell* opinion:

> A father's choice to enter a burning building is not voluntary where he must choose between entering the building and failing to save his child. The bond between a parent and a child is the strongest human bond. In situations that otherwise would constitute assumption of the risk, the law should not penalize a plaintiff for fulfilling the duties of a parent to a child.
>
> Further, our law places the highest value on human life, and the highest form of courage is to risk one's own life in an attempt to save the life of another. The doctrine of assumption of the risk was not designed to penalize one who demonstrates this kind of courage.
>
> We must remember, after all, that it was the defendant's negligence that placed the plaintiff in the position of having to choose between the threatened harm and an option of equal or greater evil. A defendant cannot subject the plaintiff to such a Hobson's choice and then defend against his own negligence by pointing to the plaintiff's decision.

If the *Cantwell* opinion contains this language, could you formulate a broader holding? What holding might you formulate if you focus primarily on the first paragraph? What if you focus primarily on the second paragraph? The third? Which paragraph would allow you to formulate a holding that will accommodate the Gregorys' concern about their kitchen?

The first paragraph grounds the result in the particular obligations of a parent to a child. From that paragraph, you could formulate a holding that applies to parents, not just fathers. You might even be able to formulate a holding that would apply to property damage if protection of the property was a clear parental duty. But the Gregorys' dilemma did not involve parental duty, so the holding you could formulate from the first paragraph would not help the Gregorys very much.

The second paragraph grounds the holding in the special value we place on trying to save human life. From that paragraph you could formulate a holding not limited to a parental obligation, but it still might not cover property damage.

The third paragraph, however, grounds the holding in the observation that the defendant's negligence has caused the necessity to choose between two bad options. That paragraph describes the situations that call for this result as those in which the defendant's negligence has forced the plaintiff

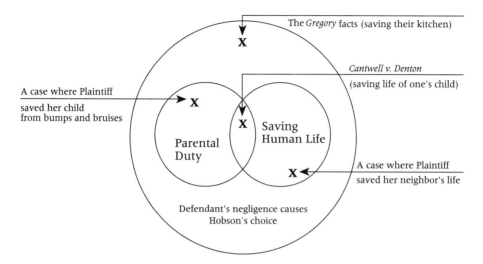

Figure 2-2
Situations covered by each rule formulation.

to choose between the threatened harm and an equal or greater harm. The third paragraph would allow you to formulate a broader holding like this:

> *Holding*   Assumption of the risk requires a voluntary choice. When the defendant's negligence forces the plaintiff to choose between the threatened harm and another equal or greater harm, the plaintiff's choice is not voluntary.

Figure 2-2 demonstrates how this broader holding statement would allow the Gregorys to argue that their decision to continue driving did not constitute assumption of the risk.

We have seen in this section that case analysis is inherently subjective. It is no wonder that holding statements differ so widely from each other. At the beginning of your law study, you may find this subjectivity unnerving, but it provides lawyers with wonderful opportunities for advocacy on behalf of clients. In the practice of law, you will find that you are grateful for it.

EXERCISE 2-2

Write a statement of the holding for a case your professor has assigned. If your professor has not assigned a case for this exercise, use the well-known contracts case, *Lucy v. Zehmer*, found in Appendix E.

D. Holdings Versus Dicta

We are now ready to explore the last important topic explaining the common law process—the distinction between *holdings* and *dicta*.[11] This distinction is important because only an opinion's holding is binding on future courts.

---

11. The full term is *obiter dictum*, literally meaning "a remark made in passing." "Dictum" is singular; the plural form is "dicta."

The doctrine of stare decisis does not apply to dicta. A judge in a future case may *choose* to follow dicta but is not bound to do so.

The holding of an opinion is limited to the court's statements resolving the question(s) *actually at issue in that case*, that is, statements on issues necessary to the result reached. The court might make many other statements about the law, statements other than those necessary to explain the decision. Such statements of law not essential to the outcome of that particular case are *dicta*. They are not part of the holding.

An example will be helpful here. Assume that you are reading a contracts opinion dealing with whether a communication without a price would constitute a valid offer. In that opinion, the court might have made some statements about other legal issues. In the course of the opinion, the judge might have stated that a valid contract requires acceptance and consideration. However, the judge did not decide that particular case by considering whether there had been a valid acceptance or sufficient consideration. Those were not the issues the parties raised. Instead, the question before the court and the basis for the result was whether there had been a valid *offer*. Therefore, any statements the judge might have made about *acceptance* or *consideration* would be dicta.

In the prior example, the dicta were statements about principles of law. However, statements about how the law might apply to hypothetical facts can constitute dicta as well. For instance, in a case deciding whether a driver's 65 mph speed was unsafe, a court might say, "A speed of 65 miles per hour would have been unsafe if road conditions had been wet or icy." If road conditions in the pending case were dry, any statements of the legal result for wet roads would be dicta.

Remember that the primary purpose of distinguishing holding from dicta is to decide whether a future court is *bound* by the language. While dicta is not binding, a lower court will often give the dicta of a higher court great deference. Many trial and intermediate appellate court judges consider it their role to apply the law as the higher court would, and dicta is a strong indication of what the higher court would hold. Take care, however, not to mislead the court or another lawyer by presenting dicta as if it were part of the holding.

While the distinction between holding and dicta is sometimes clear, as in the contracts example above, it is often debatable. You will not always know for sure whether a certain statement of law was necessary to the court's decision. For instance, consider again the *Cantwell* language in the prior section. If you are trying to persuade the judge that the Gregorys did not assume the risk of injury to their engine, you probably will draw the *holding* from the third paragraph. However, if you represent Jerico, no doubt you will argue that the statements in the third paragraph are *dicta*. You will argue that the narrower statements in the first and second paragraphs were all that were necessary to decide *Cantwell* and therefore that the broad statements in the third paragraph are "mere dicta."

Once again we see that case analysis is inherently an interpretive project. If you are looking for certainty in the law, you are bound to feel frustrated, for no language can capture completely the whole of human experience. It is this very flexibility of interpretation, however, that provides the opportunity for advocacy.

EXERCISE 2-3

Read the following hypothetical opinion. For each statement that follows it, decide whether the statement is part of the holding or dictum. Be prepared to explain your answers.

> This is an action to decide the rightful owner of a painting, which was allegedly given by Harrison Crenshaw to his daughter Alecia Green on her 25th birthday. According to the record below, on the date of Green's birthday, Crenshaw hosted a party for his daughter in his condominium. He told her in the presence of the guests at the party that the painting was hers. Crenshaw said that she could have the painting as soon as he found another to replace it. One month later, before the painting was delivered, Crenshaw died. The trial court held that Crenshaw had made a valid gift to Green. We disagree.
>
> To constitute a valid gift of personal property, the donor must manifest his intention to make the gift and the item must be physically delivered unless physical delivery is not practicable. Physical delivery is not practicable if, for instance, the item is in another city, or locked in a safe deposit box in a bank closed for the weekend, or too heavy to move without arranging moving assistance. This painting, however, was hanging on the wall not ten feet away. It is small and light, and it was hanging freely on a hook. Physical delivery is required when the item can be so easily removed and handed over. Therefore, there was no valid gift of the painting.

1. An item must be physically delivered unless physical delivery would be impracticable.
2. An item locked in a safe deposit box in a bank closed for the weekend need not be physically delivered.
3. A small, light, freely accessible item must be physically delivered in order to complete a valid gift.
4. To constitute a valid gift of personal property, the donor must manifest his intention to make the gift.

IV. THE WEIGHT OF AUTHORITY

No doubt you already have noticed many different kinds of authorities cited in the cases you are reading and in the note material in your case books. Some of these authorities are actually "law," and some are not. Some of them would bind a particular court, and some would not. Some would trump another authority, and some would not. The principles that govern these questions are critically important for your understanding of law.

A. Primary Authority Versus Secondary Authority

The first important distinction among authorities is the question of which actually constitute "law." Some do, and some are simply commentary on the law or suggestions about what the law ought to be. Authorities that actually constitute law are called "primary authorities." Authorities that merely explain or comment on these primary authorities are called "secondary authorities."

Primary authority is created by an entity that has the legal power to create law, and it takes one of the forms used to create law. Four basic kinds of law exist: (1) federal and state constitutions; (2) case law; (3) statutes; and (4) regulations or rulings issued by governmental agencies. Situations to which Michigan law applies will be governed by the Michigan Constitution and by the statutes the Michigan legislature enacts. They will be governed by the case law the Michigan courts create. They will be governed by the administrative law the Michigan state agencies create. They are also governed by applicable federal constitutional provisions and federal case law, statutes, and administrative law. All of these sources are primary authority.

Secondary authority comes in many forms. You may have encountered some secondary sources already, such as treatises or hornbooks on particular subjects, legal encyclopedias, or law review articles. These sources are created by private individuals, organizations, or businesses. They may help you locate primary authority or understand it better once you have found it. For some, respect for the author or for the drafting process may persuade a judge to defer to the source's content, but those private individuals, organizations, or businesses do not have the authority to create law. Thus, if the source is not a constitution, a statute, a case opinion, or an agency pronouncement, a court is not required to follow it.

Relationships Among Primary Authorities. Each jurisdiction has a constitution, a set of statutes, a body of case law, and a body of administrative regulations. The relationships among these primary authorities are, in a sense, hierarchical. Applicable constitutional provisions constrain all other authorities. Thus, a state statute or case opinion found to violate that state's constitution will not be followed. Properly enacted statutes constrain both case law and administrative regulations or rulings. Thus, a judge must follow a properly enacted statute and may not simply disagree and rule according to her own views. The court does, however, have the authority to interpret the meaning of a constitutional provision or a statute and to decide whether it applies to the situation before the court. The ability to interpret the text and decide whether it applies gives the courts broad powers to define even statutory law. Case law constrains an administrative agency. The agency cannot decline to follow an applicable binding court decision.

EXERCISE 2-4

For each question below, which authority carries more precedential value? Assume that the authorities listed in each question address precisely the same issue, that all are in the same jurisdiction, and that each is valid in all respects. Be prepared to explain your answers.

1. A state statute or an opinion of that state's highest court?
2. An agency regulation or a state statute?
3. A state constitutional provision or a state statute?

4. An opinion of the state's highest court or a ruling by a state agency?
5. A state constitutional provision or an opinion of that state's highest court?

B. Mandatory Authority Versus Persuasive Authority

In our discussion of primary authorities we identified what is actually law, but not all primary authorities will bind every court. To decide which primary authorities will bind a particular court, we must explore another distinction— the distinction between mandatory and persuasive authority. An authority is mandatory in a particular court if it binds that court. An authority is merely persuasive if it does not bind that court. The judge may choose to be persuaded by it, but the judge has a choice.

For instance, an Iowa case would not bind a Texas trial court on an issue of Texas law. The Texas court may find the Iowa opinion persuasive, perhaps because of the strength of its reasoning or because the judge who wrote the opinion is particularly well respected, but the Texas court would not be *required* to follow it. Thus, in the Texas trial court, the Iowa opinion would be *persuasive* authority, not mandatory authority.

On the other hand, an applicable opinion of the Texas Supreme Court would bind the Texas trial court. The Texas Supreme Court is the highest appellate court in the state, and the Texas trial court is bound to follow a Texas Supreme Court opinion absent some reason to think that the opinion is no longer viable. Thus, the Texas Supreme Court opinion is *mandatory* authority for the Texas trial court. Similarly, a Texas statute would be *mandatory* authority for any Texas court. Here are the basic principles for identifying mandatory case authority, divided according to whether the issue is a matter of state law or federal law:

On issues of state law, the decisions of a state's highest court are mandatory authority for all other courts of that state as well as for all federal courts applying that state's law. It may surprise you to learn that federal courts can be bound by state courts. However, a state's highest court has the ultimate authority on matters of that state's law. No federal court, not even the United States Supreme Court, can control the state's highest court on matters of that state's law.

Decisions of a state's intermediate appellate courts are binding on trial courts within the geographic boundaries of the intermediate appellate court's jurisdiction. In many states, the decision of an intermediate appellate court also binds any trial court whose own intermediate appellate court has not ruled on the issue. Decisions of federal courts or courts from other states are persuasive but not mandatory on matters of state law.

On issues of federal law, decisions of the United States Supreme Court are binding on all federal and state courts in the country. Decisions of the applicable intermediate federal appellate court are binding on all federal district courts in that circuit. Decisions of other circuits are persuasive only.

Decisions of federal intermediate appellate courts and federal trial courts on issues of federal law are not mandatory authority for state courts. However, as a practical matter, state courts generally give the opinions of those courts significant weight. This is particularly true of state courts within the geographical boundaries of the particular federal court.

EXERCISE 2-5

Gauging the Relative Weights of Authorities

Your firm represents Kay Lang, who sold a piece of commercial property located in Los Angeles to Adam Kornfeld. Kornfeld claims that Lang failed to disclose to him the true condition of the property, and he has filed suit against her for damages in the state trial court. You are researching whether under California law a seller of real property has a duty to disclose to the buyer the condition of the property.

You have found the following authorities: (1) Which are primary authorities? (2) For each authority, describe the precedential value it likely will carry for the dispute between Kornfeld and Lang. Use the following choices: binding; very persuasive; moderately persuasive; slightly persuasive; no persuasive value.

A. An opinion of the California Supreme Court deciding the duty of a seller to disclose to the buyer the condition of the property;

B. An article in the University of California at Los Angeles (UCLA) Law Review discussing the applicable California rule on the seller's duty to disclose to the buyer the condition of the property;

C. An opinion of the United States Court of Appeals for the Ninth Circuit applying the applicable California rule on the duty of a seller to disclose to a buyer the condition of the property;

D. A California statute on the duty of a seller to disclose to a buyer the condition of the property;

E. An opinion of another California state trial court applying the California rule on the duty of a seller to disclose to a buyer the condition of the property;

F. A section from a California legal encyclopedia explaining the applicable California rule on the duty of a seller to disclose to a buyer the condition of the property; and

G. An opinion of the United States Supreme Court applying the California rule on the duty of a seller to disclose to a buyer the condition of the property.

C. Other Characteristics Affecting the Persuasive Value of Cases

The degree of deference a court will give to any particular case will be affected in more subtle ways by additional factors, including the following:

The relative level of the issuing court. The more prestigious the court, the more persuasive its opinions. For instance, a decision of the United States Supreme Court is powerful persuasive authority, even when it is not mandatory.

The date of the opinion. All other things being equal, more recent opinions carry more persuasive value.

The strength of the opinion's reasoning. A well-reasoned opinion is more persuasive than a poorly reasoned one. An opinion that explains the rationale of the decision rather than simply announcing it is more persuasive than an opinion that simply applies existing legal authorities without exploration of the policy rationale for the rule.

The subsequent treatment of the opinion by other authorities. The more the case has been followed by subsequent cases, the greater its precedential value. The more it has been discussed approvingly in treatises or law review articles, the greater its precedential value.

The number of other jurisdictions that follow the same approach. If a majority of jurisdictions follow this court's approach, the opinion's precedential value is increased. We refer to the approach of the majority of jurisdictions as the "majority rule" and to a minority approach as the "minority rule."

Whether the court's statements about the issue are part of the holding or dicta. As Part III in this chapter explained, statements that are dicta are not as persuasive as statements that are part of the holding.

How factually similar the opinion is to the facts of the present situation. The more similar the facts of the precedent case and the pending case, the more sure the judge can be that the authority was meant to apply to situations like the pending case.

The number of subscribing judges. Most federal intermediate-level appellate cases are decided by a panel of the court, often three judges. Far less frequently, a case will be decided by all judges of that court (the court sitting "en banc"). En banc opinions are binding on future panels of the same court. Other courts generally find them more persuasive than panel decisions. Unanimous opinions are more persuasive than split decisions. A majority opinion generally is more persuasive than a concurring opinion, which is in turn more persuasive than a dissenting opinion.

Be careful with concurring or dissenting opinions. If the statement of law you are interested in is part of a disagreement between the concurring or dissenting opinion and the majority opinion, the statement in the concurring or dissenting opinion may actually establish that what it says is *not* the law. After all, the opinion is disagreeing with the majority opinion on that point (or agreeing for different reasons), and it is the majority opinion that establishes the law.

En banc opinion	An opinion issued in a case that was heard by all of the judges of the court.
Majority opinion	An opinion subscribed to by a majority of the judges who heard the case.
Concurring opinion	An opinion that agrees with the result reached by the majority opinion but for reasons different from or in addition to those of the majority opinion.
Dissenting opinion	An opinion that disagrees with the result reached by the majority opinion.

Whether the opinion is published. If the opinion does not appear in an official collection of published opinions (an official case reporter), it is not "published." In most jurisdictions, an unpublished opinion has no precedential value, and many courts have local rules that prohibit citing an unpublished opinion.

The reputation of the particular judge writing the case opinion. Some judges have earned significant respect personally, separate from the position they hold. The opinions of those judges may have added persuasive value.

Trends in the law. If you can discern a trend among other courts in the nation or in your state, opinions consistent with that trend may have greater precedential value than inconsistent opinions. For instance, if, over the past several years your state's highest court has been extending the liability of manufacturers in various situations, a case opinion consistent with that trend may have more precedential weight than an opinion that questions that trend.

PART TWO

Reading and Analyzing the Law

CHAPTER 3

Briefing and Synthesizing Cases

To understand case law, a lawyer must read and interpret the written decisions of judges. The lawyer looks for cues from the language of the opinion, evaluating the meaning and significance of each cue and synthesizing the results. Thus, the lawyer creates an interpretation that synthesizes the facts, the result, and the judge's explanation of that result. One can even say that a lawyer "constructs" the law through this interpretive process. The starting point for learning this interpretive process is the case brief.[1]

I. INTRODUCTION TO CASE BRIEFING

A case brief is a method for reading, analyzing, and making notes about a case. Formats and preferred methods for case briefing vary widely, partly because case briefs are personal study tools. People process information differently, so they develop personalized study methods that best accommodate their own learning styles.

Briefing formats differ also according to the legal task to be performed. When you brief a case for your torts class, your most immediate goal is to be ready to answer classroom questions about the case. Your torts professor may have given you a format to use, or you may be able to devise your own format based on your observations of the kinds of questions your professor tends to ask.

When you brief cases for a legal writing assignment, however, your purpose is different in several ways. First, you have a hypothetical client with a set of facts and a specific legal question to answer. Having a discrete task means you can focus your case brief on the aspects of the case most applicable to your client's facts. Second, you will be reading many cases on a particular legal point, not just one or two. Your assignment will require you not only to understand the case you are reading but also to understand how it relates

---

1. The term "brief" also is used to refer to a formal court document a lawyer submits to a judge to advocate for a favorable ruling in a case. A case brief often is called simply a "brief," so some confusion of terminology is possible. Usually, though, the context will clarify the meaning.

to a number of other cases on the same point. This broader task requires you to notice additional features about the case. Third, you will be writing a document (perhaps an office memo or a memorandum of law) describing the case and referring to its language. Therefore, you will need to be able to find the case again, and you will need to take more careful notes about the parts you anticipate describing in your office memo or memorandum of law. These notes will save you time when you are writing, and they will save you from committing plagiarism.[2]

The following section sets out a suggested format for briefing the cases you read as part of your legal writing assignment. You may find that much of this format also works well in your other courses. The key is to remember that case briefing is a personal study tool, so adapt the format freely to fit your own learning style and your particular analytical task.

II. A FORMAT FOR CASE BRIEFING

Read the case through once before you start to write, perhaps underlining or highlighting a bit. Then read the case again, this time making the following notations:

CASE BRIEF
1. Case Name, Court, Citation, Date
2. Facts
3. Procedural History
4. Issue(s)
5. Applicable Rule(s) of Law
6. Holding(s)
7. The Court's Order
8. Reasoning
9. New Information
10. Questions, Comments, and Speculations

Case Name, Court, Citation, Date. You will need to know the name of the court and the date so you can examine how this case fits with other cases and gauge its precedential value for your assignment. Also, correctly recording these pieces of information during your research stage will save you time and frustration when you start to write.

Facts. Describe in your own words the facts of the case. You need include only the facts that pertain to the legal issues relevant to your assignment. For example, if the case concerns a dispute over whether a person revoked her will before she died, normally you will not need to include facts about what

---

2. See Chapter 1, section IV.

property she owned or about the cause of her death. You would include those facts only if they should pertain to the question of whether she had revoked her will.

Procedural History. The procedural history is the story of the case's progress through the litigation process. If the case is on appeal, include the procedural posture of the trial court decision being appealed, such as a decision on a motion to dismiss, a motion for summary judgment, some other kind of motion, a jury verdict, or a judgment after a bench trial.

Issue(s). The issue is the legal question the opinion resolves. Usually, the opinion tells you how the court thought the governing rule of law applied to the facts of that case, so you can state the issue in those terms. You can use either a question or a phrase beginning with "whether." Here is an example of an issue statement:

Can a testator effectively revoke a will by marking a large "X" across only the first page of a five-page will and not signing or initialing the "X"?

Focus on the part of the governing rule that actually was at issue in the case. For instance, assume the case concerns a dispute over whether a testator had revoked her will before she died, as in the issue statement above. The parties were before the court to find out whether there is a valid will, but an issue statement that broad would not help you isolate the precise point on which this larger question turned: whether the existing will had been revoked.

Some opinions decide only pure questions of law[3] and do not apply law to facts. In such a case, the issue statement simply poses the legal question the court answered, for example:

Whether Illinois law allows recovery for the wrongful death of a fetus.

If the issue relates to how a term in a statute will be defined or applied, your brief should identify the statutory language at issue. A good place to do that is here in the issue statement, for example:

Whether the "nighttime" element of the burglary statute is satisfied if the entry occurred 20 minutes before sunrise.

Applicable Rule(s) of Law. This section will help you begin to understand the legal principles (rules of law) governing your issue. A rule of law is a

---

3. See Chapter 2, Section II.

statement of the legal test the court will apply to resolve a legal issue. Here is an example of a governing rule of law for deciding the will revocation issue:

> To revoke a will, a testator must have the intention to revoke and must take some action that demonstrates that intent.

The court may state some other legal rules in order to provide context for the issue it actually will decide. Feel free to note these also. That legal context will help you understand the law governing your assignment, and when you begin to write your memo or brief, you may need to provide the same kind of context for your reader. If so, that information will be readily available in your case briefs.

Holding(s). As we saw in Chapter 2, the holding is the court's decision on the particular legal issue plus the important facts—the facts that seem to make the most difference for the result. If your issue statement included a sufficient description of the key facts, you need not repeat those facts in the holding statement. If not, include facts in the statement of the holding. The combination of your issue statement and your holding statement should include the key facts and the court's decision on the legal issue. For example:

> A testator can effectively revoke a will by marking a large "X" across only the first page of a five-page will and not signing or initialing the "X" if the other evidence of the testator's intent is sufficiently strong.

Notice the difference between a holding and the governing rule of law. The rule sets out the legal test the court will use to decide the case. The holding states the court's conclusion about whether the facts of the case meet that legal test.

If the issue is a pure question of law, you need not include the facts unless the answer to the question depends on a certain set of facts. For instance, if the issue is "Does State *X* allow recovery for the wrongful death of a fetus?" (a pure question of law), the answer (holding) might include facts: "Recovery for the wrongful death of a fetus is permitted if the fetus was medically viable at the time of the injury."

The Court's Order. After deciding the legal issue, the court either will take some action itself or will order that a person or another court take some action. For instance, a trial court might grant or deny a motion or might order the clerk to enter a judgment. An appellate court might affirm or reverse the lower court's ruling and might remand the case to the lower court for further proceedings. Note the legal result of the court's decision under this category of your brief.

Reasoning. Usually, a court uses its written opinion to explain the reasons for its decision. These reasons will be important to you as you work on your assignment. They will give you important clues about how the court might decide future cases, and they can provide you with effective arguments for your client. Chapter 11 identifies the major forms of legal reasoning, but whether you use those names or not, note in your case brief the court's reasons for its decision.

Pay particular attention to the court's *policy rationales.* Policy rationales justify a decision based on what result will be best for society at large. Courts realize that their rulings will affect the way people act in the future. They want to apply the law in ways that will encourage desirable societal results or discourage undesirable results. For instance, a court might adopt a particular legal rule because that rule will reduce the number of disputes resulting in litigation or because it will encourage people to think more carefully before entering into a contract. Including policy statements in your brief will help you understand whether and how the court's decision might apply to future cases. The opinion is likely to apply to future cases that raise these same policy concerns.

New Information. This category is optional, but it can be especially help-ful when you are working on a legal writing assignment. It provides a place to record what you learned about the rule or its application that you did not know before you read this case. Notice especially anything about this case that could apply in some way to your assignment. Perhaps this opinion modified or expanded the rule. Perhaps the court discussed a part of the rule you have not seen discussed so thoroughly before. Perhaps the court phrased the governing rule in a way particularly helpful to your client's facts. Perhaps the opinion explains the historical developments in this area of the law. You will notice more information in the opinion if you consciously look for new information, and you will be better able to use that information in your assignment if you have made note of it in your case brief. Here are some tools that will help you find new information about a rule:

1. *Notice what the court said about the rule.* In most opinions, the author gives the reader some explanation of the rule before applying it to the facts of that particular case. Here, the author's primary goal is to tell the reader about the rule. Begin with this part of the opinion. The *court's* explicit explanation of the rule gives you the most basic new information from the case.

2. *Notice how the court applied the rule.* After you have examined carefully what the court *said* about the rule, look at how the court *applied* the rule to the facts before it. You might expect an opinion to state and explain a rule of law and then to apply that rule of law exactly as the opinion just explained it. Often, that is exactly what happens. But sometimes the court's *application* of the rule differs from the court's explanation of it. One of the best ways to understand the rule is to observe how the court applied it. A court "holds" what it *does,* not what it *says.*

3. *Notice how the court did* not *apply the rule.* After you have observed how the court applied the rule, ask yourself how the court did *not* apply it. A court's unexplained silence rarely can be characterized as a binding rule of law. However, judicial silence can have persuasive value if the most likely reason for the silence is that the ignored topic is not a part of the relevant legal analysis. For instance, in a child custody case, if the facts state that one spouse is Christian and one spouse is Moslem but the opinion does not mention

religious differences, you may be able to infer that religious differences will not be relevant to custody decisions.

After all, your goal here is to figure out what rule was governing the judge when deciding the case and how that rule would apply to your client's facts. If you are wondering whether a certain fact true of your client's situation would affect the outcome, ask yourself whether that kind of fact seemed to affect the judge's ruling in the earlier case.

4. *Notice any facts the court emphasized.* When a court sets out the facts or applies the law, it sometimes will emphasize a particular fact. Usually, the court's explanation of the law will tell you why the court found that fact important. However, sometimes a court will emphasize a fact without explicitly explaining the fact's significance. Even if the court did not directly explain whether or why that fact was important, the opinion's emphasis on it implies that the judge found it legally significant.

5. *Find out what leading commentators have said about the case.* Case opinions actually make law, but a wealth of secondary authorities exist. As we saw in Chapter 2, secondary authorities are explanations of the law written by legal commentators. Secondary authorities have persuasive value, depending on factors such as the reputation of the author, the level of detail of the discussion, and the recency of the writing. If you are working with a well-known and influential case, commentators may have discussed it. Finding secondary authority can help you understand the case and its significance for your assignment.

Questions, Comments, and Speculations. Finally, note any questions, speculations, or thoughts of your own about the case and how it might apply to your assignment. It is common to have passing thoughts and questions as you read a case. These thoughts, speculations, and questions are the first steps toward a clearer understanding of the applicable law and how it might apply to your client. If you do not record them, you are likely to forget them.

A Sample Case Brief

A sample case brief appears in Appendix E, along with the case itself. Read the case and the case brief.

EXERCISE 3-1

Prepare a case brief for a case your professor has selected. Bring your brief to class, and be prepared to discuss it. If your professor has not assigned a case, brief *Lucy v. Zehmer*, found in Appendix E.

III. SYNTHESIZING CASES

Case briefing will help you understand a single case, but a lawyer faced with multiple authorities must do more than analyze each authority separately.

Such a discussion would be little more than reading a series of case briefs. Instead, she must explain how the cases fit together to create the law governing her client's issue. She must compare the authorities to find and reconcile any seeming inconsistencies and to combine the content of the authorities so she can present a unified statement of the governing rule of law. Therefore, after you have identified the cases that will be important to your analysis, you must consider how they fit together. This process is called "synthesizing" cases.

A. Using Consistent Cases

Sometimes the cases will use similar language to state the governing rule and will apply that rule consistently. Or perhaps some jurisdictions follow one rule while others follow a different rule. However, the cases within each jurisdiction are consistent with each other. In either of these situations, it will not be difficult to combine the language of the cases into one explanation of the law with a consistent explanation of how the courts have applied it. Simply identify the points you want to make about the law and its application, and select and discuss the cases that best illustrate each point. Usually those points will include each element or factor and may include other observations about how the rule is usually applied. For example, recall our rule on whether a person had effectively revoked her will:

> To revoke a will, a testator must have the intention to revoke and must take some action that demonstrates that intent.

Your written analysis would discuss each element (intention and action) separately. For each element you would identify several cases that best explain that element and discuss them in your description of that element.

Similarly, if jurisdictions are split between two different approaches, your written analysis would discuss each approach separately. For each approach, you would identify several cases that best explain that approach and discuss them in your description of that element. For instance, assume you are writing an office memo on the question of whether parents can recover for the wrongful death of a fetus. You might find that some jurisdictions do not permit recovery at all, while others permit recovery if the fetus was medically viable at the time of the injury. You would explain to your reader that jurisdictions disagree and then discuss separately each of the two approaches. For each approach, you would select and discuss the several cases that best illustrate that approach.

B. Reconciling Seemingly Inconsistent Cases

Cases in the same jurisdiction are not always consistent, however. If you find seemingly inconsistent cases in the same jurisdiction, and if these cases will be important for your analysis, you must try to reconcile them. Reread carefully all of the language in both opinions, and also look for later cases that may resolve the inconsistency. Even if the later cases do not mention the inconsistency, these later cases will probably articulate and apply a rule. As you study the way these later cases articulate and apply the law, you will probably find clues about how to reconcile the cases.

One possibility is that the later case implicitly overruled the earlier case. As we saw in Chapter 2, a court can overrule an earlier opinion implicitly, however, by ignoring the earlier opinion and reaching a result inconsistent with the earlier opinion. Another possibility is that the seemingly inconsistent legal rules are meant to apply to different situations. Perhaps one rule is meant to be an exception to the other. In either case, the rule in one of the cases will apply to your client's situation while the other will not. This explanation handily resolves the inconsistency. Analysis that leads to a conclusion that the two opinions apply to different situations is called "distinguishing" cases.

Finally, you may be able to study the language of each opinion and find meanings in the text that will allow you to read the two cases consistently. Identify the seemingly inconsistent aspects of the opinions. Then reread the opinions carefully, exploring whether you can imagine a possible explanation that would reconcile the statements.

Inconsistencies in Rule Statements. Cases can seem inconsistent because they appear to state two different legal rules. For instance, assume that a lawyer is representing Sharon Watson, a sales employee of Carrolton Company, headquartered in Atlanta, Georgia. Watson had sold Carrolton to its present owners. She remained employed by Carrolton and signed a covenant not to compete, an agreement promising not to compete with Carrolton in certain ways for a certain period of time after the termination of her employment. Watson is considering leaving Carrolton to form a new business that would compete with Carrolton. She needs to know whether Carrolton would be able to enforce the covenant against her.

The lawyer researches the issue and finds *Coffee System of Atlanta v. Fox*[4] and *Clein v. Kapiloff*[5], two Georgia cases dealing with enforcement of covenants not to compete. In *Fox*, the court uses the following language to articulate the rule governing when a covenant is enforceable:

> A covenant not to compete is enforceable if all of the following elements are reasonable: the kind of activity restrained; the geographical area in which it is restrained; and the time period of the restraint.

If *Fox* were the only authority, the lawyer would use this rule to analyze Watson's question. He would analyze the reasonableness of each of the identified characteristics of the Watson covenant. But *Fox* is not the only authority.

---

4. 176 S.E.2d 71 (Ga. 1970).
5. 98 S.E.2d 897 (Ga. 1957).

The lawyer also found *Clein*, and there the court seems to articulate the governing rule differently. In *Clein*, the court stated:

> A covenant not to compete is enforceable if it is reasonable. The test for determining reasonableness is whether the covenant is reasonably necessary to protect the interests of the party who benefits by it; whether it unduly prejudices the interests of the public; and whether it imposes greater restrictions than are necessary.

Fox and *Clein* seem to lay out different rules. There seem to be two different legal standards governing the enforceability of covenants not to compete. Novice legal writers may be tempted to analyze the Watson issue by describing and applying, one at a time, the "rules" set out in *Fox* and in *Clein*. The discussion would first give a sort of "case brief" of *Fox*, describing the facts, the "rule" language that court used, and the result. The discussion would then apply the "rule" from *Fox* to the Watson facts. Then the discussion would do the same thing with *Clein*, setting out the "rule" language from that case and applying that "rule" to the Watson facts. The organizational structure would look something like this:

> Is the Watson covenant not to compete enforceable?
> 1. The rule in the *Fox* case: The covenant is enforceable if
>   a. the kind of activity restrained is reasonable;
>   b. the geographical area of restraint is reasonable;
>   c. the duration of the restraint is reasonable.
> 2. The rule in the *Clein* case: The covenant is enforceable if
>   a. it is reasonably necessary to protect the employer's interests;
>   b. it does not unduly prejudice the interests of the public; and
>   c. it does not impose greater restrictions than are necessary.

This approach is problematic, however. The lawyer needs to know *Georgia's* rule of law on enforcing covenants not to compete. Determining Georgia's rule is the most important analytical task. Organizing by the separate cases here would give the client two possible rules and two possible outcomes. Yet our legal system contemplates that a jurisdiction ordinarily will have only one rule of law on a particular issue so people can know what the law is and how it will apply to their conduct.

The lawyer must try to reconcile these seemingly inconsistent statements in *Fox* and *Clein*. After rereading the cases several times and carefully considering the court's possible meanings, the lawyer might conclude that the language in *Fox* identifies the particular terms that must be reasonable while the language in *Clein* identifies the criteria the court will use to judge whether those terms are reasonable. In other words, each contract term (kind of restraint, area of restraint, and duration of restraint) must meet the three criteria identified in *Clein*. This reconciliation salvages precedential value for each case and combines them into one unified statement of the jurisdiction's legal rule. Here is a rule statement that reconciles *Fox* and *Clein*:

> A covenant not to compete is enforceable if the kind of activity restrained, the geographical area of the restraint, and the duration of the restraint are reasonable. Reasonableness is judged according to whether the restraint is necessary to protect the employer's interests, does not unduly prejudice the interests of the public, and does not impose greater restrictions than are necessary.

This reconciled rule statement might produce an analysis organized like this:

> Is the Watson covenant not to compete enforceable?
> The covenant is enforceable if its terms are reasonable according to the following criteria:
> **A.** Are its terms necessary to protect the employer's interests?
>   **1.** The kind of activity;
>   **2.** the geographical area;
>   **3.** the duration.
> **B.** Do its terms unduly prejudice the interests of the public?
>   **1.** The kind of activity;
>   **2.** the geographical area;
>   **3.** the duration.
> **C.** Do its terms impose greater restrictions than necessary?
>   **1.** The kind of activity;
>   **2.** the geographical area;
>   **3.** the duration.

Inconsistencies in Results. You may find cases that seem to apply the same governing rule to seemingly similar sets of facts but reach puzzlingly different results. To reconcile them, search for differences in the facts that might adequately explain these results.

Consider this example: To establish adverse possession of land, a claimant must prove several things, one of which is "possession." The kind of possession that will ripen into title is gauged by the kind and degree of the claimant's use of the land. Here are summaries of two hypothetical cases dealing with the issue of whether the kind and degree of use was sufficient. Do they seem inconsistent? If so, can you reconcile them?

> *Allen v. Baxter:* Fifteen years ago, Anne Allen bought Lot A in a suburban neighborhood. Lot B, the vacant and overgrown lot next door, was owned by Jacob Baxter. Allen built a house on lot A and moved in. In 1981, Allen began gardening on Lot B. During the eight-month growing season, she worked in the garden nearly every day, growing vegetables for herself and her neighbors. During the four remaining months, she seldom went on the lot. The court held that this use did not establish a sufficient degree of "possession" for the purposes of adverse possession.

Clay v. Davidson: Fifteen years ago, Charles Clay bought a lakeside lot in a resort area. The lot already contained a cabin, and Clay built a dock. Every year since then, he has spent about six weekends a year and two weeks during the summer at the cabin. He has now discovered that the legal description of the lot was incorrect in that it actually describes the lot next door. Darlene Davidson is the actual record title-holder of the lot Clay thought to be his. The court held that Clay's facts established a sufficient degree of "possession" for the purposes of adverse possession.

The results in these two cases seem inconsistent. The degree of possession in *Allen* seems much greater than the degree of possession in *Clay*. Allen was physically present on the land for many more days of the year than was Clay, and Allen did more to the land than did Clay. Yet the court held that Clay possessed the land to a sufficient degree, and Allen did not. Reconciling these cases requires you to search for differences that could explain this seeming inconsistency. Perhaps the court will be satisfied with a lesser degree of possession in the case of vacation property, where an owner would not be expected to be in possession year round. Perhaps the court counted the continuous presence of Clay's improvements as part of Clay's possession. Or perhaps the court will require a greater degree of possession in the case of a possessor who knows she does not have record title. Any of these explanations could reconcile *Allen* and *Clay*.[6]

EXERCISE 3-2

Synthesizing and Reconciling Rule Statements

Synthesize (and reconcile where necessary) the following four summaries of case opinions setting out the requirements for recovery under the attractive nuisance doctrine. Use the cases to formulate one rule of law. For each part of the rule you formulate, identify the case(s) you would cite for support of that part of the rule. Remember that often you can formulate different rules from the same set of authorities.

Bell v. Grackin (state's highest appellate court, 1959)

Facts. A piece of wire was lying in a neighbor's yard. A child walking by saw the wire and went into the yard to get it. As he was playing with the wire, the child bent it and then let it go. The wire recoiled, hitting the child in the eye. The child sought recovery from the neighbor based on the doctrine of attractive nuisance. The court denied recovery, stating:

> The doctrine underlying the attractive nuisance cases applies only where the instrument or artificial condition is within itself inherently dangerous even while being used properly, such as weapons, explosives, or power tools. It would be extending the doctrine entirely too far to apply it to such commonplace objects as a piece of wire, a pencil, a coat hanger, or a hammer, all objects so commonplace as to be found around any house or yard, but not dangerous

---

6. If you study adverse possession in your property class, you may learn more about how to reconcile these two cases. The purpose of this exercise is simply to give you some practice in *imagining possible reconciliations.*

in themselves, although they might be attractive to children and capable of inflicting injury if misused.

Andersonville v. Goodden (state's intermediate-level appellate court, 1961)

Facts. A neighbor's pickup truck was parked unattended in the neighbor's yard. A child came into the yard to sell the neighbor candy bars for a school fund-raising project. The child saw the truck, climbed on it, fell, and impaled himself on a hook on the end of a chain dangling from the rear of the truck. The child sought recovery from the neighbor based on the doctrine of attractive nuisance. The court denied recovery, stating:

> The attractive nuisance doctrine was developed for the benefit of children coming upon property even though trespassing. However, the courts of this state have been reluctant to extend the doctrine beyond its restricted application to situations in which the dangerous instrument is found to be one of actual and compelling attraction for children. The courts have not expanded the doctrine to cases where the instrument or artificial condition did not actually draw the children onto the property.

Newcomb v. Roberts (state's highest appellate court, 1982)

Facts. A swimming pool was located in a backyard with no fence, unshielded from view. A child visiting next door and playing hide-and-seek came into the backyard seeking a hiding place. She hid behind a utility shack for a while. Then she began to wonder whether her friends were still looking for her. She decided to go investigate the status of the game. As she was leaving the backyard, walking alongside the pool, she accidentally fell into the pool and suffered serious injury. She brought suit against the property owner under the doctrine of attractive nuisance. The court allowed recovery, stating:

> A landowner is liable for physical harm to trespassing children by an artificial condition if the place where the condition exists is one upon which the possessor knows or has reason to know that children are likely to trespass; if the risk posed by the condition is one that children, because of their youth, will not realize; and if the landowner fails to exercise reasonable care to eliminate the danger or otherwise to protect the children. This landowner should have known that neighborhood children were likely to trespass and that such children would not appreciate the risks posed by a swimming pool. The landowner did not enclose the pool in a fence or take any steps to shield the pool from view. Thus, the landowner is liable for the injuries to the child.

McDaniels v. Lanier (state's highest appellate court, 1987)

Facts. A natural pond lay behind a house located on two acres of property. The pond was visible to passersby, and no fence prevented access. A child saw the pond and decided to swim in the pond. The child suffered abdominal cramps and drowned. The court denied recovery, stating:

> An owner who has reason to know that children are likely to trespass is liable, under the doctrine of attractive nuisance, for injuries sustained by a child if the risk is one that children will not appreciate and if the owner has failed to exercise reasonable care to protect the child [cite to *Newcomb*].

[handwritten annotations at top:]
(1959) (HC)
Bell
child w/ wire, hurt
only applies to 'instrument'
'artificial condition' inherently dangerous
No attractive nuisance

However, here the condition that caused the injury was a naturally occurring condition rather than an artificial condition. While landowners have a duty to protect trespassing children from artificially created conditions on their property, they do not have the duty to protect trespassing children from naturally occurring conditions. Such a duty would often require landowners to take unreasonable or impossible actions such as fencing off huge tracts of land. Thus, the owner is not liable for the injuries to the trespassing child.

EXERCISE 3-3
Reconciling Facts

You are researching an issue dealing with the requirements for making a valid gift. The cases explain that to make a gift, the donor must physically deliver possession of the item to the donee if possible. All of the cases you first find are similar to *Elder v. Fisher* below. Then, you find *Galloway v. Harris*. Does *Galloway* seem inconsistent with *Elder* and the cases like it? If so, how? Can you imagine how you might reconcile *Elder* and *Galloway*?

Elder v. Fisher. Janice Elder had a ruby ring, which she kept in her safe deposit box at a local bank. She wanted to give it to her sister, Darlene, for her birthday. Janice took Darlene to lunch and gave her a birthday card. The card read, "You're the best sister anyone could have. From this moment on, my ruby ring is yours. Meet me at the bank Wednesday at noon, and I'll get it out of the safe deposit box." Janice died on Tuesday, and her executor, Fisher, refused to turn over the ring to Darlene, claiming that no valid gift had been made because the ring was in the same town as the donor and donee but had not been physically handed over. The court held that actual physical delivery was required and that no valid gift had been made.

Galloway v. Harris. Chester Galloway wanted to give his daughter Jane an oil painting that was hanging over his mantel. He gave Jane a birthday party, and in the presence of the guests, he gave Jane a birthday card. Inside the card was a note declaring that the painting was her gift. Chester said that he wanted to keep the painting in place until his house sold and then he would bring it to her. Before Chester's house sold, he died. Jane claimed that the painting was hers, and Chester's executor (Harris) claimed that no valid gift had been made because the painting was in the same room with the donor and donee and had not been physically handed over. The court held that actual physical delivery was not required and that the painting was Jane's.

[handwritten annotations at bottom left:]
(1961) (MC)
Andersonville
Burning lot
attractive nuisance must
have lured child there
No attractive nuisance

McDaniels (1957) (HC)
d/n apply to nat. occurring
conditions

[handwritten annotations at bottom right:]
New combe   (1982) (HC)
Open swimming pool
Rule: to prove AN ① Lo knows or has reason
to know that kids will trespass
② risk kids won't recognize
③ Lo does not exercise reasonable care
to elim danger
Attractive nuisance

CHAPTER 4

Interpreting Statutes

While the roots of the American legal system remain in the common law, the 1930s saw the beginning of "an orgy of statute-making".[1] Today, most legal issues are controlled or significantly affected by statutes. Thus, your skills of statutory analysis will be crucial to your success as a lawyer. The skills basic to statutory analysis are (1) reading the statute; (2) identifying the issues; and (3) interpreting the statute's language.

I. READING STATUTES

The starting point for reading a statute is understanding the legislature's relationship to the courts. As we saw in Chapter 2, an applicable statute binds the courts of that jurisdiction, but a court has the authority to interpret the statute's language. Once a court has interpreted the statute, the doctrine of stare decisis applies, and the court's interpretation binds all other courts for whom the opinion is mandatory authority. If the legislature disagrees with the court's interpretation, the legislature is free to amend the statute to clarify its intended meaning. The court is then bound once again, this time by the newly-amended statute.

Also, as we saw in Chapter 2, a court has the authority to rule on the constitutionality of the statute. On the question of constitutionality, the court has the last word. The legislature can amend the statute to cure the constitutional infirmity the court identified, but the legislature cannot enact another statute declaring the original statute constitutional. A statute that has been held unconstitutional will not be enforced within the jurisdiction of the court that issued the opinion.

Within the boundaries set by these interlocking roles, courts must read statutory language and tell litigants whether the statute applies to their situation, and if so, what that language means. To advise clients and represent litigants, therefore, lawyers must read statutes precisely, accurately, and

---

1. Grant Gilmore, *The Ages of American Law* 95 (Yale U. Press 1977).

sometimes creatively. You can think of the questions critical to this inquiry as similar to the famous five W's that guide a journalist:[2]

THE FIVE W's OF READING A STATUTE

Who?	Whose actions are covered?
What?	What kinds of actions are required, prohibited, or permitted?
When?	When was the statute effective?
Where?	Where must the actions have taken place to be covered?
What then?	What consequences follow?

Often, the scope of the material you must read closely is larger than the specific statutory provision you first identify. If you are dealing with an act containing individual separately-numbered provisions, you must read carefully at least the following parts of the act:

READ THESE PARTS OF A STATUTE

1. The language of the individual provisions that appear to deal directly with the legal issue;
2. The language of any other individual provisions expressly cross-referenced by the directly-applicable provisions;
3. The titles of these individual provisions and of the entire act;
4. Any set of definitions applying to the individual provisions or to the act as a whole;
5. Any statement of purpose and any preamble to the individual provisions or the act as a whole;
6. If length is not prohibitive, read the entire act;
7. If the entire act is too long to read, at least read carefully the titles of all other individual provisions to identify any that might relate to the issue at hand;
8. The dates on which the act as a whole and the individual provisions were enacted and on which they became effective;
9. All of the same information for any amendments to important provisions;
10. If available, read the same information for any prior versions of important provisions (to understand what changes the legislature intended to make when it enacted the current version).

Read each of these parts of the statute word by word and phrase by phrase, paying attention to every detail. Reading a statute is more like reading an algebraic formula than it is like reading standard prose. Each word and punctuation mark is important. Even the internal tabulation (numbering or lettering) can be significant. Pay particular attention to words that signal structural information.

---

2. A journalist asks "five W's and an H": who, what, when, where, why, and how.

SOME WORDS THAT SIGNAL STRUCTURAL INFORMATION

and	include	unless	other
or	limited to	outweighs	shall
either	except	all	may

Also, notice whether any list set out in the statute is meant to be exclusive. The statute may tell you expressly that the list is not exclusive, using such language as the phrase "and any other factors relevant to the child's best interests." Or the statute may merely imply whether the list is exclusive, for instance, by introducing the list with a word like "including."

EXERCISE 4-1

Read this statute, and answer the questions that follow it. If you would need more information to answer the question, identify the information you would need.

> A lawyer's fee shall be reasonable. The factors to be considered in determining the reasonableness of a fee include the following: the time and labor required; the novelty and difficulty of the questions involved; and the skill requisite to perform the legal service properly; the likelihood, if apparent to the client, that the acceptance of the particular employment will preclude other employment by the lawyer; the fee customarily charged in the locality for similar legal services; the amount involved and the results obtained; the time limitations imposed by the client or by the circumstances; the nature and length of the professional relationship with the client; the experience, reputation, and ability of the lawyer or lawyers performing the services; and whether the fee is fixed or contingent.[3]

1. Client *A* asks a lawyer to handle a car accident case. The opposing party is insured by Security Insurance. The lawyer has been hoping to be placed on the list of lawyers approved to represent Security Insurance clients. In setting her fee, can the lawyer consider the fact that acceptance of the client's case may prevent Security Insurance from approving her to represent Security Insurance clients?

2. Client *B* has come to a lawyer to handle a car accident case. In setting her fee, can the lawyer consider the fact that she is certified as a Family Law Mediator?

3. In setting her fee, can the lawyer consider the fact that she is leaving for her vacation at the end of the week and therefore must finish the client's work in only two days?

---

3. Based on Model R. Prof. Conduct 1.5(a).

EXERCISE 4-2

Read this statute and answer the questions that follow it. If you would need more information to answer the question, identify the information you would need.

> A lawyer may reveal [information relating to the representation of a client] to the extent the lawyer reasonably believes necessary: (1) to prevent the client from committing a criminal act that the lawyer believes is likely to result in imminent death or substantial bodily harm; or (2) to establish a claim or defense on behalf of the lawyer in a controversy between the lawyer and the client, to establish a defense to a criminal charge or civil claim against the lawyer based upon conduct in which the client was involved, or to respond to allegations in any proceeding concerning the lawyer's representation of the client.[4]

1. How many circumstances justifying revelation of the client's information does the rule identify?
2. If the lawyer is suing the client for payment of the lawyer's fee, can the lawyer reveal information relating to the representation of the client?
3. If the lawyer has been charged by the bar association with unethical conduct in the representation of client *A*, can the lawyer reveal information relating to the representation of client *B*?
4. Assume that a lawyer is representing the husband in a divorce proceeding and she noticed that her client became angry when describing his reasons for seeking a divorce from his wife. She knows that her client owns several guns, and she fears that her client might try to shoot his wife. Can the lawyer reveal information relating to the representation of the client?

EXERCISE 4-3

Read this statute and answer the questions that follow it. If you would need more information to answer the question, identify the information you would need.

> A lawyer who has formerly represented a client in a matter shall not thereafter represent another person in the same or a substantially related matter in which that person's interests are materially adverse to the interests of the former client unless the former client consents after consultation.[5]

1. Assume that Lawyer Smith previously represented Client Jones. Prospective Client Harris has asked Lawyer Smith to represent him in a matter involving Client Jones. In your own words, make a list of what Client Jones would have to prove to show that Lawyer Smith could not accept representation of Client Harris.
2. On the facts of Question 1, make a list of Lawyer Smith's possible defenses to Client Jones's attempt to preclude the new representation.

---

4. Model R. Prof. Conduct 1.6(b).
5. Model R. Prof. Conduct 1.9(a).

3. Assume that last year Lawyer Cole represented client *A* in a car accident case. That case is now closed. Today *A*'s wife asked Lawyer Cole to represent her in a divorce proceeding against *A*. Must Lawyer Cole seek *A*'s consent to the representation? If *A* refuses to consent, can Lawyer Cole ethically accept the case anyway?

II. IDENTIFYING ISSUES

Recall that when you brief cases, you should read the whole case through once before you begin to prepare your brief. Similarly, when you are ready to identify statutory issues, read through all the material identified on page 46 in order to establish the context for your analysis and to identify the key provisions of the statute. When you have identified the provisions that will govern your issue, return to those provisions for another and even more careful reading. Read with a pen or pencil in your hand. Read the text of the statute word for word, looking for key terms that tell you what conduct the statute covers.

One way to find the key terms is to focus on the answers to the 5 W's set out on page 46. Another way is to ask yourself what someone would have to prove to show that the requirements of the statute were or were not met. If you can mark on the actual text of the statute, underline each word that tells you something about the answers to those questions. Then circle all the terms that tell you something about the relationships among the key terms (words like "and," or "or"). If you are working from hard copy library materials, write these words on a sheet of paper instead of underlining them. Here is an example:

The statute:

No cemetery shall be hereafter established within the corporate limits of any city or town; nor shall any cemetery be established within two hundred and fifty yards of any residence without the consent of the owner of the legal and equitable title of such residence.[6]

Key terms:

cemetery	hereafter	established	corporate limits
city	town	250 yards	residence
consent	owner	legal title	equitable title

Relational terms:

or	nor	and

Notice that each of the key terms raises an issue. Something other than a cemetery would not be covered by this statute, so to know whether

---

6. Va. Code, § 56 (Michie 1942), construed in *Temple v. Petersburg*, 29 S.E.2d 357 (Sup. Ct. Apps. Va. 1944).

this statute would apply to your client's facts, you must find out what the term "cemetery" means in this context. There may be a definition section in this same act, or there may be cases in which prior courts have defined the term. Either way, the term "cemetery" raises an issue you must resolve.

The same is true with the word "hereafter." The statute does not prohibit all cemeteries; it prohibits only those established "hereafter." After what? The date of the statute's passage? Or the date on which the statute became effective? What are those dates? Another issue to resolve. And what does the term "established" mean? Is a cemetery "established" when construction begins? Ends? When the cemetery first opens for business? Each key term identified above raises an issue the lawyer must resolve before the lawyer can know whether and how the statute might apply to her client's facts.

Are you surprised to find so many issues raised in one statutory sentence? Statutes are packed tightly with key terms, each of which sets out an important component of the statute and each of which raises an issue. If you were analyzing whether and how this statute applies to your client's facts, you would have at least twelve issues to consider.

One word of caution about identifying key terms: You may be tempted to treat a phrase as a single key term. For example, consider a statute providing that a donor must transfer possession of the gifted item with "a manifested intent" in order to part with ownership. You may first think of the words "manifested intent" as a single key term. However, that phrase would require the party seeking to establish the gift to prove two things, not one: (1) that the donor actually intended to part with ownership and (2) that this intent was sufficiently "manifested" to others. This phrase raises two issues, not one. Your list of key terms should treat these words separately.

One more strategy is helpful for reading statutes and identifying issues: rewriting the statute in your own words. Restating the rule in your own words is an effective tool of analysis, and you often can state the rule more simply and clearly than its original writer did. Do not, however, rephrase the *key terms* of the statute. Those terms will be defined and explained by the authorities; thus, they will have developed their own meaning, and as we saw above, that meaning is the critical question of the analysis.

EXERCISE 4-4

The Fair Housing Act, 42 U.S.C. §§ 3601-3619, prohibits housing discrimination. Underline the words or phrases that raise potential legal issues in the following portion of the Act:

> [I]t shall be unlawful . . . to refuse to sell or rent after the making of a bona fide offer, or to refuse to negotiate for the sale or rental of, or otherwise make unavailable or deny, a dwelling to any person because of race, color, religion, sex, familial status, or national origin.

III. INTERPRETING THE STATUTE'S LANGUAGE

Statutes are interpreted by case opinions. If case authority has already told you what the statute means, you can rely on that case law to the extent of its precedential value. But if no binding case law has answered your particular question, you must use other tools of interpretation. The most important of these tools are (1) the text itself, (2) the intent of the legislature, (3) the policies implicated by the possible interpretations, (4) the interpretation of any governmental agencies charged with enforcement of the statute, and (5) the opinions of other courts and of respected commentators.

The Text Itself. The most important inquiry is the "plain meaning" of the text itself. When the plain meaning is unambiguous, a court generally will give effect to the plain meaning unless the result would be absurd. Look first at the plain meaning of the statute's text. Also look for other parts of the statute or act that may tell you more about the language you are concerned with, such as the section explaining the act's purpose. Many acts contain separate definition sections. Even when your term is not defined, other parts of the statute may give you clues about what the term means.

The Legislature's Intent. Often, the text of the statute will be unclear. In such a case, many courts will try to decide what the legislature intended by the text's language. This search for the legislature's intent is problematic at best. The statute was probably enacted by a large group of elected officials who were serving in that office some years ago. The particular language you are concerned with may have been the result of political compromise, and various factions of the legislature may have had vastly different intentions surrounding that language. Quite possibly, your question never occurred to them at all. How can one decide the intent of the legislature as if the legislature were an entity with one mind? Yet, when a statute's language is unclear, a court applying the statute will have to have some basis for a decision. In such a circumstance, the court often will try to discern the legislature's intent.

Many courts are willing to consider the legislative history of the statute as evidence of legislative intent. Legislative history consists primarily of the documents or other records generated by the legislative body during its deliberations about the bill that ultimately became the statute. Legislative history comes in many forms, such as committee reports, speeches, witness testimony, or studies introduced into the record. Your research text will tell you more about legislative history and how to find it.

Policy. The fourth tool for statutory interpretation is analysis of the policy concerns implicated by a particular construction of the statute. Some implicated policies probably were part of the legislature's intent, but the legislature may not have foreseen all the policy concerns. Issues of interpretation implicating these other policies may arise. If the legislature has not spoken on the issue, the court is free to consider its own view of which possible interpretation of the statute would produce the best overall results for society.

In addition to the policies specifically applicable to a statute, some *kinds* of statutes carry a general policy leaning applicable to all statutes of that particular kind. These policies call for either a strict or a liberal construction of that kind of statute. The most common of these policies are:

- Statutes that change long-standing case law (statutes "in derogation of the common law") should be strictly construed. (A statute is strictly construed when it is read narrowly, so that it changes the legal environment as little as possible.)
- Statutes intended to remedy a problem ("remedial statutes") should be liberally construed to accomplish their remedial purpose. (A statute is liberally construed when it is read broadly to include more kinds of situations than a narrow reading would allow.)
- Statutes making certain conduct a crime ("penal statutes") should be narrowly construed, out of concern for the rights of the citizen-accused.

Finally, courts are guided by the general policy that, if possible, the meaning of a statute should be construed in a way that will render the statute constitutional.

Agency Interpretation. When enforcement of a statute is assigned to a particular agency, that agency must decide what the statute means in order to enforce it. Courts often look to this agency as the entity with the most expertise in the relevant issues and thus may give deference to the agency's interpretation. The court also may consider the interpretation of an agency that has no authority to enforce the statute but nonetheless works with the statute routinely. Look for agency interpretations in the agency's regulations, in the agency's decisions, and in case law.

Commentators and Other Courts. Finally, courts may recognize persuasive value attaching to the opinions of other courts and of respected commentators. The persuasive value of another court's opinion depends on the factors identified in Chapter 2. The persuasive value of a commentator's opinion depends on the reputation of the commentator and on the commentator's well-reasoned reliance on the other tools of construction.

IV. CANONS OF CONSTRUCTION

To decide how to construe a statute, a court also may consider commonly accepted maxims of interpretation known as "canons of construction." Here are some of the most generally applicable:

- Read the statute as a whole.
- Give effect to rules of grammar and punctuation.
- Construe technical terms technically and ordinary terms in their ordinary sense.
- When the same language is used in various parts of an act, the language is presumed to have the same meaning throughout.
- Where general words (such as "and any other") follow a list, the general words should be construed to refer to things similar to the items in the

list. This principle is sometimes called the principle of "ejusdem generis," meaning literally "of the same genus."

- Modifying words or phrases refer to the possible referent immediately prior to the modifier.
- Where a statute from state X is adopted in state Y, the construction given the statute by the courts of state X should be followed in state Y.
- If the statute does not contain an exception for a particular situation, the courts should apply the statute to that situation.
- Absent clear indication, the court should presume that the legislature did not intend to enact a statute that impairs fundamental and commonly held societal values.
- Specific description of one or more situations in the text of a statute implies the exclusion of other kinds of situations not mentioned.
- Different statutes on the same legal issue (statutes "in pari materia") should be read consistently, especially where the legislature intended to create a consistent statutory scheme.
- Sometimes the courts of state X will have interpreted a particular word or phrase in a certain way. If, subsequently, the legislature of state X enacts a different statute using that word or phrase, the language in the new statute should be interpreted as having the meaning previously given it by the courts.
- Although not technically part of the statute's text, such items as titles, preambles, and section headings are persuasive evidence of legislative intent.
- Sometimes courts will have construed the language of a statute in a particular way. Subsequently the legislature may amend the statute in ways that change or clarify other issues but do not address the issue the courts have interpreted. A later court may conclude that the legislature's lack of action to change the judicial construction is evidence of the legislature's approval of the court's construction.

Where courts have relied upon these maxims, they are treated as legal principles in and of themselves. Therefore, when you rely on one of them as part of the analysis of a rule, cite to a persuasive case opinion that adopts that maxim if you can. Even if you cannot find case authority adopting the maxim, however, a court still will be willing to consider the maxim's logic.

None of these guidelines for interpreting statutes will provide a certain answer. As a matter of fact, when you apply several, they may support contradictory results.[7] However, courts generally will consider these guidelines, so they will help you to predict what a court might decide or to persuade a court to interpret a statute favorably for your client.

---

7. Karl N. Llewellyn, *Remarks on the Theory of Appellate Decision and Rules or Canons About How Statutes Are to Be Construed,* 3 Vand. L. Rev. 395 (1950).

CHAPTER 5

Forms of Legal Reasoning

Lawyers and judges use a number of kinds of logical reasoning to argue and decide cases. They reason by relying on a statement of the law, like a statute or a common law rule articulated in a case (rule-based reasoning). They reason by comparing the facts of earlier cases to the facts of the present case (analogical reasoning). They reason by pointing to a desirable social or economic result, like promoting economic efficiency (policy-based reasoning). They reason by alluding to norms of conduct and customary expectations common in our society, such as how we expect people to act in certain circumstances (custom-based reasoning). They reason by appealing to a moral principle such as honesty or fairness or a political principle such as equality or democracy (principle-based reasoning).

In practice, these forms often overlap, but it is helpful to identify them separately in this chapter so that you can learn to recognize them and to use them in your own analyses. Mastering their use is one of the most important goals of a law school education.

This chapter will also cover one more important way lawyers advocate for a result: narrative. Today, we usually use the term "reasoning" to describe only logical processes like those described above, but an earlier understanding of "reasoning" was much broader. It included processes that transcend logical arguments and may even resemble intuition. For lawyers and judges, the most powerful of these nonlogical processes is narrative. No matter what understanding of the term "reasoning" one prefers, lawyers and judges know that narrative functions just as the logical forms do, to justify and persuade. Therefore, this chapter includes narrative along with the logical forms of reasoning. Together, these forms will provide you with a powerful set of tools for analyzing legal issues and for advocating for a particular legal outcome.

I. RULE-BASED REASONING

Rule-based reasoning is the starting point for legal analysis. It justifies a result by establishing and applying a rule of law. It asserts, "X is the answer because *the principle of law* articulated by the governing authorities mandates it."

> **RULE-BASED REASONING**
> Harold Collier should not be bound by the contract he signed because he is a minor, and *A v. B* establishes that minors do not have the capacity to execute binding contracts.

Example of Rule-Based Reasoning
"[T]he only lawful means to dispossess a tenant who has not abandoned nor voluntarily surrendered . . . is by resort to judicial process. . . . Applying [this principle of law] to the facts of this case, we conclude, as did the trial court, that because Wiley failed to resort to judicial remedies against Berg . . . , his lockout of Berg was wrongful as a matter of law." *Berg v. Wiley*, 264 N.W.2d 145, 151 (Minn. 1978).

EXERCISE 5-1
Rule-Based Reasoning

Your client owns rental property. She wants to know whether she can refuse to rent to unmarried couples. Read the following statute and write one paragraph that uses rule-based reasoning to answer her question.

> It shall be unlawful to refuse to sell or rent after the making of a bona fide offer, or to refuse to negotiate for the sale or rental of, or otherwise make unavailable or deny, a dwelling to any person because of race, color, religion, sex, familial status, or national origin. 42 U.S.C. § 3604(a) (2000).

II. ANALOGICAL REASONING (Analogizing and Distinguishing Cases)

Analogical reasoning is another major form of legal reasoning. The most common variety of analogical reasoning justifies a result by making direct factual comparisons between the facts of prior cases and the facts of the client's situation. The comparison can demonstrate factual similarities (leading to a similar result) or factual differences (leading to a different result).[1] A comparison that points out similarities asserts, "X is the answer because the facts of this case are just like the facts of *A v. B*, and X was the result there." Comparing cases to point out similarities is often called "analogizing" cases.

---

1. Comparisons that show differences are often called "disanalogical" or "counteranalogical" reasoning. For simplicity, however, we will use "analogical" reasoning to refer both to pointing out similarities and pointing out differences.

ANALOGICAL REASONING
(Similarities)
Harold Collier should not be bound by the contract he signed because, like the defendant in *A v. B*, he is only sixteen, and in *A v. B* the defendant was not bound by the contract she signed.

A comparison that points out differences asserts, "Even though X was the answer in *A v. B*, that is not the appropriate answer here because the facts in this case are different from the facts in *A v. B*. Comparing cases to point out differences is often called "distinguishing" cases.

ANALOGICAL REASONING
(Differences)
In *C v. D*, the minor was bound by his contract. However, Harold Collier's situation is unlike the situation in *C v. D* because there the defendant had signed a statement asserting that he was nineteen, thus deliberately misrepresenting his age. Harold Collier, however, never made any statement about his age. Therefore, the result in *C v. D* does not control Collier's case.

Example of Analogical Reasoning

"[In *Fahmie*,] property was conveyed to [Fahmie], who had no knowledge of the installation of the culvert [or the violation of state law]. Fahmie made application to the development commission to make additional improvements to the stream and its banks. It was then that the inadequate nine foot culvert was discovered, and the plaintiff was required to replace it.

The case before us raises the same issues as those raised in *Fahmie*. Here, the court found that in 1978 the wetlands area was filled without a permit and in violation of state statute. The alleged violation was unknown to the defendant and was discovered only after the plaintiff attempted to get permission to perform additional improvements to the wetlands area." [The court went on to assert that the result in the pending case should be the same as the result in *Fahmie*.] *Frimberger v. Anzellotti*, 594 A.2d 1029, 1033 (Conn. 1991) (ellipses omitted).

EXERCISE 5-2
Analogical Reasoning

Your client's mother has just died, and a dispute has arisen over who owns the mother's dining room table and the set of eight matching chairs. Your client, James, has told you this story: His mother was 80 years old when she died, and her neighbor, Martha, had often taken her to the store or the doctor. Martha has now produced a thank you note from the mother, dated six months before her death, in which the mother wrote, "Dear Martha, I can't thank you enough for all your help through the years. I want you to have my dining room table and chairs. You can come get them anytime you want."

You have found a relevant case, *Elder v. Fisher*, which is summarized below. Write a paragraph using analogical reasoning to argue that the attempted gift is not valid. Then switch sides and write a paragraph pointing out differences between *Elder* and Martha's claim, to demonstrate that *Elder* does not mean that Martha should lose.

> *Elder v. Fisher:* Janice Elder had a ruby ring, which she kept in her safe deposit box at a local bank. She wanted to give it to her sister, Darlene, for her birthday. Janice met Darlene and several friends for lunch. In the presence of the friends, Janice said to Darlene, "You're the best sister anyone could have. From this moment on, my ruby ring is yours. Meet me at the bank Wednesday at noon, and I'll get it out of the safe deposit box." Janice died in a car accident on Tuesday, and her executor, Fisher, refused to turn over the ring to Darlene, claiming that no valid gift had been made because donor had not physically handed over the ring. The court held that actual physical delivery was required and that therefore no valid gift had been made.

III. POLICY-BASED REASONING

Policy-based reasoning justifies a result by analyzing which answer would be the best for society at large. It asserts, "X is the answer because that answer will encourage desirable results for our society and discourage undesirable results."

POLICY-BASED REASONING
Harold Collier should not be bound by the contract he signed because he is only sixteen, and people that young should be protected from the harmful consequences of making important decisions before they are mature enough to consider all the options. Further, contract defaults are likely when minors undertake contractual obligations, and contract defaults dampen economic growth and decrease productivity levels.

Example of Policy-Based Reasoning
"To approve this lockout [of a defaulting tenant by a landlord] . . . merely because in Berg's absence no actual violence erupted while the locks were being changed would be to encourage all future tenants, in order to protect their possession, to be vigilant and thereby set the stage for the very kind of public disturbance which it must be our policy to discourage. . . . " *Berg v. Wiley*, 264 N.W.2d 145, 150 (Minn. 1978).

EXERCISE 5-3
Policy-Based Reasoning

Your client signed a one-year lease for an apartment, but before he moved in, he lost his job. Without the job, he was unable to afford the rent, so he

[handwritten margin notes at top:]
Elder
— sisters
— ring in safety deposit box
— tells sister verbally to meet at bank on certain date
Hold: no valid gift, no phys. gift

notified his landlord that he would not be able to take the apartment after all. The landlord has refused to rent the apartment to any other tenant and is holding your client responsible for the entire year's rent. Write a paragraph setting out a policy-based argument in favor of your client. You can consider both the economic effects and the social effects of a rule that allows landlords to do what this landlord is doing.

IV. PRINCIPLE-BASED REASONING

[handwritten margin notes:]
Martin
— donor = elderly woman, neighbors
— dining room set
— written note thanking Martin for 'help'
— pick up furniture when you want

Principle-based reasoning justifies a result by appealing to a broad principle or character trait valued by our society, such as a principle of morality, justice, fairness, or democracy. It asserts that "X is the answer because that answer upholds notions of morality, justice, fair-play, equality, democracy, or personal freedom."

[handwritten margin notes:]
Gifts:
oral vs written
1) better indication
2) seriousness
3) offer

PRINCIPLE-BASED REASONING
Harold Collier should not be bound by the contract he signed because enforcing contracts like his would encourage sales agents to lie and would reward unfair and dishonest sales practices.

Example of Principle-Based Reasoning
"A succession of trespasses . . . should not . . . be allowed to defeat the record title. . . . [T]he squatter should not be able to profit by his trespass." *Howard v. Kunto,* 477 P.2d 210, 214 (1970).

EXERCISE 5-4
Principle-Based Reasoning

Your client bought a house and soon discovered that the roof leaked. The seller had not made any statement to your client about the roof, but your client believes the seller knew about the problem. Up until now, your jurisdiction has not required a seller to tell a buyer about problems like this roof, so long as the seller makes no affirmative statement about the quality of the roof. You want to argue that your jurisdiction should impose a duty on sellers to disclose significant defects of which they are aware. Write a paragraph using principle-based reasoning to argue in favor of this change in the law. You can consider principles like honesty and fairness.

V. CUSTOM-BASED REASONING

Custom-based reasoning justifies a result by reliance on cultural and societal norms of behavior. It asserts, "X is the answer because that result is consistent with what we expect of people in this society." Custom-based arguments often are phrased as statements about what is and is not "reasonable." Some legal rules directly incorporate custom-based reasoning as the operative legal standard, such as the negligence standard ("the reasonable person") or the constitutional standard for judging pornography ("falls outside contemporary community standards") or rules that protect people from "undue" influence.

CUSTOM-BASED REASONING

Harold Collier should not be bound by the contract he signed because it is unreasonable to expect a minor to be able to match wits with an experienced and overreaching sales agent. In our society, people do not make contracts with minors; they deal with the minor's parent or guardian.

Example of Custom-Based Reasoning
"[T]here is no . . . reason to deny plaintiff relief for failing to discover a state of affairs which the most prudent purchaser would not be expected to even contemplate." *Stambovsky v. Ackley*, 572 N.Y.S.2d 672, 676 (1991).

EXERCISE 5-5
Custom-Based Reasoning

Your client has signed a contract to buy a house. The contract requires the seller to deliver "marketable title," which is a title a reasonable person would accept and pay fair value for. Your client has now discovered that the house extends over the lot line by one foot. The house was built in 1892, and the seller claims that he owns the extra twelve inches under the doctrine of adverse possession. Assume that you have researched the doctrine and the applicable facts, and as far as you can tell, the seller's claim appears true. Can you use custom-based reasoning to argue that, even if the seller's claim appears likely, title partially based on adverse possession instead of actual record title does not satisfy the definition of marketable title?

VI. NARRATIVE

Narrative justifies a result by telling a story whose theme implicitly calls for that result. Narrative uses the components of a story (characterization, context, description, dialogue, theme, and perspective) to appeal to commonly shared notions of justice, mercy, fairness, reasonableness, and empathy. In this sense, narrative is closely related both to principle-based reasoning and to custom-based reasoning, but narrative is far more contextual, placing these other forms of reasoning in a specific situation. Narrative tells the client's story in a way that encodes but does not directly articulate the commonly held principles and values on which these two logical forms rely.

The governing rule might directly adopt a legal standard easily communicated as a narrative theme. For instance, assume that the applicable rule about the enforcement of contracts made by minors allowed enforcement only if the other party to the contract did not use "undue" influence to convince the minor to enter into the contract. Narrative would use storytelling techniques such as description, dialogue, characterization, perspective, and context to establish that the other party's conduct was or was not "undue."

> **NARRATIVE**
> **(where the use of undue influence is an issue in the governing rule)**
> Harold Collier should not be bound by the contract he signed because Jenkins, a car dealer for twenty-two years, discouraged Harold from calling his parents to ask advice and told him that another purchaser was looking at the car at that very moment. Jenkins lowered his voice, said, "Tell you what I'll do. I'll knock off $1,000 just for you—just because this is your first car. But you can't tell anyone how low I went. This will have to be our secret."

Even if the applicable rule does not articulate a legal standard based on a particular narrative theme, however, narrative still persuades. A narrative demonstrating the fairness of a particular result can convince a judge to exercise any available discretion in favor of the client, to create an exception to the general rule of law, or to reinterpret or overturn the rule. The law is not insensitive to justice, mercy, fairness, reasonableness, and empathy, even when those commonly shared values are not directly incorporated in the legal rule. As a matter of fact, those notions underlie much of the more abstract rationales in policy-based or principle-based reasoning. Narrative can serve as a powerful partner with policies or principles, providing a real-life example of the policy or principle that justifies the desired result.

For example, recall that the rule prohibiting enforcement of contracts made by minors is supported by the policy rationale that minors should be protected from the harmful consequences of making important decisions before they are mature enough to consider all the options. Narrative reasoning can bolster that policy point:

> **NARRATIVE**
> **(consequences to minor not part of rule, but part of policy behind rule)**
> Harold Collier should not be bound by the contract he signed because he is only sixteen; he has never before shopped for a car; he was pressured by a sophisticated sales agent; he did not have the benefit of advice from any advisor; and the car purchase will exhaust the funds he has saved for college.

Each form of reasoning has persuasive power, and each has particular functions in written legal analysis. As we shall see in Part III of this book, rule-based reasoning establishes the structure of the analysis and organizes the written discussion. Within that structure, a complete analysis includes reasoning based on applicable rules, analogies, policies, principles, norms, and narrative. In addition to its role in the written legal analysis, narrative is paramount in the written fact statement.

Begin to notice the kinds of reasoning you find in the cases you read, the arguments you hear your classmates and your professors make, and your own analysis of hypothetical questions. By next year at this time, your skills in using all of the logical forms of reasoning will have increased dramatically.

EXERCISE 5-6

Make a photocopy of section I-A of the sample office memo found in Appendix A. In the margin of the photocopy, identify each form of reasoning you find, and be prepared to explain your labeling.

PART THREE

Writing the Discussion of a Legal Question

CHAPTER 6

The Writing Process and Law-Trained Readers

Now that you understand the legal authorities and the kinds of legal reasoning you will be working with, it is time to turn your attention to the document you will write and to the reader for whom you will write it.

I. THE WRITING PROCESS

Writing is a process with distinct stages and distinct goals at each stage. Each writing stage serves an important function as you work toward a finished document. This chapter identifies five main stages of a writing task and invites you to use each stage consciously as an opportunity to strengthen your writing.

STAGES OF THE WRITING PROCESS
1. Reading and analyzing the materials.
2. Creating an annotated outline.
3. Writing a working draft of the analysis.
4. Converting that analysis into a document designed for a reader.
5. Editing for style and technical correctness.

This section will describe each stage, and writing process hints will be included at appropriate points throughout the rest of the book. For easy identification, this margin symbol will mark those process hints in future chapters. Two caveats about this description of the writing process are in order, however. First, writing processes are as personal as signatures and fingerprints. The stages presented here represent a common way of approaching a writing task, but your own process will be unique to you. What is important is that you find places in your *own* writing process for the *activities* described here.

Second, the writing process is recursive. While you are working on the tasks of one stage, you often will find yourself returning to the tasks of an earlier stage and anticipating those of a later stage. Writing requires you to circle back again and again as you come to understand more about your legal issue, your client's facts and goals, and the available legal strategies. Your willingness to construct, dismantle, and reconstruct your document will be crucial to achieving a good written product.

Stage 1: Reading and Analyzing the Materials. Start by reading carefully all parts of your assignment, paying particular attention to the assignment's articulation of the issue(s). If you have any trouble understanding the issues, try writing them out in your own words and comparing them to the issue statements in the relevant case law. In a law office, you will be encouraged to talk to the assigning lawyer to clarify any confusion over the scope of the issue. In law school writing, to the extent permitted, clarify any questions with your professor.

Then read all of the relevant legal sources, briefing the cases and taking notes on the statutes as Chapters 2-5 explained. Use a separate sheet of paper for each source so you can sort them later. Be sure to keep your legal issue in mind, and look particularly for the ways in which each legal source might tell you something about your legal issue. You are looking generally for answers to the following questions:

KEY INFORMATION ABOUT LEGAL AUTHORITIES
1. What is the governing rule?
2. What do its important terms mean?
3. What are some examples of facts that have satisfied the rule's requirements?
4. What are some examples of facts that have *not* satisfied the rule's requirements?
5. What policies or principles does the rule serve?

Make a note about each thought or question that occurs to you, whether you think it might have merit or not. There will be time later for sorting and discarding. This is the time for wide, creative perception.

Stage 2: Creating an Annotated Outline. At some point, you must arrive at an outline of your analysis. It is ideal if you can create the outline before you begin to compose a draft, even if later you find you must change it. Start by formulating and outlining the governing rule. Then use a version of the rule's outline to create the main categories of your outline. Chapter 7 will explain this process in more detail, but an example here may help. Assume that you have outlined a rule setting out the requirements for revoking a will. The outline of that rule gives you a good starting outline for a written discussion of that issue. Under each element, you would discuss whether your client's facts establish that element.

OUTLINE OF WILL REVOCATION ISSUE
To revoke a will, a testator must
1. have the intention to revoke, and
2. take some action that demonstrates that intent.

Once you have the main categories in place, select one of your authorities and ask yourself what it tells you about the first category (the intention to revoke). Does it help you answer any of the five questions we identified in the box labeled "Key Information About Legal Authorities"? If so, write that information on your case brief or other notes for that authority. *Note the page number on which you find the noted information.* You will have to cite to it when you begin to write, and you will save valuable time if you do not have to look for it again. Then move to the second category (an action demonstrating that intent), and go through the same process. Does this legal authority tell you any of the five kinds of information about the second category? Go through this process with each authority, keeping in mind that some authorities will give you information about more than one category.

When you have finished examining each authority, gather all relevant information under the appropriate categories. Use a separate sheet of paper for each category. For each point you have learned, write a complete sentence expressing that information. For instance, under the "intent" category, you might write: "The testator must intend to revoke the will now, not in the future." Under the third subcategory of the "action" element, you might write: "The action must not be consistent with any interpretation other than the intent to revoke." These sentences will be the bases for the *thesis sentences* of your paragraphs. And as we shall see in Chapter 21, good thesis sentences are crucial.

Now you are ready for the last step in the outlining stage: selecting the authorities you actually will discuss in your analysis. For each piece of information you have listed, select the sources that give you the best support or the most important information for that point. Notice that you do not select the *authorities* you will discuss until you have identified the *points* you plan to make. This writing strategy will help you organize according to the relevant substantive points and not simply list and describe cases.

One more point about outlining your analysis: Outlining comes easily for some people; others find it difficult. If you are in the latter group, there is good news and bad news. The bad news is that a tight, linear structure is essential for a good office memo or brief. The good news is that you do not have to create that structure first. Many people find that they must write a very rough draft before they are ready to create an outline. Writing before you outline usually takes longer, but often the resulting outline is more reliable. The key is finding the method that works best for your own writing process.

Stage 3: Writing a Working Draft of the Analysis. Your first job as a writer is working out your own analysis of the issue. Your primary purpose in writing a working draft is to use the writing process as an analytical tool. Dean and former Judge Donald Burnett put it this way:

> Clear expression . . . is not merely a linguistic art. It is the testing ground for ideas. Through the discipline of putting an argument into words, we find out whether the argument is worth making. . . . The secret . . . is to start verbalizing early—while there is still time to learn from the discipline of forming ideas into words. You must begin by identifying your client's goal and the issues to be resolved. Each issue is defined by a cluster of facts and governing

legal principle. If you cannot articulate this nexus of law and fact, you do not yet have a grasp of the case.[1]

Your working draft is where you "grasp the case." It guides, deepens, and tests your analysis, and it forms your ideas into the kind of structured, linear reasoning that lawyers must master. Ultimately, your analysis will take the form of a document designed to communicate with your reader, but do not worry yet about creating that document. First concentrate on working out your own analysis.

Write out your analysis, putting flesh on the outline's bones. Chapters 7-10 will explain how to organize the material. In the working draft stage, focus your attention on the substance and structure of your analysis. Each time you write a statement about what the law is or what an opinion said, note a source and page number. While you are writing your working draft, you need not stop to look up the rules explaining how to cite correctly. The revision stage will give you the chance to correct citation form, spelling, punctuation, and legal usage. In the working draft stage, do the best you can on those matters, but do not let them distract you from your primary task at this stage: creating a solid analysis of your issue.

Try to arrive at the end of Stage 3 with enough time to put down the document for a while. Then return to your draft and revise it, based on what you see when you read with fresh eyes.

Stage 4: Turning the Analysis into a Document Designed for Your Reader. After your analysis is solid, turn your attention toward your reader. The working draft of your analysis will become the Discussion section of your office memo or the Argument section of your brief. In Stage 4 you will check your organization to be sure that it will meet your reader's needs. You will complete the document by writing its statement of facts and its other components.

Stage 5: Editing for Style and Technical Correctness. In this last stage, turn your attention to the fine points of writing. Edit to achieve clarity and correct citation form, punctuation, and grammar. These technical matters are the most easily visible criteria for judging writing. Readers will notice these matters first and draw from them conclusions about the skill and care of the writer. A sloppy document causes a reader to doubt the document's substantive accuracy.

Suggestions for Consciously Using the Writing Process. First, be alert for signs that you need to revisit earlier stages. Although the completed document should take the reader on a linear journey toward the document's conclusion, you will find that the process of creating the document is far from linear. Rather, the process returns you again and again to earlier stages to reconsider earlier decisions. The willingness to reconsider earlier writing decisions and to revise existing material is one of the hallmarks of a good writer.

Second, experiment with different writing strategies, and observe your own writing process. What works well for you at each stage? Do you work

---

1. Donald L. Burnett, Jr., *The Discipline of Clear Expression*, 32 The Advocate 8 (June 1989).

better if you dictate a draft first? Does free-writing help you? How about charts or colored pens? Each writer's creative and analytical processes are unique. Part of your goal in your first few years of legal writing should be to observe as much as you can about your own process so that you can adopt writing strategies that work for you.

Third, be patient. On your first few writing assignments, take the stages in order without trying to combine or compress them. Your goal on these first assignments is to let each stage of the writing process teach you some critical skills. Soon you will have developed those skills well enough to speed up each stage. You will learn to customize each stage to fit your own skill level, the complexity of the assignment, and your own unique creative processes.

Fourth, master the general principles before you decide to try something new. This introductory course on legal writing teaches the basic principles that operate in most situations. First master the basic substantive and organizational principles covered in this course. Soon you will develop the judgment to know when and how you can depart from them.

Finally, start early. Good writing takes time—almost always more time than the writer first expects.

II. LAW-TRAINED READERS

A. Focus on the Reader

The goal of an office memo or a brief is to communicate with a reader. As a matter of fact, you can think of a memo or brief as a conversation with your reader. As in any conversation, the better we know our conversational partners, the more effectively we can communicate. The characteristics of your reader will govern many of the choices you make as a writer.

We do not have to be reminded to write to a reader. Whether we realize it or not, we always write to *someone*, but sometimes we find that we are writing to ourselves rather than to the real reader. We are having a conversation with ourselves. Or we may write to the real reader but with inaccurate or incomplete information about that person. We forget to stop before we write and ask, "Who is this person, and what is she likely to be concerned about?"

When you undertake a legal writing task, you may not know your reader well—perhaps not at all. But you can still write with a fairly accurate focus on this unfamiliar reader because law-trained readers share certain characteristics. Even in large cities, lawyers and judges live in a legal community that shares certain values, customs, and forms of expression. Understanding these values, customs, and forms of expression will help you present your message effectively.

The general characteristics of law-trained readers in this chapter introduce you to the study of readers, but do not just accept the principles that follow. Notice your own reactions when you read. Try to be a participant-observer of the reading process. Your observations of your own reactions as a reader will be your best writing teacher. Observe too the other law-trained readers you know. This way, as the years of your legal practice go by, your writing will become better and better.

B. Attention Levels

Before a speaker can communicate, the audience must be listening. Here is some information about the attention levels of law-trained readers:

1. A reader's attention is finite. Even the most diligent reader will run low or run out.
2. A reader's investment in the nuances of the topic may not be as great as the writer's. Although the law-trained reader will have a particular need to understand the material, these readers are extraordinarily busy. The judge has many other cases and does not have a personal investment in this one. The senior partner has many other obligations and depends on the memo-writer to analyze thoroughly but communicate succinctly.
3. A reader's attention is not evenly distributed. It is greatest in the first several pages, and it decreases rapidly from then on.
4. Readers generally save some attention for the conclusion. They are willing to invest attention there, but only if they can locate the conclusion easily and if the conclusion is clear and compelling enough to warrant the investment.
5. Although readers spend more attention on the document's first few pages and on a compelling conclusion, attention levels revive a bit at internal beginnings and endings, like the start of a new issue or the last few paragraphs of a statement of facts. This revival is more likely if the new issue is marked by a heading or subheading.
6. Stories, especially real life stories, are engrossing. Many readers pay more attention to facts than to abstract legal concepts. This means, for instance, that attention levels are higher in the middle of an effective Statement of Facts than in the middle of the Argument or Discussion

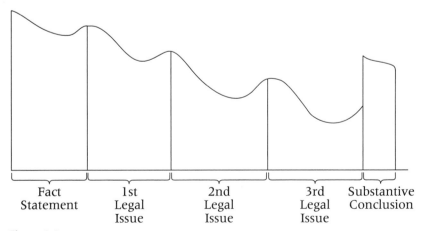

| Fact Statement | 1st Legal Issue | 2nd Legal Issue | 3rd Legal Issue | Substantive Conclusion |

Figure 6-1
Attention Levels

section. It also means that, even in the middle of a Discussion or Argument section, a reader's attention level will rise a bit when the material begins to apply law to fact.

7. A reader's attention level is lowest about three-fourths of the way through the Discussion section of an office memo or the Argument section of a brief.

These observations about readers underlie an important writing principle: Placement of material is one of the important decisions a writer must make. A good writer places the most important parts of the analysis where the reader can find them quickly and give them first priority for her attention.

C. Road Maps

Most readers want a road map—some sense of where they are and where they are headed. But law-trained readers have an even greater need for an organizational structure. Here's why:

1. A reader's first priority is to understand the law. A law-trained reader's first step in the process of understanding the law is an outline. This process of learning and applying law set out in outline form is how most lawyers and judges studied law. It is basic to the way law-trained readers think. In the first few semesters of law school, this learning style and thinking process probably came more naturally to some than to others, but by the end of law school virtually all lawyers approach legal analysis by some variation of this method. This process is one of the primary components of "thinking like a lawyer."

2. Lawyers and judges do not read the law out of intellectual curiosity but because they have a problem to solve. They are looking to your memo or brief to help them solve it. This means that your discussion of the law must be clearly and closely tied to the facts and issues of the case. Your organizational structure serves as the continuing reminder of how your legal discussion relates to the problem to be solved.

3. A law-trained reader reads skeptically, constantly assessing the strength and accuracy of the analysis and the credibility of the writer. The most visible part of the analysis, the part the skeptical reader first evaluates, is its organization. Here the law-trained reader expects to find the outline of the law. If a reader doubts the organization of the analysis, the reader wonders whether the content of the analysis is reliable.

4. At some point in their legal education or practice, law-trained readers have studied many of the more common rules of law. Such readers will be used to thinking of those rules in a familiar order or structure. Even if a reader is not already familiar with a particular rule of law, a statute or a leading case may set out the rule in a particular structure. A law-trained reader will be expecting to analyze the issue in this familiar order or structure. Law-trained readers are not comfortable with organizational surprises, and an uncomfortable reader is an unreceptive reader.

D. Readers as Commentators

It is easy to assume that writing is a one-way street, with the discourse all flowing in one direction. We tend to think that we, as writers, are the only speakers. We think this because we cannot hear anyone else talking. In reality, the most important party to the conversation, the reader, *is* talking, but we can't hear her. Each of us has a voice in his or her mind—an opinionated, skeptical, and talkative "Commentator." We've already observed this character at work because when a writer mistakenly begins writing to herself, she is writing to her own internal Commentator.

The reader has such a Commentator too, and that little voice will chatter at every opportunity. The Commentator will be saying things like "No, that's not right, because . . . " or "What in the world do you mean by that?" or "But wait, where is the discussion about . . . ?" Think of yourself as a reader. Haven't you been reading this chapter listening to both the written word and to your own Commentator?[2]

The reader's Commentator will not remain completely silent, and there is nothing the writer can do to change that. The Commentator's participation can even be helpful. Yet each time the Commentator speaks, the reader must listen to two voices at once; the writer must compete with the Commentator for the reader's attention.

The writer, then, has two objectives: (1) The writer wants to keep the reader's Commentator relatively quiet, resolving its concerns at the points where they arise, and (2) when the Commentator does speak, the writer wants it to be saying "OK," "right," "yes," point by point by point. As a writer, you must anticipate the Commentator's chatter before the conversation occurs and try to preempt that chatter. Your goal is to craft your side of the conversation to keep the Commentator as quiet and agreeable as possible.

E. Judges as Readers

Judges share the characteristics of other law-trained readers. Their attention is finite. They are busy and impatient with delay in getting to the bottom line. They generally focus more attention on the beginning and end of a document or a section than on the middle. They find facts engrossing. They want a road map. They value clear organization that sets out the rule of law. But judges tend to have some additional characteristics as well. Here are some other observations about how judges read.

1. Although any law-trained reader is a skeptical reader, testing the analysis at each step, a judge is particularly so. This skeptical testing is the heart of a judge's job. Girvan Peck explained it by describing judges as "professional buyers of ideas."[3] However, even a skeptical judge will be less skeptical of the analysis of a lawyer known for careful and honest

---

2. If so, be grateful to your Commentator. The sort of critical reading the Commentator inspires is essential to legal analysis. When you are studying the law and writing about it, your own Commentator is your best friend.

3. Girvan Peck, *Writing Persuasive Briefs* 77 (Little, Brown Co., 1984).

work than of the analysis of a lawyer with a poor reputation for either competence or candor.

2. Because judges are human, a judge who is already convinced of the equities of your position will be more receptive to your legal arguments. This judge will *want* you to be right on the law. This human desire can help to overcome a little of the judge's natural skepticism.

3. Most of us are more willing to accept the analysis of one whom we like and of one who has been considerate of our needs. This is true of judges as well. This does not mean that judges decide cases on the basis of social and political connections. But a lawyer who treats the judge professionally, with respect and consideration, will be a more effective advocate than the lawyer who does not.

4. As public servants with public responsibilities, judges are concerned about the policy implications of their decisions. However, trial judges and judges serving on intermediate appellate courts often see their role as requiring them to apply the law the way the jurisdiction's highest court would. Not only do judges prefer hearing that they were right, but reversals often mean having to deal with the case again. A judge's goal is to resolve cases, not protract them.

    Therefore, trial judges and judges serving on intermediate appellate courts are most persuaded by authorities that help them predict how the higher court would decide the question. For judges at these levels, policy arguments are less persuasive than clear mandatory authority. Judges serving on the highest appellate court in the jurisdiction are much more amenable to policy arguments than are their colleagues on lower courts.

5. Because most judges plan to spend many years on the bench, they take a long-term view of each legal issue. Judges are concerned about how an individual ruling may constrain or empower them in future cases.

6. Lawyers as a group tend to be personally conservative (though not necessarily politically so). This is particularly true of judges. Because of the public nature of their job and the fact that they are seen as safeguarders of public morality, lawyers who become judges tend to be conservative in their personal lifestyle.

7. People tend to cling more tenaciously to conclusions they think they have reached by themselves than to those asserted by others. Judges are no different. Thus, when a judge notices that the writer is using a particular technique for persuasion, the technique loses its effectiveness. Heavy-handed use of a persuasive technique usually hurts more than it helps. The most effective persuasive techniques are invisible to the reader.

8. A reader who feels pushed will resist. An effective legal argument will not push an unwilling reader down a path. Rather, an effective legal argument will place the reader at a vantage point that allows the *reader* to see and choose the best path. Thus, as a brief writer, you must decide how far you can take the judge without losing the judge's cooperation in the process. The consequences of pushing a judge to accept an unreasonable argument go beyond the judge's rejection of the *un*reasonable parts of the argument. The judge will tend to reject the *reasonable* parts of the argument as well.

9. Judges read briefs in order to decide between legal positions. When such readers are presented with categories, particularly categories identified with point headings, they tend to keep score. They may not even realize they are doing it, and they often will not observe that the rhetorical effect of keeping score is to weight each category equally. Knowing this tendency can help a writer select an organizational plan and decide how to subdivide the argument.

10. As decision-makers encounter arguments one by one, they tend to label each argument as "weak" or "strong" before going on to the next argument. Decision-makers are more likely to be convinced by one strong argument than by a series of weaker ones. Also, a strong argument will lose some of its force if it follows or is followed by weak arguments on the same point.

11. The reader's perception of the strength of the first argument affects the reader's perception of the strength of the arguments that follow. As law-trained readers, judges expect to find the strongest argument first. Unless the judge knows of a reason the weak argument had to be discussed first, the judge will presume that the strongest argument is first and thus that subsequent arguments are even weaker.

12. Judges often relate to the lawyers who practice in their courts in much the way that parents relate to children. If you are a parent, you know that there is nothing quite as tiresome and irritating as constant fighting and bickering among children. Most judges have little tolerance for bickering and blustering lawyers. Judges prefer to focus on legal issues rather than personalities.

13. One final observation about judges: The judge may skim the briefs and then ask a law clerk to read and summarize them. The impact of a law clerk on the brief-reading process is a bit of a wild card, but there are two general observations that you should keep in mind. First is the relative inexperience of most law clerks as compared to most judges. Remembering this inexperience will help you to take care not to leave out steps in the analysis on the assumption that your reader is an expert on your issue. Second, although these readers are often inexperienced, they also tend to be bright. Many judicial clerks served on their school's law review and received much of their formative training in that context. Thus, they expect the details of a brief to be right. They tend to draw conclusions about the reliability of the analysis based on the lawyer's attention to these details. They may well scrutinize every aspect of your brief more thoroughly than a busy judge could.

F. Law Professors as Readers

Your primary readers for law school documents will be law professors. Undoubtedly, these professors already understand a great deal about the relevant area of law and about the particular authorities on which your analysis will be based.

Ordinarily, a writer should tailor the document to the reader's pre-existing knowledge. If the writer is certain that the reader knows some of the relevant information, the writer would refer generally to the information only when necessary to put new information in context. However, law school writing is a different matter. Unlike most readers, your professor is not reading to learn particular information. Instead, your professor is reading to evaluate what information *you* have learned and how well you can communicate it. If the information is not set out in your document, your professor will not know whether and how well you understand it.

Therefore, in law school writing, assume that you are writing to a law-trained reader who has no particular expertise in the area you are discussing. Your goal is to include the information your professor wants to evaluate without explaining more than the assignment asks.

CHAPTER 7

Large-Scale Organization: Creating an Annotated Outline

An annotated outline is the most reliable method for making your legal analysis complete and coherent. Without it or its equivalent, you are likely to miss issues and to wander off track as you write. Also, it will provide the structure of the discussion section of your memorandum. If you have carefully prepared the annotated outline, writing the memorandum will flow easily. Your topic headings, thesis sentences, and case citations in support of your explanation and application of the law will already be laid out. This chapter first explains how to identify the structure of a legal rule and to write it out in outline form. Then, the chapter explains how to use that structure to create an annotated outline for your particular assignment.

I. RULE STRUCTURES

Rules of law adopt particular structures. Familiarity with these structures will help you in several important ways. First, recognizing a rule structure is a method for quickly deepening your understanding of the rule. This study tool will work well for virtually all of your law school classes. If you are preparing a course outline for contracts, for instance, your outline will be more effective if you consciously outline the legal rules you are studying. Second, the rule's structure will become the basis for the large-scale organization (the outline) of your memo or brief, or even the relevant part of your contracts final exam.

Therefore, when you formulate a legal rule from a case opinion, try to express it in an outline format. Use any version of traditional outline form, with roman numerals, large case letters, arabic numerals, and small case letters, as necessary. If the rule takes the form of a simple list, you can denote the list using arabic numbers. This outline of the relevant rule will allow you to focus your analysis on each element in an orderly way, not forgetting any element and not confusing your analysis of any one element with that of any other element.

As you gain experience in outlining legal rules you will notice certain common rule structures. Becoming familiar with these common structures early in your legal training will help you to recognize them quickly and to outline the rule and your legal analysis more easily.

A Conjunctive Test. This kind of rule sets out a test with a list of mandatory elements. For example, consider the following rule: To revoke a will, a testator must have the intention to revoke the will and must take some action that demonstrates that intent. The outline for this rule would set out each of the required elements like this:

> To revoke a will, a testator must
> **1.** have the intention to revoke and
> **2.** take some action that demonstrates that intent.

A Disjunctive Test. This kind of rule sets out an "either/or" test. It identifies two or more subparts and establishes a certain result if the facts fall within any *one* subpart. For example, consider the following rule: A lawyer shall not collect a contingent fee in a criminal matter or a divorce. You might outline the rule like this:

> A lawyer shall not collect a contingent fee in either of the following kinds of cases:
> **1.** a criminal matter or
> **2.** a divorce.

Notice that the difference between the first two rule structures lies in the introductory language specifying whether all subparts are required or whether any single subpart is sufficient.

A Factors Test. This kind of rule sets out a flexible standard guided by certain criteria or factors.[1] Some rules condition the legal result on a more or less objective standard. A burglary statute, for instance, defines burglary using a number of fairly objective criteria. Was it a dwelling? Did it belong to another? Did the defendant enter it? However, some rules condition the legal result on a much more flexible standard, giving more discretion to the decision-maker. To keep judges from being totally arbitrary and to help them exercise their discretion wisely and uniformly, rules using flexible standards often identify factors or criteria to guide the decision-maker. Here is an example of such a rule:

> Child custody shall be decided in accordance with the best interests of the child. Factors to consider in deciding the best interests of the child are: the fitness of each possible custodian; the appropriateness for parenting of the lifestyle of each possible custodian; the relationship between the child and

---

1. Some scholars use the term "rule" to refer only to fairly objective, concrete legal tests and use the word "standard" to refer to more flexible tests like a factors test or a balancing test. To avoid confusion, however, we will use the term "rule" to refer to both kinds of legal tests.

each possible custodian; the placement of the child's siblings, if any; living accommodations; the district lines of the child's school; the proximity of extended family and friends; religious issues; any other factors relevant to the child's best interests.

Placed in outline form, the rule would look like this:

> Child custody shall be decided in accordance with the best interests of the child. Factors to consider in deciding the best interests of the child are:
> 1. the fitness of each possible custodian
> 2. the appropriateness for parenting of the lifestyle of each possible custodian
> 3. the relationship between the child and each possible custodian
> 4. the placement of the child's siblings, if any
> 5. living accommodations
> 6. the district lines of the child's school
> 7. the proximity of extended family and friends
> 8. religious issues
> 9. any other factors relevant to the child's best interests

Notice the critical difference between this rule structure and a conjunctive test (a rule with mandatory elements). In a conjunctive test, all of the subparts must be met, but here the subparts are just factors to consider rather than separate individual requirements. One or more can be absent from a particular case without necessarily changing the result. The decision-maker has the discretion to gauge the relative importance of each factor.

A Balancing Test. This kind of rule balances countervailing considerations against each other. A rule setting out a balancing test is also inherently flexible, so such a rule often includes factors or guidelines to assist the decision-maker in weighing each side of the balance.

For example, consider this dispute over legal procedure. Prior to trial, parties in civil litigation try to obtain information from each other by using interrogatories (written questions directed to another party and calling for answers under oath). Sometimes, the party receiving a set of interrogatories will object to certain interrogatories, arguing that answering would be unduly burdensome. To decide whether the party must answer the interrogatories, the judge applies the following rule:

> A party must respond to properly propounded interrogatories unless the burden of responding substantially outweighs the questioning party's legitimate need for the information.

To measure "burden," the judge might consider a number of factors, such as the time and effort necessary to answer; the cost of compiling the information; any privacy concerns of the objecting party; and any other circumstances particular to the objecting party's situation. To measure "legitimate need," the judge might consider a number of other factors, such as how important the information would be to the issues of the trial, whether the information would be available from some other source or in some other form, and any other circumstances relating to the party's need for the information. Placed in outline form, the rule would look like this:

A party must respond to properly propounded interrogatories unless the burden of responding substantially outweighs the questioning party's legitimate need for the information.

A. The burden of answering:
1. the time and effort necessary to answer
2. the cost of compiling the information
3. any privacy concerns of the objecting party
4. any other circumstances raised by that particular party's situation

B. The questioning party's need for the information:
1. how important the information would be to the issues of the trial
2. whether the information would be available from some other source or in some other form
3. any other circumstances relating to the party's need for the information

Compare this rule structure with the factors test. In a factors test, the decision-maker gauges a single interest, for example, "the best interest of the child." In a balancing test, the decision-maker balances two competing and different interests, comparing the strength of each interest against the other. In the discovery rule above, these two interests are the burden of answering and the need for the information.

A Defeasible Rule. A defeasible rule is a rule with one or more exceptions. Here is an example of a rule with an exception:

A lawyer shall not prepare any document giving the lawyer a gift from a client except where the gift is insubstantial or where the client is related to the lawyer.

Placed in outline form, the rule would look like this:

A lawyer shall not prepare any document giving the lawyer a gift from a client except
A. where the gift is insubstantial or
B. where the client is related to the lawyer.

Again, notice that the critical distinction between this structure and the others lies in the introductory language defining the subparts as exceptions to a general principle. Notice also that you can accurately articulate some rules using different structures. For instance, do you see how you could easily articulate this rule using a disjunctive rule structure?

A Simple Declarative Rule. A simple declarative rule contains no elements, factors, or other subparts. For example, if you are analyzing the validity of an unsigned will, you might be dealing with a rule like this:

> To be valid, a will must be signed.

If you have looked carefully and find no subparts, factors, or other criteria for applying the rule, you can assume that your rule is a simple declarative rule. In such a case, your structure will be a simple one-point structure. However, take care to assure yourself that your rule has no lurking elements or other subparts. Overlooking elements or other subparts is a common mistake for beginning legal writers.

Rules Combining Several Structures. Some rules use more than one rule structure. Such a rule will use a larger structure like one of the examples set out above. However, the rule's subparts may use another rule structure. For instance, consider this rule governing attacks on the credibility of criminal defendants who testify at trial:[2]

> Evidence that the accused previously was convicted of a crime shall be admitted if the crime involved dishonesty or false statement or if the crime was punishable by death or imprisonment in excess of one year and the conviction's probative value outweighs its prejudicial effect.[3]

This rule uses the disjunctive (either/or) structure for its larger structure, like so:

> Evidence of a prior conviction may be admitted if it falls within either of the following categories:
>
> **A.** if it involved dishonesty or false statement, or
>
> **B.** if it was punishable by death or imprisonment in excess of one year and its probative value outweighs its prejudicial effect.

Notice, however, that subpart B contains two requirements (the punishment requirement and the comparison of probative value to prejudicial effect). Notice also that the inquiry about probative value and prejudicial effect is a

---

2. At a trial, the judge decides what testimony or documents can be "admitted" into evidence by applying the rules of evidence in effect for that court. If the judge refuses to admit a document into evidence, that information cannot be considered when deciding the case.

3. *See* Fed. R. Evid. 609(a) (paraphrased).

balancing test. What's more, the cases interpreting this rule probably describe the factors to be considered in gauging "probative value" and "prejudicial effect." Thus, a more detailed outline of the rule might look like this:

Evidence of a prior conviction may be admitted if it falls within either category A or category B:

A. if the conviction involved dishonesty or false statement; or

B. if both of the following are true:

1. the conviction was punishable by death or imprisonment in excess of one year; and

2. its probative value outweighs its prejudicial effect

    a. probative value is gauged by:
    [List factors set out in the cases.]

    b. prejudicial effect is gauged by:
    [List factors set out in the cases.]

EXERCISE 7-1

Outlining a Rule

For each of the following excerpts from case opinions, formulate a rule and write it out in outline form using one or more of the rule structures described above.

1. *Issue: When can an otherwise legally insufficient contract still be enforced?*

"[W]here one party has by his words or conduct made to the other a promise or assurance which was intended to . . . be acted on accordingly, then, once the other party has taken him at his word and acted on it, the party who gave the promise cannot afterward be allowed to revert to the previous relationship as if no such promise had been made." *Wheeler v. While*, 398 S.W.2d 93, 96 (Tex. 1965).

2. *Co-owners of property can ask the court to partition their property if they no longer wish to own it jointly and if they cannot agree on a manner of division. Normally, the court partitions the property by dividing it and awarding part to one co-owner and part to the other ("partition in kind"). Issue: When can a court order the sale of the property (and the division of the proceeds) rather than dividing the property itself?*

"[P]artition by sale should be ordered only when two conditions are satisfied: (1) the physical attributes of the land are such that a partition in kind is impracticable or inequitable; and (2) the interests of the owners would better be promoted by a partition by sale . . . . [In considering the practicability of partition in kind, the court can consider such matters as] the situation and location of the parcel of land, the size and area of the property, the physical structure and appurtenances on the property, and other factors." *Delfino v. Vealencis*, 436 A.2d 27, 30-31 (1980) (citations omitted).

II. CREATING AN ANNOTATED OUTLINE

As you know, outlines divide material into topics and organize them, using levels to show how the topics relate to each other. The first level of distinction is reserved for the broadest categories. The second level represents the largest distinctions within each of the broad categories. Those second-level topics can be subdivided even further. We begin with the first level of distinction for a legal analysis: the legal question(s) you have been asked to address.

A. The First Level: The Legal Questions You Have Been Asked to Address

Your writing assignment probably identified the legal question or questions you are to address. If you have been asked to analyze whether William Levitt's actions constituted burglary, you have been asked to address only one legal question. But if your assignment also asks you to address whether his statement to Delores Corbitt, his alleged common law wife, will be admissible at trial, you have been asked two legal questions. The first question will be governed by the rule identifying the elements of burglary. The second question will be governed by a different rule—a rule of evidence.

Use your outline's first level of distinction (roman numerals) to identify the separate legal questions you have been asked to address. At the outline stage, you can phrase these issues as questions or, if you are ready, as your answers to the question. In the example above, the outline's first level of distinction would be:

I. Do William Levitt's acts constitute burglary?
II. Will Levitt's statements to Delores Corbitt be admissible at trial?

If you have been asked only one question, use a roman numeral "I" for that question, and do not be concerned that you will not have more than one roman numeral. Let the use of the roman numeral assure you and your reader that this is the issue you were given and, therefore, that this is the point of connection between that question and your own analysis.

B. The Second Level: Governing Rules

Whether or not your assignment identifies separate legal questions, your research might reveal that the answer will depend on two different legal issues governed by two different legal rules. Your assignment might ask, "Can our client succeed in a claim for negligence against the other driver?" This is one legal question. However, you might discover that its answer will depend on the answers to two separate legal questions governed by two separate legal rules: (1) whether your client can establish the elements of a negligence claim; and (2) whether the applicable statute of limitations has expired.[4] If your answer to the question will require analysis under two different and unrelated legal rules, use the next level of distinction (upper case letters) to represent the discussions of these two different rules.

For instance, in our prior example, assume that the second question (admissibility of Levitt's statements) will require analysis using two different governing rules: the rule of evidence that prohibits admission of statements made to a common law spouse and that jurisdiction's rule defining a valid common law marriage. Our outline now looks like this:

I. Do William Levitt's actions constitute burglary?
II. Will Levitt's statements to Delores Corbitt be admissible at trial?
    A. Are Levitt and Corbitt married according to common law?
    B. Are statements to a common law spouse admissible at trial?

C. The Third Level and Beyond: The Rule's Structure

Use your outline of the governing rule(s) to form the next levels of your discussion's outline. For instance, in our example, the next levels under the roman numerals might produce the following outline:

I. Do William Levitt's actions constitute burglary?
    A. breaking
    B. entering
    C. dwelling
    D. of another
    E. in the nighttime
    F. intent to commit felony therein
II. Will Levitt's statements to Delores Corbitt be admissible at trial?
    A. Are Levitt and Corbitt married according to common law?
        1. intent of both parties to be married, and
        2. actions holding themselves out to the community as husband and wife.
    B. Are statements to a common law spouse admissible at trial?
        [Statements made to a common law spouse are privileged and therefore not admissible unless the privilege is waived.]
    C. Has Levitt waived the privilege?

Notice that your research on the admissibility of statements to a common law spouse has yielded a defeasible rule (a rule with an exception). The rule is

---

4. Statutes of limitation prescribe the time limits within which a claim can be brought.

a simple declarative statement with one exception: "The statements are inadmissible unless the defendant has waived the privilege." Therefore, you have discovered another subissue: whether Levitt waived the privilege. You must return to your research to learn what kinds of acts would constitute a waiver. When you find the rule that governs waiver, you will use it to structure section C in the outline.

Thus, the outlines of the relevant rules provide the organization for your working analysis of each issue. Using this outline, your analysis of the burglary question would discuss each element separately, completing the discussion of one element before proceeding to the next. Then you would proceed to the admissibility question and follow the same process there.

D. Omitting Issues Not in Dispute

You may already know that some of the categories on your outline will not be issues in your assignment. For instance, in the burglary example, the "nighttime" issue probably would not be disputed if the entry of the building occurred at 2:00 A.M. You can revise your outline now to delete the "nighttime" category, but you cannot forget the issue just yet. You will need to explain to your reader your reasons for not addressing that element. Chapter 10 will describe how and where to give your reader this information.

To be sure you do not forget the element, you can leave it in its place on your working draft outline and simply skip it when you start to write. After you have written out the other parts of your analysis, you will use your working draft to create the document designed for your reader. At that point, you will be doing some rearranging of the sections anyway, so revising the outline then would be convenient. For example, as Chapter 10 will explain, it probably will be appropriate to place the most dispositive element first in your discussion, and you may not know which element will be most dispositive until you have written out your analysis.

Leaving the category in its place temporarily can be a good idea for another reason. Legal conclusions often turn out to be less obvious than they first appeared. Only after you have researched both law and facts will you be ready to predict how the rule will apply to your client. Only then will you know for certain whether you can treat any parts of the rule as undisputed.

E. Uncertainty About Which Rule Your Jurisdiction Will Adopt

You may find that your jurisdiction has not yet adopted a rule governing your particular issue. Or perhaps your jurisdiction's rule reflects an unwise approach to the issue, and your client's interests would be served best by the adoption of a different rule. If you are writing an office memo, you will have to predict what rule the court probably would adopt. Then you can analyze the disposition of your client's particular issue, assuming that your prediction is correct. You may also need to analyze the result if the decision-maker adopts the other rule. Your working draft outline might look like this:

> **A.** If the court adopts rule *A*, what will be the result?
> **B.** If the court adopts rule *B*, what will be the result?
> **C.** Which rule is the court most likely to adopt?

In section C, in an office memo, you will need to compare the two rules to predict which rule the court is likely to adopt. In a persuasive brief to the court, you will be arguing which rule the court should adopt. In either case, you will need to address the relative strength of the authority supporting each rule.

F. Annotating Your Outline

Your working outline now provides the structure for your discussion of the authorities. The next step is deciding which authorities you will discuss under each point in the outline and for what purpose. Chapter 6, pages 66-68, described this process. If you have not yet read those pages, do so now. Remember that you should write a complete sentence expressing each relevant point you have learned about the rules of law. *Do not select the authorities you will use until you have identified the points you will make. This way you will find yourself organizing according to the relevant substantive points and not simply listing and describing cases without using them to make a relevant point.*

For each of the following exercises, draft an outline for a discussion of the legal issue. Assume that the "rules" set out below are the rules you have formulated from the applicable authorities.

EXERCISE 7-2

Facts: Joe Barrymore and Reynold Manitoba, fans of different hockey teams, came to blows in a discussion of the relative merits of their teams. Barrymore came out the loser, with four broken ribs. The fight ended when Manitoba pushed Barrymore into a cleaning closet and padlocked the door. Barrymore has come to your firm to find out whether he can sue Manitoba for battery and for false imprisonment.

Rules:

- Battery is the intentional infliction of a harmful or offensive bodily contact.
- A contact is harmful if it causes pain or bodily damage.

- A contact is offensive if it would be damaging to a reasonable sense of dignity.
- To meet the requirement of intent for a battery claim, the defendant need only have intended to make the contact; intent to harm is not necessary.
- A defendant has committed a false imprisonment if he intentionally confined the plaintiff within boundaries set by defendant.

EXERCISE 7-3

Facts: Upon her graduation from Kelly Technical College, Shakira Matthews began looking for a job in computer repair. She used the services of Grisham Employment Services. Matthews, an African-American woman, has begun to suspect that Grisham has known of employment opportunities in her field and has not disclosed those opportunities to her. She has come to your law office to learn if the law gives her any recourse. You have researched Title VII of the Civil Rights Act of 1964 and found the following provisions:

Rules:

- The term "employment agency" means any person regularly under-taking with or without compensation to procure employees for an employer or to procure for employees opportunities to work for an employer and includes an agent of such a person. 42 U.S.C. § 2000e(c) (2000).
- It shall be an unlawful employment practice for an employment agency to fail or refuse to refer for employment, or otherwise to discriminate against, any individual because of his race, color, religion, sex, or national origin. . . . 42 U.S.C. § 2000e-2(b) (2001).

[handwritten note:] Q: ISSUES: Is it unlawful for an employment agency to fail to disclose opportunities to client persons on basis of client's race or gender

CHAPTER 8

Small-Scale Organization: Explaining the Law

After you have a large-scale structure for your discussion, the next step is to write out the analysis, putting flesh on the bones of this structure. Chapters 8 and 9 will explain how to discuss a single legal issue. Chapter 10 will explain how to put the discussions of multiple issues together into one cohesive analysis.

What do we mean by a "single issue"? You will find that phrase used differently in many contexts, but for our purposes, we mean the analysis of a single element of a rule. For instance in the burglary example, each of the elements of the crime of burglary would raise a separate issue.

I. AN OVERVIEW OF THE PARADIGM FOR LEGAL ANALYSIS

A legal issue is analyzed by first identifying and understanding the governing rule and then applying that rule to a particular set of facts. First you must *explain* the rule; then you must *apply* that rule to the facts. Here is an overview of the basic paradigm:

PARADIGM FOR A WORKING DRAFT

Rule Explanation
1. Conclusion: State your conclusion about the issue.
2. Rule: State the applicable rule of law.
3. Rule Explanation: Explain the rule.

Rule Application
4. Rule Application: Apply the rule to your client's facts.
5. Conclusion: Restate your conclusion.

This chapter describes the rule explanation half of this paradigm. Many new legal writers are not sure what rule explanation covers. They also may think they have explained the rule more thoroughly than they actually have. These difficulties can be eased if, after the introductory paragraph (described below), you do not allow discussion of your client's facts (the second half of the paradigm) to slip into the first half of the paradigm—your explanation of the rule itself. Mixing explanation and application leads to confusion in identifying rule explanation. If you keep application out of the spot reserved for explanation, you will learn what rule explanation is *not*, which is vital to learning what rule explanation *is*.

Separating the halves of the paradigm also will help you accurately evaluate your own writing. Often a writer states the rule and then proceeds to write several pages about the rule and how it applies to the facts. The discussion seems thorough, but how can the writer tell? An accurate self-evaluation requires checking the depth and breadth of both halves of the reasoning process, and that is difficult to do when the two halves are intermixed. As a discipline, you might want to draw a line on your working draft between the rule explanation and the rule application. The line will remind you to keep your discussion of your client's facts below the line.

Keeping the halves distinct does not mean that while you are engaged in the process of writing the paradigm you must complete rule explanation before you attempt to write any rule application. For early versions of the working draft, you can write more freely. Many writers find this unstructured prewriting helpful. Using the paradigm means simply that at the conclusion of your writing process, the document should reflect distinct sections for rule explanation and rule application.

EXERCISE 8-1
Identifying and Labeling the Parts of the Paradigm

Read the "Facts" section of the office memo in Appendix A. Then read and photocopy section A of the office memo (a single-issue discussion). In the margins of the photocopy, identify and label each part of the paradigm.

II. STATING THE CONCLUSION

Law-trained readers are impatient to learn your answer, so the first thing your reader will want to see is your conclusion. If you already know what your conclusion will be, put it in a sentence and use that sentence as the section heading. Then write an introductory paragraph (sometimes called a "thesis paragraph"[1]) in which you state your conclusion again in two to three sentences. Place this paragraph immediately after the heading. In these sentences, your reader should learn (1) the issue to be decided; (2) your conclusion on that issue; and (3) your basic reason for that conclusion, if you can state it succinctly. Often the governing rule will be implicit in this statement, but

---

1. Shapo, Walter, and Fajans, *Writing and Analysis in the Law*, 131 (Revised 4th ed., Foundation Press, 2003).

you need not state it directly here, because you likely will be stating it as the first sentence in the next paragraph.

For example, assume that your firm represents Linda Pyle, who recently bought a tract of land to use as a commercial horse stable. A lawyer from another firm, Howard Gavin, represented Pyle in the land purchase transaction. After buying the land, Pyle discovered that a neighboring quarry owned an easement across her property, and the use of the easement is interfering with the stable's operation. Pyle has come to a partner in your firm, and the partner has asked you to research whether Gavin's failure to check the title for possible easements constituted legal malpractice. Here is an example of the beginning of the written discussion of this issue:

I. Linda Pyle has a strong claim for legal malpractice against Howard Gavin.

Howard Gavin committed legal malpractice in his representation of Linda Pyle because he did not meet the required standard of professional skill and diligence. The representation called for a basic task common to general practitioners, and the problem could have been prevented simply by doing thorough research.

If you are writing a brief to the court, probably you will already know what your conclusion will be. If you are writing an office memo, however, and if the issue is a close one, you may not be sure what your conclusion will be until you have progressed further in the writing process. If you are not yet sure, you can state the issue here rather than the conclusion, and proceed with writing your analysis. Once you have a solid draft, rewrite the heading and the first paragraph to provide your reader with the information above.

III. STATING THE GOVERNING RULE

Next, state the governing rule. Follow it with citations to the primary source(s) for the rule. Here is a rule statement added to our example:

I. Linda Pyle has a strong claim for legal malpractice against Howard Gavin.

Howard Gavin committed legal malpractice in his representation of Linda Pyle because he did not meet the required standard of professional skill and diligence. The representation called for a basic task common to general practitioners, and the problem could have been prevented simply by doing thorough research. A lawyer has a duty to provide a client with representation that meets or exceeds the standard of *professional skill and diligence commonly possessed and exercised by a reasonably prudent lawyer* in this jurisdiction. *Jacobson v. Kamerinsky* [citation].

Usually the rule statement should be the first sentence in the first paragraph after the introductory (thesis) paragraph. Occasionally, however, an issue is complex enough to require a little context or clarification before stating the rule. If so, *briefly* set out the necessary context or clarification, but get to the rule statement as quickly as you can. Not only will your reader be impatient to learn the rule, but the discipline of concisely stating the rule immediately after the conclusion is an important part of your analytical process. It forces you to articulate the focal point of the first half of the analysis, and it focuses your attention on the rule you are about to explain.

After you have typed your statement of the rule, look for the key term or legal standard. The primary task of your rule explanation is to define that term or standard. Just for the working draft, you may want to use italics for these key words so you can easily refocus your attention on them.

IV. EXPLAINING THE RULE: FIVE COMPONENTS

The third step is explaining where the rule comes from and what it means. Rule explanation usually includes five components. Generally, these components are so closely interrelated that you will not be able to break them out and perform them sequentially. While you are explaining one, you will also be explaining another, so do not use this list as an organizing tool. Instead, use it to evaluate your rule explanation for its completeness:

1. Show how the authorities demonstrate that the rule is what you say it is. Often you can do this by setting out the relevant content of the authorities (facts and holdings of cases or key provisions of statutes). Sometimes, if you have had to formulate the rule by synthesizing or reconciling authorities, as Chapter 3 described, you may have to explain your synthesis or reconciliation.

2. Explain the rule's purpose or the policies it serves. The way the rule will apply to your client's facts will be influenced by the rule's purpose and the policies it serves, so your reader will need to understand these underlying rationales. Chapter 11 explains this part of rule explanation in greater detail.

3. Explain how the rule has been applied in the past. Interpreting the language of a rule requires attention to how courts have applied it and how they have not applied it. What are some examples of cases in which the rule's requirements have been met? Have not been met?

4. Explain any additional characteristics that will affect how the rule may be applied. Is this rule to be liberally or strictly construed? Are there burdens of proof or presumptions that may affect how the rule will apply to future cases? Does the rule require an elevated level of proof, like clear and convincing evidence? Will expert testimony be required?

5. *To the extent necessary, explain any other possible understanding of the rule.* If another reasonable interpretation of the rule exists, your reader will want to know it. In persuasive writing you need address only those competing theories that your adversary has or will raise or that you think the judge may wonder about. In predictive writing, you should address any competing interpretation that is reasonably likely to arise. The explanation of another possible interpretation is sometimes called "counter-analysis" or "counter-explanation."

Match the depth of your discussion to your assessment of the strength of this second interpretation. If it is possible but unlikely that a court would adopt it, cover it briefly. However, if the choice between the interpretations is a closer call, discuss the counter-analysis in more detail, and explain why it is not the best or most likely interpretation.

V. GUIDELINES FOR RULE EXPLANATION

Here are some guidelines to keep in mind as you write the rule explanation section:

Use all relevant tools of statutory and case law analysis. Review the tools for case law and statutory analysis described in Chapters 2-4. Remember that the value of the information they yield is not simply in reporting (restating) it for your reader, but rather in *using it to make a point about the rule.*

Limit your explanation to those topics that will be relevant to the way the rule will apply to your client's facts. When you explain what the rule means, do not include everything one might ever want to know about the rule. Include only the information that may pertain to your client's situation. This focus will save your reader's patience, and it will save you writing and editing time. Since you have not yet written the section *applying* the rule to your client's facts, you will have to anticipate the application you have not yet written. After you write the application section, you may need to return to the rule explanation section to add or delete topics of rule explanation. Your goal is to match the coverage of the explanation section to the coverage of the application section.

Use only very short quotes of key language. If you force yourself to use your own words for the information you find in the sources, you will understand that information better, and you may be able to state it more clearly than the original writer did. Remember that your analysis must do more than simply retype material from the sources. Analysis begins only when you draw theses from the material in the sources and explain the reasoning that supports your theses.

Order your discussion of the authorities according to their importance, placing the most important authorities early in the discussion. Case authorities are important to an analysis primarily by virtue of their precedential value generally or by the similarity of their particular facts to your client's facts.

Articulate factors or guidelines. When you discuss the cases that are similar factually, try to discern and articulate any factors or guidelines that seem to be operating when the courts apply the rule to these kinds of situations. Sometimes such information will be described explicitly by the courts; sometimes you will have to infer it from other comments the courts have made or from the way the courts have applied the rule.

Do not use authorities just to fill up space or to prove that you have read them. Rather, demonstrate that you have the lawyerly skill of identifying the *key* authorities and analyzing them thoroughly.

Include a description of the rule's historical development if (1) the development is important for understanding the rule's current form; or (2) the rule's current form does not decisively answer your question, but the rule's history establishes a trend that can help you predict or persuade. If you choose to describe the rule's development, tell your reader why. Otherwise, a law-trained reader will become impatient with what may seem like an unnecessary history lesson.

Choose an appropriate option for using cases. You have three options for using cases: (1) using only a citation to the case; (2) using a citation with a parenthetical summary; and (3) using a case with an in-text illustration.[2] Choose among them according to your assessment of the importance of the point you are making. Here are examples of each:

Citation only:
One who is a minor at the time of making a contract can disaffirm the contract within a reasonable time after reaching the age of majority. *Woodall v. Grant,* 9 S.E.2d 95 (Ga. Ct. App. 1940).

Citation with a parenthetical summary:
A minor is estopped from disaffirming a contract if the minor knowingly misrepresented his age at the time he made the contract. *Woodall v. Grant,* 9 S.E.2d 95 (Ga. Ct. App. 1940) (minor did not knowingly misrepresent his age when he signed without reading a contract representing that he was an adult).

Citation with an in-text illustration:
A minor is estopped from disaffirming a contract if the minor knowingly misrepresented his age at the time he made the contract. *Woodall v. Grant,* 9 S.E.2d 95 (Ga. Ct. App. 1940). In *Woodall,* the minor had signed a brokerage contract to purchase stock options, and the contract contained a representation that the purchaser had attained the age of majority. However, the minor had signed the contract without reading it. The court reasoned that the law does not require a minor to read a contract and does not enforce the same

---

2. Michael R. Smith, 1991 Course Handouts, "Techniques for Using Authority in a Memo," on file with the author.

consequences on a minor as it would on an adult in the same circumstance. The court held that the minor had not knowingly misrepresented his age and, therefore, that he was not estopped from disaffirming the contract.

VI. ORGANIZING A PURE QUESTION OF LAW

Occasionally your issue will be a pure question of law. You have a pure question of law if the assignment asks you to analyze only *what the law is* in your jurisdiction and does not ask you to apply that law to your client's facts. For example, you might be asked, "In this jurisdiction, can a husband be forced to testify against his wife?" In such a case, your analysis will consist primarily of rule explanation, culminating with your conclusion about the question of law ("A husband cannot be forced to testify against his wife").

Or perhaps the assignment might ask you to apply the law to your client's facts, but there is no real question about the result of that application. For example, you might be asked "Can Mr. Studdard be forced to testify against Mrs. Studdard?" Once you have explained that a husband cannot be forced to testify against his wife, the application of that rule to Mr. Studdard is clear. In that case, your analysis will consist almost entirely of rule explanation. You will spend most of your time explaining the rule. At the end of the rule explanation, you can apply the rule to Mr. Studdard, but you probably will not need to do more than announce that as Mrs. Studdard's husband, Mr. Studdard will not have to testify.

Here is an example of a working draft of a rule explanation for the Pyle/Gavin issue.

A WORKING DRAFT OF RULE EXPLANATION	
I. Linda Pyle has a strong claim for legal malpractice against Howard Gavin.	Conclusion
Howard Gavin committed legal malpractice in his representation of Linda Pyle because he did not meet the required standard of professional skill and diligence. The subject matter of the representation is common to general practitioners, and the problem could have been prevented with thorough research.	Conclusion plus facts
A lawyer has a duty to provide a client with representation that meets or exceeds the standard of professional skill and diligence *commonly possessed and exercised by a reasonably prudent lawyer in this jurisdiction. See Jacobson v. Kamerinsky.* [citation]	Rule and citation
In *Jacobson*, the lawyer failed to file a timely claim before the medical malpractice screening panel. By statute, a medical malpractice claim cannot be pursued unless it has been filed before the screening panel within the applicable time limit. [citation] Therefore the client's claim was barred. Because a reasonably prudent lawyer would research and comply with the statutory requirements for bringing a particular kind	Key facts from cited case
	Holding from cited case

of claim, the court held that the lawyer was liable to his client for the losses that resulted from the failure to file the claim. [citation]

One gauge of the prudent lawyer standard is whether the task is something general practitioners are familiar with doing. In *Jacobson*, the court had pointed out that the enactment of the screening panel requirement had been widely publicized in newspapers, electronic media, and the state bar journal. However, the court explained that even without publicity, a prudent lawyer would comply with filing requirements because filing lawsuits is something general practitioners are familiar with doing. [citation] Therefore if the task is familiar to general practitioners, the court need not ask whether the particular lawyer should have been aware of the particular requirement. | Thesis sentence (a characteristic the court found significant)
Key facts
Court's statement about those facts
How court's statement supports thesis

Another gauge of the prudent lawyer standard is whether the error could have been prevented by research. In *Jacobson,* the court observed that an "error in judgment" does not constitute malpractice. [citation] While *Jacobson* did not expressly define the difference between an error in judgment and a breach of the prudent lawyer standard, the court distinguished the *Jacobson* facts from an "error in judgment" by pointing out that in *Jacobson* the correct answer would have been apparent had the lawyer done the necessary research. [citation] Therefore, although a prudent lawyer can make an error in judgment, a prudent lawyer does not make errors preventable by proper research. | Thesis sentence (another significant characteristic)
Disclosure that thesis is an inference
Reasoning from the court's observation about the facts

The "prudent lawyer" standard is not reduced for lawyers operating outside their area of special knowledge. In *Jacobson,* the lawyer-defendant had been in practice only ten weeks when he accepted the medical malpractice case. The court held that the lawyer's lack of experience did not excuse his failure. [citation] Clients should be entitled to at least the minimum standard of skill and diligence, according to the court. [citation] Also, a contrary rule would offer no incentive to lawyers to gain necessary knowledge or experience. [citation] | Thesis sentence (how rule applies to a particular situation)
Relevant facts
Holding on this point
Court's two policy reasons

The standard probably would not be affected by facts indicating that the lawyer intended to be particularly careful, or that he was otherwise skilled and diligent, or that he was a well-respected partner of a well-respected firm. Although no facts like these were present in *Jacobson*, the court's language and policy statement explained in the previous paragraph would seem to apply to this question as well. | Thesis sentence anticipating an issue
Disclosure of lack of similar facts
Reasoning (policy)

It is unclear whether the court would rely on expert testimony or would make its own judgment about what a prudent lawyer would do in a particular set of circumstances. This question was not at issue in *Jacobson*. However, the opinion does not mention the testimony of any expert witness, and the court's statements that a prudent lawyer would research the requirements for bringing a claim seemed to be statements of the court's own opinion rather than statements based on someone's testimony. The court's repeated references to the standard as "the minimum" that "any client should be entitled to expect" [citations] seem to indicate that the court considered itself competent to decide the standard. | Thesis sentence (evidence required)
Disclosure of no express authority
Inferring a point from the court's language

Thus, whether certain conduct falls short of the "prudent lawyer" standard appears to be determined on a case-by-case basis, by what the judge thinks a prudent lawyer would do. However, two ways to gauge whether the failure falls below the standard are: (1) whether the task is something general practitioners are familiar with doing; and (2) whether the problem could have been prevented by doing proper research.

Summary of points made in rule explanation

EXERCISE 8-2

Writing the Rule Explanation

Write out the rule explanation section for the following memo assignment, using *Lucy v. Zehmer*[3] as your only authority. One of the most common errors in legal writing is rushing into rule application before writing a sufficiently thorough rule explanation. Thus, this exercise, which requires you to write the rule explanation section only, is good practice.

Facts. Virginia Ryan is the owner of an antique shop. She has come to your firm, relating the following story and asking your firm to advise her.

Ryan is acquainted with Stewart Kaplan and his older sister, Julia Kaplan. Stewart and Julia are not on good terms. Their mother recently died, bequeathing to Stewart an old quilt and to Julia their deceased father's World War II medals. During the settling of the estate, relations between Stewart and Julia became even more strained when Julia gave the medals to a local historical organization without offering them first to Stewart. Stewart had a strong sentimental attachment to the medals because his father used to let him play "war" with them as a child, and he believes that Julia gave them away on purpose to spite him.

Ryan knew the facts of the dispute about the war medals, and she knew that the relationship between Stewart and Julia was strained. Ryan did not get along well with Julia either, and she and Stewart felt a common bond in this respect.

Several weeks after learning of Julia's disposition of the medals, both Stewart and Julia happened to attend a community carnival. Stewart saw Ryan there, and said to her, "Let's have a little fun." Ryan said, "OK. What do you have in mind?" Stewart said, "Follow me. We'll give my dear sister a scare." He took Ryan by the arm and led her to within earshot of Julia. Stewart winked at Ryan and, in a stage voice, offered to sell her the old quilt. Ryan said she was interested and asked what price Stewart had in mind. Stewart said, "How about $150?" Ryan said, "That's pretty steep for an old quilt. How about $25?"

Both Stewart and Ryan could tell that Julia had heard the conversation from the beginning. However, Ryan believed that Stewart was serious about selling the quilt. Stewart and Ryan continued negotiating the price, through several offers and counter-offers, finally settling on a price of $75. "Done!" said Stewart, winking at Ryan. He said, "Let's do this right. Here, let me write out the terms." He wrote, "Stewart Kaplan hereby sells to Virginia Ryan the old quilt he inherited from his mother for the price of $75." They both signed it. Still enjoying the game,

---

3. 84 S.E.2d 516 (Va. 1954). Opinion reprinted in Appendix E.

Stewart said, "Wait, we need today's date and the date I'll deliver the quilt to you." He inserted the date and added, "Delivery to occur next Wednesday." He also wrote, "Thanks for playing along. This was fun." Both parties initialed the additional writing, and Ryan put it in her pocket. She told Stewart that it was great doing business with him, that she had to get home to make supper, and she left.

The following Wednesday Ryan called Stewart to tell him that she had the check ready and to ask when he planned to deliver her quilt. Stewart stuttered that he had never actually intended to sell the quilt. Ryan said, "I thought that you wanted to get revenge on Julia." "Yes," said Stewart, "but just by letting her know how it feels to be ignored." "Well, that's not what I thought. I thought you wanted to get revenge by selling the quilt. I want that quilt, Stewart. It is an antique, and $75 is a fair price. Besides I already promised it to one of my customers."

Ryan wants to know whether she can enforce what she thought was Stewart's agreement to sell the quilt. An attorney in the firm has asked you to analyze Ryan's question. The attorney has instructed you to assume that a judge would find that Ryan genuinely believed that Kaplan was serious.

Issue. Can Ryan enforce a contract for the sale of the quilt?

Checklist for Rule Explanation

State the Conclusion

State your conclusion on the issue and your basic reason, if you can state it succinctly.

State the Applicable Rule of Law

Place the rule statement immediately after the introductory paragraph.

Explain Where the Rule Comes From and What It Means

- Did you show how the authorities demonstrate that the rule is what you say it is?
- Did you explain the rule's purpose or the policies it serves?
- Did you explain how the rule has been applied in the past?
- Did you explain any additional characteristics that may affect how the rule will be applied?
- If necessary, did you explain any other interpretation of the rule?

Tools for Using Case Authority
- Setting out the facts of the case
- Explaining what the court held about the rule
- Explaining any important dicta
- Explaining how the court applied the rule
- Where appropriate, explaining how the court did *not* apply the rule
- Pointing out any facts the court emphasized
- Explaining what legal commentators have said about the case or the rule

Tools for Interpreting Statutes

- Explaining the statute's plain meaning
- Applying any relevant canons of construction
- Explaining the legislature's intent
- Explaining the policies implicated by the possible interpretation(s)
- Explaining the interpretation of any governmental agencies charged with enforcement
- Explaining the interpretations of courts and respected commentators

General Principles

- Cite a source for each statement of a rule, a holding, the court's reasoning, or facts from a case.
- Do not discuss your client's facts in this section.
- Order your discussion of the authorities according to their importance.
- Articulate any factors or guidelines.
- Identify the *key* authorities and analyze them thoroughly.
- Include historical development if helpful for prediction or persuasion.
- Choose wisely among the options for using cases.

CHAPTER 9

Small-Scale Organization: Applying the Law

Now that you have explained the rule, you are ready to apply it to your client's facts. Remember that this half of the paradigm uses the deductive format of syllogistic reasoning—that is, applying a general, often abstract principle to a particular situation and arriving at a conclusion.

General principle (from rule explanation section)   Covenants not to compete are enforceable if the duration, the geographical scope, and the nature of the activity restrained are reasonable.

Application to particular facts   These three terms of the Watson/Carrolton covenant are reasonable.

Conclusion   Therefore, the Watson/Carrolton covenant is enforceable.

Although rule-based reasoning is still important in this second half of the paradigm, narrative, analogical reasoning, policy and principle-based reasoning, and custom-based reasoning are at least as important to rule application.

I. TWO APPROACHES TO WRITING THE APPLICATION SECTION

Since the point of the paradigm is to apply the rule you have just explained, the rule application section should track the rule explanation section. Each aspect of the rule you described in the rule explanation section should now be applied to your client's facts. Thus, some writers use the rule explanation section as their outline as they write the rule application section. If you use this approach, simply work your way through the application section by applying each point you discussed in the explanation section. This way you are sure to apply the rule you just explained instead of allowing your application section to wander.

You may find, however, that a slightly different approach works better for you. Although a written legal analysis ultimately should be framed in tightly reasoned logic, you may find that rigid allegiance to the structure of the rule explanation section stifles your own writing process. If you choose to open your early drafts to a broader writing process, you can begin writing the rule application section by focusing on the narrative (the facts) without looking back to the rule explanation section. You will have the rule in mind, but more impressionistically so. This strategy frees you to think like a storyteller and to focus more on the narrative themes the key facts suggest, and on the policies and principles they implicate. Be sure to compare your client's facts to the facts of precedent cases, pointing out relevant similarities and differences.

When you have a draft of each section, revise them both so the rule explained in the first half matches the rule applied in the second half. Perhaps you will need to add application of a point you discussed in rule explanation but forgot to apply in the application section. However, just as often, you will need to return to the explanation section to add or edit the discussion of a point you had not noticed until you began to write about your client's facts. No matter which way you approach the writing process, the end result should be the same—a logical analysis built upon a narrative theme.

II. CONTENT OF RULE APPLICATION

Although the organization of each rule application section will be unique to the rule and the facts involved, here are some general principles to keep in mind:

1. *Begin with a sentence or two stating your factual conclusion*, for example: "A judge would probably find that a reasonably prudent lawyer in Howard Gavin's situation would have checked the title for easements."
2. Then *apply each point from the rule explanation section*, keeping the most important points early in the discussion.
3. For each point, *write a thesis sentence* stating how that point will apply to your client's case.
4. In one or more paragraphs following each thesis sentence, *use your client's facts to explain why your thesis sentence is accurate.* If your role is predictive, explain the inferences and factual conclusions you think a judge or jury would draw from these facts. If your task is persuasive, use the facts to set out and support the inferences you want the court to draw.

   Use common sense. Imagine the situation your client has described to you. What would it have looked like? Seemed like? What other things might have been true if these are the facts? What additional unconfirmed facts might you be assuming? How might the scenario look to a judge or a jury? What facts would be important to a judge or a jury? Could someone else take the same facts and characterize them differently—that is, paint a different picture using the same facts?
5. Where possible, *support your thesis with direct fact-to-fact comparisons.* Identify the factual similarities between your client's situation and relevant precedent cases, explaining how these similarities demonstrate your points. Also, identify any significant factual *differences*, and

explain the point they demonstrate. Chapter 11 explains this important reasoning skill more thoroughly.

6. If helpful, *apply the rule's underlying policies to your client's situation.* Your client's facts may raise the precise concerns the rule was designed to address. If so, a court will be more likely to apply the rule strictly to your client's situation. A court will be less likely to limit the rule or to apply an exception. A court will be more likely to resolve doubts of application in favor of achieving the policy results the rule seeks. Conversely, if your client's facts do not raise the policy concerns the rule was designed to address, the court will be less willing to apply it strictly to your client.

   Reread the sample office memo in Appendix A, this time noticing particularly the uses of policy to help predict a result. A similar use of policy can persuade as well.

7. In an office memo, *identify any unknown facts that would be important to a resolution of the legal issue.* The assigning attorney will need to know if potentially important facts are missing from the analysis.

8. Where necessary, *refute any alternative rule applications.* In Chapter 8, we saw that you sometimes need to address and refute alternative interpretations of the rule. Just so, in the rule application section, there may be alternative views of how the rule might apply to your client's facts. This process is sometimes called "counter-application" or simply "counter-analysis." In predictive writing, your reader will need to understand these alternative views. In persuasive writing, you will need to address and refute your opponent's position.

   Note the difference between counter-analysis in the two stages: In the rule explanation stage, the theories disagree over what the rule means. Here, the alternative theories disagree over how the rule should apply to the facts. In either case, however, do not let your analysis become lost in your focus on counter-analysis. Good writing and effective advocacy call for keeping your own explanation and application of the rule at the center of the conversation.

9. *Re-state your conclusion.* After you have worked through your explanation of how the rule applies to your client's facts, restate the conclusion. If the analysis has been long or complex and your document will not have a separate "Conclusion" section, summarize the key reasons supporting the conclusion.

III. COMMON TROUBLE SPOTS IN RULE APPLICATION SECTIONS

The three most common weaknesses in rule application sections are (1) failing to apply the rule as the first half of the paradigm explained it, (2) asserting the predicted outcome without sufficiently explaining the reasoning that supports the prediction, and (3) failing to realize the diverse possible interpretations of the facts. Understanding these three weaknesses will help you avoid falling victim to them in your own analysis.

We have already discussed in some detail the first common weakness: failing to apply the rule as it was explained. Yet this is such a common difficulty that it merits a reminder. Be sure to complete the rule application section by matching its coverage and approach to the explanation section. Equally important, be sure to revise the rule explanation section to reflect the deepened and sharpened rule understanding you gained by writing out the factual analysis. This double-checking of rule-based and narrative reasoning against each other is an example of why both are critical to good legal writing.

The second common weakness may result from a belief that the application of the rule to the client's facts is so obvious that no explanation of the supporting reasoning is necessary. Nearly always this belief is erroneous. Explaining the supporting reasoning is particularly important since sometimes this process shows the writer that the application may not be as obvious as it first appeared. Even in cases where the application is clear, *some* explanation of the supporting reasoning is necessary.

The third common weakness is failing to realize the diverse possible interpretations of the facts. Sometimes this weakness results from forgetting to think independently and realistically about the facts. Many writers new to law study fall into the trap of assuming the infallibility of the inferences that someone else—like the client or the requesting attorney—has drawn from the facts. Yet, rare is the set of facts that does not support diverse inferences and interpretations.

Another and more insidious cause of this weakness is the difficulty of imagining multiple interpretations simultaneously. Perhaps an analogy will demonstrate how hard this can be. Look at Figure 9-1. You may have seen a graphic like this before. Do you see the old woman in this graphic? Do you see a young woman as well? Your brain can organize the black and white shapes of the graphic into a picture of either, but most of us can only see one at a time. More pointed for our purposes, once your brain has organized the sections to display one figure, it is difficult to find the other figure at all. Imagining diverse interpretations of facts is at least as hard as imagining diverse interpretations of these black and white shapes.

Not "seeing" these diverse interpretations of the facts is the most difficult weakness for a writer to diagnose and cure. If your assignment permits, ask others to help you imagine diverse interpretations of the facts. Present a friend or colleague with a simple chronology or other sanitized version of the facts rather than with your written description of them.[1] Your goal is to learn what story someone else might see in the facts, especially someone who has not first seen the story through your or your client's eyes.

If you must work alone, you must think both critically and creatively about the facts. Try to imagine how the various other parties to the situation would describe it. Imagine how you would describe it if you were representing those parties. Imagine how the facts might appear to someone who disliked your client and was therefore looking for an interpretation different from your client's position. This task will never be easy, and it will be particularly difficult in your early years of law study and practice. However, each year of law practice will improve your ability to see diverse interpretations of a set of

---

1. Take care not to breach client confidentiality. *See* Model R. Prof. Conduct 1.6.

Figure 9-1
How Old Is This Woman?

facts. Take the opportunity presented by your first few writing assignments to begin practicing this lawyering skill.

Here is an example of rule application for the Pyle/Gavin issue.

PYLE/GAVIN EXAMPLE—RULE APPLICATION ADDED

I. Did Howard Gavin commit legal malpractice in his representation of Linda Pyle?   Issue

    Howard Gavin committed legal malpractice in his representation of Linda Pyle because he did not meet the required standard of professional skill and diligence. The subject matter of the representation is common to general practitioners, and the problem could have been prevented with thorough research.   Conclusion plus facts followed by rule and citation

    A lawyer has a duty to provide a client with representation that meets or exceeds the standard of professional skill and diligence commonly possessed and exercised by a reasonably prudent lawyer in this jurisdiction. *Jacobson v. Kamerinsky*. [citation] [*See* pp. 95-97 for the rest of the rule explanation.]

A judge would probably find that a reasonably prudent lawyer in Howard Gavin's situation would have checked the title for easements. Receipt of title is, after all, the heart of the transaction, and carefully checking the title would be critical to evaluating the title the purchaser would receive from the seller.

Thesis sentence stating factual conclusion

The duty to check the title carefully would be particularly clear in a situation like Gavin's where the client has asked specifically whether there would be any problem with using the land for a particular purpose. A prudent lawyer would know that the use of real property can be limited either by law (such as by a zoning regulation) or by private agreement (such as an easement or a restrictive covenant recorded against the title). The client's specific question should have flagged the issue for Gavin, making Gavin's error even less excusable than the error in *Jacobson*. In *Jacobson,* the client did not ask a question that should have reminded the lawyer of the possible problem; yet the lawyer's error constituted professional malpractice anyway. [citation]

Thesis sentence applying Gavin's particular facts

Reasoning from factual comparisons

Further, both of the *Jacobson* gauges point toward liability. Representing a party to a real estate transaction probably falls within the group of tasks a general practitioner is familiar with doing. Basic real estate transactions are as common in the general practice of law as filing law suits. Nor was Gavin's omission a mere error in the exercise of professional judgment. The need to look for an easement would have been apparent if Gavin had done adequate *legal* research, and the easement itself would have been apparent if he had done adequate *factual* research. Just as in *Jacobson*, Gavin's error could have been prevented by proper research.

Thesis sentence applying points from rule explanation

Comparing facts

Applying 2nd point and comparing facts

Since the standard is not reduced by virtue of facts particular to the lawyer's experience, Gavin's relative inexperience and his lack of real estate expertise will not affect the legal result. Nor will his status in the bar or his usual skill and diligence. However, these facts do add to the equities of his case, especially since a judge in this jurisdiction would probably be aware of them. Although those facts should not change the ultimate result, they probably mean that the judge will not be happy about having to rule against Gavin. The evidence at trial will have to establish the cause of action clearly.

Thesis sentences dealing with other facts

Flagging the human impact

Finally, this evaluation that Gavin's representation fell below the prudent lawyer standard is based on an assumption that the standard can be judged without expert testimony. Additional research would be necessary to check this assumption. If the standard must be evaluated by reference to expert testimony, it will be necessary to consult with an expert.

Pointing out a necessary qualification

The claim that Gavin breached the applicable standard of care is strong. The subject matter of the representation is common to general practitioners. The problem could have been prevented with proper research. If Pyle is interested in pursuing the matter further, our next step should be the completion of our research on the need for expert testimony.

Conclusion Statement Summary of most important points

IV. EVALUATING YOUR DRAFT

Once you have completed a working draft of both halves of the paradigm, evaluate the draft. If possible, put it away for a day to let your mind clear. Then go through this procedure:

1. *Check the paradigm.* Mark off and label each part of the paradigm. Check to be sure that each part is there and in its proper order. Be sure that rule explanation and rule application are not intermixed.
2. *Evaluate the depth of rule explanation.* Ask yourself how well settled the rule is and how much explanation is necessary to clarify the rule's meaning.
3. *Evaluate the depth of rule application.* Have you written out a complete discussion of how the rule would apply to your client's facts and what inferences a judge or jury might draw from them? Watch particularly for rules that include an element pertaining to someone's state of mind or rules that set out a flexible standard (such as "a reasonable person" or "the best interests of the child"). When such a rule governs your client's issue, you probably will need to do significant factual analysis in the application section.
4. *Evaluate the content and internal organization of rule explanation and rule application.* First, confirm that the rule you explained is the rule you applied. Now, examine each section in smaller chunks. Identify the blocks of text devoted to particular substantive points, using labels in the side margin as do the sample drafts in this chapter and in Chapter 8. Is your organization logical? Does it communicate good ideas clearly?
5. *Check your perspective.* Remember the difference between predicting and persuading. If you are writing a predictive document, maintaining an objective perspective can be difficult. Many writers find themselves slipping into advocating their prediction rather than objectively evaluating it. After you have written your working draft, set it aside and then reread it to be sure you have not begun inadvertently to write as an advocate.

EXERCISE 9-1
Recognizing Analogical Reasoning

In the sample office memo in Appendix A, identify each instance of analogical reasoning (analogizing and distinguishing cases).

EXERCISE 9-2
Writing the Rule Application

Write a working draft of your analysis of the issue set out in Exercise 8-2. If you already wrote out a rule explanation section, simply complete the working draft by adding the rule application. Pay special attention to using analogical reasoning (analogizing and distinguishing cases) in your rule application.

Checklist for Rule Application[2]

State Your Factual Conclusion
- Use one or two sentences to state your conclusion about how the rule applies to your client's facts and, if feasible, the most important reasons supporting that conclusion.

Apply the Rule to Your Client's Facts
- Be sure the content of the rule explanation and rule application sections are consistent and that you applied the rule you explained.
- Compare the key facts from the case authorities to the key facts of your client's situation, noting the legally significant similarities and differences.
- Explain the inferences and factual conclusions a judge or jury could draw from your client's facts.
- In the draft of an office memo, identify any unknown facts that would be important to a resolution of the legal issue.
- Evaluate the appropriateness of the factual discussion's depth.

State Your Conclusion
- Restate your factual conclusion in one sentence.
- If the analysis has been long and complex or if your document will not have a separate "Conclusion" section, include a brief summary of the primary reasons supporting the conclusion.

---

2. *See* the end of Chapter 8 for checklist for the rule explanation half of the paradigm.

CHAPTER 10

Discussing Multiple Issues: Putting It All Together

Chapter 7 explained how to use the question(s) you have been asked and the relevant governing rules to create the outline for your analysis. Chapters 8 and 9 explained how to write the analysis of each single issue identified on your outline. This chapter explains how to finish writing the analysis, connecting these single-issue discussions and putting them in the order your reader will prefer. With very little revision, this completed analysis will become the "Discussion" section of your office memo or the "Argument" section of your brief to the court. Here is an overview of an analysis of multiple issues:

THE MULTI-ISSUE PARADIGM

1. Heading stating your overall conclusion on a legal question
   [An "umbrella section" introducing the subsections to follow.]
   A. Heading stating your conclusion on the first issue
   - Conclusion
   - Rule statement and explanation
   - Rule application
   - Conclusion on this issue
   B. Heading stating your conclusion on the second issue
   - Conclusion
   - Rule statement and explanation
   - Rule application
   - Conclusion on this issue
   [Add discussions of any other issues.]
   Overall conclusion

I. ORDERING FOR YOUR READER

A. Accounting for Elements Not at Issue

Recall from Chapter 7 that your outline did not have to cull out the elements not at issue. Now that you have completed your study of the authorities and how they apply to your client's facts, you can finalize the selection of elements requiring discussion. Remove from your draft the headings for any elements needing no discussion, but make a note of them. You will need to explain to your reader why you are not discussing them. Section II below will explain where and how to give your reader this information.

B. Selecting an Order for the Remaining Issues

Now that your analysis is complete, you have the information you need to select the order your reader will prefer. The three most common choices for the order of single-issue discussions are (1) important issues, (2) threshold issues, and (3) familiar order.

1. Important Issues. The important-issues approach places subheadings in the order of importance to the reader and to the analysis.[1] An issue can be important because it is likely to be dispositive. For instance, any burglary element the state cannot prove would be dispositive since the state must prove all elements to win a conviction. The issues most likely to be dispositive usually should be discussed first.

A subissue can be important even if it would not be dispositive alone. For instance, in a factors test, usually no one factor is dispositive; yet the particular circumstances of a case may make some factors more important to the analysis than others. A child custody dispute is a good example. The court will consider many factors in deciding custody. Rarely will one factor be dispositive alone, but several may be especially important. All other things being equal, discuss these first.

Organizing according to importance is an effective tool to help your reader manage a number of issues or subissues. The most important issues are placed where the reader's attention and patience are greatest. The time a busy reader must invest is minimized. The reader can choose how far into the analysis to read and with what degree of care. It assures the reader that the writer's analysis is complete enough to identify the most important issues.

2. Threshold Issues. A threshold issue is one that determines the direction of the analysis from that point on. For instance, assume that a rule of law tells you that if a business is a lending institution, it may not do certain things. The issue of whether your client is a lending institution within the meaning of that rule determines the direction of the analysis from that point on. If your client is *not* a lending institution, the rule prohibiting certain conduct does not apply to your client, and the analysis can move on to any other rules that may apply to your client. But if your client *is* a lending institution, the rule does apply, and the analysis must continue to determine

---

1. The importance to the reader and the importance to the analysis should be the same unless the writer and the reader have differing views of the analysis. If the writer suspects a difference, the writer should either (1) use the introductory paragraphs to convert the reader to the writer's view of the analysis or (2) order the subpoints by their importance to the *reader's* analysis.

whether your client's proposed conduct falls within the category of conduct prohibited by the rule. Thus, the issue of whether your client is a lending institution is a threshold issue.

When you are analyzing a legal question that includes a threshold issue, consider placing the threshold issue first. The reader probably will expect the analysis to begin with the threshold issue. Also, a reader's attention and patience are limited. If you conclude that the threshold step in the analysis is not met, the reader need not devote as much attention to later steps.

Occasionally, however, you may be working with a rule where the analysis of the threshold issue is complex and your answer to a remaining issue makes the complex analysis of the threshold issue unnecessary. For instance, perhaps the issue of whether your client is a lending institution—and therefore whether the statute would apply to your client at all—is a close and complex question. However, even if the statute applies to your client, the statute rather clearly would not prohibit your client's proposed conduct. If this second conclusion is relatively clear and easily explained, your reader may prefer that you organize by importance. Simply explain your organizational choice in the introductory paragraphs. Your reader will appreciate your organizational choice if she understands your reasons.

3. Familiar Order. Many rules of law are familiar to law-trained readers, and the elements of those rules are often listed in a certain familiar order. Often the familiar order is the order the rule uses. Common law burglary is a good example. The definition of burglary is traditionally stated as "the breaking and entering of the dwelling house of another in the nighttime with the intent to commit a felony therein." On a burglary issue, a law-trained reader will be accustomed to thinking of the elements in the order recited in that sentence.

Even if no rule establishes a familiar order of elements, the custom of ordering issues chronologically may establish a familiar order. If the subissues pertain to events occurring in a chronology, a law-trained reader probably will expect to analyze the issues in that order. For instance, contracts issues are often ordered by the chronology of events constituting the formation and performance of the contract: offer, acceptance, modification, and performance. Unless the reader's other needs require a different choice, order your discussion in the way the reader is expecting.

II. UMBRELLA SECTIONS

All the subsections are in place now, but you need introductions so your reader will understand what will follow and why. We will call these introductions "umbrella sections." Umbrella sections are appropriate wherever the analysis is broken down into subsections. Take a moment to read an example of an umbrella section between "I" and "A" in Appendix A.

The umbrella section can serve four main functions. First, it provides a place to *state the governing rule(s)* so the reader has a road map of the analysis to follow. If you use it for this purpose, provide a citation to the main authority establishing the rule, and include any other information important to how the rule functions. For instance, one party will carry the burden of proof. The rule may require a higher-than-normal level of proof (for example, clear and convincing).[2] Some rules come with a presumption of one variety or another.[3] Some come with policy "leanings" (for instance, case law stating that doubts are to be resolved in favor of the criminal defendant). The procedural posture of a case, such as a motion for summary judgment, a motion to dismiss, or an appeal from a jury verdict, may impose a particular standard more favorable to one party. A canon of statutory construction may call for a strict reading of a particular kind of statute. If the authorities have mentioned any such information, you can include it here.

Second, an umbrella section can *identify elements not at issue.* For each undisputed element, ask yourself whether your conclusion will be readily apparent to your reader or whether the reader will require some (although perhaps simple) analysis in order to be satisfied on the point. Make this decision based upon your assessment of (1) your reader's existing knowledge of the law, (2) the degree of your reader's faith in you as a legal thinker and writer, and (3) your reader's need for certainty. Make these assessments conservatively. If you are in doubt, err on the side of treating an issue as disputed.

If you conclude that an issue is not genuinely disputed, say so. And if your reasons may not be obvious to your reader, provide a cursory explanation of the basis for your conclusion—just enough to reassure the reader that your reasons for this conclusion are consistent with the reader's understanding.

Third, the umbrella section *identifies the remaining issues and explains the order in which you will address them.* Explaining your choice of structures is particularly important if your structure is different from the one the reader expects.

Finally, if necessary to prevent confusion, *identify any related legal issues not covered by the analysis.* If a reader might assume that your analysis includes all relevant legal issues pertaining to the question but it does not, be sure to say so. For example, the requesting attorney may have asked you to analyze claims under only one statute, but claims might exist under other statutes as well. In such a case, clarify that your memo covers only possible claims under the identified statute. Your reader will appreciate this clarity, and you will be protected from later misunderstandings.

Often the umbrella section is fairly simple. For instance, in the burglary example, the umbrella section would state the rule defining burglary and cite to the statute establishing it. One item of rule explanation applies to all

---

2. The most common standard for a burden of proof in a civil case is proof by the preponderance of the evidence. That means that the party bearing the burden need only present stronger evidence than that of the opposing party in order to win. However, in a criminal trial, the prosecution must meet a higher standard of proof—proof beyond a reasonable doubt. In some circumstances, a party may be required to prove certain facts by a higher standard than a mere preponderance, but not beyond a reasonable doubt. Courts often refer to this intermediate standard as "clear and convincing evidence."

3. In the determination of most legal and factual issues, the decision-maker starts from a neutral posture. However sometimes, as a matter of policy, the law will impose a "presumption" supporting a certain result. For instance, the law imposes a presumption that service of process in a judicial proceeding has been accomplished lawfully. In such a case, the decision-maker presumes the truth of the presumption until sufficient evidence to the contrary has been offered.

elements: the burden of proof. If several of the elements are not disputed, the umbrella section would explain their omission and explain organizational decisions. The umbrella section need contain nothing else. It would look like this:

---

1. Jamison's actions probably do not establish the elements of burglary.

To obtain a burglary conviction, the state must prove that Jamison's conduct constituted a breaking and entering of the dwelling house of another in the nighttime with the intent to commit a felony therein. [citation] The state must prove each of these elements beyond a reasonable doubt. [citation] The only elements in dispute are the nighttime element and the intent element. Since the nighttime element is most likely to be dispository, this memo discusses it first.

A. Jamison probably did not enter the building in the nighttime.
- Conclusion
- Rule & rule explanation
- Rule application
- Conclusion on nighttime element

B. The state probably can prove that Jamison intended to commit a felony inside the dwelling.
- Conclusion
- Rule & rule explanation
- Rule application
- Conclusion on nighttime element

Here is an umbrella section for a discussion governed by several separate rules.

---

1. The Foster car sale probably included a warranty.

In [name of jurisdiction], warranties governing U.C.C. transactions are set out in [citation]. Non-U.C.C. warranties are set out in [citation]. Because these warranty provisions differ in critical ways, the first question this memo will discuss is whether U.C.C. warranties would apply to the Foster transaction.

The first section concludes that U.C.C. warranties probably will govern the Foster transaction, so the second section discusses the application of those provisions to that transaction. However, because the application of U.C.C. warranties is a close question, the final section of the memo discusses the possible application of non-U.C.C. warranties to that transaction.

Notice that this umbrella section does not attempt to state the warranty rules. Both rules are complex, and each will be the subject of its own subsection. What the reader needs in this umbrella section is a road map of the organization to follow. With this map, the reader will know exactly where to look for the rule statements.

An effective umbrella section provides the reader with the context for the analysis, and it clears away the underbrush—the issues that the reader need not consider. It provides a road map for the remaining issues and explains the organizational choice to follow. In other words, the introduction meets the reader where she is, deals with her immediate needs, and leads her to the starting point of the analysis.

III. THE CONCLUSION

If the format of your document permits, write a conclusion pulling together the results of each separate analysis and setting out the ultimate conclusion on the question presented. Include a summary of the primary reasons for the overall conclusion. Chapter 12 explains the Conclusion section of an office memo, and Chapter 14 explains the Conclusion section of a brief to the court. Chapter 13 explains the format for a letter to a client.

IV. EDITING SUBSECTION LENGTHS

Now that you have your organization in place, check the length and complexity of each of the subsections. If several subsections are short, you may choose to combine them. Remove the original subheadings, leaving the material under one heading that covers it all. Within that new and larger section, use clear transitional phrases or sentences to mark the beginning and end of your discussions of each subissue. Do not be too hasty to obscure the rule's structure like this, however. Law-trained readers generally are less troubled by short sections than by confusion about rule structure.

If a subsection strikes you as particularly long and complex, consider further subdivisions with headings. These subdivisions can reflect different lines of authority, different tests set out in case law, rule explanation versus rule application, or any other points of division that would be helpful to the reader. For length, use three pages as a rough outside limit. Headings and subheadings will constitute your reader's road map. Most busy readers want to orient themselves in the text at least every three pages or so. Also remember that reader attention wanes between subheadings and can be renewed with a subheading.

Finally, check your headings and subheadings to be sure they communicate your conclusions. Headings are important to readers because they make the large-scale organization visible at a glance. They mark the reader's progress through the analysis, so the reader always knows where she has been and where she is headed. They mark the spots where the reader might choose to invest a bit more attention. They assist the reader in evaluating the analysis itself, and through it the writer's ability and credibility. They enable the reader to consider preliminary issues with the assurance that awaited sections are coming. They allow busy readers to jump immediately to the particular section they want to review.

V. VARIATIONS OF THE MULTI-ISSUE PARADIGM

Like the paradigm for a single-issue analysis described in Chapters 8 and 9, the multi-issue paradigm provides a format you can adapt to fit each assignment. The most common adaptation of the paradigm is stating and explaining the rules for *all* elements before applying any of them to the facts. An outline for such a discussion would look like this:

I. Conclusion Statement
[Umbrella section]
   A. Rule statements and explanations
      1. First element
      2. Second element
   B. Rule applications
      1. First element
      2. Second element
   Conclusion

In some situations, you can explain all elements before applying any of them, as this outline does. The rules and rule explanations for each element may be particularly interrelated in the authorities. The distinctions among them may be minor, and separating the rule explanation sections may require you to repeat material. If the courts seem to take a more unified view of the elements, separating the rule explanation sections may even sacrifice some precision in the analysis. If your careful evaluation of the rule convinces you that these descriptions apply to your assignment, you can opt for this variation of the multi-issue paradigm. Remember, though, that the key virtue of the basic paradigm is that its structure forces you to think precisely about each element. Do not discard the advantages of that structure lightly.

EXERCISE 10-1
Identifying the Parts of a Multi-Issue Discussion

Read the Discussion section of the office memo in Appendix A (a multi-issue discussion). Make a photocopy of the memo. On the photocopy, identify and label each part of the multi-issue discussion. Include the parts of the basic paradigm within each subsection of the discussion.

EXERCISE 10-2
Writing a Multi-Issue Discussion

Write a working draft of an answer to the Question Presented below, using as your only authority the case summaries in Exercise 3-2.

Facts. Mr. and Mrs. Carillo, each 64 years old, live in a neighborhood that includes older people, middle-aged people who have teenaged or young-adult children, and people with young children. The elementary school is about two blocks away, though most children walk to school down the next street over. The closest neighbors who have children living at home are the Lupinos, three houses away from the Carillos.

About a year ago, the Carillos bought a trampoline for the use of their four grandchildren, who visit from time to time. The trampoline is located in the Carillos' backyard. The yard is not fenced, but it is surrounded by a hedge and other shrubbery that effectively shield the backyard from view. Nonetheless, the neighborhood children know that the trampoline is there because they sometimes play with the Carillos' grandchildren. All of the children know that they are not permitted to jump on the trampoline unless an adult is present.

One day last spring, nine-year-old Jimmy Lupino was playing outside with a group of friends. One of the friends remembered the trampoline and suggested to the group that they ask the Carillos if they could play on the trampoline. They knocked, but the Carillos were not home. They huddled about what to do and decided they would each take just one turn on the trampoline. They went around the back and began to take their turns. When Jimmy Lupino's turn came, he climbed on. On his fourth jump he got too close to the edge, hit the metal side of the trampoline, and broke his spine. He is now partially paralyzed.

The Lupinos have asked if your firm will represent them on a contingency basis in a lawsuit against the Carillos. In order to decide whether to accept the case on this basis, you need an idea of what claims the Lupinos might be able to bring. One of the possible claims you need to evaluate is an attractive nuisance claim.

Issue. Do the Lupinos have a reasonable chance of recovery on an attractive nuisance claim?

CHAPTER 11

Deepening Your Analysis

Now that you have an overview of the basic structure and content of rule explanation and application, we will explore some ways to deepen and strengthen your analysis.

I. MAJOR FORMS OF REASONING IN RULE EXPLANATION: POLICY AND PRINCIPLE

The main forms of legal reasoning used in rule explanation and their common uses are:

Rule-Based	Clarifying the precise language, structure, and meaning of the rule
Policy-Based	Identifying underlying rationales intended to encourage desirable results for the society at large and affecting either the rule's original purpose or the policy implications of how the rule might be interpreted
Principle-Based	Identifying any principles that the rule is intended to serve or that might constrain the rule's interpretation
Custom-Based	Identifying social norms or business customs that the rule formalizes and enforces

Once you have formulated the rule, supported your formulation with citations to authority, and shown how the courts have applied the rule in the past, you have given the basic explanation of rule. But you will need to explain the purpose of the rule in order to understand and eventually apply the rule with some degree of confidence. In most cases, policy and principle-based reasoning will be your most valuable tools in explaining the rule's purpose. Does the rule embody a broad principle valued by our society, or might its interpretation and application be constrained by such a principle? What did the creator of the rule, be it a legislature or a court, intend to accomplish? To answer these questions, you need policy and principle-based reasoning.

Policies and principles cover many kinds of concerns. Professor Ellie Margolis has identified four common categories:[1]

Policies affecting judicial administration pertain to the practical administration of the rule by the courts.[2] For example, a court's reasons for choosing a flexible factors test might include the ability to fashion a particularized fair result in each future circumstance. The choice of a more rigid rule, however, might be designed partly to maximize people's ability to predict legal outcomes and to bring their conduct into line with that prediction, thus reducing the need for litigation.[3]

Normative policies promote shared societal values. These policies can include moral considerations such as the promotion of honesty and fair dealing, social considerations such as the promotion of stability within families, and corrective justice considerations such as the placement of liability on the most culpable party.[4]

Institutional competence policies recognize the value of relying on the decision-maker who is most capable of resolving the dispute wisely.[5] Perhaps the rule is designed to encourage an appellate court to defer to the trial court because the trial judge is able to see the witnesses and evaluate their demeanor. Perhaps the rule relies on the expertise of an administrative agency staffed by presumably neutral experts in a complex field. Perhaps the rule defers to the legislature because the legislative process allows for more public input and accountability.

Economic policy rationales seek to maximize efficient resource allocation, keep economic costs in line with resulting benefits, and maintain a free market.[6] Economic rationales include such considerations as placing the liability on the party most able to obtain insurance for such losses. They also can include larger-scale economic considerations such as balancing the desire to refrain from government interference against the need for protection against practices that, in the long term, would reduce desirable competition.

As we saw in Chapter 5, these policies and principles can help you predict how a court might apply the rule to a particular set of facts, especially in a close case. Most assuredly, policy and principle-based rationales can help you persuade a court to apply the rule in your client's favor. A court will try to apply the rule in a way that advances the policies and principles the rule is designed to advance. Conversely, the court will try to avoid applying the rule in a way that impedes those policies and principles.

The first and best place to look for policy and principle-based rationales is in the authorities themselves. Often a statute or its legislative history will

---

1. Ellie Margolis, *Closing the Floodgates: Making Persuasive Policy Arguments in Appellate Briefs*, 62 Montana L. Rev. 59 (2001).

2. Margolis at p. 72.

3. *See also* Carol M. Rose, *Crystals and Mud in Property Law*, 40 Stanford L. Rev. 577 (1988).

4. Margolis at p. 74. This category is closely related to principle-based reasoning as described in Chapter 5.

5. Margolis at p. 77.

6. Margolis at pp. 78-79.

contain a statement of the purposes for the legislation. Often courts will articulate the rationales their rulings are designed to address. Secondary sources like treatises and law review articles are instructive as well. And you can use your own common sense. What are the most likely goals the legislature or the courts had in mind when they were developing the rule? What long-term results would follow if courts ruled one way rather than the other on your issue? What advantages would be produced? What dangers? To jumpstart your thinking, here are examples of some common policy rationales:

- As between two parties, the law should place the risk of liability on the party most able to prevent a loss.
- As between two parties, the law should place the risk on the party who already bears similar risks and therefore whose legal and practical situation will be least affected by the risk.
- Where the bargaining positions of certain kinds of parties are grossly disparate, the governing rule should protect the weaker party.
- The law should not impose a liability that might limit the ability of people to engage in a particular business in the future, especially if the business provides a socially desirable service.
- The rule should place the burden of proof on the party with the easiest access to the evidence.
- The governing rule should be workable in light of the practical realities of day-to-day life. It should incorporate a realistic view of human psychology and business custom.
- The governing rule should not create a legal standard that is easily subverted by knowledgeable and crafty individuals and businesses.
- Stability in the law is desirable. The law should not change unless the need for the change is clear.
- The realities of modern life have changed significantly (explain how). The law must be willing and able to change and adapt to changing circumstances.
- The law should resist the temptation to rush to the rescue when a refusal to intervene will encourage people to be diligent and responsible in handling their economic and legal affairs.
- The rule should not create additional costs for a person or an industry unless the harm to be prevented justifies the imposition of those costs.
- The governing rule should not add impediments to the free transfer of assets and the ease of doing business.
- The governing rule should be flexible enough to allow future courts to achieve a fair result in individual future circumstances.
- The governing rule should be concrete enough to insure that future adjudications will be based on objective criteria rather than on prejudices of the decision-maker.
- It is appropriate for the law to require a higher standard of conduct from a commercial party than from an individual not engaged in a particular business.
- The court should adopt a rule that is as consistent with established custom as possible since customs become established because, over time, people have discovered that they work well.

II. THE MAJOR FORM OF REASONING IN RULE APPLICATION: ANALOGICAL REASONING

In the rule application section, the focus shifts to your client's facts. Each of the forms of reasoning described in Chapter 5 can be brought into play here. You need not use all forms of reasoning in all cases, but you should not neglect to consider how each of them might serve your purpose. The structure, the specific words, and the form of the rule must be related to the situation at hand (rule-based reasoning). But the law is more than words, so you should look behind the words to consider the principles or social policies the rule serves. Consider how those principles and policies may bear on your client's story (policy and principle-based reasoning). Look for any customs, practices, or normal behavior of people in your client's situation, and consider that most rules of law probably intend to codify normative conduct, not prohibit it (custom-based reasoning). Look also for the narrative themes of your client's story, particularly those that might affect the way the rule should be applied (narrative).

All of these forms of reasoning can be helpful in the rule application section, but the most important and valuable form for connecting your client's facts to the rule is analogy. Analogical reasoning is essential to most rule application sections. Chapters 5 and 9 introduced these forms; now we will explore them in greater depth.

Analogical reasoning compares two things. A lawyer uses analogical reasoning when she compares the facts of a prior case with her client's facts, pointing out similarities that can help her predict or advocate a similar result. This process is sometimes called *"analogizing"* cases. A lawyer may also compare two cases to find differences that might call for a different result. This process is called *"distinguishing"* cases.

A. Deciding Which Similarities and Differences Are Significant

The first step in mastering the skill of analogizing and distinguishing cases is to understand what kinds of similarities and differences may be legally significant. If you have a sense of how you might use a similarity or difference, you will have a better idea of what you are looking for. A similarity or difference is legally significant if it relates to

- a term in the governing rule of law, or
- a policy or principle implicated by the rule or its application in this case.

Comparisons relating to a key term of the governing rule are the most important. The governing rule is the starting point for all legal analysis. No matter how compelling a party's case, the judge must be able to reconcile the result with the governing rule. If a factual similarity or difference would help a court decide how the rule might apply to that party's situation, the comparison will be important.

For example, in most jurisdictions, a seller of real property who knows or should know of material defects in the property must disclose those defects to a potential buyer. Notice that this rule has two elements:

A seller must disclose if:
1. the seller knows or should know of the defect, and
2. the defect is material.

Therefore, factual similarities or differences will be most important if they help the judge decide either of these two elements—what kind of "knowledge" is enough to raise the duty and how to gauge whether a defect is "material."

Similarities or differences that do not relate directly to an element of the rule but do relate to the purpose or policy behind the rule can be important as well. If applying the governing rule in your client's case would not serve the policies the rule was meant to further, a court might be willing to create an outright exception for situations like that of your client.

B. Choosing a Format for Your Case Comparison

Now that you have identified the comparisons you want to make, you need only decide how much depth you need. Professor Michael Smith has identified two formats for case comparisons: the short form and the long form.[7] Use the long form for important comparisons, for complicated comparisons, or for multiple points of comparison. In all other circumstances, you can use the short form. In either format, however, be sure to give direct, fact-to-fact comparisons. Notice how the examples below make those direct factual comparisons.

1. Short-Form Case Comparison

Begin with a thesis sentence stating the point of the comparison, and give a factual overview of the cited case, unless your reader is already familiar with its facts. Next state the specific facts that will form the basis of your factual comparison, and state the result reached in the cited case. Then use a thesis sentence to state the nature of the similarities or differences you are pointing out. Identify the specific facts from your client's situation to which you are comparing the cited case, and use that comparison to explain why the result in your client's situation should or should not be the same. Here are two examples of a short-form case comparison, one showing differences and the other showing similarities:

Differences

Buckley's representation that she was old enough to buy a car is significantly different from the representations in *Carney*. There, a minor entered

---

7. Michael R. Smith, 1992-1994 Class Handouts, "Techniques for Using Case Authority to Discuss 'Points' in a Memo," on file with the author.

into a contract to purchase a car. The minor affirmatively stated to the sales agent that he was twenty-two, and the agent recorded that information on the loan application, which the minor then signed. The court affirmed the holding that the minor had fraudulently misrepresented his age and was therefore estopped from disaffirming the contract. *Id.* at 807-808.

Buckley, however, never stated her age at all. Further, her answer, taken to mean what she intended it to mean, was not even false. The sales agent had asked her whether she was old enough to buy a car. Buckley misunderstood the question, thinking the agent was asking whether she was old enough to drive. She truthfully answered the question she thought the agent was asking. She said "yes," meaning that she was old enough to have a driver's license. Thus Buckley's facts do not constitute misrepresentations according to the *Carney* standard.

Similarities

Buckley's statement is much closer to the situation in *Woodall*, in which the minor made the representation "unknowingly." In *Woodall*, the minor did not realize that he was making a representation of majority because he did not read the form contract he was signing. *Id.* at 97. Similarly, Buckley did not realize that she might be making a representation of majority because she misunderstood the agent's question. In both cases, the requisite intent to deceive is absent. Therefore, the result in Buckley's situation should be the same as the result in *Woodall*—an order permitting disaffirmance.

2. Long-Form Case Comparison

The long-form case comparison uses an extensive in-text discussion of the case to give the reader more information about the cited case and about the relevant comparisons. Here is an example of a long-form case comparison[8] that demonstrates many factual similarities and also a factual difference:

> *Fahmie v. Wulster*, 408 A.2d 789 (1979), provides the closest analogy to Frimberger's situation. In *Fahmie*, a corporation that originally owned a parcel of property requested permission from the Bureau of Water to place a nine-foot diameter culvert on the property to enclose a stream. The Bureau required instead that a sixteen-foot diameter culvert should be installed. The corporation, however, went ahead with its original plan and installed the nine-foot culvert.
>
> The property was later conveyed to Wulster, the CEO of the corporation, who had no knowledge of the installation of the nine-foot culvert. Nine years later, Wulster conveyed the property, by warranty deed, to Fahmie.
>
> In anticipation of the subsequent resale of the property, Fahmie made application to the Economic Development Commission to make additional improvements to the stream and its banks. It was then that the inadequate nine-foot culvert was discovered, and the plaintiff was required to replace it with a sixteen-foot diameter pipe.
>
> Fahmie sued Wulster for the cost to correct the violation, claiming a breach of the deed's warranty against encumbrances. The New Jersey Supreme Court concluded that a claim for breach of a covenant against encumbrances cannot be predicated on the necessity to repair or alter the property to conform with land use regulations.

---

8. Adapted from *Frimberger v. Anzellotti*, 594 A.2d 1029 (1991).

Similarities

The *Fahmie* case is remarkably similar to Frimberger's situation. Like the plaintiff in *Fahmie*, Frimberger is also alleging a breach of the covenant against encumbrances based on the necessity of bringing the property into compliance with a state environmental land use regulation. Just as in *Fahmie*, neither the current owner nor his immediate predecessor knew of the violation of the regulation. In both cases, the violation was created by a remote owner. In both cases, this remote owner knew or should have known that he was creating a violation of the regulation. In neither case did the current owner's deed contain an exception for violations of land use statutes. In both cases, the current owner discovered the violation upon filing an application with the relevant regulatory agency to make further improvements to the property.

Difference

The only relevant difference between the two situations results in an even weaker case for Frimberger. In *Fahmie*, the state agency actually required the plaintiff to replace the inadequate culvert with the larger culvert, thus causing the plaintiff significant expense. In Frimberger's situation, however, the state agency has taken no action to require abatement of the violation. As a matter of fact, the agency has invited Frimberger to apply for an exception to the relevant requirement, a procedure which Frimberger has thus far declined to pursue. Therefore, it is even less likely that Frimberger's facts establish a breach of the covenant than did the facts in *Fahmie*.

This example has three key characteristics: Notice how specific is the discussion of the facts from each case. Notice how many factual similarities and differences are identified (find them and count them). And notice how the theses sentences provide the structure and explain the points of the comparisons they introduce. (Find the theses sentences and underline them.) Emulate these three characteristics in your own case comparisons.

EXERCISE 11-1

Analogical Reasoning

Formulate the rule of law from *Goldman v. Kane*, reprinted in Appendix E. Then read Karen Berry's facts set out in Exercise 12-3. Make a list of the similarities between Berry's facts and the facts in *Goldman v. Kane*. Make a list of the differences. Identify the similarities and differences that are legally significant for Berry's case and explain why.

EXERCISE 11-2

Policy Analogies

Assume that several months after closing, a buyer of real property discovered a major structural defect on the premises. The buyer has sued the seller, alleging that the seller knew of the defect and failed to disclose it to the buyer. You represent the seller. Assume that your jurisdiction has historically followed the older rule on this issue (a seller has no duty to disclose defects), but the state's highest court has signaled a willingness to consider imposing such a duty. The buyer's attorney will argue, among other things, that in recent years the law has imposed such a duty on sellers of personal property (goods) and that the law governing the sale of real property should be the same. What analogies can you expect the buyer's lawyer to make between the sale of personal property and the sale of real property? What arguments will the buyer's lawyer make based on those analogies? What differences might you point out, and what arguments might you make based on those differences?

PART FOUR

Predictive Writing

CHAPTER 12

Writing an Office Memo

I. THE FUNCTION OF AN OFFICE MEMO

An office memo is an internal working document of a law firm or other office. It is not designed for outside readers, although clients and others may receive a copy if the need arises. The function of an office memo is to answer a legal question, usually for a particular client in a particular situation. Often, it will be the primary basis for making a decision with both legal and nonlegal consequences. Also, the firm may have a "form file" in which it keeps, for future use, office memos dealing with particular legal questions. Therefore, your document may have a long life, may impact many clients, and may create impressions about you in the minds of many future readers.

When you write an office memo, your role is predictive rather than persuasive. You must take an objective view of the question you are asked. The client and the requesting attorney need an accurate understanding of the situation. Learning bad news later could be costly for the client, for the firm, and for you. Making an accurate prediction, then, is the function of an office memo.

II. AN OVERVIEW OF THE MEMO FORMAT

The format of a memo is designed to fit its function and its reader's needs. Since a memo is an internal document, law firms are likely to have a preferred memo format. The firm's preferred format may use various words for the section titles, it may place the sections in an order different from that described here, or it may include other sections. If your reader (your teacher or law firm) has a particular format preference, use it. If not, you can use the standard memo format this text describes. Variations in format are much less important than the accuracy and thoroughness of the analysis. The components of a standard office memo are

1. Heading
2. Question Presented
3. Brief Answer

    4. Fact Statement
    5. Discussion
    6. Conclusion (when appropriate)

Look at the sample memo in Appendix A to locate and review each component.

Heading. The function of the heading is to identify the requesting attorney, the writer, the date, the client, and the particular legal matter.

Question Presented. The Question Presented identifies the question(s) you have been asked to analyze. It allows your reader to confirm that you have understood the question(s). It also may remind a busy reader of the question(s) he or she asked you to analyze.

Brief Answer. The Brief Answer provides your answer quickly and up front. The reader then can decide how much attention to invest in the explanation that follows.

Fact Statement. This section sets out the facts on which your answer is based. You probably obtained the facts from your reader (the requesting attorney) in the first place, but your memo must repeat them. Your reader will want to be sure you have not misunderstood any important facts. Also, your reader, who has been busy working on other cases, may need a review of the facts, and other attorneys working on this case or future cases may need access to your analysis. Finally, reading your fact statement in conjunction with your legal analysis may cause your reader to realize that she has neglected to give you a critical fact.

As the writer, you have an interest in reciting the facts as well. Your legal analysis will be based on the facts as you understand them. If the facts were to change, the result might change. If you memorialize the facts you have been given—the facts on which your answer is based—you insure that your work will be evaluated with reference to those facts. No future reader will think you had access to other, different facts and therefore expect you to have reached a different answer.

Discussion. The Discussion section explains to your reader the analysis that led to your answer. Chapters 7-11 explained how to write this section.

Conclusion. You may choose to end with a Conclusion section, a summary of the main points of your analysis. A Conclusion section can be helpful in two ways. First, if the analysis has been complex, a Conclusion section can tie together and summarize the Discussion section. Sometimes, this summary can add a clarity that the Discussion alone may not be able to achieve. Also, a Conclusion can increase your reader's options for deciding how much attention to invest in understanding the details of your analysis. A Conclusion would be a summary with more detail than the Brief Answer but not as much as the Discussion. Therefore a law-trained reader could read your Brief Answer first, then proceed to your Conclusion for somewhat more depth, and finally read your Discussion for even more depth. After reading each section, your reader can decide how far and how deeply to read on.

III. DRAFTING THE HEADING

Draft a heading in the format of standard business interoffice communications:

TO:	[Name of requesting attorney]
FROM:	[Your name]
DATE:	[Date]
RE:	[Include client's name, the file number, the particular legal matter, and a phrase identifying the particular issue.]

The date is important to both you and your readers. Your readers need the date because the law is subject to change and because your readers may refer to your memo months or even years later. The memo's date will tell them whether and for what period of time the analysis in your memo must be updated. You need the date because you want your work to be evaluated on the basis of the law to which you had access, not later developments you could not have known.

The "Re" section should identify the client and the file number, both for your current reader and so the memo can be returned in case it is later separated from the file. This section also should identify both the legal matter you are working on and the particular issue you have been asked to analyze. Identify the legal matter because your firm may be handling a number of matters for this particular client and your reader will want to know at a glance which of those matters your memo concerns. Identify the issue because this legal matter may raise many issues that will be the subjects of office memos. Your reader will want to know at a glance which issue your memo analyzes.

Here is an example of a heading:

TO:	Ramon Caldez
FROM:	Marcia Willingham
DATE:	March 17, 2003
RE:	Sharon Watson (file #96-24795); covenant-not-to-compete against Carrolton; enforceability of the covenant.

IV. DRAFTING THE QUESTION PRESENTED

The Question Presented, sometimes called the "Issue," states the question(s) you have been asked to analyze. If you have been asked only to research the state of the governing law on a particular question, without reference to a particular client, the Question Presented simply states the legal question:

> Under what circumstances does Iowa law allow recovery on a claim for the wrongful death of a fetus?

If you have been asked to apply a rule to a set of facts and predict a result—the more common scenario—drafting a readable Question Presented can be more of a challenge. The Question Presented should include both the question and the most important facts, and perhaps the governing rule as well. Here are three format options.

Format Option 1
Organize the content of the Question Presented in two sections: a statement of the *legal* question and a concise statement of the major relevant fact(s).

Can . . . [state the legal question] . . . when . . . [state the major facts]?

This format does not state the rule of law as part of the Question. Here is an example:

> Can Carrolton enforce the Watson covenant-not-to-compete when the covenant prohibits Watson from making sales contacts for three years and applies to the three counties closest to Carrolton's headquarters?

Common verbs for beginning a Question Presented in this format are: "Can . . . ?" "Did . . . ?" "Was . . . ?" "May . . . ?" and "Is . . . ?" Common transitions into the factual description are: "when . . . " and "where . . . "

Format Option 2
An even simpler version of a Question Presented is the format beginning with "whether" and constituting a clause rather than a complete sentence. This format still begins with the legal question and ends with the significant facts:

> Whether Carrolton can enforce the Watson covenant-not-to-compete when the covenant prohibits Watson from making sales contacts for three years and applies to the three counties closest to Carrolton's headquarters.

When the Question Presented uses the "whether" format, the clause can be followed by a period and treated as a complete sentence although it is not.

Format Option 3
A third format option is the "under/does/when" format. This format usually results in the longest and most complex Question Presented, although it allows for a shorter Brief Answer (the succeeding section). The Question Presented is longer and the Brief Answer shorter because this format puts

the statement of the law in the Question rather than in the Answer. Here is an example:

Under the Georgia common law rule that allows covenants-not-to-compete only when the area restrained, the activities restrained, and the duration of the restraint are reasonable, can a covenant-not-to-compete be enforced when the covenant prohibits the covenantor from making sales contacts, for three years, and applies to the three counties closest to the headquarters of the covenant's beneficiary?

The middle verb can vary, using the same common verbs identified above: "can," "did," "was," "may," or "is."

Format Option 4
The factual descriptions of any of these formats can be expanded to include the key facts on both sides of the question. Since a memo's analysis should be as objective as possible, an explicitly balanced description of the key facts can be helpful both to your reader and to you. It gives the reader a quick overview of the most important facts on both sides of the question, and it can remind you to recognize what is compelling about each side's arguments. This format is particularly appropriate when each side would want to emphasize different facts rather than simply construct legal arguments about the same facts. For instance, assume that the question is whether an airline passenger attempted to intimidate a flight crew member. Here is an example of a Question Presented that identifies key facts on both sides of the question:

Under . . . , did Mitchell Sheffield attempt to intimidate the flight crew when he left his seat, approached the door to the control cabin, and shouted at the co-pilot but never articulated any threat or attempted any violent act?

Notice that the key facts tending to show intimidation are grouped together, followed by the key contrasting facts. This structure provides an immediate overview of the factual situation. It also prompts the writer to recognize the factual arguments on both sides.

Use the format your teacher or requesting attorney prefers. If you can identify no preference, consider using the first format, since it results in a simpler, more understandable sentence and since locating the governing rule is usually part of the question you are asked to answer.

Generic Versus Specific References. No matter which format you choose, you will need to decide whether to use a general or a specific Question Presented. For example, the Format Options 1 and 2 above refer specifically to Watson and Carrolton, while Format Option 3 does not. Option 3 is phrased as a generic legal question without direct reference to Watson or

Carrolton. Here is an example of a generic Question Presented drafted in Format Option 1:

> Can a covenant-not-to-compete be enforced where the covenant prohibits the covenantor from making sales contacts for three years and applies to the three counties closest to the headquarters of the covenant's beneficiary?

You will find proponents of both the generic and the specific Question Presented. The specific Question Presented directly states the question the requesting attorney wants to know. The senior attorney who requested the memo is not asking an academic legal question; rather he wants to know the fate of a particular client—Sharon Watson. While this memo may someday be placed in the firm's memo file and be examined by a future reader for purposes of another case, the primary function of this memo is to answer a question about the *present* client.

The abstract version of the Question Presented refers to the parties involved by characterizing them rather than by naming them. When the requesting attorney reads this characterization, he probably will have to stop as he reads it to substitute in his mind the names of the parties in place of the characterizations. He also will have to ask himself whether the characterizations accurately refer to the parties in this particular case because if they do not, then the answer set out in the memo may not apply to these parties. But the question of whether the law set out in the memo applies to these parties is part of what the senior attorney wants *you* to analyze *for* her.

Finally, as a practical matter, a Question Presented that uses the parties' names rather than characterizations of the parties generally uses fewer words and is more easily readable. Notice how this is true for the examples above. Since some Questions Presented must include a great deal of information, finding ways to reduce the number of words and to simplify the sentence structure can be helpful.

On the other hand, a busy attorney with a heavy caseload may not remember the names of the parties as easily as the characterizations (the landlord, the contractor, the lender). If you suspect that your reader is not familiar enough with the case to remember the names, either use generic references or use names with characterizations in parentheses, like this:

> Can Carrolton (the beneficiary) enforce the Watson covenant-not-to-compete when the covenant prohibits Watson (the former employee) from making sales contacts for three years and applies to the three counties closest to Carrolton's headquarters?

Again, use the phrasing you think your teacher or requesting attorney will prefer. As with most other writing decisions, your assessment of your reader's starting point should be the most important factor.

Degree of Detail. Try to limit the Question Presented to one readable sentence. Packing both the legal issue and the major facts into one readable sentence can be quite a challenge. If your draft of the Question Presented is unwieldy, first use the editing techniques described in Chapter 21. If those techniques do not allow you to achieve a readable sentence, consider shortening the facts you include. If all else fails, use two sentences. Two clear sentences are better than one confusing sentence.

Assuming the Answer in the Question Presented. Avoid stating the Question Presented in a way that assumes the answer. For instance, in the Watson/Carrolton case, the following Question Presented assumes the answer:

> Can Carrolton enforce the Watson covenant-not-to-compete when the covenant prohibits Watson from making sales contacts for an unreasonable length of time and applies to an unreasonable geographic area?

According to the governing rule, a covenant with unreasonable terms is not enforceable. But the requesting attorney did not ask merely what rule governs the issue. The requesting attorney has asked how the rule applies to Watson's facts. She has asked whether the Watson terms are unreasonable, so do not phrase the Question Presented so as to assume the very question you are to answer.

EXERCISE 12-1

For each of the following Questions Presented, use a different format. Use specific references for one and generic references for the other.

a. Draft a Question Presented for an office memo addressing Ms. Ryan's question in Exercise 8-2.
b. Draft a Question Presented for an office memo addressing Ms. Pyle's question introduced in the hypothetical on page 91 and continuing with the working draft of the analysis on pages 95-96 and 105-106.

V. DRAFTING THE BRIEF ANSWER

The Brief Answer gives your busy reader the answer quickly and right up front. Since Questions Presented come in several formats, their Brief Answers do as well. A Brief Answer responding to a Question that does not articulate the rule of law (those described in formats 1 and 2 on page 130) should state the answer forthrightly ("yes," "probably yes," "no," or "probably not"). The remainder of the Answer should set out, either directly or indirectly, the rule of law governing the issue and a summary of the reasoning leading to the answer. We will assume that you have concluded that Carrolton will be able to enforce the Watson covenant. Your Brief Answer might be:

> Probably yes [**forthright statement of the answer**]. A covenant-not-to-compete is enforceable under Georgia law if the activity restrained, the geographic area of the restraint, and the duration of the restraint are all reasonable [**statement of the governing rule of law**]. Several Georgia courts have held that covenants restraining sales contacts are nearly always reasonable as to the activity restrained. Georgia courts have also held covenants reasonable when the duration of the restraint was up to three years and when the area restrained included up to ten counties [**summary of reasoning**].

Brief Answers that respond to Questions in the third format on pages 130-131 (Questions that have already stated the law) can be shorter. When you are using this format, state the answer in the first few words ("yes," "probably yes," "no," or "probably not"). Then state, in several complete sentences, the reasons for your answer, like so:

> Probably yes [**forthright statement of the answer**]. Several Georgia courts have held that covenants restraining sales contacts are nearly always reasonable as to the activity restrained. Georgia courts have also held covenants reasonable when the duration of the restraint was up to three years and when the area restrained included up to ten counties [**summary of reasoning**].

Generic Versus Specific References. Use references that match those in the Question Presented. If you used the parties' names in the Question, use them in the Brief Answer. If you used characterizations in the Question Presented, use those characterizations in the Brief Answer as well.

Degree of Detail. An average length for a Brief Answer is one moderate paragraph (about one-third to one-half of a double-spaced page). The function of the Brief Answer is compromised when the Answer is much longer than that. Occasionally, you will be dealing with a rule that is so complex that even a Brief Answer will take more space, but usually not. Try to limit this section to a maximum of five sentences, like the example above.

Degree of Certainty. For many memo assignments, deciding your degree of certainty is daunting. Perhaps the answer seems clear and certain. Have you simply received an easy, straightforward assignment? Or have you missed another possible way to construe law or facts? Perhaps you think the answer could go either way, and you cannot decide which is more likely; yet you know that the requesting attorney wants an answer, not a coin toss.

There is no easy solution to this discomfort. You are just beginning the lifelong project of developing the legal judgment to gauge the certainty of a predicted result. With experience, you will get better at making these judgments, and in practice you will be able to discuss the law and the facts with other attorneys. For the time being, you must research and analyze thoroughly and then make the best judgment you can.

When you are struggling with the question of the degree of certainty of your answer, keep in mind the possible spectrum:

| Certain | Almost certain | Probable | Equally likely to go either way |

Think carefully before you choose an answer on either end of the spectrum. Some issues actually have certain answers, but before you conclude that yours is one of them, be sure you have done a complete and accurate legal and factual analysis. Some issues actually will be a coin toss, but before you conclude that yours is one of them, ask yourself whether you are simply resisting the discomfort of having to make a prediction in an uncertain area.

Finally, once you decide where your answer fits on the spectrum, communicate that decision clearly in the Brief Answer. Search your draft of the Brief Answer for the words that will tell your reader your degree of certainty, and be sure that you have not sent mixed signals within the Brief Answer itself or between the Brief Answer and the Discussion section.

Here is how the office memo looks so far:

TO: Ramon Caldez
FROM: Marcia Willingham
DATE: August 17, 1996
RE: Sharon Watson (file #96-24795); covenant-not-to-compete against Carrolton; enforceability of the covenant.

QUESTION PRESENTED

Can Carrolton enforce the Watson covenant-not-to-compete where the covenant prohibits Watson from making sales contacts for three years and applies to the three counties closest to Carrolton's headquarters?

BRIEF ANSWER

Probably yes. Carrolton should be able to enforce the Watson covenant. A covenant-not-to-compete is enforceable under Georgia law if the activity restrained, the geographic area of the restraint, and the duration of the restraint are all reasonable. Several Georgia courts have held that covenants restraining sales contacts are nearly always reasonable as to the activity restrained. Georgia courts have also held covenants reasonable when the duration of the restraint was up to three years and when the area restrained included up to ten counties.

EXERCISE 12-2

For each of the Questions Presented you drafted for Exercise 12-1, draft a corresponding Brief Answer.

VI. DRAFTING THE FACT STATEMENT

In drafting the fact section, your primary tasks are (1) selecting which facts to include, (2) organizing those facts in an effective way, and (3) remembering your predictive role.

A. Fact Selection

Often you will know many facts about a particular client's situation. However, your busy reader will want to know only two kinds of facts: (1) facts relevant to the question presented and (2) background facts necessary to provide context for these legally relevant facts. Contextual facts will come to you naturally as you write, so we will focus on identifying the legally relevant facts.

Relevant facts are those that help you decide how the rule of law will apply to your client's situation. For instance, for a covenant-not-to-compete issue, the relevant facts are those that tell you about the kind of activity restrained, the geographic scope, and the duration of the restraint.

Writing your working draft already has given you a good sense of the facts that will be relevant to the issues. Especially as you wrote the "rule application" section of your analysis, you considered how the legal rule would apply to your client's situation. Review your Discussion section to make a list of these relevant facts. Consider each subissue separately so your thinking will be more precise and focused. While your list certainly should include all facts you discussed in your analysis, do not limit your list to those facts. Let the process of reexamining each part of your legal discussion be an occasion for double-checking your fact application. You may be surprised at how often you will see a fact in a significant new way when you are working on the fact statement.

Also, include any facts that may have a powerful emotional impact on the decision-maker, even if those facts are not technically relevant to the legal issues. Remember that judges and other decision-makers are human. Few of us can separate completely our objective legal analysis from our reaction to compelling parts of a story. While legally irrelevant facts theoretically should not affect a result, judges may be more swayed by these inevitable responses than theory contemplates. For instance, in a divorce case, the judge deciding property issues might be influenced by knowing that one spouse has seriously battered the other spouse, even if the applicable law does not make fault relevant to property division. If your case includes an emotionally powerful fact, do not ignore it, especially if the legal rule you are working with gives the decision-maker some discretion.

Finally, include facts only. Save the coverage of legal authorities and arguments until the Discussion section. For cases already in litigation, include the current procedural posture of the case and, if relevant, a summary of the procedural history.

As you compile your list of known relevant facts, ask yourself what other facts you would like to know—what unknown facts might affect your prediction? Once again this will serve both your reader's purposes and your own. First, even if the requesting attorney has not asked you to identify important unknown facts, she almost certainly will appreciate ideas about factual investigation. Second, you will find that legal analysis and fact investigation are inextricably intertwined. Often the process of identifying important unknown facts will yield new insights about rule application, rule explanation, or both. Fact identification is yet another opportunity to deepen your analysis of the question presented.

Use your assessment of the requesting attorney's preference to judge whether and how to pass on a list of unknown facts. One fairly easy way would be to attach the list at the end of the memo as a helpful and practical bonus for your reader, but one that does not interrupt the flow of the material your reader is expecting. If an unknown fact is particularly important, you might even mention it in the Fact Statement. Your goal is to provide your reader with all appropriate information, placed at the most helpful spot.

B. Organization

Once you have identified the facts, think about how you want to organize them. Normally your first paragraph should identify your client and briefly describe the client's problem or goal. This paragraph will give your reader a context for the facts that follow. The first or the last paragraph should describe the current status of the situation, including the procedural posture of any litigation. For the material between, the most common format choices are organizing chronologically, or topically, or using a combination of the two.

Chronological Organization. If the legal analysis has not identified complex and distinct factual topics, if the order of events is particularly important, or if there are a number of factual developments in the story, a simple chronology may be best. For instance, turn back to the description of the Ryan/Kaplan facts in Exercise 8-2. Notice how those facts are organized. The legal issue there is whether a reasonable person would have thought that Kaplan was serious. The story has a number of factual developments, and the chronology is particularly important. Therefore, a chronological organization works well.

Topical. When the facts are complex and cover a number of topics, or when they include more description than plot, a topical organization may work best. For example, consider these facts:

Janet Harbin represented Marcel Myers in a divorce proceeding. Myers made some statements to Harbin that caused Harbin to fear that Myers might physically injure his estranged wife. Harbin disclosed these statements to a police officer. Subsequently Myers filed a disciplinary complaint against

Harbin. Assume that under the applicable ethical rule, a lawyer may reveal information if the lawyer reasonably believes that disclosure is necessary to prevent the client from committing a criminal act that is likely to result in imminent death or substantial bodily harm.

Here, chronology may not be important. The facts might simply describe topics: Myers' statement, the circumstances surrounding it, the possible consequences of it, and Harbin's reaction to it. If we had more detailed facts about each of those topics, perhaps each topic might become one or more paragraphs. This would be an example of a topical organization.

Combination of Chronological and Topical. If, as is common, the facts have characteristics of both patterns, using a combination may be the best approach. Turn back to the Carillo facts in Exercise 10-2. There, some of the facts have chronological importance, but many are descriptive. Notice how they fall roughly into four topics: (1) an introduction of the Carillos and a description of their neighborhood; (2) facts surrounding the purchase of the trampoline, its purpose, its placement in their yard, and the rules for its use; (3) the events on the day of the accident; and (4) the present status of the matter. The overall organization of that fact statement is topical, devoting a paragraph to each factual topic. However, the topics appear chronologically, and the facts within the third topic are presented chronologically.

Identifying format choices will be helpful as you organize your first few fact statements. Many writers find it best to write a preliminary draft, letting the story unfold according to the writer's intuition. Then they can identify the format that emerged, evaluate where it works and where it does not, and edit it in a second draft. Your goal is to use the format that will best meet your reader's needs for clarity and logical presentation.

Remembering Your Role. As you begin to write the Fact Statement, be particularly attentive to your role. Remember that both your legal analysis and your factual description must be as objective as possible. Watch for the tendency to try to prove something by the way you tell the story. Here are three techniques that will help you resist this role confusion:

1. Use neutral language and objective characterizations wherever possible. Rather than writing, "the defendant was speeding through the school zone," write instead "the defendant was traveling 40 MPH through the school zone." Rather than writing, "Wade brutally beat the victim," write instead, "Wade struck Baker on the head several times, resulting in multiple lacerations and a concussion."
2. Include the unfavorable facts. Do not focus primarily on the facts that support your prediction. You may have to remind yourself to identify and include these unfavorable or conflicting facts, but the discipline will help you stay in role.
3. Where appropriate, identify one or two important unknown facts. Pointing out a potentially important but currently unknown fact will help counteract the unconscious tendency to slip into describing the facts with more certainty than a balanced, objective perspective would support.

EXERCISE 12-3

Critique the following Fact Statement, using the criteria described above and any others you choose. Then write an improved version.

Fact Statement. On March 1, 1996, our client Karen Berry, a lawyer, loaned $50,000 to her client, Morgan Cox. Cox was to use the money to purchase a lot in order to construct a warehouse for his wholesale distribution company, ABC Distributing. The loan was to be repaid over ten years. As security for the loan, Berry took a mortgage on the lot and assumed a 51% partnership status in ABC. The partnership documents give Berry both control over ABC and joint ownership with Cox of all company assets.

ABC had been operating out of leased space, but the lease would soon expire, and the owner had served notice that the lease would not be renewed. ABC had only four months to vacate the leased premises. Berry had learned of this fact during the course of her representation of Cox and ABC in the negotiations to renew the lease. Upon learning that the owner had decided not to renew the lease, Berry suggested to Cox that he buy a particular lot in the heart of the industrial district and build a warehouse on the lot. Cox responded that he did not think he could come up with the necessary funds. Berry offered to loan him $50,000 at 8% per annum. She said that as security she would take a mortgage on the lot, and she would assume 51% partnership status in ABC.

The law requires that Berry refrain from misrepresenting or concealing any material fact. Berry knew that the lot was close to one of the routes proposed for a planned interstate connector. She knew that the value of the lot would increase if that route was chosen for the highway. Berry says that she told Cox about this possibility. Whether Cox will confirm Berry on this point is presently unknown.

On the matter of the $50,000 loan, Berry says that she explained the transaction to Cox. However, she says that Cox already understood the proposed transaction clearly since he has over twenty years of business experience. Cox has a Masters degree in Business Administration, and he was at one time a licensed real estate broker. Clearly, with this kind of background, Cox should have been aware of the nature and effect of the proposed transaction. Being sure that the client is aware of the nature and effect of the proposed transaction is one of the key elements required by *Goldman v. Kane.*

Shortly after completing the transaction Berry discovered that Cox had a gambling problem and was draining ABC of its cash. The business was in serious trouble. Fortunately for Berry, she was able to dissolve the partnership agreement before she incurred significant liabilities. Since Cox was in default on the loan payments, Berry foreclosed on the lot. She did not claim interest in any other company asset.

Within a month after Berry took title to the lot, the proposed connector route nearest the lot was selected for the new highway. Two months later Berry sold the lot for $80,000. Cox has filed a disciplinary grievance against Berry, alleging that Berry violated the ethical rule governing a lawyer's business transactions with a client.

VII. DRAFTING THE CONCLUSION

If your Discussion section is relatively short and clear and if your teacher or requesting attorney does not have a preference, you need not add a separate Conclusion section. A Conclusion section should not simply repeat the Brief Answer. However, if your analysis has been complex or multifaceted, a Conclusion section can tie together and summarize the Discussion. It also can increase your reader's options for deciding how much attention to invest in understanding the details of your analysis. A Conclusion should go into more detail than the Brief Answer but not as much as the Discussion.

Checklist for an Office Memo

Heading
- Have you included the name of the requesting attorney, your name, the date, the client's name; the file number; and a phrase identifying the particular legal matter and issue?

Question Presented
- Have you made an appropriate choice of format?
- If you chose the "legal issue/major facts" format, did you state the legal question in the first half of the sentence and the significant facts in the second half?
- If you chose the "whether" format, did you state the legal question first and the significant facts second, all in a clause and ending with a period?
- If you chose the "under/does/when" format, did you state the rule, then the legal question, and then the significant facts?
- Have you made an appropriate choice of generic or specific references?
- Have you edited to achieve one readable sentence?
- Have you maintained an objective perspective?

Brief Answer
- Have you stated the answer in the first several words?
- Have you included a statement of the rule if the Question Presented did not already state it?
- Have you stated a summary of the reasoning leading to the answer?
- Have you chosen either generic or specific references to match the Question Presented?
- Have you kept the Brief Answer to a maximum of one-third to one-half a double-spaced page?
- Have you taken a position, even if you are not sure?
- Have you avoided sending your reader mixed signals about how sure you are of your answer?

Fact Statement
Fact Selection
- Have you included all legally significant facts?
- Have you included sufficient factual context?
- Have you included any major emotional facts?
- Have you avoided including discussion of legal authority?
- Have you avoided drawing legal conclusions?

Organization
- Have you identified the client and the client's situation at the beginning of the Fact Statement?
- Have you selected an appropriate organization (chronological, topical, combination) for the facts?
- Does your last paragraph give the facts closure and lead into the Discussion section by explaining the procedural posture of the legal issue or by some other device?

Role
- Have you maintained neutral language and objective characterizations?
- Have you included both favorable and unfavorable facts?

Discussion
Umbrella Section
- Have you summarized the rule, setting out all subparts and clarifying how they relate to each other?
- Have you included any important information about how the rule functions generally, such as a burden of proof or a relevant presumption?
- Have you identified any genuinely undisputed issues and, if necessary, provided a cursory explanation for why they are not in dispute?
- Have you stated the order in which the remaining issues will be discussed, explaining the reason for this organizational choice?
- If necessary to prevent confusion, have you identified any related legal issues not covered by the memo?

Analysis
- Have you selected an appropriate order for the issues?
- Have you checked section lengths, combining or dividing subsections where appropriate?
- Are your headings complete thesis sentences?
- Have you placed a thesis paragraph at the beginning of the discussion of each issue?
- Have you also used the checklists at the ends of Chapters 8 and 9?

Conclusion
- Have you added a Conclusion section only if your reader prefers or the Discussion has been long and complex?
- Is your Conclusion more detailed than the Brief Answer but significantly less detailed than the Discussion?

CHAPTER 13

Writing Professional Letters

Letters and e-mail messages are critical to a lawyer's reputation. Lawyers write far more letters and e-mail messages than office memos or briefs, and these less formal communications are seen by many people—people with whom the lawyer must maintain a key professional relationship and people the lawyer will never meet. Unlike oral communications, letters and e-mail messages can have a long life. They often are copied and distributed well beyond the original audience, and they are read and reread long after a human voice would have died away.

Perhaps even more important, self-disclosure is nearly impossible to avoid when you write a letter. The genre is by far the most personal kind of writing lawyers do, and inevitably, the reader of a letter forms opinions about the character and personality of the writer. These opinions may not be true, but they become part of the lawyer's reputation anyway.

Of course, letters and e-mail messages are important substantively as well. Key information is conveyed in both media. Clients make decisions based on their lawyer's letters and e-mails, and lawyers are exposed to malpractice liability when a letter or e-mail is inaccurate or misleading.

This chapter introduces professional letter-writing.[1] The first section discusses the general characteristics of professional letters. Succeeding sections introduce the most common kinds of letters lawyers write: letters to clients (retainer letters, informal advice letters, status reports), letters to other lawyers (demand letters and confirming letters), and transmittal letters. For each, we will explore the three most important considerations in letter writing: the purpose, the reader, and the content.

I. GENERAL CHARACTERISTICS OF PROFESSIONAL LETTER WRITING

Readers. Because letters are more personal than office memos or briefs, it is especially important that a letter writer consider the needs and characteristics of

---

1. For easier reference, we will include both electronic and paper communications in the term "letters."

her reader. Lawyers write letters to diverse people in diverse circumstances. These circumstances often are highly charged emotionally, and the lawyer may have a number of delicate purposes for the communication. Therefore, a letter writer must fine-tune her understanding of her reader.

The writer must consider three kinds of facts about her reader. First, what does this reader already know and understand? This question includes both general knowledge and legal knowledge. The reader may be a well educated and experienced business person who knows nearly as much about the legal environment of her business as does the lawyer. The reader may be another lawyer or a judge. The reader may be uneducated or developmentally disabled or not fluent in English. The writer would communicate the same information to all of these readers in very different ways.

Second, what is this reader's current mental and emotional status? All emotions, especially anxiety, fear, grief, and anger, affect the way people receive and process information. A writer must be sensitive not only to which emotions the reader may be feeling, but also to the causes of those emotions. The content of the letter may touch on some of those causes, and the writer will need to decide how to handle those subjects appropriately.

Third, what is this reader's personality? If the reader is a client, does this client prefer to be treated formally or informally? Does he want a calm, wise counselor or an impassioned advocate? Does he want an empathetic lawyer or a one who is businesslike and efficient? The purpose of asking these questions is not to enable the writer to be someone she is not. Every good lawyer possesses all of these traits and more. Nor will the writer always choose to present a persona consistent with the reader's preferences. The lawyer must decide which traits will serve the client best in the present situation, and knowledge of the reader is the first step toward making that decision.

Substantive Purposes. Every letter has at least one substantive purpose. Letters are used primarily (1) to convey information or advice objectively; (2) to document information for the protection of the client and the lawyer; and (3) to persuade someone to do something. For these substantive purposes, you will need the same analytical skills you have already been learning: accurate content, good organization, and clarity of expression.

Relational Purposes. Every letter also has at least one relational purpose. Relationally, letters are used primarily (1) to establish and maintain a good relationship; (2) to communicate the writer's competence; and (3) to establish professional boundaries. For these relational purposes, you will need the analytical skills set out above plus one more important writing skill—the careful use of tone.

Tone. The letter's tone is the primary way the writer communicates two important kinds of information: the writer's personality and character traits and the writer's opinion of the reader. A letter's tone usually reflects particular character and personality traits of the writer. Some traits are appropriate in nearly all situations, traits like trustworthiness, knowledge, skill, experience, reliability, and diligence. Other traits are appropriate in some but not all situations, traits like warmth, empathy, passionate advocacy, detachment, coolness, efficiency, and measured rationality. A lawyer should never appear sarcastic or contemptuous and should never appear to act out of anger.

Tone is created primarily by content choices, attention to detail, word choices, placement choices, and sentence formats. Content choices and attention to detail help establish many of the most important traits of the lawyer: trustworthiness, knowledge, experience, skill, reliability, and diligence. Traits relating to more personal aspects of the relationship often are more subtle. Here are some examples of methods for creating a warm tone (friendly, kind, empathetic, encouraging) or a cool tone (detached, efficient, rational, stern).

WARMER TONE	**COOLER TONE**
Beginning and ending the letter with content establishing a personal connection.	No content establishing a personal connection.
Word choices without connotations of blame, fault, criticism.	Word choices that are sharp, blunt, biting.
Words with more syllables and soft initial sounds; sentences with longer phrases.	Shorter words with hard consonant sounds; shorter sentences with powerful verbs and vivid nouns but fewer adjectives and adverbs.
Contractions (only when informality is appropriate).	No contractions.
Mutual references using the pronoun "we" to underline the relationship.	Liberal use of the pronoun "you" to underline the distinction between the writer and the reader.
Tempering any uncomfortable subjects with offsetting indirect assurances that the writer likes and respects the reader.	Discussing uncomfortable subjects without any reassurances.
Using passive voice for uncomfortable subjects.	Using the active voice for uncomfortable subjects.
Placing uncomfortable subjects in the middle of the letter or in the middle of a paragraph.	Placing uncomfortable subjects early in the letter and at the beginning of a paragraph.

Letters as Public Documents. Before we begin considering particular kinds of letters, one word of caution is helpful. Because letters are addressed to particular readers and are not usually filed in court, it is easy to think of them as private documents. But any document that goes outside your office is or may one day become a public document. You may find your letter appended as "Exhibit A" to a court document or presented against you or your client in a future dispute or settlement negotiation. Never write a letter that you would cringe to see again in another context. If you are angry, do not mail a letter until you either have calmed down or had another lawyer review what you have written. Do not click on your e-mail program's "send" icon in the heat of the moment.

II. LETTERS TO CLIENTS

A. General Considerations

Purposes. Letters to clients are used for all three substantive purposes. Lawyers write client letters to communicate legal and procedural information and advice. For example, they write status letters to update clients on developments in their cases. They write formal and informal opinion letters to explain the results of legal and factual research the firm has conducted. And they write to convey the lawyer's professional judgments and to advise clients about decisions the clients must make. These letters often cover both legal and nonlegal matters.

Lawyers also write to clients to document information in case an issue about that information should arise in the future. For example, a lawyer should write a letter confirming the oral transmission to a client of any important information, such as a settlement offer, a deposition date, a trial date, or the fee agreement. The letter will help the client remember the information and help the lawyer demonstrate that she met her professional duty to inform her client of that information.

Finally, lawyers write to persuade their clients to do something or to refrain from doing something. While the lawyer's primary persuasive role occurs outside the client/lawyer relationship, the lawyer sometimes must persuade her client as well. The lawyer may advocate for particular decisions regarding legal and extra-legal matters, and sometimes the lawyer must persuade the client to act within the law or within moral boundaries.

Client letters are also used for all three relational purposes. Almost always the lawyer intends that a client letter will help establish and maintain a good relationship. Letters can be extraordinarily effective for this purpose because letters effectively carry relationship messages and because clients typically reread their lawyers' letters many times. Carefully written letters also effectively communicate the writer's competence. Nearly all clients can distinguish a sloppy letter from a careful letter. The letter itself is powerful proof of the lawyer's ability and diligence.

Finally, lawyers sometimes must write to establish professional boundaries with clients. A client may disregard a fee agreement or other policies of the firm; may be overdependent on the lawyer in inappropriate ways, or may desire an unprofessional relationship. In any of these situations, the lawyer's letters would include a boundary-setting purpose.

B. Retainer Letters

Retainer letters, sometimes called "engagement letters," are written to document the beginning of a representation. A good retainer letter must achieve a delicate balance between establishing a positive relationship and setting boundaries. On the one hand, the lawyer hopes the letter will leave the reader glad to have selected the lawyer. The reader should feel confident that the lawyer's loyalties are not divided between the client's needs and the lawyer's own welfare. The reader should sense that the lawyer and the client will function as a team working toward the same goal.

On the other hand, the letter informs the client about a number of uncomfortable but necessary subjects such as fees, costs, and perhaps allocation of decision-making authority and conditions under which the firm can withdraw. Achieving this balance can be a daunting task, one which will require wise selection of coverage and careful attention to tone. Since we have already discussed the topic of tone, this section will focus primarily on content.

Formalities. Use the standard business format for dating and addressing the letter: the recipient's name; his title and business name, if appropriate; and the address. Include a "Re" line on which you identify the legal matter. You can include your own file number, but include also any identifier your recipient uses as well (Your file #12345"). Unless your relationship with the client is on a less formal level, use the courtesy titles of "Mr." and "Ms." Conclude the letter with any standard business closing such as "very truly yours." Type your name under the place where you will sign the letter, and include your title or law firm name beneath your name.

First Sentence and Last Sentence. Begin with an appropriate expression of pleasure at the opportunity to serve the client. Much of the body of the letter will have to set out contract terms, so you risk sounding like an adversary rather than a counselor and advocate. Therefore, a warm beginning and ending are especially important.

Coverage Decisions. Some topics should always be covered in a retainer letter, while coverage of other topics should depend on the client and the legal matter. A retainer letter should usually do the following:

1. *Identify the client.* If the client is a single person, client identification is a simple matter and usually is handled implicitly by addressing the letter to the client and referring to the client as "you" in the body of the letter ("The firm of X, Y, and Z will be pleased to represent you in your efforts to . . ."). The client's identity can be less clear, however, in the case of a corporation, a partnership or other group, a married person, a minor, or a mentally disabled person. In any circumstance where the identity of the client might need clarification, be sure to resolve that ambiguity in the retainer letter. It may be sufficient to name the client, or you may need to identify specifically certain people or entities you are *not* representing. ("We understand that we will be representing only Hamlin Roofing, Inc. and that any individual defendants will retain separate counsel.")

2. *Identify the legal matter.* Clarify the scope of your representation, especially if there could be any misunderstanding. In a discrete litigation,

the scope of the representation is usually clear, but sometimes one law suit is related to others, or the litigation may be related to a separate transactional matter. Be sure that you and your client agree about what is your responsibility and what is not. ("We will represent you in the law suit Ms. Robbins plans to file against you in Ada County District Court. However, you should retain separate counsel to handle any coverage dispute you may have with the insurance company.")

3. *Set out the fee, possible expenses, and payment expectations.* Usually lawyers charge an hourly rate, a fixed fee, or a contingent fee. In the case of an hourly rate or a fixed fee, set out the amount of the rate or the fee. In either case, the lawyer may require payment of an initial amount (sometimes called a "retainer") and also may require that additional advance payments ("refreshers") be made routinely as the credit balances are reduced. Clarify any retainer and refresher requirements. Also clarify your billing cycles and your expectations regarding when payments will be made.

A contingent fee is a fee charged only if certain results are obtained. Usually the fee is a certain percentage of any funds recovered. If no funds are recovered, no fee is charged. The retainer letter should set out the percentage of the contingent fee. If the percentage will vary depending on how far into the litigation process the matter proceeds, explain clearly the points at which the percentage will change and what the new percentage will be. ("The fee will be 30 percent of any funds recovered prior to filing suit, 40 percent of any funds recovered after trial begins, or 50 percent of any funds recovered after the filing of any appeal.")

No matter what kind of fee arrangement you have agreed upon, be sure to explain any other expenses the client will be expected to pay and whether those expenses will be deducted before or after a contingent fee is calculated. ("The contingent fee will be calculated based on the gross recovery. Any litigation expenses the firm has incurred will then be deducted from your portion of the recovery. Litigation expenses customarily include expert witness fees, court filing costs, deposition transcript charges, or professional copying services.")

4. *Clarify when the representation will begin.* Both you and your client should understand when your responsibility for the legal matter will begin. If the representation will not begin until some event occurs, identify the event clearly. ("As soon as we receive the signed fee agreement, we will start work on the case.")

5. *Possible conflicts of interest.* If you or your firm previously represented any party involved in the present matter, you probably should disclose this prior representation to your new client. If these prior representations did not involve the present matter, you probably can represent the new client.[2] However, your present client may later discover the past relationship and feel deceived. Even if the ethical rules do not require it, disclosure is usually the best choice.

6. *Termination of the representation.* Some firms prefer to explain the circumstances under which the firm might choose to withdraw, including circumstances in which the client does something to prompt the withdrawal,

---

2. Model R. Prof. Conduct 1.9.

such as not cooperating or not paying fees or costs on time. If you have some reason to believe that this client might engage in that kind of conduct, perhaps you will want to cover the subject in the retainer letter.

However, if you have no reason to believe the client will be a problem, it may be best to omit this topic. Under ethical rules, you can usually withdraw in either of these circumstances whether or not you have covered the matter in the retainer letter.[3] And a reasonable client who always pays his bills is likely to feel insulted at being threatened in advance for conduct he would not dream of committing. To the client, it seems that the most likely reason for including that warning is the lawyer's belief that he is the sort of person who might fail to cooperate or pay his bill. No one wants to work with a lawyer who holds that opinion of him.

Formats. The letter itself can contain all the terms of the representation, or the letter can accompany a separate document (a fee contract or a firm brochure for new clients) that contains your firm's standard terms. This latter format allows you to minimize the strain on the relationship caused by the need to discuss uncomfortable subjects. The letter can contain personalized information establishing good relations and move directly into substantive matters dealing with the legal matter, while the enclosure can cover most of the off-putting subjects in a less personal way. Appendix D provides a sample retainer letter containing in its body the terms of the representation. Here is a sample retainer letter referencing an enclosed fee agreement:

[date, recipient's name and address, and "re" line]

Dear Ms. Gomez:

Thank you for your selection of Harris, Felton, and Cox to represent Best Auto Repair in its possible zoning litigation against the City of Decatur. We look forward to working with you toward a successful resolution of the current zoning dispute. I am enclosing two copies of our firm's standard fee agreement, which sets out the fee terms we discussed and includes our standard operating procedures. If the terms and procedures meet with your approval, please sign and return one of the copies. When we have received the signed agreement, we can begin work on the case.

As we discussed this morning, our first step will be to meet with Ms. Ferrar to explore the City's particular concerns about the proposed commercial use of the lot. Then we will research the City's legal position and report to you what we have learned. With that information in mind, you can decide whether to attempt an administrative solution or proceed directly to litigation.

Once again, thank you for the opportunity to serve you. If you should have any questions or concerns at any point in the process, please feel free to call.

Very truly yours,

Keith Salter
Attorney at Law

---

3. Model R. Prof. Conduct 1.16(b)(5).

C. Advice Letters

Lawyers write two kinds of advice letters. Formal advice letters (usually called "opinion letters") and informal advice letters. Opinion letters are formal documents communicating a lawyer's legal opinion. They are commonly required for particular kinds of transactions, as a form of assurance to the parties of their legal situation. The requirements for these opinion letters often are highly specialized and beyond the coverage of this course.

Informal advice letters, however, are common, important, and well within your present ability. Here is a summary of the content and organization of an informal advice letter. Use your understanding of your reader to help you decide the appropriate level of formality for the letter. Refer to the advice letter in Appendix D for an example of each of the following components.

Opening Paragraphs. Begin with any personal material that is appropriate for your relationship with this client in this particular matter. For instance, assume that you are probating the estate of your client's deceased wife and that during your last conversation with your client, he told you that his children were having difficulty adjusting to their mother's death. You might begin with an expression of hope that the children are doing better. Do not manufacture a stilted opener, however. Simply respond genuinely to your client, as one human being to another.

Then set out a summary of the question you have analyzed. Usually you can summarize the question in one paragraph or less, though a complex question might take more space. If you think your reader is ready, provide a summary of your conclusion here as well. If you think your reader will be more receptive to your conclusion after reading your reasoning, postpone your conclusion.

Fact Summary. Usually you should include a fact summary to be sure that your client understands the facts on which you base your conclusion. If your understanding of the facts is incorrect or incomplete, the client can advise you. Your responsibility for the accuracy of your conclusions is limited to the circumstances of which you were aware. If different circumstances develop in the future, you will not be held accountable for a conclusion not meant to apply to those other circumstances.

Legal Analysis. Explain the results of your research and the legal conclusions you have reached. Use your understanding of your reader to help you decide the appropriate level of detail for this explanation and the degree to which you can use legal terms. Follow roughly the paradigm for legal analysis; that is, explain the governing rule and then apply it to your client's situation. If the analysis must cover several separate topics, feel free to use headings to help you mark the transition from one topic to the next. Clear organizational markers help readers manage new, frightening, or complex material.

Advice. You may have been asked simply to provide a legal conclusion, such as whether certain conduct would be legal. If so, your analysis in the prior section will have answered the question adequately. However, you may have been asked a broader question, such as "Should I sue my employer for salary discrimination?" The answer to that question certainly includes one or more legal questions aimed at learning whether the client has a legally viable claim.

But the question also asks you to help the client think about the personal and professional consequences of bringing a claim against a current employer. If the answer to the broader question is complex or sensitive, you might prefer to discuss it in a personal meeting with your client, perhaps summarizing your advice after the meeting. If the answer to the broader question is more straightforward, however, you can communicate it here, at the end of your legal analysis. Feel free to organize the components of your advice according to simple topics, such as advantages, disadvantages, likelihood of success, and time frame.

D. Status Letter

Not only do ethical rules require lawyers to keep clients informed,[4] but good relations with clients demand frequent communication. This need is even greater if the fee arrangement requires monthly billing. Clients hate to receive nothing but bills from their lawyers. If you are billing your client monthly, include with the bill a status letter explaining what has happened on the case that month. Knowing that you will have to report to your client also provides a good discipline for you to attend to the case appropriately.

If you are not billing the client monthly, report to your client at the intervals your client prefers, within reason. If the case is in litigation and your client is the plaintiff, monthly reports are appropriate. If your client is the defendant, if your strategy is to allow the case to lie dormant, and if the plaintiff's attorney has done nothing on the case for quite a while, you could wait longer between status letters. Your goal is to keep the client informed and reassured of your attention to the matter, but not to cause the client to think that you are billing him for too many unnecessary letters.

Report the developments in the case at a level of detail appropriate for your client. You need not explain the intricacies of a discovery dispute to a lay client unless the client will need to know the precise legal grounds for the dispute. To the extent that you explain procedural developments to lay clients, try to use clear, simple language. An example of a status letter is found in Appendix D.

One final word about status letters: Do not avoid telling your client bad news. Many a lawyer has gotten into disciplinary trouble for pretending that a case was proceeding well instead of disclosing unfavorable results. Ultimately, your client will learn the truth, and the consequences will be worse if you appear to have tried to hide the situation.

III. LETTERS TO OTHER LAWYERS

A. General Considerations

Lawyers also write many letters to lawyers for other clients. These letters may convey straightforward procedural information (like the time and place of a deposition) or substantive material (like a demand letter or a settlement offer). Two important considerations apply to all of these letters: the importance of careful writing and the importance of tone.

---

4. A lawyer shall "keep the client reasonably informed about the status of the matter." Model R. Prof. Conduct 1.4(a)(3).

Careful writing (including careful legal analysis) is important primarily because lawyers have a professional obligation to do good work on behalf of a client. Also, a lawyer's reputation among other lawyers and judges is critical to a successful career. A reputation is formed largely by the quality of the work other lawyers observe. Among the most visible work products are the letters lawyers write to each other. For both of these reasons, then, take care with your letters to other lawyers. Be sure your analysis is complete and your writing is free of errors.

Tone is important because your ability to both represent your client well and simultaneously enjoy your job depend on establishing good relationships with other lawyers. If your working relationships are good, you will offer professional courtesies to other lawyers and receive them in return. These courtesies will benefit you and your client alike. Other lawyers with whom you are on good terms will be willing to accommodate your scheduling conflicts and will hesitate to treat you as they do not wish to be treated in return. The tone of your letters will be instrumental in establishing and maintaining these relationships.

Always maintain a polite professional tone, even if you are very frustrated with the recipient of your letter. Do not descend into sarcasm or angry rhetoric. It will not advance your client's cause, and it does not wear well in the long term. Generally, acting out of anger is a sign of weakness rather than strength. Before you write, wait until you regain your emotional equilibrium.

Formalities. Use a customary business letter format such as that described above. One added piece of information may be helpful when writing to other lawyers. Often it is appropriate to provide other people with copies of your letters to counsel. Copying your client with your correspondence is an excellent way to keep your client informed. When you send copies to other people, note the fact in one of two ways: If you want your primary recipient to know that you sent the copies and to whom, use the standard "cc" notation (for "courtesy copy") along the lower left margin and include the names of your secondary recipients. If you do not want your primary recipient to know of the copies, use "bcc" (for "blind courtesy copy") *on the copies themselves and on your file copy, but not on the original.* This way your file will reflect the fact that you sent the copies. Here is an example of the end of a letter in which the lawyer has sent copies both ways:

[date, recipient's name and address, and "re" line]

Dear Mr. James:
.... [the body of the letter] ....

Very truly yours,

Karen Kelly
Attorney at Law

cc: Benjamin Ahmad
       Home Care, Inc.

bcc: Sarah Lancaster

B. Demand Letters and Responses

Before proceeding to litigation or other enforcement mechanisms on behalf of a client, a lawyer usually sends a demand letter setting out the claims and the damages the client incurred. A demand letter can have three purposes. First, it allows the client to attempt to resolve the matter early and inexpensively. If the parties can settle the matter without resort to litigation, they usually will be best served to do so. Second, in some cases, a prevailing party can recover additional fees and costs if the prevailing party apprised the losing party of the claims prior to filing suit and thus gave that party a chance to settle the case. Third, in a few kinds of cases, sending a demand letter is a legal prerequisite for filing suit.[5]

If the opposing party is represented, the demand letter goes to the lawyer, not the party. It can be a one to two paragraph statement of the client's claim, the damages he has sustained, and the amount he seeks. If the lawyer believes that early settlement is unlikely, she may send such a conclusory demand letter. However, the lawyer may have two reasons for choosing to send a more thorough demand letter. The lawyer may believe that early settlement is possible, so she will want the demand letter to present her client's claim as effectively and thoroughly as possible. Or she may simply want to send a message to the opposing lawyer—the message that she is a diligent and skilled lawyer who intends to take this case seriously. For either reason, the lawyer may choose to send a detailed letter setting out the results of her legal and factual research. She may even include exhibits such as photographs or documents relevant to the claim or the damages suffered. Demand letters of this second kind can be as long as five or six pages with additional enclosures.

In the case of a more detailed demand letter, it is customary to begin by identifying your client, summarizing the claim against the other party, and asserting that party's liability. Then set out the facts of the case, truthfully but phrased favorably for your client. Emphasize the culpable conduct of the other party and minimize any culpable conduct of your client. Include a description of your client's damages in sufficient detail to justify the claim. Next, explain the results of your legal research, again framing it in the light most favorable for your client's claim.

Finally, make demand for a certain sum and for any nonmonetary relief your client claims, and express your hope that the matter can be settled short of litigation. Invite a response from the lawyer to whom you are writing, set a deadline by which the matter must be resolved, and indicate what action you will take if the deadline is not met.

An example of a relatively simple demand letter is found in Appendix D.

C. Confirming Letters

Often in law practice lawyers reach agreements orally. In litigation, these agreements may range from relatively unimportant procedural aspects of a case to a complete settlement agreement. In transactional matters, oral agreements may range from setting meeting times to major terms of a transaction. The more

---

5. When a demand letter is required by law, check the authorities to learn any additional requirements with which the letter must comply.

important the topic, the more likely it eventually will be reduced to writing in some formal way, but the process of drafting and signing a formal document will take time.

Therefore, whether the topic of the oral agreement is a detail or a major matter, make it the subject of a prompt confirming letter. The process of writing out the agreement will help you clarify your understanding of its terms, and your recipient will go through a similar process upon reading the letter. Then, any misunderstandings can be resolved before the parties rely on the agreement. Also, if memories fade, the confirming letter will be there in both files to clear up the confusion.

In a confirming letter, recite the terms of the agreement. Take care to get the details right. If the other lawyer has extended you a courtesy, do not forget to thank her. Here is an example of a simple confirming letter:

[date, recipient's name and address, and "re" line]

Dear Ms. Keller:
    This letter confirms the rescheduling of Mr. Burston's deposition until April 12, 2003, at 10:00. I understand that the location has been moved to your office. Mr. Burston will make every effort to bring with him the documents you requested. Thank you for agreeing to the later date.

Very truly yours,

Keith Salter
Attorney at Law

cc: David Burston

IV. TRANSMITTAL LETTERS

Transmittal letters (also called "cover letters") accompany documents or other enclosures provided to clients, other lawyers, or the court. Sometimes the letters include an explanation of the enclosures or instructions about what to do with them. The letters provide a tangible record of the transmission for your file, and they allow you to provide explanation or instruction in a form the recipient can keep and review as necessary.

Transmittal documents are notorious for stilted, obtuse language. Some lawyers still write "Enclosed please find ..." followed by a parade of "herewiths" and "saids," strung together in long, nearly indecipherable sentences. Instead, use normal twenty-first century English words and syntax, for example:

[date, recipient's name and address, and "re" line]

Dear Ms. Cantrell,
    I have enclosed drafts of your will and the trust agreement for your son. Please read these drafts, and let me know if you have any questions or concerns. You can

> sign the final versions of both documents in my office when we meet on Monday. By law, you will need two witnesses not related to you. Members of our staff can serve as your witnesses, or you can bring witnesses of your own choosing.
> I look forward to seeing you next week.
>
> Very truly yours,
>
> Keith Salter
> Attorney at Law

Clearly set out any explanations or instructions your reader will need. If there are more than two enclosures, tabulate the list or format the list in a way that will help your reader tell at a glance what is enclosed. Here is a sample letter to a lay person familiar with the litigation process:

> [date, recipient's name and address, and "re" line]
>
> Dear Ms. Gomez,
> I am enclosing for your review the following discovery documents received today from Air Mart, Inc.:
>
> First Set of Interrogatories
> Requests for Production of Documents
> Requests for Admission
> Notice of Deposition (Francis Hawley)
> Notice of Deposition (James Bainley)
>
> Please calendar the dates of the depositions, and let me know if any schedule conflicts arise. Our response to the written discovery is due on May 5. We can discuss those responses when we meet next week.
>
> Very truly yours,
>
> Keith Salter
> Attorney at Law

If the transmittal letter accompanies documents mailed to the court, do not forget to send a copy to all other parties (through their lawyers). Indicate that you have done so by using a "cc" as explained in section IIIA. Ethical rules prohibit any ex parte[6] (private) communication with a judge about a pending matter,[7] so you will need to demonstrate to the judge that you have included all parties in this communication. The "cc" format shows the judge that you have complied with your ethical duty.

---

6. Literally "on one side only."
7. Model R. Prof. Conduct 3.5.

PART FIVE

The Shift to Advocacy

CHAPTER 14

Introduction to Brief-Writing

The briefs you write will be vital to your clients. The outcome of most cases depends on the judge's rulings on numerous legal questions arising during the litigation. Most of those questions will be decided after you have filed a brief, and the judge usually will be influenced more by your brief than by any other form of argument you make. Therefore, for your client's sake, your brief must be thorough, well written, accurate, honest, free of technical errors, and in compliance with the court's rules.

Your brief-writing will be important to you as well. Your reputation as a lawyer will be built, in significant part, by the care you take in brief-writing. And reputation is more than just a personal matter; it is an integral part of your professional effectiveness. Over the course of her career, a lawyer with a reputation for honest and careful work will be able to accomplish much more for her clients than a lawyer with a reputation for dishonesty or slipshod work. Thus, every brief you write is a document with persuasive impact, for good or for ill, not only for your current client but for all your future clients. So write as if your practice depends on it, because it does.

We begin our study of briefs with some important general principles. First, we examine more closely the ethics of brief-writing. Then the chapter identifies the most common kinds of writing assignments and provides suggestions for how to handle each. Then we consider the characteristics of judges as readers. Finally, the chapter describes the common components of trial-level and appellate briefs and how to format these documents.

I. ETHICS AND THE ADVOCATE'S CRAFT

Language and justice are distinctive attributes of humanity. Instead of growling and gesticulating naked aggression or craving, human beings reason with language toward resolutions that are just, compassionate, and practical. This connection between language and justice made rhetoric an honored study and practice in classical antiquity, a study and practice whose foundations were formed, in part, by ancients such as Socrates, Aristotle, and Cicero. In writing a brief, today's lawyer takes her place within that honorable tradition. Reasoned argument in the quest for justice is not a mere trade performed for pay, but a craft in the Aristotelian sense, and its right practice helps sustain and advance our common humanity.

Many of the ethical principles that govern the right practice of brief-writing are codified in the professional rules governing lawyers. Chapter 1 covered many of these duties, but a reminder and some additional explanation is in order here:

1. A brief-writer must not knowingly make a false statement of law.[1] This means, for example, that the writer must not assert that a particular case stands for a proposition of law when no reasonable interpretation of the case would yield that proposition. It also means that the writer cannot fail to disclose that a case has been reversed or overruled. Many law-trained readers maintain that citing an authority is an implicit representation that the writer has read the authority itself (not just the headnotes). Citing an authority you have not read and updated is unprofessional and extraordinarily risky. Never do it.

2. A brief-writer must not knowingly fail to disclose to the court directly adverse legal authority in the controlling jurisdiction.[2] The writer is not required to disclose the adverse authority if it has been disclosed already by other counsel. However, omitting the authority from an opening brief cannot be justified by the argument that the lawyer was simply waiting to see if opposing counsel would raise it in reply.[3]

Disclosure is not only ethically required, but it is strategically wise as well. If you wait for the opposing lawyer to raise the adverse authority, you forgo the chance to be the first to interpret the authority and explain its impact. Allowing opposing counsel the first shot at interpreting the authority means that you start out behind and must make up that lost analytical ground.

The scope of the duty to disclose can be articulated in several ways, most often focusing either on the question of whether the case is one that the judge should consider or on the more subjective reactions of a "reasonable judge." In a pre–Model Rules Formal Opinion, the ABA Ethics Committee adopted both articulations:

> The test in every case should be: Is the decision which opposing counsel has overlooked one which the court should clearly consider in deciding the case? Would a reasonable judge properly feel that a lawyer who advanced, as the law, a proposition adverse to the undisclosed decision, was lacking in candor and fairness to him? Might the judge consider himself misled by an implied representation that the lawyer knew of no adverse authority?[4]

The ABA Model Rule expressly requires disclosure only if the authority is in the controlling jurisdiction, but some jurisdictions broaden the requirement. For instance, the New Jersey Supreme Court has required, on federal questions, disclosure of adverse decisions of any federal court.[5]

---

1. Model R. Prof. Conduct 3.3(a)(1).
2. Model R. Prof. Conduct 3.3(a)(3).
3. *Jorgenson v. County of Volusia*, 846 F.2d 1350 (11th Cir. 1988) (applying Fed. R. Civ. P. 11).
4. ABA Committee on Ethics and Professional Responsibility, Formal Op. 280 (1949).
5. *In re Greenberg*, 104 A.2d 46 (N.J. 1954).

3. A brief-writer must not knowingly make a false statement of fact or fail to disclose a material fact when disclosure is necessary to avoid assisting a criminal or fraudulent act by the client.[6] The duty to refrain from false statements of fact applies throughout the brief, not merely to the section of the brief labeled "Statement of Facts" or "Statement of the Case."[7]

4. A brief-writer must not assert a legal argument unless there is a nonfrivolous basis for doing so. A position that argues for an extension, modification, or reversal of existing law is not frivolous. When defending the accused in a criminal matter, it is not frivolous to require that every element of the case be established.[8]

A claim is not frivolous merely because the lawyer believes that probably it will fail.[9] But when a lawyer cannot "make a good faith argument on the merits of the action" the claim is frivolous.[10] The attorney's subjective belief is not sufficient to meet the standard. The test is whether a reasonable, competent attorney would believe that the argument could have merit.[11] The meaning of "frivolous" in this context often is subject to debate, even among experienced lawyers. In the early years of law study, while you are still observing the kinds of arguments that do and do not have persuasive value for judges, you may feel particularly at sea with this standard. When you suspect that you may be approaching the line, consider doing two things: (1) Ask a more experienced lawyer whether the argument might be frivolous.[12] (2) Ask yourself (and the more experienced lawyer) whether making such a marginal argument is good strategy, even if the argument is permissible. If you are wondering whether the argument is so weak that it might be considered frivolous, your position may be stronger without it.[13]

5. A brief-writer must not communicate ex parte[14] **with a judge about the merits of a pending case, unless the particular ex parte communication is specifically permitted by law.**[15] In the context of brief-writing, this means that you must provide each party (through counsel, if any) with a copy of your brief. Court rules require certification that you have done so.[16]

6. A brief-writer must not intentionally disregard filing requirements or other obligations imposed by court rules.[17] Virtually all courts operate under rules of procedure that set out the applicable time deadlines and format requirements for your brief. Many courts impose page limits, and some prescribe the margins and number of permissible characters per inch. You can

---

6. Model R. Prof. Conduct 3.3(a)(1) and (2).

7. *See* Chapter 16.

8. Model R. Prof. Conduct 3.1.

9. Model R. Prof. Conduct 3.1 cmt. 2.

10. *Id.*

11. *See, e.g., Beeman v. Fiester*, 852 F.2d 206, 211 (7th Cir. 1988).

12. Take care not to violate any honor code regulations pertaining to your law school assignment or your duty of confidentiality to a client.

13. *See* Chapter 6, section IIE.

14. Ex parte, in this context, means without notice to other parties in the litigation.

15. Model R. Prof. Conduct 3.5.

16. *See* Fed. R. Civ. P. 5(a).

17. Model R. Prof. Conduct 3.4.

guess the purpose behind these rules. It may be tempting to change the font or ignore the margin requirements so that you can file a longer brief, but it is neither ethical nor wise to do so. Resist the temptation, both in practice *and* in your legal writing course.

II. JUDGES, BRIEFS, AND PERSUASION

In your brief-writing, judges are your primary readers, so keep in mind their needs and expectations. Review the description of judges in section IIE of Chapter 6. Judges serve an important and difficult role, and respect for their position requires a respectful tone and the formality befitting the position and the task at hand. Do not use contractions, colloquialisms, slash constructions ("and/or"), or note-taking abbreviations. Do not use humor, for the job you are doing is serious work.

The judge should find your brief clear and in control of the material, respectful of the court, and focused on issues rather than personalities. Here are some editing strategies to help you send these important messages.

Tabulate. When your document deals with several items (such as elements of a rule, factors, guidelines, categories of facts), consider tabulating the items.

> A lawyer has a responsibility to undertake legal service in the public interest. Among the possible avenues of service are (1) free or reduced-fee representation of the poor, (2) free or reduced-fee representation of public service organizations, (3) participation in activities designed to improve the legal system, or (4) financially supporting legal services programs.

Tabulating not only helps your reader navigate through the substance of your text; it also demonstrates to your reader that you are in control of the material. Your reader will be more willing to follow you along your line of reasoning if the reader finds you an effective leader.

Use short forms of reference. Where helpful, create shortened forms of reference for people and things your text refers to often. This is another technique for sending the message that you are in control of the material. Introduce the shortened reference at the earliest feasible occasion, and maintain consistency of reference from then on. If you will use several shortened references, consider a paragraph or footnote early in the text introducing all of them.

> This brief will refer to Defendants Carter, Colham, Tellerhoff, and Winston, in combination, as "the owners" and to Defendants Allen, Rakestraw, and Vernon, in combination, as "the managers." The brief also refers to 42 U.S.C. § 2000e-17 by its popular name, "Title VII," and to 42 U.S.C. § 1983 by its popular reference, "Section 1983."

Where possible, select a shortened reference that will facilitate your theory of the case. Avoid references that will work at odds with your theory of the case.

Add explanatory parentheticals to citations. Before finalizing your brief, review your citations to identify any authorities that could use an explanatory parenthetical.[18] A citation might profit from a parenthetical if you are not discussing its facts and reasoning in the text. Look for cases you are citing cursorily, either as support for a minor and uncontested proposition or as additional authority for a proposition principally supported in some other way. You can use the parenthetical to quote a nugget of language or to provide relevant facts that serve as examples of your point. Here is an example of each:

An effective quotation. After a discussion of several cases dealing with the evidentiary significance of racial statements by supervisors, the writer places this citation:

> *See also Slack v. Havens*, 7 F.E.P. 885, 885 (S.D. Cal. 1973), *aff'd as modified,* 522 F.2d 1091 (9th Cir. 1975) ("Colored folks are hired to clean because they clean better").

An example supporting a minor point: To support a sentence expressing a minor and uncontested point, the writer uses these two citations:

> Courts have held that a defendant who resides out-of-state cannot be lured into the state by fraud or trickery and then served with process. *McClellan v. Rowell,* 99 So. 2d 653 (Miss. 1958) (petitioner told his ex-wife that his mother was dying and wanted to see the couple's child one last time); *Zenker v. Zenker,* 72 N.W.2d 809 (Neb. 1955) (plaintiff told defendant that his presence was needed to convey certain real estate).

Purge your document of vague references. Avoid references like these:

this matter	with regard to
it involves	it deals with
it pertains to	it concerns

Writing peppered with these phrases forces the reader to struggle to understand the reference and to wonder whether the writer is in control of the material.

Do not tell a court what it "must" do or what it "cannot" do. Use less confrontational language when referring to limits on the court's authority or power. For instance, avoid:

> The Court must reverse the trial court's order ...
> The Court cannot grant the defendant's motion ...
> The Court is not permitted to consider subsequent negotiations ...

Here are some better options:

a. Shift the focus to a tactful statement of another court's error:

> The lower court erred in ordering that ...

---

18. *See* Chapter 8, section V.

b. Use a passive-voiced verb (to avoid identifying the court as the actor); substitute "should" for "cannot"; and switch to a permissive statement (what the court *should* do) rather than a prohibitory statement (what the court *should not* do):

> The defendant's motion should be denied ...

c. Focus on the rule that governs the issue rather than on the entity that must follow the rule:

> The rule allows consideration of subsequent negotiations only where ...

Edit out signs of negative emotion. Cool reason is much more persuasive than sarcasm or anger. Cool reason says to your reader, "The law and the facts are on my side, so I do not have to be disturbed by the opposing side's position."

Focus on the judge rather than on the opposing party or the opposing lawyer. A brief-writer's focus can be distracted by becoming caught up in seeing the litigation as a battle with opposing parties or their lawyers. Do not let your day-to-day contact with the parties and their lawyers cause you to forget that the primary focus of your brief must be the *reader* (the judge).

Moderate any exaggerations of the law, the facts, or the inferences. A necessary part of the advocacy process is the shift from an objective perspective to a partisan perspective. But a brief-writer still must evaluate the final draft of the brief with an objective eye, being careful not to overstate the law or the facts. Remember that a reader who suspects that the advocate has exaggerated one point will doubt all of the writer's other points as well.

III. THE COMPONENTS OF A TRIAL-LEVEL BRIEF

While formats for trial-level briefs vary with the customs of the court and the law firm, the variations are seldom substantively significant. This chapter describes a standard format for a trial-level brief. Refer to the sample trial-level brief in Appendix B for examples of the components described here:

Case Caption and Title of Document. The function of the Caption is simply to identify the court, the case, and the document, for example:

IN THE UNITED STATES DISTRICT COURT FOR THE
SOUTHERN DISTRICT OF TEXAS

CAROLINE MacDONNELL and
BARBARA JAMES,
     Plaintiffs,
  v.
ELLIS PEST CONTROL, INC., and
FORREST MICHIE,
     Defendants.

Civ. No. 99-8636

BRIEF IN SUPPORT OF PLAINTIFFS' MOTION TO COMPEL
THE PRODUCTION OF DOCUMENTS

The Caption must include the docket number (the case number assigned by the court[19] and the name of the document. In many courts, the captions of cases with multiple parties need list only the first plaintiff and the first defendant followed by "et al."[20] Court rules may require additional information such as the name and address of the attorney or the name of the assigned judge. The Caption can appear on a separate cover sheet or simply at the top of the first page of the brief.

Introduction. The Introduction (sometimes called a "preliminary Statement") introduces the judge to (1) the nature of the case; (2) the parties; (3) the motion or other procedural event that has led to filing of the brief; (4) the party's requested relief; and (5) the primary legal points justifying that relief. All of this information must be conveyed concisely, usually in one or two paragraphs. Here is an example of an Introduction:

INTRODUCTION

This is a sexual harassment action brought against Ellis Pest Control, Inc., and its President, Forrest Michie, by Caroline MacDonnell and Barbara James, former employees of the corporate defendant. The action alleges violations of Title VII of the Civil Rights Act of 1964, 42 U.S.C. § 2000(e) *et seq.* (1988), and related contract claims.

Plaintiffs file this brief in support of their motion to compel defendants' response to plaintiffs' Requests for Production of Documents, properly filed and served on May 14, 2003. The requests seek production of plaintiffs' employment files and all documents referring to any evaluations of the plaintiffs' job performance. Defendants refuse to provide any of these documents, despite the reasonableness and clearly permissible scope of the requests.

---

19. *See* Fed. R. Civ. P. 10(a).

20. *Et al.* is an abbreviation for *et alii,* meaning literally "and others." *See* Fed. R. Civ. P. 10(a) and 7(b)(2).

Statement of Facts. This section sets out the facts relevant to the legal issues addressed by the brief, as well as the context necessary for understanding those facts. The Statement of Facts is an important opportunity for advocacy, requiring skillful and careful drafting. Chapter 18 explains how to draft a Statement of Facts.

Question(s) Presented. The Question(s) Presented section states the legal issues addressed by the brief and the factual context in which they have arisen. The questions are phrased favorably to your client's position, suggesting a decision in your favor. Some lawyers include Questions Presented in trial-level briefs and some do not. Chapter 15 of this book explains how to draft Questions Presented.

Argument. The Argument section contains your fully articulated argument on the legal issues. In drafting the argument, you will be drawing on the analytical material in Chapters 3-5 and the organizational material and writing process information in Chapters 6-11. Chapter 16 provides some suggestions and important reminders for drafting this section.

Remember one special characteristic of trial judges, however. Trial judges are constrained by mandatory precedent. They primarily want to know what those precedents are and how they apply to your case. Authorities from other jurisdictions hold less interest for trial judges, most of whom do not see themselves as free to change the law. Therefore, right up front, the trial judge wants to know whether there are mandatory authorities on your issue, and if so, what they are. Use authorities from other jurisdictions only to fill in any gaps in your jurisdiction's mandatory authority and only after you have explained to the judge why you are presenting these otherwise extraneous authorities.

Conclusion. The Conclusion refers to the arguments set out in the body of the brief and states that the requested relief should be granted. It is followed with a courtesy closing like "Respectfully submitted," a signature line, and the typed name, address, and telephone number of the signing attorney.

Two schools of thought exist on the content of conclusions. The more traditional approach is a pro forma statement of the precise relief sought:

For the foregoing reasons, the Court should grant the Defendant's Motion to Dismiss.

However, if court rules and local customs permit, consider a Conclusion that gives you one last opportunity for advocacy. This sort of Conclusion should still be short—no more than half a double-spaced page. But it could gather together the most compelling arguments in support of the result you seek. Here is an example of a more substantive conclusion:

Therefore, as this brief has demonstrated, the circumstances of this case render the covenant's terms unreasonable. The covenant would protect Carrolton to a

> degree far greater than necessary, while devastating both Ms. Watson's fledgling business and her personal finances. Further, it would significantly infringe the public's interest in reasonably priced health care equipment, merchandise vital to the community's well-being. For these reasons, Carrolton's Motion for Summary Judgment should be denied.

Certificate of Service. Ethical rules prohibit ex parte contact with the judge about the merits of a legal matter.[21] Court rules require copies of all filings to be served upon all parties, via their attorneys.[22] The Certificate of Service demonstrates compliance with these rules. The Certificate is placed either after the Conclusion or on a separate page at the end of the brief. It certifies that copies of the brief have been mailed or delivered to the attorneys for all parties. For an example of a Certificate of Service, see the last page of the sample trial brief in Appendix B.

IV. THE COMPONENTS OF AN APPELLATE BRIEF

An appellate brief is a working document for the court, so its sections and format are designed to make it a useful and efficient tool for the judges and law clerks who will work on the case. Requirements for appellate briefs largely are determined by court rules, which vary from court to court. This section describes a standard set of sections and formatting practices. Follow these instructions unless your assignment requires different sections or formats.

Cover Page. The cover page of an appellate brief usually is printed on colored paper of a heavier stock than the rest of the brief. Court rules determine the color of the cover page according to the kind of brief. For instance, the cover sheet on the appellant's brief might be blue while the cover sheet on the appellee's brief might be red. These colors allow the court and the law clerks to distinguish the briefs easily and quickly. On the cover sheet, place the case caption, the docket number, the document's title, and the lawyer's name, address, and telephone number (see page 165). Use the sample appellate brief in Appendix C as an example of how to format this material on the page.

Table of Contents. Include all subsequent sections of your brief in the Table of Contents along with the page numbers on which they appear. These section titles (such as "Table of Authorities") should appear in initial caps here, though they will appear in all caps in the body of the brief. The Table of Contents also includes the point headings and subpoint headings, allowing a busy judge to skim the Table for a quick summary of the major points of the argument. Point headings should appear in the Table of Contents in the same typeface as they appear in the text of the Argument, that is, all caps,

---

21. Model R. Prof. Conduct 3.5(b).
22. *See, e.g.,* Fed. R. Civ. P. 5(a).

single-spaced, and not underlined. Similarly, subheadings should appear in the Table of Contents as they appear in the text, that is, in initial caps and underlined. The first page of the Table of Contents should be numbered as page one.

Table of Authorities. Here, provide the titles and citations for all authorities on which you rely in the brief as well as the page number(s) on which they appear in the Argument. If an authority appears on numerous pages, use the term "passim" in place of a page number. Organize the authorities according to categories with labels, such as Cases, Constitutional Provisions, Statutes, Administrative Regulations, Law Review Articles, and Miscellaneous. Beneath each category, the authorities should appear in alphabetical order.

Question(s) Presented. The Question(s) Presented section states the legal issues addressed by the brief and the factual context in which they have arisen. The questions are phrased favorably to your client's position, suggesting a decision in your favor. Chapter 15 will explain in detail how to draft Questions Presented.

Additional Sections. Some courts may require other sections, such as the following: Opinion Below (a complete sentence providing the court with the citation to the opinion from which the appeal is taken); Jurisdictional Statement (a complete sentence providing the citation to the statute on which appellate jurisdiction is based); and Constitutional and Statutory Provisions Involved (a section setting out the text of and the citation to any constitutional provision or statute important to the resolution of the issues). See Appendix C for examples of these sections.

Statement of the Case. The Statement of the Case is the customary title for the fact statement of an appellate brief. Chapter 18 will explain how to draft a fact statement. You can use subheadings in a complex fact statement, including a section labeled "Statement of Facts" and a section labeled "Procedural History."

Summary of the Argument. Summarize your argument here, allotting approximately one paragraph per issue. Often the judge will read the Summary of the Argument either first or immediately after reading the Question Presented, so this section provides an early opportunity for advocacy. Phrase your summary as persuasively as possible, pulling together your most important points. In an appellate brief, your Conclusion will be a one-sentence, pro forma request for relief, so the Summary of the Argument functions as a substantive conclusion would.

Argument. The Argument section sets out your argument in its complete form. Draw on the analytical material from Chapters 3-5, the organizational and writing process material from Chapters 6-11, and the brief-writing material in Chapters 14-19. Most court rules require an appellate brief to identify the appropriate standard of review for each legal issue the court will decide. Even if you have included a separately labeled section for the standard of review, you may want to state the relevant standard early in the Argument section, especially if it is favorable for your argument. Chapter 16 will provide some important suggestions and reminders about writing this section.

Conclusion. The Conclusion of an appellate brief is a one-line, pro forma request for the relief you seek, for instance: "For the foregoing reasons, the judgment of the District Court should be reversed and the case should be remanded to the District Court for a new trial."

CHAPTER 15

Questions Presented and Point Headings

Two of the potentially most persuasive parts of a brief are the Questions Presented and the Point Headings. This chapter explains their function and tells you how to draft them effectively.

I. WRITING THE QUESTION PRESENTED

A Question Presented should both apprise the judge of the legal issue to be decided and begin persuading the judge to decide that issue in your client's favor. To draft a Question Presented that accomplishes both purposes, the writer must walk a fine line between neutrality and overzealous advocacy. The goal is to draft a Question that accurately states the issue *and* suggests a favorable answer. For example, here are examples of Questions Presented from opposing briefs:

QUESTION PRESENTED

Is a covenant-not-to-compete enforceable where the covenant was a bargained-for term of the sale of a business, where the term was negotiated as part of the agreement to allow the seller to continue working for the business, and where the sale specifically included the company's customer lists and good will?

QUESTION PRESENTED

May an established business enforce a covenant-not-to-compete where the covenant would eliminate all competition within the market area and where the prohibited activity would affect only four percent of the covenant-holder's profits?

Notice how each accurately recites the legal issue and several key facts while suggesting an answer favorable to the client for whom the brief is written.

Drafting a Question Presented is like creating a haiku. Each of these literary forms requires meticulous attention to word selection and placement, sentence structure, and theme. Unlike poetry, however, no one would argue that obscurity of message is desirable for a Question Presented. Rather, a Question Presented should be a powerful sentence that is easily understandable on first reading.

Keep reworking the Question Presented for readability and subtle persuasiveness. Use the techniques presented in Chapter 21. Try to achieve a concise, clear, and direct style, and a persuasive framing of the Question. The following are some particular suggestions for the Question Presented

Format for a Pure Question of Law. A Question Presented for a pure question of law is a straightforward statement of the legal issue. It should identify the particular legal issue, rather than simply asking whether one side's position is correct. For instance, the first of the following Questions simply asks whether one party's position is correct, without identifying the legal issue. The second actually poses a legal question.

> Can Dole bring a claim for malicious prosecution?

> Can a criminal defendant bring a civil action for malicious prosecution prior to the resolution of the criminal proceedings that give rise to the claim?

Format for a Question Requiring the Application of Law to Facts. If your legal issue will require the judge to apply the law to your client's facts, your Question Presented should include both law and facts. You can think of the Question in two parts, the first part stating the legal issue and the second part stating the key facts.

> Can . . . [state the legal question] . . . where . . . [state the major facts] . . . ?

Both of the examples on pages 171 use this format. Common verbs beginning the Question Presented are: "May. . . ?" "Does. . . ?" "Is. . . ?" and "Did. . . ?" Common words used for the transition to the second part of the Question, referring to facts, are "when" and "where."

A Question Presented also can be phrased as a clause beginning with "whether" and ending with a period:

QUESTION PRESENTED

Whether a large, established business can enforce a covenant-not-to-compete where the covenant would eliminate all competition within the market area and where the prohibited activity would affect only four percent of the covenant holder's profits.

References to Parties. To refer to the parties, a Question Presented can use (1) the parties' names (2) generic descriptions (property owner, retailer, buyer, lessor) or (3) procedural titles (plaintiff, defendant, appellant, respondent). Procedural titles require the judge to remember who the parties are in this particular case. Thus, they make the Question less readily understandable and, for this reason, some court rules instruct the lawyers to avoid procedural titles.[1] You can use procedural posture, for example:

---

1. *See* Fed. R. App. P. (28)(d).

> Can a criminal defendant bring a civil action for malicious prosecution prior to the resolution of the criminal proceedings that give rise to the claim?

In such a case, the procedural title is actually the generic description of the kind of person to whom the question would pertain.

In other cases, the better choices are generic descriptions or the parties' names. Choose the alternative that will be clearest and that better serves your strategy. Sometimes, using the parties' names can serve the strategic function of humanizing the parties and the legal issues in dispute. Using names can serve a practical function as well, allowing the drafter to use fewer words. For instance, in the third example above, the generic description "an established business" is longer than the name "Carrolton" would have been.

On the other hand, using generic descriptions may allow the writer to give additional helpful information about the party. For instance, in the Carrolton example, the generic description allowed Watson's lawyer the chance to convey some helpful information about Carrolton—that it is an established business. In such a situation, the additional information may be worth the added length. Experiment with both alternatives and select the one that works best for your particular case.

Do Not Avoid the Actual Question the Judge Must Decide. Some writers are tempted to assume the answer to the question the judge must decide, like so:

> May Carrolton enforce the terms of the covenant-not-to-compete where the terms are unreasonable?

Neither party argues that Carrolton can enforce a covenant with unreasonable terms. The governing case law clearly states that Carrolton cannot, and neither party is asking the court to change that rule. Rather, the question the judge must decide is *whether the terms are reasonable.* Perhaps the drafter of this Question Presented was hoping that the assumption would slip past the judge, but it will not. Write a Question Presented that addresses the actual legal issue.

Phrase the Question in a Way That Suggests a Favorable Answer. Generally, a question that suggests an affirmative answer is more persuasive than a question that suggests a negative answer.[2] Sometimes, however, other rhetorical factors can outweigh the advantage of calling for an affirmative response. For instance, a structure that asks, "Can *X* force *Y* to do *Z*?" implies that *X* is being oppressive to *Y*, simply by virtue of the structure of the question.

---

2. John C. Dernbach et al., *A Practical Guide to Legal Writing and Legal Method* 221 (2d ed., Rothman & Co. 1994).

The structure invites the reader to respond with a resounding "No." For example, consider this Question Presented:

> Can an employer, in order to collect urine samples, force employees to urinate in the plain view of a supervisor?

Do Not Overdo the Advocacy. Some court rules require that Questions Presented not be argumentative. Even in the absence of such court rules, overzealous advocacy is counterproductive. It causes the skeptical reader to discount the material because the writer's agenda is too heavy-handed. The goal is to state the question in a way that allows the *facts* to speak for themselves. Facts persuade more effectively than bluster and puffery ever can. Here is a Question Presented that has crossed the line into argumentativeness:

> Can a reckless defendant, whose callous conduct caused the death of a precious new life, escape liability for wrongful death just because the baby's guardians had not yet completed an adoption proceeding?

To avoid argumentative Questions Presented, limit adjectives and adverbs, using facts instead of such descriptors. Edit out language that smacks of name-calling. Stick to facts the opposing party cannot dispute.

> Can legal guardians recover for the wrongful death of a child when the guardians had raised the child as their own for four years, had instituted adoption proceedings two years prior to the child's death, and had believed, reasonably and in good faith, that a final adoption decree had been issued?

Drafting More than One Question. A brief can raise several questions and thus have several Questions Presented. In such a case, draft a separately numbered Question Presented for each legal question. Place these Questions Presented in the order in which the issues will appear in the Argument section.

EXERCISE 15-1

Critiquing Questions Presented

1. Review the Carillo facts in Exercise 10-2. Assume that the matter is now in litigation. Critique these two versions of the Question Presented drafted by the lawyer for the Lupinos. Then write a better version.

Version 1 Can the Carillos maintain an attractive nuisance in their backyard?

Version 2 Does a trampoline constitute an attractive nuisance?

2. Assume that a construction firm, M & L Construction, and one of its customers, Quincy Development, contracted for the construction of a shopping center. The construction contract contained an arbitration clause prohibiting each party from suing the other over "disputes pertaining to M & L's performance of the construction contract" unless the parties first went through nonbinding arbitration of their dispute. Construction began. About two months later, Quincy decided that M & L was not keeping to the construction schedule, and it withheld one of the scheduled interim payments. M & L has filed suit without going through arbitration, taking the position that the nonpayment is not a dispute that is controlled by the arbitration clause. The following Question Presented appears in Quincy's brief arguing for dismissal. Critique it.

> Is the plaintiff's interpretation of the arbitration agreement fundamentally flawed?

3. Review the Guzman facts in Exercise 17-1. Critique these two versions of the Question Presented appearing in a brief filed by the lawyer for Guzman. Write an improved version. The issue is whether the premises have become unsuitable for the purposes for which they were leased.

Version 1 Has an apartment become unsuitable for use as a dwelling when the utility services are unreliable?

Version 2 Has a slumlord constructively evicted poor tenants who cannot afford to move elsewhere when he callously forces children to live with rats and without heat, water, and toilet facilities?

II. POINT HEADINGS

A. Identifying Point Headings

Usually, *a point heading* is the statement of your argument on a *dispositive* legal issue—that is, an independent and freestanding ground that entitles your client to the relief you seek.[3] Here is an example of a point heading:

> I. THE WATSON COVENANT SHOULD BE ENFORCED BECAUSE ITS RESTRICTIONS ON DURATION, NATURE, AND SCOPE ARE REASONABLE.

To tell if your argument on an element or set of elements is an independent ground for the relief you seek, ask this: If the judge agrees with me on *only* this component of the rule, is that enough? If yes—if the judge would not need to consider other legal issues before granting the ruling you seek—then your argument on that component of the rule is an independent ground. A heading that states your conclusion on that component is a point heading.

---

3. Richard K. Neumann, Jr., *Legal Reasoning and Legal Writing: Structure, Strategy, and Style* 359 (5th ed., Aspen L. Bus. 2005); Helene S. Shapo, Marilyn R. Walter, Elizabeth Fajans, *Writing and Analysis in the Law* 396 (Revised 4th ed., Foundation Press 2003).

This definition will be clearer if we look at an example. In a burglary case, the state must prove *all* of the elements to win a conviction. Thus, a defense attorney's brief need only show that any one of these elements is missing in order to show that the state cannot prove the burglary charge. In that brief, each challenged element will constitute an independent ground for the desired result. If the attorney challenges the state's proof on three elements ("nighttime," "intent," and "of another"), the defense attorney will have three independent, freestanding ways to win. The defense attorney can prevail by persuading the judge on any *one* of these elements. Therefore, the argument on each element will constitute a *point,* and the defense attorney's brief will contain three point headings.

However, the prosecution's brief in response must argue that the state can prove all of the elements of burglary. The state cannot obtain the ruling it seeks (submission of the case to the jury) simply by showing that the facts will prove any *one* element; the prosecutor's brief must show that the facts can prove *all* of the challenged elements. In the prosecutor's brief, then, each challenged element will be a subpoint. The prosecutor's brief will have only one *point* heading—a point arguing that all elements are provable. As in an office memo, having only one roman numeral is fine. The roman numerals will identify for the judge the freestanding arguments that entitle your client to the result you seek.

As we said, a point heading is generally a freestanding ground that will entitle your client to the relief she seeks. In brief-writing, this is not a rigid rule, but rather a custom and a general principle of persuasion. In most cases, your reader will expect you to follow this method, and your case usually will be more persuasively presented if you do. Rarely will you have three freestanding grounds for relief that would be more persuasively argued under a single point heading. Instead, you will want to emphasize each by giving each its own point heading. You will want the judge to know at a glance that you are correct for three independent reasons, not just one.

Occasionally, however, you may choose to treat an issue as a point heading even if it is not a freestanding ground for relief. You may want to consider this organizational variation if your case falls into one of the following categories:

- When you have a major threshold issue;
- When you are responding to a brief that has given that issue its own point heading;
- When you must win on two weighty issues that are very different from each other.

Arguing an Important Threshold Issue. Recall that a threshold issue is one that determines the direction of the analysis from that point on.[4] For instance, the question of which standard of review is appropriate would be a threshold issue. The court must decide how much deference to give to the trial court's opinion before the court can consider what decision it will make on the issues you raise.

---

4. *See* Chapter 10, section IB.

The question of which law will govern your legal issue would be a threshold issue. Perhaps the court will have to decide whether the law of state *A* or the law of state *B* will govern the situation. Or perhaps your client's legal duty would be different depending on whether a particular statute applies to your client. For instance, under Title VII, an "employer" must not discriminate on the basis of religion.[5] The question of whether your client is an "employer" as defined by the act would constitute a threshold question.

An evidentiary or procedural issue may be a threshold issue. The court may have to decide an evidentiary or other procedural issue before it can consider your argument on the merits. The court may have to consider whether a particular document was properly admitted into evidence before that court can consider whether the trial evidence was sufficient to support the trial court's opinion.

If you have a threshold issue such as one of these, and if you do not have much to say about it, you can simply include it in the umbrella section of another point heading. But if you have a great deal to say about it, you may want to give it a point heading of its own.

Mirroring the Organization of the Opening Brief. If you are filing a brief in response to another brief, you may find that the judge's understanding of your arguments will be improved if you adopt the organizational structure of the opening brief. If the judge will have read your opponent's brief, which uses three point headings, you can consider whether to respond by giving each of those three issues its own point heading in your brief as well. Be careful, though, not to concede structural decisions to your opponent too easily. Sometimes structural decisions carry important implications for persuasion.

Arguing Two Major Issues. Occasionally you will have to win on two weighty issues, and the analysis of each of those weighty issues will be quite different in nature. For instance, you may have to argue that a particular statute is constitutional and also that your opponent breached its terms. While you will have to win on both of those issues, you may find that each is a very large issue, that you have a great deal to say about each, and that the nature of your argument for one is quite different from the other (constitutional principles in one case and statutory construction principles in the other). In such a case, you may want to give each of those weighty issues its own point heading. However, do not rush into the decision to separate them. Quite often, your argument on each will be strengthened by a closer association with the other, an association you can emphasize by positioning them as subpoints under a common point heading.

B. Drafting Point Headings

Headings and subheadings provide the structure of your Argument. They also serve as a tool of persuasion. They can persuade because they assert your position in compelling language; they make visible the persuasive structure

---

5. 42 U.S.C. §2000e-2(b) (2001).

you have selected for your rule and your argument; and they allow the judge to find a quick summary of your entire argument by reading only the point headings and subheadings, either in a Table of Contents or by paging through the body of the Argument itself.

Ideally, a point heading should identify, expressly or implicitly, three things: (1) the result you seek; (2) the part of the rule that justifies that result; and (3) the key facts supporting that result.[6] The heading should phrase these items of information as assertions of their correctness. One way to learn to draft point headings is to think of them in halves. The first half asserts the correctness of the result you seek. The second half identifies, at least implicitly, the part of the rule that justifies that result and adds the key facts:

DRAFTING A POINT HEADING

_____

[Identify the ruling you seek, asserting its correctness.]

because

_____

[Identify the part of the rule justifying the result and the key facts.]

Here is an example of a burglary point heading. Notice how the second half of the point heading implicitly identifies the part of the rule that determines the desired result and asserts a conclusion about it:

A BURGLARY POINT HEADING

The burglary charge should be dismissed
[Identify the ruling you seek, asserting its correctness.]

because

the testimony of the bartender and other bar patrons establishes that
Mr. Shaffer arrived at the house earlier than thirty minutes past sunset.
[Identify the key facts and state how they establish the correctness of the ruling.]

When the point heading must cover more than one element, placing the key facts for all those elements in one sentence may result in an unwieldy heading. In that situation, move the facts for each element into the subheading dealing with that element. For example, here are the prosecutor's headings for a brief responding to the defendant's challenge of three elements. Since the prosecutor must win on all three challenged elements to prevail, the point heading must cover all three elements, but there are separate *sub*headings for each. Notice that the subheadings expressly identify the components of the rule to be addressed in that subsection and add the key facts.

---

6. If the issue is a pure question of law, not requiring fact application, then you have no facts to add. However, the heading should still state the supporting rationale.

> **I.** THE BURGLARY CHARGE AGAINST THE DEFENDANT SHOULD NOT BE DISMISSED BECAUSE THE EVIDENCE AT TRIAL WILL ESTABLISH ALL OF THE ELEMENTS OF BURGLARY.
>
> **A.** The evidence will show that the crime occurred in the nighttime because it occurred at 6:45 P.M., more than thirty minutes past sunset.
>
> **B.** The evidence will show that the defendant intended to commit a felony when he entered the house because he alluded to his intent to batter Mrs. Shaffer before he left the bar for her home.
>
> **C.** The evidence will show that the dwelling was not the defendant's own because he had waived his claim to the premises and did not retain any right of access.

As you write out the body of the Argument, you will develop even more clarity about which facts are compelling. Revise your point headings to reflect these new insights.

One last point: This section began by stating that point headings "ideally" should include key facts. A situation is less than ideal, however, when the key facts, stated in isolation from other facts and from your explanation of them, are not persuasive. Sometimes the facts of a particular case are persuasive only in a particular context. Or perhaps they require some explanation before their significance will be apparent to the judge. In either case, including the key facts in the point heading probably will hurt rather than help your effort to persuade the judge. In either case, then, leave the facts out of your point heading.

Similarly, a point heading for a pure question of law[7] usually would not include your client's facts. For a question of law, the court will only be deciding what the law is, not how that law applies to your client's facts. In place of facts, however, the point heading should assert the key argument(s) supporting your position on the question of law before the court. Here is an example of a point heading for a pure question of law:

I. THE STATUTORY PROCEDURE FOR DECIDING ZONING AMENDMENT APPLICATIONS COMPLIES WITH DUE PROCESS REQUIREMENTS BECAUSE IT PROVIDES FOR A PETITION FOR RECONSIDERATION AND A SUBSEQUENT APPEAL TO DISTRICT COURT.

EXERCISE 15-2
Evaluating the Content of Point Headings

Facts. Several years ago Clifford Foodman defended Carson on hit-and-run charges. Now Foodman is defending a new client, Janoff, on a contract dispute. Carson is the plaintiff in this new case. Before accepting Janoff's case,

---

7. *See* Chapter 16, section IA.

Foodman wrote to Carson explaining that there appeared to be no relationship between the two representations and inviting Carson to raise any concerns he had about Foodman's acceptance of Janoff's case. Carson did not respond. Carson has now filed a motion to disqualify Foodman from representing Janoff. One of the issues raised by this motion is whether Carson's failure to respond to Foodman's letter constituted consent to Foodman's representation of Janoff.

Read the following versions of the "consent" point heading for Foodman's brief. Identify the point heading that best includes the information a point heading should contain. For the others, identify which part is missing.

a. Carson consented to Foodman's representation of Janoff when he did not respond to Foodman's letter.

b. The motion to disqualify should be denied because Carson did not respond to Foodman's letter.

c. The motion to disqualify should be denied because Carson consented to the representation.

d. The motion to disqualify should be denied because Carson's failure to respond to Foodman's letter constituted consent to the representation of Janoff.

C. Editing Point Headings for Readability and Persuasion

1. Editing for Readability

Often the inclusion of all desirable information in a point heading results in a long, complex, and confusing sentence. Yet a point heading cannot persuade a judge of something she cannot decipher. And readability is especially important for point headings because the format for point headings (all capital letters) already hinders readability.

If you are struggling with readability, use all relevant editing techniques in Chapter 21 to help simplify and clarify the heading. As a quick checklist, here are some of the techniques most likely to help tame a point heading.

1. *Keep the subject and the verb close together.* In other words, avoid intrusive phrases and clauses.
2. *Avoid nominalizations.* Nominalizations are noun forms of verbs. "Investigate" is a verb; "investigation" is a nominalization. Nominalizations require more words and make sentences harder to understand.
3. *Avoid unnecessary passive-voiced verbs.* Passive verbs make the sentence's subject something other than the actor. These verbs generally require more supporting words and make sentences harder to understand.
4. *Keep the facts and reasoning at the end of the sentence.* Placing the desired result first and the facts and reasoning second often results in a more readable point heading.
5. *Avoid vague words.* Vague words cause the reader to puzzle over the writer's meaning. Purge your point headings of words like these:

this matter	with regard to
it involves	it deals with
it pertains to	it concerns

6. *Avoid negatives.* Negatives, especially multiple negatives, can make a sentence harder to understand.

If you have tried all available editing techniques and still cannot produce a readable point heading, the best solution is to remove one of the items of information. Decide which one, based on persuasiveness and on your assessment of your reader's needs. If the key facts are particularly persuasive, remove the relief requested or the part of the rule at issue. The facts may sufficiently imply the part of the rule at issue, or perhaps the judge is already well aware of the nature of the relief you seek. Regardless, an easily readable point heading that asserts the party's legal argument but lacks supporting facts is more persuasive than a point heading that includes the facts but cannot be understood.

EXERCISE 15-3
Editing Headings for Readability

Edit the following headings to make them more easily readable. Use the techniques identified in the prior section and in Chapter 21.

1. It is clear that Crawford's actions of sitting peacefully in the parking lot of an open store, entering the store and leaving therefrom without incident, and driving lawfully out of the parking lot do not give rise to a reasonable, articulable suspicion of criminal activity to make a valid stop of said defendant.

2. The Defendant's Motion to Dismiss should be granted in as much as the contract involved provided that the escrow account under consideration could be closed by the escrow agent at the point in time when at least three days have passed from the date the notice of default was issued by the lender.

3. The Motion to Attach Assets should be denied because the Court should take into consideration the defendant's reduced line of credit and the unavailability of other sources for cash for the purpose of operating the business during the litigation in this matter.

4. The Motion for Summary Judgment filed by the Defendants, Mr. and Mrs. Carillo, should not be denied due to the fact that the evidence will show that the injured child understood the danger involved in a trampoline.

5. There is no reasonable, articulable suspicion to justify a stop of Salavar where the testimony of the officer is contradicted on virtually every point, where the officer has no facts to support a claim of criminal activity, and where the officer only witnessed Salavar's car in an area of criminal activity and therefore the Defendant's Motion to Dismiss should be granted.

6. The leased premises, which are subject to the constant threat of very disruptive demonstrations, are not suitable with regard to the purpose for

which they were leased, and therefore the lessees have been constructively evicted.

7. A minor who induces another to enter into a contract with him by making a false representation of his age is estopped from a disaffirmance of the contract if the other party demonstrated reasonable and justifiable reliance on the minor's representation.

2. Editing for Persuasion

Editing for persuasion is the final step in the process of drafting point headings. Here are three rhetorical strategies particularly applicable to point headings.

1. Affirmative Language Versus Negative Language. Most briefs focus on certain conduct: Is the conduct lawful? Proper? Desirable? Sometimes the writer can articulate the client's position either by using affirmative language or negative language. In addition to being more readable, affirmative language generally is more forceful and appealing than negative language. Here are examples of two point headings, one using affirmative language and one using negative language.

> *Negative language*   Carrolton's Motion for Summary Judgment should be granted because Watson is unable to show that the terms are unreasonable or that she has not breached those terms.
>
> *Affirmative language*   Carrolton's Motion for Summary Judgment should be granted because the terms of the covenant-not-to-compete are reasonable and the uncontested facts establish Watson's breach.

2. Varying the Structure of the Point Heading. The point heading structure described in this chapter is the easiest structure for learning to draft a readable point heading. It begins with the relief you want and follows with the facts and law supporting that relief. After you have a little practice with drafting point headings, however, you can vary the formula and sometimes achieve a more persuasive version. For instance, consider these versions of a burglary heading. What differences in effectiveness do you notice?

> *Version 1*   The burglary charge against Mr. Shaffer should be dismissed because the alleged breaking and entering occurred at 6:15 P.M., which was earlier than thirty minutes after sunset.
>
> *Version 2*   Because the alleged breaking and entering occurred at 6:15 P.M., which was earlier than thirty minutes after sunset, the burglary charge against Mr. Shaffer should be dismissed.
>
> *Version 3*   The alleged breaking and entering occurred at 6:15 P.M., which was less than thirty minutes after sunset, and therefore the burglary charge against Mr. Shaffer should be dismissed.

Tinker with the structure of the point heading until you are satisfied that it is as persuasive as it can be.

3. Phrasing Alternative Arguments. When you have more than a single point heading, one or more of the headings may be an alternative argument, presented in case the judge does not agree with the first argument. The challenge here is to avoid seeming to reduce the credibility of the first argument by making an alternative argument. The following example demonstrates this flaw:

> I. THE LAW OF THIS JURISDICTION DOES NOT ALLOW RECOVERY FOR THE WRONGFUL DEATH OF A FETUS, EVEN IF THE FETUS IS VIABLE AT THE TIME OF THE INJURY.
>
> II. THE LAW OF THIS JURISDICTION ALLOWS RECOVERY FOR THE WRONGFUL DEATH OF ONLY A *VIABLE* FETUS, AND THE LAWRENCE FETUS WAS NOT VIABLE AT THE TIME OF THE INJURY.

In this pair of headings, a strong first argument is followed by a second argument that seems to undercut the first. Rather than undercutting your own best argument, phrase alternative arguments *in terms that assume the correctness of the first argument.* One way to do this is to restate the first argument expressly, like this:[8]

> I. THE NEGLIGENCE CLAIM IS BARRED BY THE STATUTE OF LIMITATIONS BECAUSE THE PLAINTIFF DID NOT FILE THE COMPLAINT UNTIL FOUR YEARS AFTER THE ALLEGED NEGLIGENT ACT.
>
> II. NOT ONLY IS THE CLAIM BARRED BY THE STATUTE OF LIMITATIONS, BUT THE PLAINTIFF'S ASSURANCE THAT HE WOULD NOT PURSUE AN ACTION BARS THE CLAIM UNDER THE EQUITABLE DOCTRINES OF ESTOPPEL AND WAIVER.

Reiterating the first point in the course of making the second can make the second heading unwieldy, however. Another way to avoid seeming to disavow the first point heading is to use, in the second heading, a verb tense that communicates that any assumption of a flaw in the first point is contrary to fact:

> I. THE LAW OF THIS JURISDICTION DOES NOT ALLOW RECOVERY FOR THE WRONGFUL DEATH OF A FETUS, EVEN IF THE FETUS IS VIABLE AT THE TIME OF THE INJURY.
>
> II. EVEN IF THE LAW *DID* ALLOW RECOVERY FOR THE WRONGFUL DEATH OF A VIABLE FETUS, THE LAWRENCE FETUS WAS ONLY IN THE FOURTH MONTH OF GESTATION, AND THEREFORE WAS NOT VIABLE.

Notice the use of the subjunctive verb "did." The subjunctive is used when stating something contrary to fact. Therefore, the first clause of the alternative heading affirms your assertion of the first heading rather than disavowing it.

D. Identifying Subheadings

Use the rule's structure and your annotated outline[9] to create any additional subheadings you desire. Look at the rule's structure first. For example, if the

---

8. Modified from Girvan Peck, *Writing Persuasive Briefs* 135-136 (Little, Brown Co. 1984).
9. *See* Chapter 7.

rule is a factors test such as the child custody rule on page 79, you can allocate subheadings to each of the factors your brief will discuss.

If the rule does not identify subheadings like factors, you can create your own subheadings based on your major arguments on the point. For instance, if your point heading is a question of statutory interpretation, you can allocate subheadings to the major canons of construction you use or the major policy rationales you assert. Here is an example of such a set of subheadings:

I. THE COURT SHOULD DISMISS THE COMPLAINT BECAUSE THE PLAINTIFF LIED ON HER EMPLOYMENT APPLICATION AND UNDER 42 U.S.C. §2000e, A PLAINTIFF CANNOT RECOVER IF SHE OBTAINED HER JOB UNDER FALSE PRETENSES.

   A. The Plain Meaning of the Statute Establishes That Only an Employee Who Has Acted in Good Faith Can Recover.

   B. The Legislature Did Not Intend to Allow a Windfall to an Employee Who Lied on the Application.

   C. Construing the Statute to Allow Recovery Would Encourage Applicants to Lie and Would Undermine Employers' Efforts to Employ Trustworthy Employees.

As Chapter 10 explained,[10] use three pages as a rough maximum for a section or subsection. Readers prefer to orient themselves every three pages or so, and new section headings will revive waning attention levels.

---

10. *See* Chapter 10, section IV.

CHAPTER 16

Writing the Argument Section

I. ARGUMENTS FOR DIFFERENT KINDS OF LEGAL ISSUES

Legal issues, including legal writing assignments, come in several varieties. Drawing on the material in earlier chapters, this section will identify the major kinds of legal issues and provide suggestions for how to handle each. Some of these categories overlap, so be sure to read each section to learn if your assignment falls into more than one category.

A. A Pure Question of Law

Some legal issues raise a pure question of law. You have a pure question of law when the only issue meaningfully before the court is *what the law is*—when there is no meaningful issue before the court about *how that law will apply to the facts*. The application of the law to the facts either is not before the court or is essentially uncontested. You can have a pure question of law before either a trial court or an appellate court.

For instance, assume you are representing a plaintiff in a wrongful death action arising from an automobile accident in which your client's wife was killed. At the time of the accident, your client's wife was pregnant with the couple's second child, and the unborn child also died. The defendant might file a motion to dismiss part of your client's claim, arguing that the law in your jurisdiction does not allow recovery for the death of an unborn child. You would file a brief arguing that the law does allow recovery. Both briefs deal with a pure question of *law*. The question of how that law will apply to the *facts* of the case is not yet before the court. That will be a question for the jury to decide.

The same issue also could come before the court on uncontested facts. For instance, the defendant might move for summary judgment in this same wrongful death claim, arguing that the law in your state allows recovery for the death of an unborn child only if the fetus was viable at the time of the injury. If your client's unborn child clearly was not viable at the time of the injury, your only response to the defendant's motion can be to argue that the law does (or should) allow recovery for a fetus not yet viable. You will be arguing a pure question of law—whether the law in your jurisdiction allows recovery for a fetus not viable at the time of the accident. The way the law will apply to your client's facts is not in dispute. The court need only decide the question of law.

For a pure question of law, your introduction or umbrella section will explain to your reader, if necessary, why the facts are not at issue. Then you will proceed with rule explanation. The core of your issue is *what* the law requires—what the governing rule is in this jurisdiction. Once your rule explanation section has proven and explained this governing rule, your work is done. You need not add a rule application section in the usual sense.

You still may be able to use your client's facts to help you persuade the judge on the question of law, however. Consider using your client's facts in your rule explanation section, to demonstrate any policy rationales or important principles on which you rely. You might be able to strengthen these policy or principle-based rationales by showing the results of each possible interpretation of the law in situations like your client's. This strategy would be an exception to the normal practice of avoiding discussion of your client's facts in the rule explanation section.

B. An Issue of Statutory Interpretation

You have an issue of statutory interpretation when the primary question before the court is what a particular statutory provision means and especially when little case law has arisen defining the provision. In such a situation, the court must interpret the statute itself rather than relying on interpretations other courts have given. The issue may arise because the statute does not directly address your client's legal question or because the statute addresses the question in ambiguous language.

For issues of statutory interpretation, you should use all the relevant tools from Chapter 4. Start with the statutory text—the language and punctuation of the provision itself and other related provisions; any definitions of terms; the titles of the provisions; and the name of the act itself. Consider any arguments you can make from the legislative history or from other indicia of the legislature's intent. Discuss any favorable interpretations by other courts, by an enforcing agency, or by law review authors or other commentators. Argue from any helpful canons of construction. Do not forget to rely on policy and principle-based reasoning. In matters of statutory construction, these arguments can be particularly persuasive.

C. An Issue of Common Law Case Synthesis

You have an issue of common law case synthesis when you must combine holdings of several cases to formulate the governing rule, to discern the factors courts examine when deciding an issue under the rule, or to discern any exceptions to the rule. For issues of case synthesis, find arguments by using all of the tools in Chapters 2, 3, and 4. Consider the following:

- Which cases are most similar to your client's case;
- Whether any of the opinions have subsequently been followed, over-ruled, or questioned;
- Distinctions between a holding and dicta;
- The breadth of the holdings;
- Differences in the precedential values of the cases;
- Differences in the procedural histories of the cases;
- The depth of the courts' analyses and the quality of the courts' reasoning processes;
- The age of the various opinions;
- The weight of authority in your own jurisdiction and in others;
- The evaluations of commentators;
- The comparison between the rule the court announced and the way the court ruled on the facts before it;
- The facts the courts emphasized;
- Any rulings the court declined to make, either expressly or by implication;
- Whether any of the opinions are concurring or dissenting opinions; and
- Whether cases, reviewed chronologically, establish a trend.

For issues of case synthesis, sensitivity to the varying precedential values of cases is critical. The judge will want you to focus on the mandatory authorities and on the cases from the highest courts in your jurisdiction.

Again, do not forget to consider policy and principle-based reasoning. Not only will judges consider the policies and principles implicated by various understandings of the rule of law, but some of the cases whose holdings you must synthesize may raise policy and principle concerns that are different from or closely similar to your client's situation. Those policy and principle-based comparisons can help you justify placing more reliance on some cases than on others.

D. A Case of First Impression on Your Jurisdiction

You have a case of first impression if the courts of your jurisdiction have not addressed the legal question you must brief. Usually, the issue has been decided in other jurisdictions, although perhaps inconsistently. For federal issues, this situation is sometimes called a "circuit split," meaning that the circuit courts have issued inconsistent opinions on the questions.

For an issue of first impression, research the holdings of the other jurisdictions to identify the approach most favorable to your client, and argue that this approach is the best. Use all the tools set out in section C above to show why your proposed approach is best and why the other approaches are inferior. If more jurisdictions have adopted the approach you prefer, be sure to point out that the "weight of authority" supports your position. Where possible, use analogies to align your case with similar cases from favorable jurisdictions. Rely on any secondary authorities that have compared the diverse approaches and supported the approach you prefer. You can include interdisciplinary sources that support your position. Also, use policy and principle-based reasoning. When a court must rule on a case of first impression, policy and principle considerations are among the most important parts of your analysis.

E. Seeking a Change in the Law

You have an issue asking for a change in the law when the existing law in your jurisdiction is not favorable for your client and you must ask the court to change the rule or to create an exception to it. The strategies for handling such an issue are similar to those used for a pure question of law (section A above) and a circuit split (section D above). You must honestly disclose the existing state of the law but show the court why a change is appropriate. Therefore, your job is to point out the infirmities of the existing rule, propose the change you desire, and explain why your proposal is better. Courts hesitate to change the law without careful thought because the law should be stable and because citizens plan their lives and businesses in reliance on the law. Therefore, address these concerns directly if you can. Also, state clearly the change you propose. A court cannot effectively consider changing the law without understanding the exact nature of the change you request.

Again, policy and principle-based rationales are persuasive. You may draw on persuasive authority from other jurisdictions, the opinions of legal scholars in secondary sources, and available interdisciplinary sources. If you can, use your client's facts as an example of the infirmities of the old rule and the advantages of the rule you propose.

F. An Issue Applying Law to Fact

You have an issue applying law to fact when the issue will be resolved primarily by how the court applies the applicable law to your client's facts. Issues of application of law to fact often arise when the governing rule is a factors test or a balancing test or when the language of the governing rule is vague enough to invite speculation about how it might apply to your client's fact. A classic example is the standard for defining negligent conduct: the "reasonable person." If you have taken torts, you probably have had many debates about what conduct would be reasonable in particular circumstances. These debates raise issues of application of law to fact.

Analogical reasoning (analogizing and distinguishing cases) is by far the most important tool for issues such as these. Your analysis should provide the judge with as many examples as possible of cases in which courts have applied the governing rule to situations like your client's and ruled as you hope your judge will rule. Focus primarily on opinions from courts in your jurisdiction. Use opinions from other jurisdictions in a supporting role if necessary to bolster your jurisdiction's case law.

Explicitly state the similarities between your client's facts and the facts of the favorable cases. Distinguish unfavorable cases by showing relevant factual differences. Show similarities or differences of policy and principle as well, thus further aligning your client's case with the favorable cases and distinguishing it from the unfavorable cases. Custom-based reasoning can be effective to show that your client's actions were consistent with customary practices and that the actions of other parties strayed beyond those bounds.

II. HONING YOUR ARGUMENT FOR THE COURT'S ROLE

The roles of trial court judges and appellate court judges differ significantly. Effective arguments target precisely the role of the judge who will be reading the brief. Let's review the most important differences.

A. The Trial Judge

Most trial judges share the characteristics described in Chapter 6, section IIE. They are busy, skeptical, and impatient with squabbling. They want to make good decisions that accurately apply the law in their jurisdiction and achieve a fair result. More than any other characteristics in a brief, they want clarity, brevity, and accuracy.

Because trial judges have heavy case loads, they usually are not familiar with individual cases in the pretrial stages, when most of your briefs will be filed. They may or may not be familiar with the law on your legal issue, depending on how often that issue has arisen in prior cases. Therefore, do not assume that your judge knows the facts and circumstances of your case or even that the judge knows the law on your issue. Your brief must give the judge the factual and legal background necessary to decide your issue.

Finally, trial judges are constrained by mandatory precedent. They primarily want to know what those precedents are and how they apply to your case. Authorities from other jurisdictions hold less interest for trial judges, most of whom do not see themselves as free to change the law. Therefore, right up front, the trial judge wants to know whether there are mandatory authorities on your issue and, if so, what they are. Use authorities from other jurisdictions only to fill in any gaps in your jurisdiction's mandatory authority and only after you have explained to the judge why you are presenting these otherwise extraneous authorities.

B. Appellate Judges and the Appellate Process

Both a trial-level brief and an appellate brief are written to persuade a judge to rule favorably on one or more legal issues. But on appeal, the lawyer's job is more complicated and more difficult. First, the appellate court will not review the entire proceeding below. The court will review only the issues the appellant's lawyer has identified for appeal and see only the portions of the trial record the lawyers have designated to be included in the record on appeal.[1] Therefore, the appellant's lawyer must first comb the record of the proceedings below to identify issues that may have been decided wrongly.

It may not be enough, however, that the appellate court would have decided the case differently had it been sitting in the trial judge's place. Rather,

---

1. The appellee's lawyer can cross appeal, identifying additional issues for review. For easier reference here, we will refer only to the role of the appellant's lawyer.

as section II explains in greater detail, reversal of some kinds of cases would require a finding that (1) the trial judge applied the wrong law, or (2) the record below cannot reasonably be read to support the decision below, even if all inferences are interpreted in the appellee's favor. Further, not every clear error of law or fact will result in appellate relief, but only those that might have made a difference in outcome ("reversible" error). Nor can any additional evidence be submitted,[2] though the appellate court may rely on extrinsic information in making policy judgments.[3] The appellate court will be evaluating whether the record below adequately supported the lower court's decision, so the relevant facts are those that were before the lower court.

Not only does the decision-making process differ on appeal, but the roles and perspectives of the judges differ as well. Appellate judges, especially those sitting on the highest appellate level of their jurisdiction, see themselves as responsible for the law's development. They are more willing to reevaluate the wisdom of a governing rule and therefore more willing to consider policy and principle-based reasoning. Still, they understand the value of stability and the legitimate need of citizens to rely on legal rules. Therefore, they find analogical reasoning (analogizing and distinguishing cases) persuasive because they want their rulings to be consistent with similar prior rulings, if possible. Although they are just as persuaded by stories as are trial judges, they are seeing only the "cold" record, not the actual witnesses, and so will tend to defer to the lower court's subjective interpretations.

Important similarities remain, however. All of the characteristics attributed to trial court judges above apply to appellate judges as well. They are busy with heavy case loads. They want to issue good, just rulings. More than anything else in a brief, they want clarity, brevity, and accuracy.

III. SUGGESTIONS AND REMINDERS

Umbrella Section. If your brief will analyze several rules or several elements of a rule, begin with an umbrella section.[4] An umbrella section should be concise—generally limited to one or two short paragraphs. Its primary function is to introduce the components of analysis that follows. You can use an umbrella section at the beginning of the Argument section (before the first roman numeral) to introduce the roman numerals or after a point heading to introduce subparts within that point heading.

The content of an umbrella section depends on the particular situation and on your own writing decisions. Among the uses for an umbrella section are the following: (1) summarizing the rule and citing the controlling authority defining the rule; (2) providing any favorable principles affecting the application of the rule, such as presumptions, burdens of proof, elevated levels of proof (such

---

2. There are some exceptions to this rule, but none that need concern us here.
3. Ellie Margolis, *Beyond Brandeis*, 34 U.S.F. L. Rev. 197 (2000).
4. Chapter 10, section II, explains umbrella sections in more detail.

as clear and convincing evidence), or policy leanings;[5] (3) explaining the status of any elements not discussed in the brief; (4) providing a one- or two-sentence summary of your argument on each element; and (5) resolving any potential resistance to the order in which you will discuss the issues.

The Standard Paradigm. Since a brief is an advocacy document, it asserts positions (conclusions) at numerous points. The argument begins with a statement of the conclusion the writer hopes the judge will reach. This conclusion, in one form or another, appears in the point heading for that issue, as Chapter 15 explains. It also may appear in the first paragraph of text beneath the heading.[6] A version appears at the beginning of the rule application section, right before the writer shows how the client's facts establish the conclusion. Finally, the conclusion appears at the end of the argument on that issue. This repetition contributes to an orderly route through rule-based reasoning. Also, subtle repetition is an effective technique for emphasis.[7] Here is an overview of the paradigm for the persuasive analysis of a single issue:

Conclusion
- State the conclusion you want the judge to reach on this issue (your thesis).
- Place it in the point heading and in the first paragraph.
- Succinctly state the most important reasons supporting your conclusion.

Rule Statement
- State the applicable legal rule.
- State it in the form and structure most favorable to your client's position.

Rule Explanation
- Explain where the rule comes from so the judge is satisfied that your rule statement is accurate.
- Explain what the rule means and how it applies to your client's facts.
- Explain these characteristics of the rule in the terms most favorable to your client's position.
- Rebut any counter-explanation you can weaken by a preemptive discussion.

Factual Conclusion
- State the conclusion you want the judge to reach about how the law applies to your client's facts.

Rule Application
- Discuss how the rule applies to your client's facts.
- Emphasize the favorable facts and de-emphasize or justify the problematic facts.
- Rebut any counter-application you can weaken by a preemptive discussion.

---

5. *See* Chapter 10.
6. *See* the example on p. 319-320.
7. Mary Barnard Ray & Barbara J. Cox, *Beyond the Basics: A Text for Advanced Legal Writing* 2nd ed. 183 (West 2003).

> **Conclusion**
> - Restate your conclusion.
> - Unless the discussion has been short, summarize the key points supporting the conclusion.

Separating Rule Explanation and Rule Application. Remember that rule explanation generally should remain distinct from rule application, with rule explanation coming first. All of the reasons we saw earlier for keeping rule explanation separate from rule application still apply, but in persuasive writing another important reason applies as well. Presenting the reader with rule explanation first and separate from rule applications capitalizes on a principle of persuasion: Readers are more persuaded by ideas they have first thought of themselves than by an idea first asserted by another.[8] This is especially true when the reader knows that the person doing the asserting is an advocate with an admitted persuasive agenda.

The strategy goes like this. The reader first reads the brief's fact statement and has those facts in mind when reading the rule explanation. During the rule statement and explanation, the reader will be thinking of those facts and anticipating rule application. The reader's Commentator[9] will be applying each point the writer is explaining about the rule to those facts. Presenting rule explanation first, without explicit application to the facts, allows the rule explanation to lead the reader to the desired conclusions about rule application, *before the writer asserts those conclusions.* Then, when the writer reaches the rule application phase, she is only asserting the conclusions the reader has already reached on his own.

Variations on the Paradigm. Occasionally, later drafts can alter the normal paradigm by combining the rule explanation section for each element into one comprehensive explanation of the rule and then combining the rule application section for each element into a comprehensive application of the rule. If you think that your situation may call for this approach, review the description of this variation in Chapter 10, section V. However, resist using this variation for the first draft. Let the discipline of separately writing out the rule explanation and rule application for each individual element help you deepen your understanding of that element. After you have mined the depths of possible arguments for each individual element, you can decide whether a combined discussion is appropriate.

Working Labels. As you write your early drafts, feel free to use working labels to help you stay on track and to help you evaluate your early drafts.

Thesis Sentences. Remember to use thesis sentences wherever you can. Since thesis sentences assert positions, they are even more important for a strong *argument* (in a brief) than for an accurate *prediction* (in an office memo).

---

8. *See* Chapter 6, section IIE.
9. *See* Chapter 6, section IID.

Citations to the Record. An appellate brief must refer only to facts that are a part of the court record.[10] When the brief recites a fact, it must cite to the location of the fact in the record. The same is true for certain kinds of trial-level briefs. Insert these cites to the record now, as you write your early drafts. Including the citations as you write will save you valuable time later.

Writing the Fact Statement First. You may find it helpful to write out a draft of the Statement of Facts[11] before writing a draft of the Argument section. If you are having trouble getting started, this strategy may help. Also, you may find that immersing yourself in your client's story is excellent preparation for the more linear reasoning required in the Argument section.

EXERCISE 16-1

Labeling the Components of the Paradigm

Make a photocopy of the Argument section of the brief in Appendix B. Locate and label the parts of the umbrella paragraph and, for each issue, the sections of the standard paradigm.

IV. REBUTTING YOUR OPPONENT'S ARGUMENTS

As we saw in Chapter 1, lawyers write both opening briefs and briefs responding to the briefs filed by others. Lawyers often need to rebut their opponent's arguments, both in their own opening brief, where they anticipate opposing arguments, and in responsive and reply briefs filed after those opposing arguments have been made. Often lawyers must rebut both an opposing *explanation* of the law and an opposing *application* of the law to the current situation.

Lawyers struggle with how to treat counter-argument in an opening brief.[12] On the one hand, the writer wants to respond to the arguments she anticipates. On the other hand, she does not want to raise arguments the opposing party might not have thought of or articulate them better than the opposing brief would have. (This concern applies to adverse *arguments*, but not to directly adverse *authorities*. As you know, the lawyer has a duty to disclose directly adverse authorities in the controlling jurisdiction.) Nor does she want to sacrifice her affirmative stance—the primary advantage of the opening brief—by turning her own brief into a defensive document. Resolving these strategic questions is always a case-by-case task, but here are some helpful guidelines:

1. Include counter-argument in an opening brief when you are relatively sure that the opposing brief or the court itself will raise the argument

---

10. *See* Chapter 18, section IB.
11. *See* Chapter 18.
12. An opening brief is the first brief filed on an issue. Usually one side files an opening brief, and the opposing party files a responsive brief. Then, generally, the party who filed the opening brief has an opportunity to file a reply brief. *See* Chapter 1, section II.

and when you can weaken it by a preemptive discussion. More often than not, a well-crafted preemptive discussion will weaken an opponent's argument.

2. Usually, the most effective forms of counter-argument do not draw attention to opposing argument by labeling it as such ("The defendant may argue that . . . However, . . . "). Rather, the counter-argument disproves opposing arguments primarily by affirmative proof of the writer's own position ("The Defendant's actions constituted negligence [explain why]. The unreasonableness of the behavior is not justified by . . . or by . . . [explain why].")

3. Articulate your position on that argument in more detail than you use to articulate the opposing party's argument. Detail is a technique for emphasis, and lack of detail is a technique for deemphasis.[13]

4. Do not place an identified counter-argument ahead of your own affirmative argument. Rather, place it after you have made all of your own points. Otherwise, your brief will take on a defensive tone and will lose much of its rhetorical power.

5. After you have a draft of the argument, compare the space devoted to counter-argument with the space devoted to affirmative argument. The great majority of the draft should be devoted to your own affirmative argument.

6. If your opponent has used rhetoric that is either excessive or particularly effective, consider ways to defuse that opposing rhetoric. Confront excessive rhetoric if you think that, left unconfronted, it may influence the judge. Confront particularly effective rhetoric if you can devise a way to remove the rhetoric's power. Usually the best way to remove the power of rhetoric is by using the law or the facts or both. For example:

> Defendant's brief contains broad general conclusions such as "preemptive effect . . . is firmly established in the case law," a "comprehensive network of agency regulations," "pervasive nature of the regulations," and the agency's "specifically stated intent." Def. brief 4. The support and analysis of these grandiose phrases and broad-brush conclusions consists simply of three agency source materials, plus an extensive reliance on one district court opinion, Simon. We now show these authorities do not support these statements. . . . [14]

---

13. Mary Barnard Ray & Barbara J. Cox, Beyond the Basics: A Text for Advanced Legal Writing 176 (West 1991).

14. Irwin Alterman, Plain and Accurate Style in Court Papers 125-126 (Student ed. ALI-ABA 1994).

CHAPTER 17

Standards of Review

Effective appellate advocacy requires careful attention to the standard of review. First, the standard of review often is a vitally important threshold issue shaping how other issues will be decided. Also, the standard of review determines the language in which you frame the issues, especially in your point headings.

The standard of review defines the level of deference the appellate court must give to the trial court's decision on the issue(s) appealed.[1] Can the appellate court freely decide the question on its own, without any regard for the decision of the trial court? This standard would be good news for the appellant, who objects to the trial court's decision. It would be like starting over, as if the trial court had never decided the question. Or must the appellate court give some level of deference to the trial court's decision? This more limited standard would be good news for the appellee, who agrees with the trial court's decision. This standard increases the odds that the trial court's decision will prevail. The question of which party will have the good news, and just how good the news will be, depends on the kind of trial court decision being appealed.

I. CATEGORIES OF TRIAL COURT DECISIONS

In a trial before a judge, the judge must decide both the law and the facts. A trial judge also must decide many discretionary questions, often procedural in nature. Errors in making any of these decisions—decisions of law, decisions of fact, or decisions left to the court's discretion—can lead to an appeal. The following sections describe these categories of decisions and the standard of review and policy rationale applicable to each.

Questions of Law. A pure question of law can be decided without reference to the facts of the case at all. Does this jurisdiction recognize a claim for the wrongful death of a fetus? Within what time period must a notice of appeal be filed? Must a contingent fee agreement be put in writing? Must a will be

---

1. *See generally* Ruggero J. Aldisert, *Opinion Writing* 53-69 (West 1990); Daniel J. Meador, *Appellate Courts: Structures, Functions, Processes, and Personnel* 154-226 (Michie Co. 1994); Alan D. Hornstein, *Appellate Advocacy in a Nutshell* 31-36 (2d ed., West 1998).

signed? These are all purely questions of law. They can be researched and answered without reference to any particular set of facts.

A trial court's decision on a pure question of law is subject to de novo review by an appellate court. De novo review allows the appellate court to grant no deference to the trial court's opinion. The appellate court is free to substitute its own opinion on the question of what the jurisdiction's law provides.[2] The principle of stare decisis encourages the appellate court to pay some deference to existing common law, but this deference is unrelated to whether the lower court adopted and applied that law. Therefore, an appellate court need not give any deference even to a trial court ruling that is *correct*—correct in the sense that it accurately states the rule of law at the time of the lower court's decision. Depending on the level of the appellate court and on the nature of the issue being appealed, the appellate court may decide that the trial judge was right in concluding what the law *was*, but that the law *ought* to be something else. The appellate court might take the opportunity presented by this case to announce a change in the law.[3] As a matter of fact, the primary rationale for the de novo standard is the recognized function of appellate courts to make new law.

Questions of Fact.   A pure question of fact is a question that can be decided on the basis of only the evidence in the record. What the law is has absolutely nothing to do with the question. What speed limit was posted? Did the defendant enter the building? Is the signature on the contract that of the plaintiff? These are all purely questions of fact. They can be decided without reference to any rule of law. You could have decided such questions long before you came to law school.

A trial *judge's* decision of a pure question of fact usually is subject to review using a "clearly erroneous" standard.[4] To overturn a trial judge's decision using the clearly erroneous standard, an appellate court would have to decide that, while *some* evidence supporting the decision may exist in the trial court record, the appellate court "is left with the definite and firm conviction that a mistake has been committed."[5] It is not enough that the appellate court would have made a different decision. As long as the lower court's decision is plausible, given the record as a whole, the opinion must be upheld.[6]

The most common policy rationales for the clearly erroneous standard are (1) the better opportunity of trial courts to judge the credibility of witnesses and the weight to be accorded to testimony; (2) the function assigned to trial courts as the primary fact finders; (3) the inadvisability of expending judicial resources on duplicating functions and responsibilities; (4) the unfairness of requiring the parties to convince two different courts of their facts; (5) the concern for crowded appellate dockets; and (6) the advantage of a trial judge's expertise in fact-finding.

A *jury's* decision on a pure question of fact usually is subject to an even more limited standard of review—a *competent evidence* standard. If the jury was

---

2. *See, e.g., Watzek v. Walker,* 485 P.2d 3 (Ariz. Ct. App. 1971).
3. Whether that change in the law will apply to the case then before the court is a separate legal issue that is the subject of a separate body of law.
4. *See* Fed. R. Civ. P. 52(a).
5. *Anderson v. City of Bessemer,* 470 U.S. 564, 573 (1985).
6. *Id.* at 573-574.

properly instructed and if the record contains some modicum of competent evidence supporting the jury's decision, the appellate court must allow the jury's decision to stand.[7] In other words, the appellate court's only function in reviewing a jury verdict is to be sure that the jury's verdict is not irrational, given the trial evidence.[8] In addition to some of the same policies supporting the limited review of a judge's fact-finding, the primary rationale for this competent evidence standard, the most limited of reviews, is the parties' constitutional right to a trial by jury.

Mixed Questions of Law and Fact. Identifying purely factual or purely legal questions and the corresponding standards of review is fairly straightforward. The matter becomes more complex, however, when the question involves a mixture of law and fact. For example, consider the following example drawn from a case in which the plaintiff is suing the defendant for damages arising from a car accident. Here are some questions of *fact* and the trial court's decisions on them:

Question of Fact	*Trial Court's Answers*
What speed limit was posted?	55 MPH
What speed was the defendant traveling?	65 MPH
Was it raining?	yes
Did the driver signal before changing lanes?	no

Here is a question of *law* and the trial court's decision on it:

Question of Law	*Trial Court's Answer*
What is the duty of care owed by an automobile driver to other drivers?	A driver must exercise the degree of care that would be exercised by a reasonable person under those same circumstances.

Having decided the *facts* and decided the relevant *law*, the trial court now decides *how the law applies to the facts of this case.*

Mixed Question of Law and Fact	*Trial Court's Answer*
Is driving 65 MPH in the rain when the speed limit is 55 and not signaling the intention to turn [facts] consistent with the degree of care that would be exercised by a reasonable person under those same circumstances? [law]	No

---

7. *See, e.g., I.M.A. v. Rocky Mountain Airways, Inc.,* 713 P.2d 882 (Colo. 1986).

8. Robert J. Martineau, *Fundamentals of Modern Appellate Advocacy* 133-134 (Lawyer's Co-op 1985).

Now, assume that the defendant appeals. She does not disagree with the trial court's answers deciding the speed limit, her speed at the time of the accident, whether it was raining, and whether she signaled. Assume also that she does not disagree with the trial court's answer defining the duty of care owed to other drivers. Rather, she disagrees with the trial court's decision that driving at that speed under those conditions and changing lanes without signaling *was inconsistent with* the way a reasonable person would drive. In other words, she disagrees with the way the trial court applied the law to the facts. This is a disagreement about a mixed question of law and fact.

For a mixed question of law and fact, the reviewing court must decide whether to use a de novo standard (the standard for questions of law) or a "clearly erroneous" standard (the standard for questions of fact). Usually the court chooses the standard on a case-by-case determination of whether factual questions or legal questions predominate in the particular issue before the court. The majority of mixed questions are subjected to de novo review, and mixed questions of constitutional law are nearly always subject to de novo review.[9] Questions of negligence generally are subjected to "clearly erroneous" review.[10]

Questions within the Trial Court's Discretion. A trial judge has no discretion about whether to apply the relevant rule of law. A trial judge has no discretion about whether to decide the facts of the dispute and be bound by those facts in resolving the case. However, during the course of a legal proceeding, a trial judge must decide many other questions, questions that the applicable rule of law leaves within the judge's discretion.

The governing rule and relevant authorities may identify factors or guidelines to help the judge know *how* to make the decision, but the governing rule and relevant authorities do not tell the judge *what* to decide. Instead, the rule recognizes that the best answer to that particular question will differ from situation to situation and will depend on circumstances that no single rule of law could anticipate, describe, and evaluate.

Questions left in the trial court's discretion are usually either matters of equity or matters of procedure and case management. For instance, in some circumstances, a party who has filed an answer must obtain the judge's permission before she can amend that answer.[11] Case law construing the applicable rule may give the judge some guidelines about when to give permission, but under most court rules, the decision is left to the judge's discretion. The trial judge's duty in making such decisions is to refrain from acting unreasonably or arbitrarily.

This scope of authority gives a trial judge broad latitude, and, correspondingly, it gives appellate courts a narrow role in reviewing these decisions. An appellate court is not free to overturn a trial judge's decision merely because the appellate court would have made a different decision. To overturn a decision left to the trial court's discretion, the appellate court must hold that the decision was an abuse of discretion.[12] As long as the trial court's decision

---

9. *See, e.g., United States v. McConney,* 728 F.2d 1195 (9th Cir. 1984) (en banc).
10. *Id.*
11. *See, e.g.,* Fed. R. Civ. P. 15(a).
12. *See, e.g., Napolitano v. Compania Sud Americana De Vapores,* 421 F.2d 382 (2d Cir. 1970); *Kern v. TXO Production Corp.,* 738 F.2d 968 (8th Cir. 1984).

was not unreasonable or arbitrary, the appellate court must affirm it. Some lawyers evaluate the "abuse of discretion" standard as allowing roughly the same degree of deference as the "clearly erroneous" standard for reviewing facts.[13] Others view abuse of discretion as allowing slightly more latitude on appeal than does a "clearly erroneous" standard.[14] Still other lawyers believe that abuse of discretion actually covers several subtle sublevels of deference.[15]

Policy rationales justifying the "abuse of discretion" standard include (1) the need for flexibility in case management; (2) judicial economy and the crowded appellate docket; (3) judicial comity, that is, a judge's respect for the decisions of other judges; (4) the ability of the trial judge to assess the circumstances firsthand; (5) the need for flexible rules of law to address satisfactorily all possible circumstances; and (6) the need to support the trial judge's authority and control of her own courtroom.

II. ADVOCATING A MORE FAVORABLE STANDARD OF REVIEW

Section A sets out the general rules that usually determine the appropriate standard. Courts, however, do not always follow the general rule; the first and best way to identify the appropriate standard of review for your case is to look for opinions issued by the court deciding your case. Search for cases deciding issues similar to yours, and see what standard of review the court used in those cases. If you are relying on appellate cases from your own jurisdiction for some of your argument on the merits of your case, those cases probably also mention the appropriate standard of review for the issues your brief addresses. If not, look for cases on your issue from other appellate courts, and look for opinions from your own jurisdiction on similar issues. Find out what the standard is, what it means, and how it might apply to a case like yours.

It should go without saying that an advocate should look for authority, including policy arguments, supporting the most favorable standard of review possible. Where doubt exists as to the proper standard, an appellant should argue for the *least* restrictive standard—a standard that maximizes the appellate court's authority to overturn the challenged decision. An appellee should argue for the *most* restrictive standard—a standard that limits the appellate court's authority to overturn the trial court's ruling. On pure questions of law, the de novo standard of review is well settled, and few, if any, distinctions will affect it. On pure questions of fact, the "clearly erroneous" or "competent evidence" standards are fairly well settled too. However, an advocate may still be able to influence, subtly, an appellate court's application of the standard for reviewing fact-finding. For instance, in an appropriate case the lawyer might point out that the evidence was entirely documentary (requiring no assessment of witness credibility) or that the evidence was uncontested. In either situation, the policy rationales listed above would be less relevant.

---

13. *See, e.g.,* Robert J. Martineau, *Fundamentals of Modern Advocacy* 138 (Lawyer's Co-op 1985).

14. *See, e.g.,* Ruggero J. Aldisert, *Opinion Writing* 65 (West 1990).

15. Maurice Rosenberg, *Standards of Review,* in Arthur D. Hellman, ed., *Restructuring Justice* 48-49 (1990).

However, the standards applicable both to mixed questions of law and fact and to questions left to the trial court's discretion may leave some room for advocacy. For questions that might be categorized as mixed law and fact, the advocate can sometimes influence the appellate court's decision on whether the particular question *is* a mixed question and, if so, what standard should apply to it. Should the appellate court decide by examining the nature of the particular question on appeal? If so, how does this particular question fare under such an examination? Does the *factual* aspect or the *legal* aspect predominate? Were the facts contested? Was the law well settled and construed by many cases? Were the facts established by a judge or by a jury? Does the case involve an important issue of constitutional rights?

For questions that may be left to the trial court's discretion, the advocate can sometimes influence the appellate court's decision on (1) whether the applicable rule *does* leave the question to the trial court's discretion and, if so, (2) just how much discretion the appellate court should allow the trial court to exercise in deciding this particular kind of question. Though the cases do not expressly identify sublevels within the "abuse of discretion" standard, such sublevels probably exist.[16]

So you should compare the policy rationales for the "abuse of discretion" standard to the circumstances of your case. Consider the rule that grants the trial court discretion. Use your common sense. What small points can you make to subtly convince the appellate court to narrow or widen the deference it will give to the trial court? For instance, do the authorities announce standards or factors that are to guide the trial court's discretion? Did the trial court have to make factual findings as part of the decision of the question left to its discretion? How important are the rights at stake? How possible and how desirable is it to increase the uniformity of approach among trial courts on this issue? Has the trial court deviated from a common custom or practice? Is this a relatively new question that could benefit from a period of experimentation at the trial court level before an appellate court takes a position on it? The answers to these sorts of questions can provide the raw material for influencing the way the appellate court applies the standard.

III. CONFORMING HEADINGS TO THE STANDARD OF REVIEW

The brief's point headings ordinarily should be consistent with the applicable standard of review.[17] Here are examples of headings phrased according to the appropriate standard:

---

16. A number of commentators have identified levels within the abuse of discretion standard. *See, e.g.,* Henry J. Friendly, *Indiscretion About Discretion,* 31 Emory L.J. 747, 760-762, 771-772, 783-784 (1982); *Federal Civil Appellate Jurisdiction: An Interlocutory Restatement,* 47 (2)/13, Law & Contemp. Probs. 62-63 (Spring 1984); Maurice Rosenberg, *Standards of Review,* in Arthur D. Hellman, ed., *Restructuring Justice* 48-49 (1990).

17. If the standard of review is unfavorable, you may not wish to reiterate it in each point heading. A simple acknowledgment of the standard early in the brief may be sufficient.

No competent evidence	The burglary conviction should be reversed because the record contains no competent evidence that the breaking and entering occurred later than thirty minutes after sunset.
Clearly erroneous	The judgment should be reversed because the trial court's finding of intent to discriminate was clearly erroneous.
De novo	The judgment entered on the defendant's motion to dismiss should be reversed because this jurisdiction allows recovery for the wrongful death of a fetus.
Abuse of discretion	The trial court abused its discretion when it issued a preliminary injunction prohibiting the defendant from concealing or disposing of his assets.

Notice that the de novo standard does not change the phrasing of the argument because that standard puts no gloss whatsoever on the question. That standard imposes no limitations on the appellate court's decision.

A brief is far more effective when it establishes the most favorable standard of review supportable by the authorities and makes a few points about how that standard should be applied to the pending case. Consider the policy rationales that underlie each standard of review, comparing them to the circumstances of your case. As you write the argument, make whatever points you can in favor of applying the standard most favorable to your position. As Senior United States Circuit Judge Ruggero J. Aldisert explained, "[S]tandards of review are critically important in appellate decision making."[18] Yet many lawyers forget to research the proper standard and to couch their arguments according to its terms. As a matter of fact, Judge Aldisert describes his experience of observing the "psychological block" that seems to prevent some lawyers from recognizing and dealing with the standard of review.[19] If, from the beginning of your practice, you pay careful attention to the standard of review, you will never be one of the lawyers Judge Aldisert describes.

EXERCISE 17-1
Identifying Categories of Trial Court Decisions

You are a staff attorney in the local legal aid office, which represents people who do not have sufficient income to pay an attorney. One of your clients is Sophia Guzman. Guzman has five children. Her husband died three years ago, and she has had to resort to public assistance to support herself and her children. Guzman and her children rent a two-bedroom apartment in a dilapidated building owned by A-1 Realty Co. She lives there because she cannot afford to pay higher rent elsewhere, nor can she afford the costs of moving. The building is in terrible shape, however, and Guzman believes it to be a health risk. The water and sewer system work sporadically, the power surges and wanes, and the rat population is increasing. After many complaints to the landlord, Guzman has sued the landlord, alleging constructive eviction. You are her lawyer.

---

18. Ruggero J. Aldisert, *Opinion Writing* 53 (West 1990).
19. *Id.*

Believing that the facts about the property's condition are compelling, you decided to move for summary judgment. For each of the following issues on appeal, decide whether the issue is a question of law, a question of fact, a mixed question, or a question of the trial court's exercise of discretion.

1. Assume that the trial court ruled against Guzman and in favor of A-1 Realty. The trial court held that, to prevail on a claim for constructive eviction, the plaintiff must prove that the property was unsuitable for occupancy for the purposes for which the occupancy was intended. The court decided that the apartment had been leased as a residence and that the condition of the apartment was suitable for occupancy as a residence. You have appealed the court's decision that the apartment was suitable for occupancy as a residence.

2. Assume that the trial court ruled against Guzman and in favor of A-1 Realty. The trial court held that, to prevail on a claim for constructive eviction, the plaintiff must prove that the property was unsuitable for occupancy for the purposes for which the occupancy was intended. The court's opinion stated that a dwelling with rats would be unsuitable for occupancy but that this building does not contain rats. You have appealed the court's finding that the building does not contain rats.

3. Assume that the trial court ruled against Guzman and in favor of A-1 Realty. The trial court decided that, to prevail on a claim for constructive eviction, the landlord must have intended to force the tenant to move. You have appealed the trial court's decision that a successful claim for constructive eviction must prove intent to evict.

4. In pretrial discovery, A-1 Realty refused to answer ten of Guzman's interrogatories. Guzman moved for an order requiring A-1 to answer the ten interrogatories. The trial court decided that five of the interrogatories were proper and five were objectionable. The court ordered A-1 to answer the five proper interrogatories and refused to order A-1 to answer the other five. You have appealed the trial court's order.

5. The applicable rule of procedure provides that when a motion to compel discovery is granted in part and denied in part, the court "may" apportion the expenses of bringing and resisting the motion among the parties "in a just manner."[20] In the *Guzman* case, the trial court ordered that each party bear its own expenses on the motion. Both parties appealed the court's order apportioning expenses, each arguing that the court should have required the other party to reimburse that party's expenses. Your research on this question will yield case opinions that tell you the applicable standard of review on this issue, but what is your best guess about what standard these opinions will identify?

---

20. *See, e.g.,* Fed. R. Civ. P. 37(a)(4)(C).

CHAPTER 18

Writing a Fact Statement

There is an adage among trial lawyers: If you have to choose between the law and the facts, take the facts. The adage reflects the experience of many lawyers that a judge or jury convinced of the justice of your cause will find a way around unfavorable law. Conversely, if the judge or jury perceives that justice is on the other side, favorable law may not be enough.

The Statement of Facts (sometimes called the "Statement of the Case") is the primary place where your reader's sense of justice about the case will be formed. As a general rule, narrative is more effective at creating attitudes than is intellectual analysis. *The Jungle* persuaded countless readers of the inhumanity of the meat-packing industry. *Cry, the Beloved Country* convinced people around the world of the injustice of apartheid.

Consider your own reactions. Imagine reading a well-reasoned analysis arguing that Hitler should not have imprisoned and killed European Jews. The analysis explains and applies certain abstract moral principles. Imagine your response. Now compare it to your response to *The Diary of Anne Frank* or *Schindler's List* or *Sophie's Choice*. Which would you find more powerful: the rational analysis or the stories of the people who lived the facts? Which would you remember longer? Which would persuade you more?

Stories grab us, persuade us, motivate us. Your client's story can persuade a judge, just as a movie or book can persuade you. But to be persuasive, your client's story must be told skillfully. Many lawyers believe that the brief that tells the most effective story is the most likely to prevail. But writing this key part of the brief is more challenging than writing a short story or novel. It is harder because you cannot make up desirable facts or imagine away undesirable facts, and because you must use the facts to persuade without *appearing* to do so. You must recite the facts objectively enough to be fair and yet persuasively enough to be compelling. As Professors Ray and Cox put it:

> If briefs to the court were gymnastics events, their statements of facts would be performed on the balance beam. Writing a persuasive statement is accomplished not by following one set of rules, but by balancing your use of various techniques to maintain credibility while achieving the stance needed to highlight favorable facts. It does not require the brute force of emphatic language so much as a subtle blend of strength and control of structure and detail. It involves much thought, consideration of alternatives, and monitoring

the interactions of various techniques. Yet an excellent statement of facts looks natural and effortless, just like a complex routine looks easy when performed by a skilled gymnast.[1]

I. FACT ETHICS, READERS, AND THE CONVENTIONS OF FACT STATEMENTS

A. Fact Ethics

Remember from Chapter 14 that a lawyer must not misrepresent facts.[2] Misrepresentation includes both stating facts untruthfully and omitting material facts when the result of the omission is to create a false inference. The rule further requires lawyers to disclose material facts when disclosure is necessary to avoid assisting the client in a criminal or fraudulent act.

In virtually every case, you will find some facts you wish were not there. The more material the facts are, the more you wish they would go away. But they exist nonetheless, and leaving them out of your Fact Statement will not make them disappear, for they will certainly appear in the opposing brief. Omitting them from your brief will only damage your credibility before the judge, causing the judge to wonder how much she can rely on the other facts you assert and on the legal analysis you propose. Few things make a judge angrier than feeling misled by a lawyer.

The omission of important facts also forces the judge to use the opposing party's Fact Statement, rather than yours, as the court's primary factual reference. These consequences are serious for both lawyer and client. Therefore, both good ethics and good strategy require inclusion of all material facts, whether favorable or not.[3]

B. The Conventions of a Statement of Facts

Certain formal requirements and generally accepted conventions apply to the Statement of Facts. Refer to the Statement of Facts of the briefs in Appendices B and C for examples of how a Statement of Facts employs the following conventions:

1. An appellate brief must refer only to facts that are a part of the court record. Facts cannot be added to the record.[4] Since the point of an appeal is to decide whether the lower court's decision on a certain point was supported by

---

1. Mary Barnard Ray & Barbara J. Cox, *Beyond the Basics: A Text for Advanced Legal Writing* 167 (2d ed. West 2003).
2. A lawyer shall not knowingly make a false statement of fact or fail to disclose a material fact when disclosure is necessary to avoid assisting a criminal or fraudulent act by the client. Model R. Prof. Conduct 3.3(a)(1) and (2).
3. Later sections in this chapter identify ways to neutralize or de-emphasize unfavorable facts.
4. There are rare exceptions to this rule, but none that we need worry about here.

the facts and the law *before that court,* the appellate court may consider only the factual record that was before the lower court at the time of the decision from which the appeal has been taken.

The Statement of Facts must cite the location of the fact in the record.[5] The citation allows the judge to verify that the fact actually appears in the record and to check that the writer's descriptions of the fact and its context are not misleading. Judges *do* check the facts. For an appellate brief, the most common form for these citations to the record is "R. at [page number]."

2. A Statement of Facts is a part of a legal document and retains the formal style of the rest of the brief. While a Statement of Facts tells the story of the legal dispute, its style is not like a short story. You do not want the style of the fact statement to cause the judge to wonder if she is reading fiction. Therefore, present the facts in an objective style, avoiding obvious appeals to emotion, grand description, dramatic literary devices, and other obvious attempts to manipulate the reader. The style should be dignified and courteous, never sarcastic or angry.

3. A Statement of Facts does not discuss law. It sets out all of the facts the rule makes important, but it does not explain the rule or the rule's relationship to the facts. Rule explanation and application come in the Argument section. The only exception to this convention is that the last paragraph of the fact statement may segue into the legal argument by stating the legal issue the Argument will address.[6]

4. A Statement of Facts does not contain overt argument, whether legal or factual. The facts are presented in an objective style, and the writer does not expressly assert factual conclusions. For instance, for a case involving medical malpractice, the Fact Statement might relate the patient's vital signs, the medical test results, the patient's medical history, and the nurse's observations, but the writer would not argue that the doctor breached the applicable standard of care.

Note that this restriction applies to conclusions drawn by the *writer,* but the writer *is* permitted to relate the conclusion of another. For instance, while the writer cannot assert that the doctor breached the applicable standard of care, the writer can report the testimony of an expert witness who asserted this conclusion. The testimony of the witness is a *fact* that occurred at a deposition or at trial. Reporting the conclusions of others is sometimes called "masked editorializing."[7] Quotations, used in moderation, are appropriate in a Statement of Facts, and often are effective, as section IV explains.

A Statement of Facts also can point out the *absence* of certain facts from the record. The absence of a fact from the record is itself a fact. Thus it is fair game to include in the Statement of Facts the following:

> At trial, three officers testified that they were stationed at the building's entrance between 5:00 and 6:00. However, no witness testified to seeing the janitor enter or leave the building.

---

5. Fed. R. App. P. 28(a)(7).

6. *See* section IIIB.

7. *See* Louis J. Sirico & Nancy Schultz, *Persuasive Writing for Lawyers and the Legal Profession, Second Edition,* 81 (Lexis Nexis 2001)

Pointing out a fact's absence can allow the writer to make a point about the evidence while remaining within the legitimate bounds of fact-reporting. One of the most common and most unfortunate errors lawyers make is neglecting to notice important *absent* facts.

II. DEVELOPING A THEORY OF THE CASE AND SELECTING FACTS

While some facts must be included no matter what theory of the case or theme the lawyer selects, other fact-selection decisions are tied directly to the theme the lawyer will develop. This section explores these two interrelated lawyering tasks.

A. Developing a Theory of the Case

Lawyers use the term "theory of the case" to refer to the theme they will weave throughout the facts, the theme that will explain the facts from their client's perspective. The theme should be sympathetic to the client. It should help the judge understand who the client is, why the client acted in the way he did, feels the way he does, needs the things he needs. At the least, a good theory of the case assures the judge that a ruling in favor of your client will not be unjust. At best, the theory convinces the judge that justice requires a ruling for your client.

Of course, a theory of the case must be consistent with the key facts. Creating a theory is easy when the facts are generally favorable and much more difficult when they are not. For troublesome facts, you must work even harder to see and *feel* the story from your client's perspective. Look at the sample Questions Presented for Carrolton and for Watson in Chapter 15, section I. Can you see what Carrolton's theory of the case will be? How about Watson's?

To find an effective theory of the case, try to look at the facts from your client's perspective and look for narrative themes. Professors Brian Foley and Ruth Anne Robbins have pointed out seven common kinds of narrative themes: (1) a person against another person; (2) a person against herself; (3) a person against nature; (4) a person against society; (5) a person against a machine; (6) a person against God; and (7) a person against everybody else.[8] Might one of these stock themes describe your client's struggle? If so, explore possible theories of the case that would communicate that narrative theme.

You might find that several of these themes could describe your client's story. People are complex, after all, and seldom are we motivated by only one need, feeling, or goal. For presentation of the facts in a legal proceeding,

---

8. Brian Foley & Ruth Anne Robbins, *Fiction 101: A Primer for Lawyers on How to Use Fiction Writing Techniques to Write Persuasive Fact Sections,* 32 Rutgers L.J. 459 (2001) (citing Josip Nova-kovich, *Fiction Writer's Workshop* 74-75 (1995)).

however, beware of trying to present several themes at once. The medium of a brief generally is better suited to handle one consistent theme rather than several themes intermixed. The effort to combine several themes may leave the reader with no coherent theory at all; so pick the theme that is most compelling and best supported by the facts.

The best way to find an effective theory of the case is by talking with your client. However, your client may not be good at communicating the heart of his position and may not even be consciously aware of it himself, so you will need also to use your imagination. Try to put yourself in his position. Imagine what it must have been like, what it must be like now. Try to understand who this person is and who the other key characters are. Mull it over in the shower, on your morning run, on your way to the grocery store. Try to fill in the blanks of the following statement: "This is a story about a (man)(woman) who (is) (was) . . . [describe client] . . . and who is struggling to. . . . " If you can do so without breaching client confidentiality, try telling the story orally. Go to lunch with another lawyer from your firm and tell her your client's story. Telling the story and then talking about it with another person often gives you a fresh perspective. After you have developed a clearer sense of your client and the situation, what helps you understand your client's behavior? What moves you about the story? What might move the judge?

Once you have an idea, try articulating it in a few sentences, like so:

> Carrolton bought Watson's company, the only provider of health care products in the area, and immediately began to take advantage of the company's customers by raising prices, limiting product lines, and allowing long delays for special-order items. Since the customers had nowhere else to go for their health care products, they had no choice but to pay the prices and put up with the limited service. Watson, who had continued to work at the business, had to sit by and watch as Carrolton took advantage of her neighbors and longtime customers. Many of them even thought that Watson was intentionally profiting at their expense, since she was still the customer contact person in the office—the only face her old customers saw. This situation was personally distressing to Watson. She also became increasingly convinced that it just wasn't right.

A good theory of the case should be consistent with the facts and with a common sense notion of fairness. It should explain as many of the unfavorable facts as possible, and it should cast your client in a sympathetic light.

B. Selecting and Citing to Facts

Once you have developed your theory of the case, select the facts you will include in the Statement of Facts. Include facts that fall into the following categories:

1. Facts that fit the theory of the case
2. All facts mentioned in the Argument section of the brief
3. All legally significant facts, whether favorable or unfavorable
4. Significant background facts
5. Emotionally significant facts

Note the location of each fact in the record. In the final draft of a trial-level brief, the citations should appear like so:

> On January 20, 1995, Carrolton filed a complaint in state court alleging that Watson was violating the terms of the covenant-not-to-compete. (Compl. ¶ 27.) Carrolton's Vice President, Justin Bakker, stated that the Complaint was filed within one month of Carrolton's discovery of Watson's business activity. (Bakker Aff. ¶ 14.)

III. ORGANIZATION

A. Formats

The most common organizational formats for fact statements are organizing chronologically, by topics, or by theories of the case.

Chronological. For simple facts, a chronological presentation is often best. For instance, in a simple collection matter, the facts will usually set out the events giving rise to the debt, the default, the plaintiff's demand that the defendant cure the default, and the amount owed. These simple facts are best presented chronologically.

Topical. For more complex facts, the topical format may work best. Set out the facts according to relevant topics. For example, in an employment discrimination case, the plaintiff's facts might be organized according to these topics: the nature of the defendant's business; the defendant's usual hiring process; the defendant's usual employee evaluation procedure; the procedures used in selecting employees for layoffs; the hiring process for the plaintiff's position; the terms of the plaintiff's employment; the plaintiff's employee evaluations; the business conditions that necessitated layoffs; the selection of plaintiff for layoff; the defendant's efforts to assist laid-off employees to find other jobs. The topics should be ordered logically, perhaps chronologically. For lengthy Fact Statements, consider using subheadings to help your reader follow the topics.

Theory of the Case. This format might be effective when the opposing party has some powerful facts that seem to support her position, but you have some key facts or a compelling theory of the case that will explain away those opposing facts. The format first sets out the powerful facts that seem to support your opponent's theory of the case, and then neutralizes them by setting out the facts that explain or justify the opposition's facts. For instance, in a trial brief,[9] the defendant's lawyer might organize the facts by first setting out the

---

9. A trial brief is filed shortly before trial. It gives the judge a general description of the evidence expected to be offered. It may alert the judge to expected legal disputes at trial (such as evidentiary disputes or disputes over jury instructions) and argue the writer's position on those disputes. It also may provide the judge with an overview of the elements of the various causes of action and claims for damages.

evidence the plaintiff is expected to offer and then setting out the evidence the defendant plans to offer.

Organizing by theory of the case is a more daring choice for several reasons. First, as a general rule, the beginning of a section soaks up far more reader attention than does later material.[10] Second, there is the risk that a busy judge may not finish reading the Fact Statement. Third, the writer who selects this organization is betting a large stake that the supporting facts will defeat the opposing facts. Since the format sets up such a direct and express juxtaposition of these facts, the writer had better be right.

When this organizational format works, however, it is extraordinarily effective. Having heard the worst facts and having decided that they do not necessarily mean what they seem to mean, the reader is far less likely to be impressed on reading them in the opposing brief, on hearing them at oral argument, or at trial. So, be aware that this organizational format is an option, but choose it only after careful evaluation.

B. Procedural History

No matter which format you choose, you will need to decide where to place the procedural history. Court rules or the instructions for your assignment may make this decision for you.[11] Or the rules or instructions may require a Preliminary Statement or Introduction, in which case the procedural history goes there, in its own section.

If court rules or your instructions have not identified the location for the procedural history, the two most common places for it are at the beginning or the end of the Fact Statement. At the beginning, it can help to establish the context for the facts that follow. At the end, it can serve as a natural segue into the Argument section. Either way, consider using subheadings to divide the Statement of the Case into at least two subsections: the "Factual History" and the "Procedural History." Since the procedural history will seldom comprise a compelling part of the theory of the case, using subheadings can put the dull procedural facts out of the way of the theme you hope to deliver with the facts.

IV. TECHNIQUES FOR PERSUASION

A. General Principles

1. Clarity is more important than using sophisticated techniques for persuasion. Judges will not be persuaded by a fact statement they cannot understand. If a technique impedes clarity, do not use it.

---

10. Other lawyers believe that the position of greater emphasis is the end. But nearly everyone agrees that the position of least emphasis is the middle.

11. *See, e.g.*, Fed. R. App. P. 28(a)(6).

2. Do not use a technique that the reader will notice. An effective technique must be invisible, or nearly so. Once a reader recognizes a technique, it has lost its power because the reader's attention is on the technique and not the fact. For instance, assume that you have used the technique of repetition to emphasize a favorable fact. You hoped that it would encourage the reader to realize the significance of the fact, to let it sink in. If, instead, your reader's Commentator[12] observes, "Ah, look, the writer is repeating this fact to try to get me to notice it," the reader will be thinking about the technique and the writer's goals rather than the fact. Your Fact Statement would have been more persuasive if you had not used the technique at all.

3. Do not overuse any technique. Overuse creates monotony, decreases the technique's power, and increases the chances that the reader will notice the technique rather than the facts.

4. Any technique for emphasizing one fact or group of facts deemphasizes the remaining facts. To the extent you try to use techniques of emphasis for nearly all of the facts, your strategy will fail. You have to pick the few facts you want most to emphasize and allow the others to serve as the background.

5. Some of the techniques described below are inconsistent with each other. The inconsistency does not mean that one is right and the other wrong, but only that each has its advantages and disadvantages. The writer's job is to select the technique that will work best for the needs of a particular fact statement.

B. Large-Scale Organization

The Beginning

6. Unless you know differently, assume that the judge is not already familiar with the case. The beginning of the Statement of Facts should establish the context for the facts that follow. Otherwise, the judge may find herself reading a chronological account of a series of events without knowing why these events are important. Context can be provided by a procedural history or by a short summary of what the case is about, written to be consistent with your theory of the case. Here is an example written on behalf of Carrolton:

> This is an action to enforce the terms of a covenant-not-to-compete. As part of the sale of her business to Carrolton Company, the defendant promised that for the three years immediately following the sale she would not compete with Carrolton in the three counties closest to Carrolton's headquarters. Eighteen months after the sale was completed, the defendant opened a competing business just one mile from Carrolton's office. She has been competing directly with Carrolton in the three prohibited counties ever since. This action seeks to enjoin her continued breach of the covenant-not-to-compete.

7. The reader's attention level is greatest in the first few paragraphs. When you can find a way to do so logically, capitalize on this increased attention level by selecting an organization that allows you to place there material you

---

12. *See* Chapter 6, section IID.

want to emphasize. This strategy can be consistent with a summary of the case drafted from your client's perspective, like the one above.

8. Aim for a beginning that will spark the reader's interest. Journalists call this "the lead." The conventions of a legal document do not allow for some of the more dramatic forms of grabbing attention, but you do want the reader to be drawn into the story and want to read on. For example, a prosecutor's brief might begin with the facts of the crime rather than with the procedural history of the appeal.

The Middle

9. Here is the place for the facts you want to deemphasize. Normally, a reader's attention level is at its lowest about three-fourths of the way through the section.[13]

The End

10. Readers may pay more attention to the material at the beginning, but they remember longest the material at the end. Readers tend to take a mental break to let the story sink in, and when they do, the last sentence lingers in their minds. Try to select an organization that allows you to place at the end material you most want the reader to remember.

11. The last paragraph should have the "feel" of a concluding paragraph. One way to accomplish this is to close with a transition into the legal argument to follow by identifying the legal positions staked out by the parties. Be careful not to include overt legal argument. Limit yourself to identifying the positions each side will take on the legal dispute. Avoid stating the opposing position any more favorably than you have to. Keeping in mind that the last sentence lingers in the reader's mind, end with your legal position rather than your opponent's. Here is an example of such a transition:

> The bank has admitted that it did not disclose the effective interest rate to the Turners. However, it claims that disclosure was not required, arguing that the transaction was not a "consumer loan" under the Consumer Protection Act. This brief will show that the transaction was, indeed, a "consumer loan" and that the bank's failure to disclose to the Turners the effective interest rate was a violation of the Act.

C. Paragraph Organization

12. A reader devotes more attention to the beginning and the end of a paragraph than to the middle. Put facts you want to emphasize in the first sentence or in the last clause or phrase of the last sentence. Deemphasize unfavorable facts by placing them in the middle.

---

13. Mary Barnard Ray & Barbara J. Cox, *Beyond the Basics: A Text for Advanced Legal Writing, Second Edition* 171 (West 2003).

13. Be conscious of paragraph length. In sections where you want to emphasize the facts, keep paragraphs relatively short. Where you want to deemphasize facts, let the paragraphs get longer, and put the facts you particularly want to deemphasize deep in the paragraph.

D. Techniques with Sentences

14. As a general rule, reduce clutter by using the techniques in Chapter 21 to eliminate surplusage. Clutter reduces clarity, irritates the reader, and deemphasizes the important facts. Occasionally, you can allow just a bit of clutter to surround an unfavorable fact. The clutter will reduce emphasis by lengthening the sentence and by making it less striking. Use this technique sparingly.

15. Use active verbs for emphasis and passive verbs for deemphasis or to avoid focus on the identity of the person who took the action.

a. *To encourage focus on the person taking the action:*

> Shaffer kicked in the front door of the house and attacked his estranged wife, breaking her forearm.
>
> *[Here the prosecutor wants all attention on Shaffer as he takes these violent actions.]*

b. *To avoid focus on the person taking the action:*

> Acme Health Equipment was formed and began operation on April 22, 1995.
>
> *[Here the writer seeks to deflect attention away from the person who formed and ran Acme—Watson.]*

c. *To focus on a person other than the one taking the action:*

> In the early morning of January 1, 1995, after attending several New Year's Eve parties, the defendant was stopped for a routine sobriety test.
>
> *[Here the writer is not so much trying to keep attention* away from *the police officer who stopped the defendant as to keep the focus* on *the defendant who was stopped.]*

16. Place favorable facts in main clauses and unfavorable facts in dependent clauses. Consider this sentence in a brief for Watson:

> Although Acme's business does compete with Carrolton [dependent clause], the competition only extends to three small product lines and could only impact, at the most, four percent of Carrolton's profits [main clause].

17. If an unfavorable fact *must* go in the first or last sentence of a paragraph, place the dependent clause carrying the unfavorable fact toward the interior of the paragraph. Thus, for the first sentence of the paragraph, a dependent clause carrying an unfavorable fact should go at the end of the sentence. Which party's brief would contain this sentence?

> Acme competes directly with Carrolton in the three prohibited counties [main clause], although the competition presently extends only to three product lines [dependent clause] . . . [paragraph continues by setting out the facts of the competition].

For the last sentence of the paragraph, try putting the dependent clause at the beginning:

[The paragraph has set out the facts establishing the competition.] Thus, while the competition extends only to three product lines [dependent clause], Acme directly and openly competes presently with Carrolton in the three prohibited counties [main clause].

18. Occasionally, when you want the reader to slow down and take in the significance of the material in all parts of the sentence, place a phrase or dependent clause in the middle of the sentence, interrupting the reader's usual path from the subject directly to the verb.

Watson, who admits that she is intentionally violating the terms of her covenant, asks this Court to use its equitable powers to relieve her of the consequences of her own actions.

Use this technique sparingly because it makes sentences less readable.

19. Use shorter sentences for material you want to emphasize and longer sentences for material you want to deemphasize.

Longer Sentences for Less Emphasis

On July 1, while Mr. and Mrs. Emilio and their daughter Ashley were driving south on Interstate 75 toward Valdosta, a car swerved across the median and hit the Emilio car. Mr. and Mrs. Emilio survived, although they were seriously injured. Their daughter, who had been riding in the back seat, died as a result of the injuries she sustained in the accident.

Shorter Sentences for Greater Emphasis

On July 1, Mr. and Mrs. Emilio were driving south on Interstate 75 toward Valdosta. Their daughter Ashley was riding in the back seat. A car swerved across the median and hit the Emilio car. Mr. and Mrs. Emilio survived, though seriously injured. Ashley, however, died.

E. Other Small-Scale Techniques

20. Compress the space you devote to unfavorable facts, and expand the space you devote to favorable facts. The more material you provide about the favorable facts, the more emphasis they soak up.

21. Use detail to describe the material you want to emphasize. Conversely, limit the detail of your discussion of the unfavorable facts, though of course you cannot omit any significant facts.

22. Use *visual* facts and images to describe favorable facts; avoid them for unfavorable facts. Visual images carry particular power for placing the reader, mentally, at the scene.

On July 1, Mr. and Mrs. Emilio were driving south on Interstate 75 toward Valdosta. Their daughter Ashley was riding in the back seat. A car swerved across the median and crashed into the Emilios. The front of the other car hit the Emilio car at the left rear door, precisely where Ashley was sitting, strapped in by her seat belt.

The force of the impact carried the other car's engine well into the passenger cabin of the Emilio car. It ripped Ashley from her seat belt, pinned her against the opposite door, and crushed her thoracic cavity.

Mr. and Mrs. Emilio survived, though seriously injured. Ashley, however, died at the scene.

23. Short quotations (a sentence or two) or snippet quotations (just a word or a phrase) can be powerful facts. If the words of the witness or document are particularly helpful, quote them.

> Shaffer left the bar, declaring "I'm going to go talk to my wife, and she'll need a doctor before I'm through."

Avoid overquoting, however. Overquoting will result in a disjointed story and will cause the most effective quotes to fade into the pack with the rest of the quotes.

24. When you can repeat key facts *unobtrusively,* the repetition serves to emphasize those facts or concepts. For instance, the first sentence of the paragraph might summarize the facts, and the remaining sentences could set out the facts in more detail. Or the beginning of a sentence might refer to the facts of the prior sentence as a transition.

> Marie Claxton, the expert witness who testified on behalf of Pyle, concluded that a reasonable and prudent lawyer would have checked the deed for easements. Claxton explained that deeds often contain restrictions that significantly affect the use of the property. She testified that any prudent lawyer would know that such restrictions are common. According to Claxton, Gavin's failure to check the deed fell below the standard of professional skill and diligence of a reasonable and prudent lawyer.

Do not just repeat particular facts, seemingly for no reason, however. It will bore and irritate your reader. Remember that the Argument section gives you a natural opportunity to repeat the key facts.

25. Place unfavorable facts in a favorable or mitigating context. You can juxtapose the unfavorable fact with favorable facts or you can place the unfavorable fact in a context that negates some of the unfavorable inferences the fact might otherwise invite.

Juxtaposing an Unfavorable Fact with Favorable Facts

> Although Acme's business does compete with Carrolton, the competition only extends to three small product lines and could only impact, at the most, four percent of Carrolton's profits.

Placing the Unfavorable Fact in a More Favorable Context

> While the demonstrations against the abortion clinic are disruptive to the other tenants, the landlords cannot prevent the demonstrations; nor can they force the clinic to move until the clinic's lease term expires.

26. Humanize your client. The most important way to do this is by telling the story from the client's perspective, as your theory of the case will already accomplish. Include, where possible, a description of the client's feelings, responses, and motivations. It is also helpful to refer to your client by name and use titles that communicate respect, like "Mr.," "Ms.," "Dr.," or "Officer."

It is especially important to humanize corporate clients. Remember that every story involving a corporation is really a story about people. Identify the people who took the actions, and humanize those people. Portray them in a sympathetic light by setting out the context for their actions.

27. Generally, do not humanize opposing parties. Where there is no need to use the names of opposing individuals, consider using generic descriptions instead ("the officer," "the insurance agent," "the electrician"). Generic descriptions can be especially helpful where the description has unsympathetic connotations, such as "the finance company," "the insurance company," or "the corporation." However, humanize when your theory of the case depends on showing the judge not only the sympathetic facts about your client but also the outrageously bad behavior of one or more of the opposing parties. In such a case, you may need to humanize the opposing party so you can show the outrageousness of his or her behavior.

28. Use graphic words, especially verbs, for facts you want to emphasize.

> The van *crashed into* [instead of "hit"] the taxi, and the force of the impact *shattered* [instead of "broke"] the driver's spine.

29. Refrain from name-calling. Name-calling tells your reader that you do not have good facts, so you are compelled to resort to derogatory characterizations.

30. Where possible, delete adverbs in favor of additional facts and more vivid verbs. Vivid verbs, alone, are much more powerful than a ho-hum verb with an adverb. Avoid such artificial intensifiers as "very" or "extremely."

31. Pay careful attention to common connotations of words. Choose words with helpful connotations and avoid those with unhelpful connotations.

A Word with Potentially Troubling Connotations

> Mr. and Mrs. McMann were *anxiously* awaiting the birth of their first child.
> ["Anxiously" carries the connotation of worry. Use it if the connotation helps your theory, but avoid it if the connotation either impedes the theory or may distract the reader into wondering what they were worried about.]

An Option with a Better Connotation

> Mr. and Mrs. McMann were *anticipating* the birth of their first child.

Finally, put the draft down for a few hours and then read it afresh. Try not to look for the techniques you used, but rather read openly, as you hope your reader will. Notice your reactions and fix anything that troubles you.

EXERCISE 18-1
Critiquing a Statement of Facts

Here are two fact statements for the Watson covenant-not-to-compete issue. Each fact statement has strengths. Neither is perfect. Evaluate each, identifying what works well and what could be improved. One formulation of the governing rule of law is:

A covenant-not-to-compete is enforceable if all of the following elementsare reasonable:

A. the kind of activity restrained;

B. the geographic area of the restraint; and

C. the time period of the restraint.

Another possible formulation of the rule is:

To be enforceable, a covenant-not-to-compete must be reasonable. Factors for deciding reasonableness are:

A. the needs of the restraining party;

B. the needs of the public;

C. the needs of the restrained party; and

D. any other relevant circumstances.

Which rule formulation does the drafter of each fact statement seem to have in mind?

Statement of Facts on Behalf of Carrolton

STATEMENT OF FACTS

This is an action to enforce the terms of a covenant-not-to-compete. On Dec. 1, 1994, the Defendant sold Carrolton Company to Richard Meyers, Andrea McPhane, and James Rey ("Purchasers") for $220,000. (Compl. ¶ 10.) The sale included not only Carrolton's inventory and accounts receivable, but also the company's good will in the community. (Compl. ¶ 11.) As part of the contract of sale, the Defendant promised that she would not compete with Carrolton for the three years immediately following the sale. (Compl. ¶ 13.) The covenant covers only Quincy, Herring, and Gawin Counties, the three counties closest to Carrolton's office. (Compl. ¶ 13.)

The covenant-not-to-compete was an integral part of the Defendant's sale of Carrolton to the Purchasers. (McPhane Aff. ¶ 8.) Carrolton retails in-home health care products in the Kinston, Georgia area. (Compl. ¶ 13.) Through her ownership of Carrolton, the Defendant had been engaged in the retail sales of health care products in the Kinston area for fifteen years. (McPhane Aff. ¶ 8.) On behalf of Carrolton, she had made and maintained the sales contacts necessary to a successful retailer of those products. (McPhane Aff. ¶ 9.) Her contacts and ongoing relationships with physicians and customers were part of the good will for which the Purchasers paid. (McPhane Aff. ¶ 10.) Thus, these contacts and relationships were a critical part of the sale of the business. (Compl. ¶ 14.) The covenant prohibits the defendant from making sales contacts for in-home health care products in the three counties that comprise the heart of Carrolton's marketing area. (Compl. ¶ 15.)

After the Defendant sold Carrolton to the Purchasers, the Defendant remained with the company, employed as Carrolton's General Manager. She held that position of trust for fourteen months after the sale. (Compl. ¶ 16.) On February 21, 1996, the Defendant left her position as Carrolton's General Manager and immediately opened a competing business one mile from Carrolton's office. (Compl. ¶ 17.) Since that date, the Defendant has been making sales contacts for health care products in the three prohibited counties, in direct competition with Carrolton. (Compl. ¶ 18.) The Purchasers have filed this action seeking to enjoin the Defendant's continued breach of the covenant not to compete.

Statement of Facts on Behalf of Watson

STATEMENT OF FACTS

In 1979, Sharon Watson founded Carrolton Company, a retailer of in-home health care equipment in Kinston, Georgia. (Watson Aff. ¶ 3.) Before Carrolton opened, residents of Kinston and the surrounding area had to travel seventy-five miles to the nearest retailer of health care equipment. (Williams Aff. ¶ 2.) The lack of a nearby health care equipment retailer was particularly problematic for the Kinston community because people needing in-home health care equipment are among those least able to make a seventy-five-mile trip to purchase that equipment. (Williams Aff. ¶ 3-6.) With Carrolton's opening, area residents had local access to the health care equipment they needed. (Williams Aff. ¶ 8.)

As the only retailer of in-home health care equipment in the area, Carrolton did a large volume of business. (Watson Aff. ¶ 7.) Ms. Watson believed that Carrolton's virtual monopoly brought with it an obligation not to take advantage of her customers. (Watson Aff. ¶ 9.) Thus, she used a markup of only 35 percent to ensure that her customers paid fair prices. (Watson Aff. ¶ 10.) She kept the business responsive to customer needs, making diligent efforts to fill special orders, and maintaining close communication with local physicians. (Williams Aff. ¶ 8; Watson Aff. ¶ 11.) She made certain that Carrolton was a concerned and responsible commercial citizen of the community. (Tharpe Aff. ¶ 6; William Aff. ¶ 9.)

In early 1994, a group of Atlanta investors approached Ms. Watson about the possibility of buying Carrolton. (Compl. ¶ 5.) Over the next few months, the parties discussed the terms of a possible sale. (Compl. ¶ 7.) During these conversations, Ms. Watson expressed concern about how the business, still a virtual monopoly, would be run. (Watson Aff. ¶ 12.)

In response to these concerns, the investors suggested that Ms. Watson remain with the company as General Manager and continue to manage the operation. (Watson Aff. ¶ 14.) The investors explained that they would not want Carrolton's fundamental operating policies to change, and Ms. Watson's continued management would be a way to continue the company's successful marketing approach. (Watson Aff. ¶ 15.) They explained that Ms. Watson's approach was so important to them that they would like the transaction to include the covenant that Ms. Watson would not leave Carrolton to compete in the local market for at least three years. (Watson Aff. ¶ 15.) Ms. Watson agreed, and on Dec. 1, 1994, after fifteen years of building the business, Ms. Watson sold Carrolton to its present owners. (Compl. ¶ 10.)

The terms of the sale placed Ms. Watson in the position of General Manager. (Compl. ¶ 12.) While the contract did not expressly state the reason for the terms, the parties had always discussed Ms. Watson's continued service and noncompetition covenant as a method to maintain continuity of management philosophy. (Watson Aff. ¶ 14.) The covenant prohibited Ms. Watson from competing with Carrolton's new owners in the three counties that make up Carrolton's virtual monopoly. (Compl. ¶ 11.)

Within a month after the sale, Carrolton's new owners began implementing management changes. (Williams Aff. ¶ 11; Watson Aff. ¶ 16; Tharpe Aff. ¶ 8.) They issued new pricing policies, raising the company's markup on its product lines. (Watson Aff. ¶ 16.) They ordered Ms. Watson to lay off one of Carrolton's only two other employees, and they eliminated most special orders. (Watson Aff. ¶ 17.) Eliminating these special orders effectively blocked the access of area customers to any health care products not a part of Carrolton's regular inventory. (Tharpe Aff. ¶ 9.)

In response to Ms. Watson's protests, the owners argued that these new policies maximized efficiency and company profits. (Watson Aff. ¶ 19.) They maintained that customer complaints were not important since without Carrolton, customers would have no local access to health care equipment at all. (Watson Aff. ¶ 20.)

On Feb. 21, 1996, after repeated attempts to persuade Carrolton's new owners to rescind their new policies, Ms. Watson left her position at Carrolton. (Watson Aff. ¶ 22.) Believing that Carrolton's owners had breached their assurances that Carrolton would continue being responsive to its customer's needs, Ms. Watson formed Acme Health Care. (Watson Aff. ¶ 22.) Ms. Watson incurred $75,000 in personal debt to open Acme, mortgaging her home to secure the loan. (Watson Aff. ¶ 23.) In the first two years of business Acme will do well to break even. During that time, Ms. Watson will have to make loan payments from her personal savings. (Watson Aff. ¶ 24.)

Although Ms. Watson hopes that one day Acme will represent a viable customer alternative to Carrolton (Watson Aff. ¶ 27), presently Acme competes with Carrolton in only three product lines: respiratory equipment, diabetic monitoring equipment, and wheelchairs. (Watson Aff. ¶ 25.) Even in these lines, Acme's business is just beginning. Presently, Acme carries only the products of the two leading manufacturers in these product lines. (Watson Aff. ¶ 26.) During the next nineteen months (the remaining term of the covenant-not-to-compete), Acme cannot expect to attract more than 30 percent of Carrolton's business in these product lines. Acme will have no impact on Carrolton's virtual monopoly over the twenty-two other product lines Carrolton sells. (Watson Aff. ¶ 29.)

Even if Acme meets with phenomenal success during the next nineteen months, Carrolton will still make healthy profits. (Watson Aff. ¶ 32.) During the remaining covenant term, Acme poses no realistic threat to Carrolton's business. (Watson Aff. ¶ 34.) Acme's potential threat to Carrolton is the potential end to Carrolton's virtual monopoly over the in-home health care market in the Kinston area. (Watson Aff. ¶ 35; Williams Aff. ¶ 17; Tharpe Aff. ¶ 15.) That threat to Carrolton's market position would arise, if at all, long after the covenant has expired. (Watson Aff. ¶ 36.)

Checklist for Fact Statements

Large-Scale Organization

- Does the organization present the facts clearly? Is it easy to follow?
- Does the organizational format allow you to put most of the unfavorable facts in the middle and put some of the favorable facts at the beginning and

some at the end? (The "theory of the case" format is an intentional exception to this principle.)

- Does the material at the beginning catch the reader's interest?
- If your reader needs context, does the material at the beginning provide it?
- Does the draft communicate your theory of the case?
- Does the draft include all significant facts and all facts mentioned in your Argument?
- Does the draft include enough context to allow the reader to understand the dispute and your theory of the case, but no more?
- Does the draft place the procedural history at an appropriate location?
- Does the last paragraph have the "feel" of an ending?
- Does the draft end with a sentence that you want the reader to remember?

Paragraph Organization

- Are your best facts on the outside ends of the paragraph, while your least favorable facts are in the middle?
- Does the last phrase or clause of the paragraph contain favorable information?
- Are the paragraphs with facts you want to emphasize relatively short? Are those with facts you want to neutralize longer?

Techniques with Sentences

- Are the sentences (except one or two carrying unfavorable facts) free of clutter?
- Do the passive-voiced verbs serve a purpose? Are there any actions you would like to deemphasize by changing to passive?
- Where appropriate, are unfavorable facts in dependent clauses juxtaposed with more favorable facts or explanatory context?
- Do the shorter sentences carry favorable facts? Where appropriate, are the unfavorable facts in longer sentences?
- Using brackets in the margins of the draft, identify the text that deals with favorable topics and the text that deals with unfavorable topics. How does the total allocation of space to each compare?
- Notice where you have used detail and visual images. Notice where you have not.
- Do the quotations really help?
- If you have used the technique of repetition, is it too obvious?
- How have you referred to your client? To the opposing parties?
- At spots where you are presenting favorable material, are there any verbs you can switch for more powerful or graphic synonyms?

CHAPTER 19

Using Legal Theory to Sharpen Your Arguments

If one were to apply each of the major forms of reasoning discussed in Chapter 5 to a particular case, the forms of reasoning might easily lead to differing outcomes. The question then is which form or forms will trump the others in the adversarial process? Jurisprudence—the philosophy of law—provides part of the answer to that question.

Forms of reasoning draw their persuasive force from underlying assumptions about the nature and function of law—about how cases are and should be decided. These are the questions of jurisprudence. Jurisprudence ponders such topics as what law is; where it comes from; whether it is internally consistent; whether it is or can be neutral; how we should decide new or hard cases; and whether and how law relates to morality, social values, economics, or politics.

The more you know about jurisprudence, the more it will show you practical arguments and lawyering strategies. Your own grasp of the jurisprudential basis of a form of argument and your sensitivity to the jurisprudential approach of the judge will strengthen your ability to use these forms of argument to represent your clients well. This section introduces some of the major schools of American jurisprudence and explores how these jurisprudential schools relate to the forms of legal reasoning described above.[1]

A caveat is in order. One cannot draw lines tightly defining jurisprudential schools of thought because the categories overlap and because different strains have developed within each school. Nonetheless, a broad and general description is helpful to introduce the field. With that goal in mind, here is the story of the development of American jurisprudence with particular reference to three of its most vexing questions (1) the relationship between law and morality; (2) the degree to which law is predictable; and (3) the degree to which law is, can, or should be neutral—that is, not inherently favoring any particular segment of society.

---

1. Much of the material in this section is explained more fully in Chapter 6 of an excellent book by Professors Bailey Kuklin & Jeffrey W. Stempel, *Foundations of the Law: An Interdisciplinary and Jurisprudential Primer* (West 1994).

I. NATURAL LAW

American jurisprudence began with natural law, the predominant jurisprudential school the American colonies inherited from English law. Natural law holds that law is a product of "natural reason." This natural reason has often been associated with religious thought, but natural law is actually much broader. It relies on the deepest moral instincts of humanity and attempts to justify these instincts rationally. According to natural law theory, law and morality (our beliefs about right and wrong, justice and injustice) are both grounded in natural reason and so are inevitably intertwined. An acceptable legal system must also be an acceptable moral system; that is, law should comply with standards of justice, fairness, and reasonableness. Therefore, laws can be defended or challenged on the basis of whether they are reasonable and moral.

Natural law theory favors the common law (case law) over statutes. The common law is more apt to reflect natural reason, while statutes, resulting from the political process, are thought to preempt the natural reason on which the common law was based. We saw natural law theory in action in Chapter 4, for instance, when we studied the canon of construction asserting that statutes "in derogation of the common law" should be narrowly construed.[2]

A judge with a natural law bent might therefore be willing to take more liberties when interpreting a statute or more willing to hold it unconstitutional than would a judge of another jurisprudential persuasion. The natural law judge might use some of the canons of construction to justify a result consistent with her sense of natural reason and morality. Turn back to page 53 to review the examples of canons of construction listed there. Do you see a canon that invites a kind of natural law inquiry?

A natural law judge also would be more willing to consider disregarding old or flawed precedent, justifying the decision by citing to the age of the precedent and to more recent moral development or the evolution of human understanding. By such a decision, this judge might be inviting the higher court to reconsider its earlier decision.

Forms of Legal Reasoning. Principle-based arguments are most persuasive to judges with natural law leanings. Principles of justice, fairness, reasonableness, and equity can be used to interpret rules or to challenge the strict application of legal rules. Principle-based reasoning represents a direct appeal to natural law.

Narrative reasoning is a less direct but sometimes more effective way to appeal to the values of natural law. Stories contain themes, encode principles, espouse values. The effective use of narrative, especially the narrative of the client's case, can appeal to a decision-maker's sense of justice and morality. Custom-based reasoning can also be effective, because natural law is assumed to be consistent with generally accepted practices. Aberrations from the norm are suspect.

---

2. *See* p. 52.

Although it is almost always good to organize an argument according to the structure of the rule, a natural law judge will not be overly constrained by the precise language of legal rules. Rule-based reasoning will not be strong here unless the advocate can show that the rule is a reasonable expression of a fair principle. One must not only demonstrate what the rule is but also that the rule is right.

Few judges today would be so solidly in the natural law camp that they would blatantly disregard a clear statutory mandate or a binding precedent. But if the judge has any leeway to interpret ambiguities in the rule or if the rule asks the judge to apply a flexible legal standard, our natural law judge will interpret and apply the rule in ways consistent with her understanding of natural law's abiding truths.

Strengths and Weaknesses. Natural law is attractive because it ties law to standards of justice, fairness, and reason, but it has disadvantages as well. Its two most problematic characteristics are its unpredictability and its inherent subjectivity. "Natural reason" is difficult to define or predict. And decisions resting on natural law theory historically have looked a lot like the moral perspectives of that generation's power structure. For instance, a natural law perspective might be more willing to condemn the morality of a homeless person stealing bread than the morality of the landowner who had evicted the person or the business owner who had fired him for no cause.

EXERCISE 19-1

What natural law influences do you see in the following excerpts from court opinions?

"[Requiring an adverse possessor to have known that he did not have record title to the land] rewards . . . the intentional wrongdoer and disfavors an honest, mistaken entrant." *Mannillo v. Gorski*, 255 A.2d 258, 261 (N.J. 1969).

"It cannot be expected that every purchaser will or should engage a surveyor to ascertain that the beach home he is purchasing lies within the boundaries described in his deed. Such a practice is neither reasonable nor customary. . . . [T]he squatter should not be able to profit by his trespass." *Howard v. Kunto*, 477 P.2d 210, 214 (Wash. 1970).

"We therefore hold that antiquated real property concepts which served as the basis for the pre-existing rule shall no longer be controlling where there is a claim for damages under a residential lease. Such claims must be governed by more modern notions of fairness and equity. A landlord has a duty to mitigate damages where he seeks to recover rents due from a defaulting tenant." *Sommer v. Kridel*, 378 A.2d 767, 772-773 (N.J. 1977).

"Where fairness and common sense dictate that an exception should be created, the evolution of the law should not be stifled by rigid application of a legal maxim." *Stambovsky v. Ackley*, 572 N.Y.S.2d 672, 676 (1991).

II. FORMALISM

In the last third of the nineteenth century, the Civil War had left American intellectuals disillusioned and skeptical. Further, the cultural infatuation with Darwinism and the scientific method was in full swing.[3] In that climate, the idea of "natural reason" began to seem like unprovable superstition.

Meanwhile, on the other side of the Atlantic, leading English scholars were espousing positivism, a blatant rejection of natural law in favor of the idea that law is simply whatever the sovereign decrees and is willing to enforce. Positivists are unimpressed with the common law and with the role of judges. According to positivists, statutes—through which the sovereign speaks—are the most legitimate form of law. (Do you recall this perspective reflected in some of the canons of construction discussed in Chapter 4?)

Positivism seemed to dethrone law from its natural law pedestal, and Darwinism seemed to call for a "scientific" approach to everything. In 1870, when Christopher Columbus Langdell became the Dean of the Harvard Law School, he set out to establish law as a science too. He created the case method of law teaching—the method you probably are experiencing now in most of your classes—in the hope of showing the scientific nature of law. Langdell often is described as the father of legal formalism.

For formalists, law is drawn from a set of rules ("first principles") governing recurring situations,[4] not from a set of timeless moral standards. According to some strains of formalism, these first principles resemble the laws of science, like gravity or photosynthesis. They preexist any particular articulation of them, and they can be discovered and organized according to legal categories, much like the scientific categories of animal species.

According to formalism, the judge's job is simple. He is to select the appropriate legal rule from the appropriate legal category and apply it to the facts at hand. Formalists thought that this should be a straightforward, easy process. Granted, not every case would be clear, but the more difficult cases simply signal that we legal "scientists" have more work to do. As soon as we have discovered and articulated all the first principles, all cases will be simple and clear.

Law study and legal practice still reflect the influence of formalism. We still have the West key numbering system. Legal encyclopedias and other research sources are still organized according to categories that resemble Langdell's vision. The first-year curriculum still reflects formalist legal categories, and law school pedagogy still employs the Socratic method. And as Part III of this book explained, the classic paradigm for organizing a legal discussion begins by stating and explaining a rule and then applying that rule to the client's facts. As we saw when we studied the paradigm more closely, however, the process it requires is usually far more complex and unpredictable than Langdell envisioned.

---

3. Louis Menand, *The Metaphysical Club: A Story of Ideas in America* (Farrar, Straus and Giroux 2001).

4. Bailey Kuklin & Jeffrey Stempel, *Foundations of the Law* at 149.

Forms of Legal Reasoning. For the formalist, rule-based reasoning is the heart and soul of legal rhetoric. To persuade a formalist judge, the advocate must carefully and precisely articulate the rule, offer strong authority to prove that the rule is as she has articulated it, and then carefully apply the rule to the facts of the case. But what if the literal application of the language of the rule leads to an unfavorable conclusion? All is not lost. Remember that formalism is the jurisprudential cousin of positivism. What matters is the will of the sovereign, that is, the intent of the legislature or the court that established the binding precedent. You can engage in rule-based reasoning, arguing not from the literal language of the rule but from the intent of the rule-maker.

Analogical reasoning can be persuasive to a formalist judge because it demonstrates that the judge has accurately identified the legal issue and therefore the appropriate governing legal rule. Since formalist judges believe that they should avoid decisions based on moral principles or public policy, they are not as receptive to principle-based or policy-based reasoning as such. However, you can use principle and policy arguments couched as the intent of the rule-maker. Pure formalists would be unimpressed by custom-based reasoning, considering it the weakest possible basis for a decision.

Strengths and Weaknesses. Assuming that formalism accurately describes law, it scores high on both predictability and objectivity, the two major weaknesses of natural law. Formalism recognizes that statutes and binding case law exist and that sometimes a judge is constrained to follow a clear binding rule. In such a case, the result does not depend on what the judge thinks of the litigants or on whether the judge agrees with the rule.

Formalism carries major weaknesses, however, and the most serious is inaccuracy. Simply put, legal principles cannot remove subjectivity from judging. Judges do not decide cases just by looking up rules. And even if they were willing to limit their decision-making to that mechanical exercise, rules cannot be articulated in ways that account for all human situations. Human situations are infinitely varied, and a legal system that ignores these variations would not be desirable. Rules are made of words, and words must be interpreted by human beings.

Further, formalism enshrines the articulated rule as the real decision-maker, and articulated rules, whether statutory or common law, tend to reflect and entrench the values and perspectives of the economically and socially powerful. On this score, then, formalism was no improvement over natural law. In fact, it may have been a step backward because it leaves little room for escape. Since it disallows external standards like justice and reasonableness, it provides no basis for challenging a bad or outmoded law.

EXERCISE 19-2

What formalist influences do you see in the following excerpts from court opinions?

"[The parties are co-owners of the property. The Defendant has taken possession of the property and is using it for a warehouse. The Plaintiff seeks payment from the Defendant of one-half the fair rental value of the property. The rule on occupancy by a co-owner permits each co-owner the right to possess the premises.] Thus, before an occupying cotenant can be liable for rent . . . , he must have denied his cotenant the right to enter. It is axiomatic that there can be no denial of the right to enter unless there is a demand or an attempt to enter. [Therefore, if the Plaintiff had first sought to enter into possession herself and been denied by the Defendant, she could then demand that the Defendant pay rent.]" *Spiller v. Mackereth,* 334 So. 2d 859, 862 (Ala. 1976).

"[It seems to us that] this doctrine of causa mortis [gifts given by a donor on his death bed] is in direct conflict with the spirit and purpose of [the statute requiring wills to be in writing and properly witnessed. The purpose of that statute is] the prevention of fraud. . . . We were at first disposed to confine [gifts causa mortis] to cases of actual manual delivery, and are only prevented from doing so by our loyalty to our own [prior rulings]. . . ." *Newman v. Bost,* 29 S.E. 848, 849 (N.C. 1898).

III. LEGAL REALISM

Ironically, Langdell's case method, which he had hoped would demonstrate the scientific nature of law, may have provided the most powerful evidence against his own thesis. As students and professors systematically studied cases, they began to see that the deductive application of legal rules did not account for the results they observed. What, then, did?

Oliver Wendell Holmes, Jr., a contemporary of Langdell's, began the shift toward a set of ideas that later developed into legal realism, perhaps the preeminent American contribution to jurisprudence. Holmes's famous statement is often cited as an early description of legal realism:

> "The life of the law has not been logic; it has been experience. The felt necessities of the time, the prevalent moral and political theories, intuitions of public policy, avowed or unconscious, even the prejudices which judges share with their fellow-men, have a good deal more to do than the syllogism in determining the rules by which men should be governed."[5]

Legal realists believe, as Holmes suggested, that law is made by people as the need arises. Law is not a manifestation of preexisting natural law or an objective application of rules. Our legal language still reflects this realist idea. We say that a judge "finds" facts, but we avoid saying that a judge "finds" a legal conclusion.[6] Thus, realists are willing to live with much less predictability than are formalists.

Realists also reject the assumption that law is or ever could be objective. Realism acknowledges subjectivity and may even be said to embrace it, describing law as reflecting historical, social, political, anthropological, psychological, and economic influences. Realists admit that outcomes will vary

---

5. Oliver Wendell Holmes, *The Common Law* 1 (Little, Brown & Co. 1881).
6. We say instead that a judge "holds" a legal conclusion.

according to the identity of the decision-makers and the cultural influences bearing upon them.

This reliance on the real world of place and time for law creation leads realists to believe that law should accurately reflect and effectively participate in that real world. Prior to the realist revolution, the law had become insular, largely indifferent to other disciplines. Realism called law back into dialogue with the social sciences. Therefore, realists encourage lawyers and judges to consult interdisciplinary materials such as sociology, psychology, and economics to help them decide cases.

Louis Brandeis, a legal realist who later sat on the United States Supreme Court, filed a brief in *Muller v. Oregon*,[7] relying on social science research to argue the propriety of a law limiting working hours for women. To this day, we call a brief that provides the court with social science or other interdisciplinary information a "Brandeis brief." The plaintiff's brief in *Brown v. Board of Education*[8] was just such a brief.

Legal realism forever unmasked the humanity, complexity, and malleability of the law. Realism's critique of formalism "cut so deeply into the premises of American legal thought that no amount of enlightened policy making and informed situation sense could ever really put Humpty Dumpty together again."[9] Every subsequent jurisprudential school is either an attempt to escape the implications of legal realism or to embrace them.

Forms of Legal Reasoning. Policy arguments are the life blood of realist rhetoric, especially at the appellate level. As in the natural law context, the realist court does not feel overly constrained by the words of a rule. In the natural law context, one asked the court to interpret the rule, or even reject the rule, based on external standards of justice and reason. Here one asks the court to interpret the rule, or even reject the rule, based on sound social policy. Such an argument should be supported, not by subjective speculation, but rather by solid data from interdisciplinary sources. In his classic, *The Nature of the Judicial Process*, Justice Cardozo called for more and better "Brandeis briefs."[10]

Realist judges also find analogical reasoning more persuasive than rule-based reasoning because factual comparisons contain within them the coded cultural influences that realists believe actually account for legal results. Custom-based reasoning is consistent with the realist admission of subjectivity and the impact of cultural norms.

Narrative, especially at the trial-court level, is also well-suited to legal realism. Narrative is the broadest, most flexible, and most inclusive form of persuasion. It can, therefore, do the most comprehensive job of touching all the subjective factors that, in the realist's view, actually govern the outcome of cases.

However, a realist judge, at least one with Holmes' distrust of grand principle, might be uncomfortable with principle-based reasoning, preferring

---

7. 208 U.S. 412 (1908).
8. 347 U.S. 483 (1954).
9. Elizabeth Mensch, "The History of Mainstream Legal Thought," in David Kairys, ed., *The Politics of Law* 27 (Pantheon 1982).
10. Benjamin N. Cardozo, *The Nature of the Judicial Process* (Yale U. Press 1921).

a more concrete analysis of how the proposed result actually would work in the world.

Strengths and Weaknesses. Realism acknowledges that law is a human institution, with a limited capacity for objectivity and predictability. It honestly admits the inevitable influence of the dominant culture and of powerful economic interests. For the advocate, realism sets us free from formalism's insistence on rigid, mechanical application of formulaic rules. Realism legitimates broader, more flexible approaches to legal argument.

Still, realism sometimes suffers from its own excesses. It has a conflicted relationship with external criteria such as reason, justice, and morality as standards for interpreting or applying law. True, realism grants that current notions of morality have a role to play, because current cultural norms inevitably influence law. But realism is hesitant to ask whether those cultural norms are objectively right or true. Thus, realism undermines an advocate's arguments that law should be tested by external standards. In place of these standards, realism offers an advocate the criteria of sound social policy, which can be supported by evidence that is more substantive than the abstract claims and subjective values of natural law.

Finally, realism seems to leave us without a stable ground on which to stand. Early realism often was summed up as asserting that the law depended less on precedent than on "what the judge ate for breakfast."[11] If that describes our legal system, can we have confidence in its results? And how can individual and corporate citizens plan their lives and fortunes? A purely realist analysis leaves the law without consistency, apt to shift with the wind at any moment. Realism left us in need of a stabilizing movement. To meet that need, the legal process school developed.

EXERCISE 19-3

What realist influences do you see in the following excerpts from court opinions?

"It has long been the policy of our law to discourage landlords from taking the law into their own hands, and our decisions . . . have looked with disfavor upon any use of self-help to dispossess a tenant in circumstances which are likely to result in breaches of the peace. . . . To approve this lockout . . . merely because [the tenant was absent and so no] actual violence erupted while the locks were being changed would be to encourage all future tenants . . . to be vigilant and thereby set the stage for the very kind of public disturbance which it must be our policy to discourage. . . ." *Berg v. Wiley*, 264 N.W.2d 145, 149-150 (Minn. 1978).

"[T]he requirement of delivery [to prove a valid gift] is not rigid or inflexible, but is to be applied in light of its purpose to avoid mistakes by donors and fraudulent claims by donees." *Gruen v. Gruen*, 496 N.E.2d 869, 874 (N.Y. 1986).

---

11. Bailey Kuklin & Jeffrey Stempel, *Foundations of the Law* at 155.

"[A joint tenant has long been able to sever the joint tenancy by conveying his interest in the property to a straw person and then having that straw person convey the interest back to the former joint tenant. We now hold that the joint tenant can sever by conveying directly to himself.] Common sense as well as legal efficiency dictate that a joint tenant should be able to accomplish directly what he or she could otherwise achieve indirectly by use of elaborate legal fictions." *Riddle v. Harmon*, 162 Cal. Rptr. 530, 534 (Ct. App. Calif. 1980).

"There is no sound policy reason to deny plaintiff relief for failing to discover a state of affairs which the most prudent purchaser would not be expected to even contemplate. *Stambovsky v. Ackley*, 572 N.Y.S.2d 672, 676 (1991).

IV. LEGAL PROCESS

As we have seen, formalists said that a judge could and should follow legal rules, assumed to be neutral, regardless of the preferences of the judge. Realists said that judges did not and could not do this because judges are human and because legal rules are not really neutral. The legal process school tried to find a middle ground that would recognize the realists' critique of formalism but still would curb the unpredictability of realism.

The hope lay in turning our attention to the legal process itself, especially to judicial decision-making. Perhaps careful study and development of judicial roles and systemic controls would restore some sense of predictability and objectivity in law. If the *content* of the law was not objective, perhaps we could articulate neutral standards for *how* decisions were to be made. Legal process adherents look to institutional controls (division of governmental authority, adherence to fair procedure, judicial restraint, and mandated reasoned elaboration) to constrain arbitrary judging.[12]

According to the legal process school, judges are to restrain their personal preferences in favor of neutral procedures and standards of judging. Recall that in Chapters 1 and 2 we saw several instances in which a judge's role requires just this restraint. For instance, a trial judge cannot overturn a jury's verdict simply because the judge would have decided the case otherwise. The judge can overturn the verdict only if there was no reasonable evidentiary basis for the jury's decision.

Similarly, on questions of fact, an appellate judge cannot reverse a trial judge's decision merely because the appellate judge would have decided the case differently. The appellate judge can reverse the trial judge only if no reasonable consideration of the evidence in the record would support the trial judge's decision. Legal process adherents hope that neutral standards like these will restore a sense of stability and predictability and provide protection against abuse of the judicial role.

Forms of Legal Reasoning. A judge with a legal process bent is persuaded by rule-based reasoning when the rule is binding on her court and has a clear

---

12. Bailey Kuklin & Jeffrey Stempel, *Foundations of the Law* at 159.

meaning directly applicable to the pending case. In that instance, the legal process judge will feel constrained to follow the rule and will monitor carefully her personal preferences to keep them from interfering subtly with her judicial duty. Similarly, analogical reasoning is persuasive to a legal process judge because she is concerned about procedural fairness. After all, when the facts are similar, the results should not vary from court to court.

When no clear binding rule applies or when the rule allows discretion, a legal process judge is willing to consider policy-based reasoning because it seems reliable and objective. But a legal process judge will be uncomfortable with pure custom-based reasoning because it seems too close to subjective personal preference. Principle-based reasoning will be persuasive when the principles relate to procedural fairness. Other principles may seem too abstract to be applied without subjectivity. Direct reliance on narrative is the most subjective of all, and a legal process judge will try to resist her personal reaction to the client's stories.

Strengths and Weaknesses. The legal process school succeeds in restoring some stability for the legal system. Undoubtedly, its success is limited by its necessary reliance on imperfect human beings to achieve its goals. Most judges have been thoroughly enculturated with the legal process school's description of the judicial role, however, and they try to conform to that role as best they can.

But the legal process school still does not help us find a way to explore whether the *content* of our law is consistent with fundamental principles of justice and commonly shared principles of morality. Lon Fuller, himself a natural law advocate, tried to provide a link by suggesting that a fair process with public, reasoned decision-making was itself moral,[13] but the legal process movement itself did not rush to make this connection. A movement in that direction came with the development of the fundamental rights school.

EXERCISE 19-4

What legal process influences do you see in the following excerpts from court opinions?

> "Even if we were to feel that the referee was mistaken in so weighing the evidence, we would be powerless to change the determination where, as we have seen, there is some evidence in the record to support his conclusion." *Van Valkenburgh v. Lutz*, 106 N.E.2d 28, 32 (N.Y. 1952) (dissenting opinion).

> "[The goal of our law is] to prevent those claiming a right of . . . possession of land from redressing their own wrongs by entering into possession in a . . . forcible manner. . . . The law does not permit the owner of land, be his title ever so good, to be the judge of his own rights with respect to possession . . . , but puts him to his remedy under the statutes." *Lobdell v. Keene*, 88 N.W. 426, 430 (Minn. 1901).

---

13. Lon Fuller, *The Morality of Law* (Yale U. Press 1964).

V. FUNDAMENTAL RIGHTS

By now we were entering the 1950s, and the Supreme Court, under the leadership of Earl Warren, was in a period of judicial activism. *Brown v. Board of Education*[14] and other landmark decisions were establishing principles of human rights and opening doors to political and economic power.

But where was the jurisprudential justification for this kind of judicial activism? Natural law did not provide it because the old view of natural law seemed tied to the perspectives of the established power structure, and these decisions ran counter to that power structure. Formalism did not provide it because formalism enshrines the status quo. The legal process school could help on procedural issues like due process and access to courts. But on non-procedural issues, legal process is uncomfortable with decisions that seem based on personal political preferences. We had to return to the vexing question of how law relates to broad principles like justice and human dignity. From this renewed struggle emerged the fundamental rights school.

The fundamental rights school argued that promoting justice and human welfare outweighs the need for predictability and stability.[15] Judges should be ready to apply overarching principles inherent in the law, especially if the principle has been given greater certainty through judicial interpretation. For fundamental rights proponents, the results of this decision-making process are objectively correct, not merely the subjective product of political preferences.[16]

Forms of Legal Reasoning. Principle-based reasoning is primary in fundamental rights jurisprudence, as it is in natural law. However, the principles here are not the principles that preserve the status quo, but rather the principles of liberal political philosophy that assert the rights of poor and marginalized people. Fundamental rights judges are readily guided by such principles, especially when the principle is enshrined in the constitution or other forms of law.

Rule-based reasoning remains valuable here, but in this context it is helpful to look for the principle that the law serves. A fundamental rights judge will prefer to interpret the rule in accordance with the principle. She will overturn the rule in favor of a principle only as a last resort.

Narrative reasoning works in the fundamental rights context much as it did in the natural law context. It is an indirect but highly effective way to communicate the principles and values that should guide the decision-maker. The principles comprising "fundamental rights" are persuasive when stated directly; but they gain affective force when conveyed through the warm, human medium of story, especially the client's story.

Policy-based reasoning has its place in fundamental rights jurisprudence, but it is a narrower place. The fundamental rights judge does not see herself as a free-form social engineer, but fundamental rights are meaningless unless

---

14. 347 U.S. 483 (1954).
15. Bailey Kuklin & Jeffrey Stempel, *Foundations of the Law* at 165.
16. *Id.* at 166; Ronald Dworkin, *Law's Empire* (Belknap Press 1986); Ronald Dworkin, *A Matter of Principle* (Harv. U. Press 1985).

they are grounded in social reality. So interdisciplinary sources may be needed to show how an application of the law will play out in society to either advance or undermine fundamental rights. Custom-based reasoning will generally not be very persuasive to a fundamental rights judge unless it shows that a certain right is widely recognized as fundamental.

Strengths and Weaknesses. The fundamental rights school resurrects a place for something resembling morality, reclaiming an aspirational and even a pedagogical function for law. It defines a ground of decision-making that can connect us to our past and help us mold our future. But like natural law, it suffers from the difficulty and inherent subjectivity of defining the principles to be enforced. It is vulnerable to the charge of preferencing one person's politics over another's. To the extent that the fundamental rights school seemed synonymous with liberal politics, the conservatives were ready with an alternative: law and economics.

EXERCISE 19-5

What fundamental rights influences do you see in the following excerpts from court opinions?

"This pattern of land use regulation has been adopted for the same purpose in developing municipality after municipality. Almost every one acts solely in its own selfish and parochial interest and in effect builds a wall around itself to keep out those people or entities not adding favorably to the tax base, despite the location of the municipality or the demand for varied kinds of housing. . . . One incongruous result is the picture of developing municipalities rendering it impossible for lower paid employees of industries they have eagerly sought and welcomed with open arms . . . to live in the community where they work." *Southern Burlington Co. NAACP v. Township of Mount Laurel,* 336 A.2d 713, 723 (1975).

"One should not be able to stand behind the impervious shield of caveat emptor [buyer beware] and take advantage of another's ignorance. . . ." *Johnson v. Davis,* 480 So. 2d 625, 628 (Fla. 1985).

"Confronted with a recognized shortage of safe, decent housing, today's tenant is in an inferior bargaining position compared to that of the landlord. *Park West Management Corp. v. Mitchell,* 391 N.E.2d 1288, 1292 (N.Y. 1979). Tenants vying for this limited housing are 'virtually powerless to compel the performance of essential services.' *Id.* at 1292. . . . In light of these changes in the relationship between tenants and landlords, it would be wrong for the law to continue to [hold that landlords have no duty to provide a habitable dwelling]. . . . Therefore, we now hold expressly that in the rental of any residential dwelling unit an implied warranty exists in the lease . . . that the landlord will deliver over and maintain . . . premises that are safe, clean and fit for human habitation." *Hilder v. St. Peter,* 478 A.2d 202, 207 (Vt. 1984).

VI. LAW AND ECONOMICS

Law and economics assesses legal doctrine on the basis of economic principles such as market dynamics, pricing, supply, and demand. Economics has been a part of legal analysis since the realists, but in recent years, economic analysis has become important enough to support a powerful jurisprudential movement of its own.

Proponents argue that, unlike the abstract values of fundamental rights, economic principles are concrete and objective. Some proponents would claim that economic analysis is apolitical. Law and economics emphasizes efficiency, market maximization, and the reduction of governmental controls. Early law and economic theorists argued that the law's goal should be maximizing social wealth, even at the expense of harm for individuals.[17]

wealth or welfare

The law and economics school includes a broad spectrum of approaches. For instance, some adherents still believe that law's primary goal should be wealth maximization, while more moderate proponents consider economic analysis only a component in law making, albeit an important one. Some assume that individual actors will act rationally to advance their own economic positions, while others recognize the perversities of human psychology. This breadth of exploration coupled with the badly needed economic expertise the movement encouraged has made law and economics a valuable jurisprudential movement.

Forms of Legal Reasoning. A judge with law and economics leanings would be persuaded particularly by policy-based reasoning, especially economic policy. Such a judge would be willing to interpret and apply legal rules in ways that would advance economic growth and would be ready to find seemingly analogous cases distinguishable because of differences in economic implications. Principle-based reasoning and custom-based reasoning would seem too amorphous to be of reliable help, and the narratives of the individual litigants might seem almost irrelevant unless they implicate the economic issues in the case. For a law and economics judge, rule-based reasoning should focus not on literal application of the rule's words, but on an interpretation of the rule on the assumption that its purpose is to increase social wealth.

Strengths and Weaknesses. Law and economics has offered a helpful and grounding counterweight to the fundamental rights school's abstraction and subjectivity. It has improved the economic sophistication of law and made important corrections to inaccurate economic assumptions. Its less extreme proponents have worked to improve the ways economic considerations can interact with other important considerations for the welfare of the society. In that sense, it has continued the work of the realists.

Law and economics has suffered primarily from three weaknesses: It sometimes has been too willing to credit economic conclusions not backed by sufficient research; it has been susceptible to unrealistic applications; and it

---

17. Bailey Kuklin & Jeffrey Stempel, *Foundations of the Law* at 169.

sometimes has been unwilling to admit the inherent political bias of its own perspective.

EXERCISE 19-6

What law and economics influences do you see in the following excerpts from court opinions?

> "[According to the applicable statute, a court can order the sale of co-owned property if one owner seeks partition and if division of the property cannot be made without great prejudice to the owners.] The language of this statute means that a sale may be ordered if it appears to the satisfaction of the court that the value of the share of each cotenant, in case of partition, would be materially less than his share of the money equivalent that could probably be obtained for the whole. [We give no weight to the fact that several of the cotenants have made the property their home for nearly forty years or to their interest in remaining on the family homestead.]" *Johnson v. Hendrickson*, 24 N. W.2d 914, 916 (S.D. 1946).

> "[When the markets of the nation are furnished by a business], there is great reason to give encouragement [to that business] . . . [T]he people who are so instrumental by their skill and industry so to furnish the markets should reap the benefit. . . ." *Keeble v. Hickeringill*, 3 Salk. 9 (Queen's Bench 1707).

> "Economic policies influence our decision as well. '[B]y virtue of superior knowledge, skill, and experience in the construction of houses, a builder-vendor is generally better positioned than the purchaser to . . . evaluate and guard against [and insure against] the financial risk posed by a [latent defect in the construction]." *Lempke v. Dagenais*, 547 A.2d 290, 295 (N.H. 1988) (internal citations omitted).

> "The safety of real estate titles is considered more important than the unfortunate results which may follow the application of the rule in a few individual instances." *Sweeney, Administratrix v. Sweeney*, 11 A.2d 806, 808 (Conn. 1940).

VII. CRITICAL LEGAL THEORY

One could never accuse the proponents of critical legal theory of denying its political bias. Critical legal theory admits that its own movement is all about politics, and it maintains that everyone else's is as well. For the sake of brevity and simplicity, we will include a number of diverse jurisprudential movements under the umbrella of critical legal theory, most notably critical legal studies, critical race theory, and feminist legal theory. Most of this description will focus on critical legal studies because much of its thinking is consistent with that of the other critical schools.

Critical Legal Studies (CLS) is perhaps the most direct heir of the Legal Realist School. CLS proponents consider law to be entirely subjective and political. They believe that purportedly objective legal rules actually reflect value choices that privilege politically powerful segments of society. Critical Legal Studies asserts that all legal reasoning is simply a post hoc rationalization rather than a description of a method of decision-making. Therefore, instead of articulated rules, CLS scholars trust narratives about the experiences of oppressed groups.

Ironically, CLS is willing to use a form of economic analysis too, one that asks directly about the distributional consequences for politically marginalized groups.[18] CLS supports the idea of an activist judiciary to empower such segments of society. Part of this political empowerment should be the demystification of legal processes so lay people can participate more effectively.

Critical race theory and feminist jurisprudence largely agree with CLS approaches but from an explicitly racial or gendered perspective.

Forms of Legal Reasoning. Because CLS has been largely a critique of the legal system from the outside, few CLS proponents have become judges. A judge with CLS sympathies, however, would pay particular attention to the narratives presented by the litigants and would be especially willing to explore the differing perspectives of the "outsiders." The judge also would be willing to listen to policy and principle-based reasoning to support a result that opens legal and political process and increases self-determination for marginalized groups. A CLS judge would be less persuaded by rule-based and custom-based reasoning, since each is embedded in the political and social power structure.

In comparison to the other schools of jurisprudence, CLS is less helpful as a guide to rule interpretation and application. It is most effectively used to challenge rule-based, natural law, and custom-based arguments by showing that they are masked assertions of oppressive power. It is not so much a form of argument in itself as a tool for deconstructing arguments for the status quo.

Strengths and Weaknesses. CLS has provided helpful deconstructions of law and law's origins, and it has reminded us that law must hear and represent all segments of society. It has, however, been heavy on critique and light on cure, and like law and economics, it has been vulnerable to extreme views. In the case of CLS, some of these views have advocated refusal to participate in a tainted process, but boycotting a process significantly limits one's ability to change it.

EXERCISE 19-7

What critical legal theory influences do you see in the following excerpt from a court opinion?

> "The plain truth is that the true object of the ordinance in question is to . . . regulate the mode of living of persons who may hereafter inhabit it. In the last analysis, the result to be accomplished is to classify the population and segregate them according to their income or situation in life. The true reason

---

18. *Id.* at 175.

why some persons live in a mansion and others in a shack, why some live in a single-family dwelling and others in a double-family dwelling, why some live in a two-family dwelling and others in an apartment, or why some live in a well-kept apartment and others in a tenement, is primarily economic. . . . [The ordinance furthers] these . . . class tendencies. . . ." *Amber Realty Co. v. Village of Euclid*, 297 F. 307, 316 (N.D. Ohio 1924).

VIII. THE JURISPRUDENCE OF LEGAL WRITING

We have seen a wide diversity of legal thought, just in this brief overview of some of the major jurisprudential schools, but they all have been vulnerable to one major weakness: the temptation of exclusivity. Each school has been a little too willing to think that it alone has discovered the truth. Each school has been a little too ready to reject the observations of the others.

Practicing lawyers and legal writers, however, know that exclusivity is folly. Every one of these jurisprudential schools teaches us something important about law. Each has perceived something real and true about how our legal system does and should function. And each of them needs the others' perspectives to support or temper its own.

More important for our purposes, each of these jurisprudential schools provides lawyers with important lessons about predicting what a judge might decide and about persuading a particular judge to rule in favor of a client. Sometimes you will know a particular judge well enough to tailor your arguments directly to that judge's jurisprudential leanings. However, even if you do not, imagine how much stronger your brief will be if you are careful to provide the judge with reasoning that covers the jurisprudential bases.

EXERCISE 19-8

Facts. In the past few years, the city of Annville has created a historic district in an effort to restore and preserve its architectural heritage. Several municipal programs have been implemented to encourage suburban residents to return to the city's center to live in restored older homes. A city-owned low-income housing apartment building is not far away from the historic district, and efforts are currently under way to decide what to do with it. The building is old and run down, and modern thinking about low-income housing is critical of the practice of building high-density units dedicated solely to low-income housing. Alternatives under consideration include remodeling the apartments and continuing their use as low-income housing; tearing down the apartment building and implementing a voucher system to enable low-income families to rent directly from private landlords throughout the city; and tearing down the apartment building and replacing it with city-owned low-income duplexes interspersed among private homes meant for moderate-income families.

A drug treatment clinic recently purchased property adjacent to the historic district, intending to open a drug treatment facility there. The location would be ideal because many of the clinic's present and potential patients live in the low-income apartments. At the time of the purchase, the zoning classification for that property permitted a treatment facility. Upon learning of the clinic's plans, however, residents of the historic district became fearful of the facility's effect on their neighborhood. These residents petitioned the zoning board to re-zone the block that includes the clinic's newly-purchased property. In response to the residents' petition, the zoning board has re-zoned that block to prohibit the clinic. The board notified the clinic's directors of the petition and allowed them to file a written response, but the board did not take testimony at a hearing, make any factual findings, or write an opinion that explained the reasons for the change. The following is the relevant statute pertaining to zoning changes:

> At any time after the adoption of a zoning ordinance, the zoning board may . . . amend the ordinance by a two-thirds vote of its members.

The clinic has appealed the zoning board's decision to the appropriate court, arguing both that the decision was wrong and that the procedure was faulty. Consider how the major jurisprudential perspectives might view this situation. What arguments could you use to support the clinic? What arguments would support the zoning change?

PART SIX

Style and Formalities

CHAPTER 20

Citations and Quotations

Now that you have a completed draft of the document, the next step is editing quotations and citation form. Review Chapter 1, section IV to be sure you understand why and when to cite. This chapter will explain how to cite.

I. CITATION IN LEGAL WRITING

In legal writing, as in other writing, you must cite to your sources for both words and ideas. Citation to authority has twin purposes: (1) to provide your reader with the authority that supports your assertions about the law, and (2) to attribute the words and ideas of another author to that author.

Providing your reader with authority to support your assertions about the law is essential to legal analysis and persuasive argument. Your citations should prove that the law is what you say it is and that it means what you say it means.

A citation is also your attribution to another author, recognizing that the ideas (and the words, if you are quoting) came from that author. Recall from the discussion of plagiarism on pages 9-11 the importance of careful attribution. Because a reader will attribute uncited material to you, a citation is your way of disclaiming credit for the words and ideas you did not create. Therefore, you should cite when you quote and when you paraphrase (that is, when you rephrase the authority's words).

USE CITATIONS

1. When you assert a legal principle.

"Intent is a required element of the Plaintiff's claim. *Peterson v. Taylor*, [citation]."

2. When you refer to or describe the content of an authority.

"In an earlier opinion, the court held that intent was irrelevant. *Crenshaw v. Baldwin*, [citation]."

3. When you quote.

"The court reasoned that 'the state of mind of the defendant had no impact on the extent of the damages suffered.' *Crenshaw v. Baldwin*, [citation]."

EXERCISE 20-1
Recognizing Ideas that Need Citations

Read the following passage[1] and identify the statements for which a citation is either necessary or desirable. Be prepared to explain your answers.

The lawyer has a fiduciary relationship with his or her client. The fiduciary aspect of the relationship is said to arise after the formation of the attorney-client relationship, and it applies to a fee agreement reached after the attorney-client relationship has been entered.

There are at least three reasons for imposing fiduciary obligations on a lawyer. Once the relationship is established, the client will likely have begun to depend on the attorney's integrity, fairness, and judgment. Second, the attorney may have acquired information about the client that gives the attorney an unfair advantage in negotiations between them. Finally, the client will generally not be in a position where he or she is free to change attorneys, but will rather be economically or personally dependent on the attorney's continued representation.

Several cases illustrate the contours of the attorney's fiduciary duty. In *Benson v. State Bar*, the attorney borrowed money from a current client. He "was heavily in debt, and insolvent, at the time he approached [the client] for these loans." In return for the loans, he gave the client unsecured promissory notes. In disbarring the lawyer, the court described the client's trust in the lawyer's judgment and wrote:

> The gravamen of the charge is abuse of that trust, and regardless of petitioner's contention that he never specifically recommended the unsecured loans to [the client], it is undisputed that in soliciting them he failed to reveal the extent of his preexisting indebtedness and financial distress.

In *People v. Smith*, James Smith, an attorney, was under investigation for drug use. He offered to cooperate with Colorado police as an undercover informant. He secretly recorded a telephone conversation with a former client in which he asked the former client to sell him cocaine. He then met with the former client wearing a body microphone. The recorded conversations were ultimately used to convict the former client of three felony charges. The Colorado Supreme Court held that although Smith

> no longer represented the [former client], the conduct in all probability would not have occurred had [Smith] not relied upon the trust and confidence placed in him by the [former client] as a result of the recently completed attorney-client relationship between the two. The undisclosed use of a recording device necessarily involves elements of deception and trickery which do not comport with the high standards of candor and fairness to which all attorneys are bound.

For these and other offenses, Smith was suspended from the practice of law.

---

1. Modified from Stephen Gillers, *Regulation of Lawyers: Problems of Law and Ethics* 61-62 (4th ed., Aspen 1995).

Now that you have decided *when* to cite to authority, turn your attention to *how* to cite.

II. CITATION FORM

A citation is your representation to your reader that the cited material stands for the proposition for which you cited it. It also allows a reader to find the source and provides the reader with some basic information for gauging the precedential weight the authority carries. Several commercially published citation authorities exist, and some courts have adopted their own citation rules. The two most often used sets of citation rules are the *ALWD* (pronounced "ALL-wid") *Citation Manual*[2] and *The Bluebook: A Uniform System of Citation* ("the *Bluebook*").[3]

The *ALWD Citation Manual* is a citation system designed primarily for law students, lawyers, and judges, whereas the *Bluebook* is designed primarily for academic publishing.[4] Virtually all of the common citation formats are the same, no matter which book you use. However, the more modern *ALWD Citation Manual* is easier to learn and requires no conversion of academic publishing formats to formats used by practitioners.

Learning to use one of the citation systems is unavoidable. As much as you might like to, you cannot simply copy the citations you find in the authorities your research reveals. Many citations in opinions, annotations, and secondary sources do not conform to current citation requirements. This chapter covers both the *ALWD Citation Manual* and the *Bluebook*. We begin by becoming familiar with the overall layout of both books.

A. Using the ALWD Citation Manual

1. Sections of the Manual

The *ALWD Citation Manual* contains the following sections and features:

1. *Part 1—Introductory Material:* The Manual begins with a short section expressly designed to introduce you to the book and show you how to use it. This section explains the book's organization and the "Finding Tools" that can give you quick answers to common citation questions. It also refers you to a Web site (www.alwd.org) where you can browse and download information at no charge. The site contains a section on

---

2. Association of Legal Writing Directors & Darby Dickerson, *ALWD Citation Manual, Third Edition* (Aspen Publishers 2006).
3. *The Bluebook: A Uniform System of Citation.* (Columbia Law Review Assn. et al. eds., 18th ed. 2005).
4. Because the *Bluebook* is older, many of today's lawyers were trained using it, and they may even use the name of the book as a verb. For instance, instead of saying "I have to check the citation form in my brief," a lawyer may say "I have to 'bluebook' my brief." A similar phenomenon occurred, for instance, when the brand name Kleenex™ was commonly used to refer to all brands of disposable tissues and the brand name Xerox™ was used to refer to all brands of photocopiers.

frequently asked questions and a section with updates. A particularly helpful feature of this section is the material discussing ways in which word processing software may affect citations. The section provides suggestions for handling margin settings, spacing, default settings, and quick-correct features, all of which can alter your citations in ways you did not intend. Reading these ten pages will help you understand how to use the *ALWD Manual* and how to manage your word processor.

2. *Part 2—Citation Basics*: This section gives you key general information, such as when to italicize or underline, how to select abbreviations, what to capitalize, and how to decide spacing. You'll need to be familiar with the foundational principles in this section before you look up a particular kind of citation form in later sections of the book.

3. *Part 3—Citing Specific Print Sources*: The specific citation rules covering all printed legal authorities are found in Part 3. The most commonly used are cases covered in Rule 12, statutes in Rule 14, books in Rule 22, and periodicals in Rule 23. One of the best features of the *ALWD Citation Manual* is the inclusion of Fast Formats at the beginning of each Rule covering particular sources. The Fast Format gives you, on a single page, examples of how to cite to that particular authority in all of the major circumstances in which you may need to cite it.

4. *Part 4—Electronic Sources*: This section tells you how to cite to electronic legal sources such as a World Wide Web site, cases from Westlaw and LEXIS, and CD-ROM materials.

5. *Part 5—Incorporating Citations Into Documents*: You'll find more basic information about how to use citations in this section, covering such common questions as how many and which citations to include, where to put them, in what order, how to use signals, and how to use explanatory parentheticals.

6. *Part 6—Quotations*: Pesky questions about handling citations effectively are answered here. This section covers use of quotations as they appear in the original source, alteration of quotations, and trimming quotations down to size.

7. *Appendices*: The appendices contain a wealth of important information. Appendix 1 tells you exactly how to cite all of the primary authority (like statutes and cases) from your particular jurisdiction. Appendix 2 gives you all of the promulgated court citation rules from each jurisdiction. Appendices 3-5 show you how to abbreviate almost all of the words you will need to abbreviate. Appendix 6 gives you a sample memo, so you can see a real example of how citations should appear in your final document. The Web site contains two additional appendices: Appendix 1-A (West's Regional Reporters) and Appendix 7 (abbreviations for certain federal administrative materials). Also, the Web site versions of Appendices 1, 2, 4, and 5 contain additional content.

2. How to Locate the Rules You Need

Finding the rules you need in the *ALWD Citation Manual* is not difficult. Here are the best strategies for locating particular rules or for finding out how to cite a particular source:

WAYS TO LOCATE THE RULES YOU NEED

1. For a quick way to find out how to cite a particular source, *use the Fast Format Locator on the inside front cover*. This handy list will take you immediately to the Fast Format for the source you're citing. If, for example, you want to see how to cite to a case, the Locator will refer you to the Fast Format found at the beginning of Rule 12, the rule covering cases. There, on a single page, you will find examples of how to use all of the major varieties of case cites. Then, if you need further clarification, you are already at the beginning of the section covering that source, and you can simply go further into the following pages to find out more. Notice that the *Short-Citation Locator* on the inside back cover provides a quick list of rules covering shortened citation formats.
2. If you can't find what you need by using a Fast Format, use the index, which is excellent.
3. To find larger sections of the *ALWD Manual*, such as the whole section covering electronic sources, use the Table of Contents.

B. Using the Bluebook

The *Bluebook* will intimidate you if you let it. The best way to approach the Bluebook is to cut it down to size mentally by identifying the primary parts you'll use. Notice the larger sections of the *Bluebook* as they are set out in the Table of Contents.

1. Sections of the Bluebook

1. *Introduction.* The *Bluebook* begins with an Introduction expressly designed for novices. The Introduction describes the parts of the *Bluebook* and points out the reference guides on the inside front and back covers.
2. *The Bluepages.* This section is necessary because the rest of the *Bluebook* focuses on citation form appropriate for law review publishing. The Bluepages section adapts the rules in the rest of the *Bluebook* to practitioner-writing—the kind you will be doing in your legal writing class and in practice. This section provides a table for suggested abbreviations to use in court documents and a table identifying jurisdiction-specific citation rules.
3. *Rules.* The rules themselves come next. Rules 1-9 are general rules about citation and style. They apply broadly to many citation situations. They are followed by rules dealing with citing particular kinds of sources. You will use Rules 10, 12, 15, and 16 (cases, statutes, books, and periodicals) most often.

4. *Tables*. After the rules comes a second set of tables. These are reference sources for basic information about court and reporter systems and statutory compilations for each jurisdiction as well as standard abbreviations for courts, case names, publications, and other commonly used terms.

2. How to Locate the Rules You Need

Now for ways to find the rules you need in the *Bluebook*. Here are the best strategies for locating particular rules:

WAYS TO LOCATE THE BLUEBOOK RULES YOU NEED
1. Use the *Bluebook's* index, which is quite good.
2. Use the Table of Contents.
3. When reading a particular rule, look at the listed cross-references.
4. Use the Quick Reference [for] Court Documents and Legal Memoranda set out on the last page and the *back* inside cover. (The one on the front inside cover and first page is for law review citations.)

C. Several Key Concepts

Your understanding of citation requirements will be eased by learning the following concepts right up front:

1. Citation Sentences Versus Citation Clauses. You may sometimes see references to "citation sentences" and "citation clauses." These phrases simply refer to the two places to put a citation—inside or outside a sentence of text.[5] You can put a citation inside a sentence of text, like so:

The Supreme Court has observed that employers and unions must have significant freedom in the creation of seniority systems, *California Brewers Assn. v. Bryant*, 444 U.S. 598, 608 (1980), but this freedom is not unlimited, *see, e.g., Nashville Gas Co. v. Satty*, 434 U.S. 136, 141 (1977).

Each of these citations is called a "citation *clause*" because the citation is *part* of a sentence of text and not a free-standing unit unto itself.

The cite to *California Brewers Association* is placed immediately after the part of the sentence it supports. The writer has not placed it at the end of the sentence because the writer is citing it as support for only the proposition stated in the first part of the sentence. The cite to *Nashville Gas Company* is placed immediately after the part of the sentence it supports, but the writer has not placed it outside the period because it is not cited as support for the entire

---

5. *See* ALWD R. 43.1 or Bluebook R. 1.1 and B2.

sentence. It supports only the proposition stated in the last half of the sentence.

A citation also can be placed outside the sentence of text, like so:

> The Supreme Court has observed that employers and unions must have significant freedom in the creation of seniority systems. *California Brewers Assn. v. Bryant*, 444 U.S. 598, 608 (1980).

This citation is called a "citation *sentence*" because the citation is *not* a part of a sentence of text. The citation is placed outside the period because the writer is citing the case as support for all the material in the sentence of text.

2. Typeface Requirements. The *Bluebook*'s rules (the white pages) are designed primarily for law review writing rather than for practitioner-writing. For law review writing, the *Bluebook* requires, on different occasions, large and small capitals, regular typeface, and italics. The examples and explanations in the rules section (the white pages) employ those distinctions among typefaces. Practitioner-writing is simpler, however, using only regular type such as courier and *either* italics or underscoring. Simply type everything else in regular typeface, and don't worry about the more complicated distinctions in the rules section of the Bluebook.

Unlike the *Bluebook*, the *ALWD Manual* follows the commonly accepted approach for practitioner writing.[6] Most material in a citation is presented in ordinary type. The only typeface variation is the use of italics for certain parts of a citation. The particular rule covering a particular legal source will tell you (and show you) which information, if any, to italicize, so selecting the correct typeface is easy. Notice, however, that for practitioner-writing, both the *ALWD Manual* and the *Bluebook* use the word "italics" to include either slanted type or underscoring.[7] You can use either, but don't use both in the same document.

3. Citing in Text Versus Citing in a Footnote. Law review articles are notorious for footnotes, and the rules section of the *Bluebook* provides special requirements for citations in law review footnotes. However, footnotes should be the exception rather than the rule for practitioner-writing. When practitioners *do* use a footnote, they usually use the same citation principles they have been using in the text.

D. Introduction to Citation Form

While the applicable rules are more detailed, an overview of the basic components of a legal citation will help you put the more detailed rules into a context. Here are the basic components of a citation to a case, a statute, a book, and a law review article:

---

6. Actually, the *ALWD Manual* eliminates the distinctions between academic writing and practitioner writing.
7. ALWD R. 1.1; Bluebook B.13.

BASIC COMPONENTS OF A CITATION TO A CASE
1. Case name
2. Case's location:
   a. Volume
   b. Abbreviation for name of reporter
   c. Page where the case begins
   d. Page where the cited material appears
3. Court abbreviation
4. Year

State Court Example

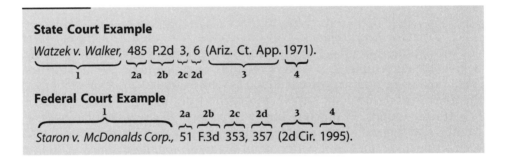

Federal Court Example

BASIC COMPONENTS OF A CITATION TO A STATUTE
1. Title number (if the code uses title numbers)
2. Abbreviation for name of code
3. Section number
4. Year the code was published

Example

BASIC COMPONENTS OF A CITATION TO A BOOK
1. Author's name(s)
2. Title of book
3. Volume number, if any
4. Section, paragraph, or page number
5. Edition number, if more than one
6. Publisher[8]
7. Year

---

8. The *Bluebook* format does not include the publisher of a book.

Example

Richard H. Chused, *A Property Anthology* 149 (2d ed., Anderson 1997).

BASIC COMPONENTS OF A CITATION TO A LAW REVIEW ARTICLE
1. Author's name
2. Title of article
3. Location of article:
   a. Volume number
   b. Abbreviation for name of law review
   c. Page where article begins
   d. Page where cited material appears
4. Year

Example

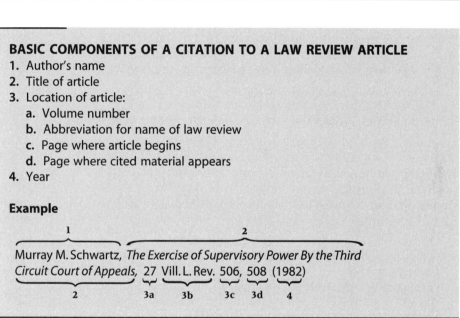

Murray M. Schwartz, *The Exercise of Supervisory Power By the Third Circuit Court of Appeals,* 27 Vill. L. Rev. 506, 508 (1982)

E. Matching the Citation to the Text

A writer tells the reader which proposition the citation establishes by the *placement* of the citation.[9] If the citation appears outside the textual sentence, standing alone as a citation sentence, the reader knows that the citation supports all of the material in the preceding sentence, like so:

> To prove a claim for sexual harassment without showing an adverse employment action, a plaintiff must show that the harassment created a "hostile or abusive work environment" and that the plaintiff indicated that the harassment was unwelcome. *Meritor Sav. Bank v. Vinson*, 477 U.S. 57, 66 (1986).

This sentence says two things: that the plaintiff must show a hostile environment and that the plaintiff must show that he or she communicated that the conduct was unwelcome. The placement of the citation to *Meritor* outside the textual sentence tells the reader that *Meritor* establishes both of these points.

However, if *Meritor* established only one of these points, the citation to *Meritor* would go inside the textual sentence and immediately after the

---

9. ALWD R. 43.1; Bluebook R. 1.1.

proposition it supports. The writer would need to cite to another authority for the other proposition, like so:

> To prove a claim for sexual harassment without showing an adverse employment action, a plaintiff must show that the harassment created a "hostile or abusive work environment," *Meritor Sav. Bank v. Vinson*, 477 U.S. 57, 66 (1986), and that the plaintiff indicated that the harassment was unwelcome [cite to the other case].

A similar situation exists when the writer has authority for one part of the sentence but no authority for the other part of the sentence. In that case, the writer should still take care to place the citation immediately after the proposition it supports, simply leaving the other proposition unsupported, like so:

> Though a plaintiff can prove a claim by showing that the harassment created a "hostile or abusive work environment," *Meritor Sav. Bank v. Vinson*, 477 U.S. 57, 66 (1986), Willingham has made no such showing in this case.

Sometimes a writer points out an aspect of an authority and then uses that aspect of the authority to reason her way to another point about that authority. The first point came from the authority but the second point did not; the second point came from the writer's own reasoning process. Once again, the writer should place the citation to the authority immediately after the point that came from the authority rather than after the writer's reasoning process, like so:

> The court has allowed recovery on an attractive nuisance claim by a child who came into the defendants' yard to hide from her friends and fell into a swimming pool while there. [The citation to *Newcomb v. Roberts* goes here.] Though *Newcomb* made no mention of the issue, the court's allowance of recovery on these facts shows that recovery no longer requires that the child be drawn by the artificial condition. [The citation to *Newcomb* does *not* go here because *Newcomb* does not say that actual attraction is no longer required.]

EXERCISE 20-2
Identifying the Text the Citation Supports

Identify the proposition(s) each of the following citations supports.

A malpractice action can be based on conduct other than a failure to exercise the proper standard of care. It also can be based on violation of a duty the lawyer owes the client as a fiduciary. For example, a fiduciary's duty of loyalty requires her to avoid conflicts of interest. *Simpson v. James*, 903 F.2d 372 (5th Cir. 1990). Ethics rules require the same, ABA Model R. Prof. Conduct 1.7-1.9 (1998), and a violation of a rule of ethics is considered evidence of malpractice, *Beattie v. Firnschild*, 394 N.W.2d 107, 109 (Mich. 1986). If a client suffers a loss as a result of a lawyer's conflict of interest, the client will be able to recover in malpractice. *Simpson*, 903 F.2d at 377; *Miami Intl. Realty Co. v. Paynter*, 841 F.2d 348, 353 (10th Cir. 1988).

Similarly, except in limited circumstances, a fiduciary may not reveal a client's confidential information to the client's disadvantage. Not only is this an ethical rule, ABA Model R. Prof. Conduct 1.6 (1998), but if a lawyer improperly reveals confidential information, a malpractice action will lie. *Tri-Growth Centre City, Ltd. v. Silldorf, Burdman, Duignan & Eisenberg*, 216 Cal. App. 3d 1139, 265 Cal. Rptr. 330 (Div. 1, 4th Dist. 1990).

Breach of fiduciary duty also can occur if a lawyer helps another agent of a client violate the agent's fiduciary duties to the client. *Avianca, Inc. v. Corriea*, 705 F. Supp. 666 (D.D.C. 1989).

F. Citing with Style and Grace

Citations in the text of a document can make the text hard to read. A reader has to jump over all the names, numbers, and parentheticals; find the spot where the text begins again and then pick back up on the message of the text. Granted, law-trained readers become fairly good at these mental and visual gymnastics, but even law-trained readers can use all the help a writer can give them. Here are some suggestions for minimizing the disruption caused by citations:

1. Case names and citations placed in the middle of the sentence make it hard to find the key parts of the sentence and combine them into a coherent thought. For instance, notice how a reader must hop through this sentence:

> A majority of the Court in *General Electric Company v. Gilbert*, 429 U.S. 125, 136 (1976), followed *Geduldig v. Aiello*, 417 U.S. 484 (1974), and held that pregnancy classifications were not gender classifications.

When possible, use the following techniques to clear the reader's path from subject to verb to object:

> a. Move the citation outside the sentence and into its own citation sentence.
> b. Move the citation to the beginning of the sentence.
> c. When the sentence contains two propositions, each requiring its own authority, consider dividing the sentence into two sentences. Then each citation can be moved outside the textual sentences.
> d. Consider moving less important material into a parenthetical in the citation.

Notice how techniques b and d have improved the readability of the sentence:

> In *General Electric Company v. Gilbert*, 429 U.S. 125, 136 (1976) (following *Geduldig v. Aiello*, 417 U.S. 484 (1974)), a majority of the Court held that pregnancy classifications were not gender classifications.

If the case name is not important, you could even move the citation outside the textual sentence, like this:

> In 1974, a majority of the Court held that pregnancy classifications were not gender classifications. *General Electric Company v. Gilbert*, 429 U.S. 125, 136 (1976) (following *Geduldig v. Aiello*, 417 U.S. 484 (1974)).

2. Avoid beginning a sentence with a citation when the citation will make the sentence hard to read. Here is an example of a sentence with this impediment and an improved version:

> *Change*   Public Law 95-555, 92 Stat. 2076, October 31, 1978, included a new §701(k).
>
> *To*   Congress added a new version of §701(k) when it enacted Public Law 95-555, 92 Stat. 2076, October 31, 1978.

3. As a general rule, avoid long string citations. *String citation* is the term lawyers use for "stringing" a number of citations together to support the same proposition. Lawyers often cite several authorities for an important proposition, but the longer the "string," the more the citations impair readability. Further, as citations are devoid of discussion, the long list seldom adds much to the legal analysis.

Generally, it is better to cite and discuss the several most important authorities and omit the others. However, string cites are appropriate when your reader needs every relevant authority or when you wish to demonstrate, graphically on the page, the overwhelming strength of support for the proposition.[10]

EXERCISE 20-3
Editing the Placement of Citations

Use the techniques described in section D to make the following passage more readable and to be sure that the placement of the citation accurately identifies the textual material it supports:

42 U.S.C. §2000e-2(a) prohibits employers from discriminating against applicants or employees based on the individual's race or sex. The act, titled the "Civil Rights Act of 1964," protects individuals of all races and both genders, not just minorities and women. *McDonald v. Santa Fe Trail Transp. Co.*, 427 U.S. 273, 280 (1976); *Hannon v. Chater*, 887 F. Supp. 1303, 1312 (N.D. Cal. 1995); *Hall v. City of Brawley*, 887 F. Supp. 1333, 1342 (S.D. Cal. 1995); *Curler v. City of Fort Wayne*, 591 F. Supp. 327, 333 (N.D. Ind. 1984).

However, the Court has never been comfortable with the issues raised by the application of Title VII to the racial majority or to men. In *United Steelworkers of America v. Weber*, 443 U.S. 193, 215 (1979), the Supreme Court upheld a voluntary race-conscious affirmative action plan, but several years later the Court held that, to be permissible, a voluntary affirmative action plan had to benefit only "actual victims of the discriminatory practice." *Firefighters Local 1784 v. Stotts*, 467 U.S. 561, 579 (1984).

Just three years later, the Court, in *Johnson v. Transportation Agency of Santa Clara County*, 480 U.S. 616 (1987), seemed to reaffirm its holding in *Weber* when it expressly followed the *Weber* holding. The Court wrote that the *Johnson* issues "must be guided by our decision in *Weber*." Id. at 627. *Johnson* dealt with a voluntary affirmative action plan designed to improve the representation of racial minorities and of women in traditionally male jobs. *Johnson v. Transp. Agency of Santa Clara County*. Id. at 627.

G. Editing Citation Form

This section assumes that you have looked up the relevant citation rules in your citation manual. What follows is an editing checklist to help you find the most common citation errors.

---

10. If you do cite to multiple authorities, place them in the order set out by ALWD Rule 45 or *Bluebook* Rules 1.3 and 1.4.

Checklist for Editing Citations

General Principles

		ALWD	*BB*
1.	Where possible, have you cited legal authority for each point you have made about the law or the authority?	pp. 3-4	B1
2.	Have you placed each citation immediately after the proposition it supports?	43.1	1.1 B2
3.	Have you placed your citations at the end or the beginning of your sentences whenever possible?	—	—
4.	Have you avoided unnecessary string citations?	43.3	—
5.	Have you minimized the number of sentences beginning with a citation?	—	—
6.	Have you italicized or underscored using an unbroken line:	1.1 1.3	B13

- Case names, titles of books, and articles?
- Signals (such as *e.g.* or *see*)?
- Phrases giving prior or subsequent history (such as *aff'd* or *cert. denied*)?
- Terms used in short citation forms to indicate a cross-reference (such as *id.*)?

		ALWD	*BB*
7.	For citing all authorities other than names of periodicals, have you closed up all adjacent single capitals, individual numerals, and ordinals (for example, ''3d''), and initials in personal names?	2.2 4.3	6.1(a)
8.	Have you left a space between single capitals and multiple letter abbreviations (for example ''F. Supp.'')?	2.2(c)	6.1(a)
9.	When you put the citation outside the sentence, have you placed a period at the end of the citation?	43.1(a)	B2
10.	When you put the citation inside a sentence, have you set off the citation with commas?	43.1(b)	B2
11.	When you have cited to several authorities together, have you separated them with a semicolon?	45.2	B2
12.	In a title, have you capitalized according to the relevant rule?	3	8
13.	Have you placed multiple authorities in the order set out by the relevant rule?	45	1.4

Quotations

		ALWD	BB
14.	For all cites to the quotation, including parallel citations, have you included the pinpoint cite to the page where the quoted material appears?	5.2(b)(1)	3.2 B5.1.2
15.	When you have used a block quote, have you placed the citation at the normal left margin on the line immediately following the block quote?	47.5(c)	5.1(a)
16.	When the source to which you are citing has quoted the material from another source, have you used an explanatory parenthetical?	47.7(c)	5.2(e)
17.	When you have added or deleted citations or indications of emphasis, have you used an explanatory parenthetical?	48.4 49.3(d)	5.2
18.	Where you have altered a quote, such as by changing a lowercase letter to an uppercase letter, have you signaled the alteration by using square brackets?	48	5.2
19.	Have you indicated an omission with an ellipsis?	49.2 49.3	5.3

Cases
Long Form

		ALWD	BB
20.	Have you used only the last names of the individual parties?	12.2(d)	10.2.1(g) B5.1.1(ii)
21.	Have you omitted all parties other than the first party listed on each side?	12.2(c)	10.2.1(a) B5.1.1(I)
22.	Have you avoided using "et al." to signal that you have omitted the names of additional parties?	12.2(c)(2)	10.2.1(a) B5.1.1.(iii)
23.	Have you used "v." (rather than "vs" or "v" or "V")?	12.2(c)(4)	B5.1.1(i)
24.	Have you abbreviated case names in citations according to the relevant rule?	12.2(e) App. 3	10.2.2 T. 6
25.	Have you placed a comma after the case name and refrained from underlining or italicizing the comma?	1.1 1.4	B5.1.1 10 B5.1.1
26.	For federal district court and circuit court cases, have you closed up the spaces in "F.3d" but left a space in "F. Supp."?	2.2 FastFormat, p. 63	6.1(a)
27.	Have you included a pinpoint cite to the page(s) of the opinion where the referenced material is located?	5.2	3.2 B5.1.2

28. Have you refrained from placing any punctuation between the page number of the case and the parenthetical?	12.1	10
29. Have you included the opinion's date in parentheses?	12.7 12.12(a)(1)	10.5
30. For cases from a state's highest court, where the state is not unambiguously conveyed by the reporter title, have you included the name of the state in the parentheses?	12.4(c)(3) 12.6(e) App. 1	10.4(b)
31. For state cases where the court deciding the case is not the highest court of the state, have you included the court's name and district or division in the parenthetical?	12.6(a) App. 1	10.4(b)
32. For cases from federal circuit courts, have you identified the circuit in the parenthetical and used the correct abbreviation for it (1st Cir., 2d Cir., 3d Cir., 4th Cir., 5th Cir., 6th Cir., 7th Cir., 8th Cir., 9th Cir., 10th Cir., 11th Cir., D.C. Cir., Fed. Cir.)?	12.6(a) App. 4	10.4(a) T. 7
33. For federal district courts, have you identified the district in the parenthetical (for example, "S.D. Cal.")?	12.6(b) App. 4	10.4(a)
34. Have you refrained from putting a comma between the date and any other information within the parenthetical?	12.6(a)(3)	10
35. For the circumstances set out in the relevant rule, have you included the subsequent history in a full citation to a case?	12.8	10.7.1 B5.1.5
36. Have you used a comma to separate the subsequent history of the case?	12.8(c)(2)	10.7.1 B5.1.3
37. Have you included an explanatory phrase in a second parenthetical (and before any subsequent history) when additional information would be helpful for evaluating the weight properly given to the authority?	12.11(a)(b) 46	10.7.1 B5.1.4
38. Where a phrase of information would help the reader understand the significance of the cited authority, have you included that information in an explanatory parenthetical?	12.11(c) 46	1.5 B5.1.4

	ALWD	BB
39. Have you complied with the relevant rule by using the appropriate signal to introduce cited authorities that:	44.3	1.2

- represent one example of many authorities standing for the same proposition? (*E.g.*)
- support the stated proposition implicitly (rather than explicitly) or in dicta? (*See*)
- support the stated proposition by analogy only? (*Cf.*)
- are compared to each other to show different results? (*Compare . . . with*)
- directly contradict the stated proposition? (*Contra*)
- contradict the stated proposition by analogy? (*But cf.*)
- provide background information? (*See generally*)

	ALWD	BB
40. Have you underscored or italicized all signals?	44.6(b)	B13
41. Have you refrained from using a signal when the authority directly supports the stated proposition?	44.2(a)	1.2(a)
42. When you are citing to a concurring or dissenting opinion, have you disclosed in a parenthetical this potential limitation on the weight of the cited material?	12.11	10.6
43. Have you indicated by parenthetical any other limitations on the weight of the cited material (for example that the cited language is dictum or that your proposition is contained in the cited material only by implication)?	12.11(b)	10.6
44. For cases available only on an electronic database, have you followed the format provided in the relevant rule?	12.7(c) 12.21(d)	10.8.1

Parallel Citations

	ALWD	*BB*
45. When more than one source is available, have you cited to the appropriate source?	12.4(a)(2)	10.3.1 B5.1.3
46. When citing United States Supreme Court cases, have you cited to the official reporter (U.S.) where possible?	12.4(b)	10.3.1 T. 1 B5.1.3

Short Forms

	ALWD	*BB*
47. Have you used a full citation the first time you cite to a particular authority?	11.1(c)(1)	B5.2
48. Have you chosen to use a short citation form with reader's needs in mind?	11.1(c)(2)	B5.2
49. When you have used *id.*, have you been referring to the case cited immediately prior to the *id.* cite?	11.3(b)	4.1 B5.2
50. Have you refrained from using *supra* to refer to a case?	11.3(b)(2) 11.4(b)(2)	4.2 B5.2

Statutes and Rules

	ALWD	*BB*
51. Have you abbreviated the statutory compilation as provided in the relevant table?	App. 1	T. 1
52. If the information would be helpful, have you given the statute's name (official or popular)?	14.2(g)	12.3.1(a)
53. If possible, have you cited to the official code rather than to an unofficial code?	14.1(b) App. 1	12.2.1 T. 1
54. Have you included in parentheses the year of the code you are citing (*not* the year the statute was enacted)?	14.2(f)	12.3.2
55. Have you identified the title, chapter, or volume number, if any, according to the relevant rule?	14.2 App. 1	12.3.1(b) T. 1
56. Have you refrained from using "*et seq.*," but rather designated the exact sections you are citing?	14.2(d)	3.3(b)
57. Have you left a space after the section symbol?	2.2(f) 6.2	6.2(c)
58. If you have cited a privately published version of the code, have you identified the publisher in the parenthetical that contains the year?	14.2(e) 14.4 App. 1	12.3.1(d) T. 1
59. If you are citing material contained in a supplement, either alone or in addition to material contained in the main volume, have you followed the format shown in the relevant rule?	8.1 8.3	3.1(c) 12.3.1(e)
60. If you are citing a statute that has been repealed or superseded, have you followed the format shown in the relevant rule?	14.3 14.4	12.6
61. If you are citing rules of evidence or procedure, have you followed the format provided in the relevant rule?	17.1-17.3	12.8.3

62.	Have you used a full citation the first time you cite to the statute?	11.1(c)(1)	B6.2
63.	If you used a short form of citation, have you followed the format set out in the relevant rule?	14.6	12.9 14.10 B6.2

Books

		ALWD	***BB***
64.	For the first citation to the book, have you used the author's full name followed by a comma?	22.1(a)	15.1
65.	If the book has more than one author, have you followed the relevant rule?	22.1(a)(2)	15.1
66.	If the book has an editor or translator, have you followed the relevant rule?	22.1(d) 22.1(e)	15.2
67.	Have you italicized the name of the book?	22.1(b)	B13
68.	Have you capitalized the name of the book as set out in the relevant rule?	3.1	8 15.3
69.	Have you cited to the latest edition and identified the edition in the parenthetical?	22.1(f)	15.4
70.	In the parenthetical, have you identified the year of publication and (if you are using the *ALWD Manual*) the publisher?	22.1(j) 22.1(i)	15.4
71.	If the cited material appears in a supplement, have you followed the format set out in the relevant rule?	8.1-8.3	3.1
72.	If you have used a short form for later citations to the same book, have you complied with the relevant rule?	22.2	15.9 B8.2
73.	Have you used a pinpoint cite to identify the page(s) on which the cited material appears?	5.2 22.1(c)	3.2(a) B8.1 B8.2

Periodicals

		ALWD	***BB***
74.	Have you provided the author's full name (including student authors) followed by a comma?	23.1(a)	15.1 16.1
75.	Have you italicized the title of the article and followed the title with a comma?	23.1(b)(3)	B13
76.	Have you capitalized the title in accordance with the relevant rule?	3.1	8
77.	Have you abbreviated the periodical as set out in the relevant table? If your periodical is not included in the list, have you used the relevant rules as your	23.1(d) App. 3 App. 5	T. 13

guides for constructing the periodical's abbreviation?

78.	Have you followed the relevant rule for spacing between the letters abbreviating the periodical name?	2.2	6.1(a)
79.	Have you included the volume number of the periodical (before the abbreviated title of the periodical)?	23.1(c)	16.3
80.	Have you identified the page on which the article begins, placing it after the abbreviated title of the periodical and refraining from using a "p." or "pp."?	23.1(e)	16.3 & 16.4
81.	Have you included a pinpoint cite to the page(s) where the cited material is found?	5.2 23.1(e)(2)	16.3 & 16.4 B9.1
82.	Have you refrained from putting a comma between the page number and the parenthetical?	23.1	16
83.	Unless the periodical uses the date for the volume number, have you included the date of the volume in the parenthetical?	23.1(f)	16.3 16.4

EXERCISE 20-4
Editing for Citation Form

Edit the following citations for correct citation form. Use the checklist in section G. If you spot an error that you cannot correct without additional information, simply note the error and identify the information you would need to correct it.

1. *Leibel vs. Raynor Manufacturing Co.*, 571 S.W. 2nd 640 (1978).
2. Brown v. New Haven Civil Service Comm., 474 F.Supp. 1256, 1263, (1979).
3. *Equal Pay Act of 1963*, 29 USC §206(d), *et seq.*
4. *Connecticut v. Winnie Teal, et al.*, supra at 444.
5. Harold S. Lewis, Jr., Litigating Civil rights and Employment Discrimination cases, 1996. (This is a book.)
6. *Humphrey v. McLaren*, 402 N.W.2d 535 (Minn, 1987). [cited in a brief filed before a trial court in Minnesota]
7. *Prandini v. National Tea Co., Id.* at 49.
8. Jack Lee Sammons, *The Professionalism Movement: the Problems Defined*, 7 Notre Dame Journ. of Law, Ethics & Public Pol. 269, 1993.
9. e.g., *U.S. Dept. of Labor v. Triplett*, 494 US 715, 716 (1990).
10. *Laffey v. Northwest Airlines, Inc.*, 567 F.2d 429, 431 (1978).

III. QUOTATIONS

The most common quotation problems are (1) failing to use quotation marks for borrowed language, (2) using too many quotations, (3) insufficiently editing quotations, and (4) making errors in the mechanics of quoting. The remainder of this chapter deals with these common quotation problems.

A. When Quotation Marks Are Required

Quotation marks are required to designate places where a writer has used the words of another.[11] Requiring quotation marks furthers several important policies.[12] First, the quotation marks ensure that the creator will have the credit (or blame) for the creation. Second, the quotation marks allow the writer to avoid claiming undeserved credit; even if the creator does not desire recognition, you should not take credit for someone else's work. Finally, the quotation marks inform readers of the source of the creation. Irrespective of the interests of the two authors, readers deserve accurate information about who created what.

For these policy reasons, quotation marks are necessary when you quote the words of another but unnecessary when you paraphrase. However, sometimes it is hard to know whether a particular passage is a quotation or a paraphrase. When are the words yours and when are they "the words of another"?

Start with the proposition that you should attempt to rephrase the thoughts of others into your own words and sentence structures. However, even if you are not looking at the source while you write, you may find that your text turns out to be similar to your source's text. This result can occur because the source uses words that are commonly used to express the idea; because the sentence structure the source used is commonplace; because without realizing it, you have been thinking of the topic in the source's words; or some combination of all three.

If the original text used the word "table" and you use it too, no one would argue that you should put quotation marks around "table" in your document. However, if your draft shares a whole paragraph in common with the original text, everyone understands that the paragraph must be designated by quotation marks or by blocking the material. Somewhere between these two extremes lies the point at which the words are those of another (and quotation marks become necessary), but no bright-line test will tell you precisely where.

The absence of a clear test is particularly unfortunate for legal writers. Legal writers rely heavily on sources, and most legal writing texts advise writers to paraphrase rather than quote the majority of those sources. If you follow this good advice, you will be doing a lot of paraphrasing. How can you know whether your paraphrase is sufficiently different from the original author's text to free you from the requirement of using quotation marks?

---

11. *Ideas* that come from another author must always be attributed to the other author. This section assumes that you are attributing the *ideas* to their source, according to proper citation form. Here we deal only with deciding when to attribute the *words* as well.

12. Copyright law can create legal requirements in addition to the policies described here.

To gauge how similar your text is to another writer's text, consider the *combined effect* of these factors: (1) the length of the common unit of text, (2) the number of units in common, (3) whether the sentence structure is the same or similar, and (4) whether the common units include language that the original author used in particularly effective ways.

Some writers use a seven-word benchmark as a starting point for measuring the length of a common unit requiring quotation marks; if seven or more words used together in your text match the text of the source, use quotation marks for those words. The benchmark recognizes the unlikelihood of a common seven-word unit appearing inadvertently in text by different authors. It also acknowledges that a passage of at least seven words is sufficiently long to merit recognition of the original author for assembling the words into a unit of text, even if it is the only common unit and even if the unit has no distinctive characteristics or particular merits. So be sure to use quotation marks *at least* for any unit of seven or more words that your text shares in common with another.

However, don't think you can avoid using quotation marks simply by changing every seventh word. The seven-word benchmark is only an approximate measure of when the writing is similar enough to require quotation marks, and it only applies when no other similarities are present. You also must consider whether there are other common units of text and whether the sentence structure is similar. Would an objective reader think that this passage is fundamentally someone else's, with just a few surface changes?

Finally, consider the nature of the common text, for you must use quotation marks for language an author has used in a particularly vivid, creative, or unusual way. Attributing the word or phrase to the original author recognizes that author's use of those words to convey the idea so effectively. For instance, the first sentence of the prior paragraph uses the words "you must use quotation marks." The words number only five, so if there are no other similarities, they probably do not constitute a phrase long enough to merit recognition of the author simply for putting them together as a unit. Nor was the author particularly original or effective in selecting those words, in combining them, or in applying them to the idea being discussed. Using these words probably would not require quotation marks attributing the words to the first author.

However, sometimes an author's use of particular words for a particular idea makes the words stand out. For instance, in *Griggs v. Duke Power Company*, Chief Justice Burger condemned employer practices that function as "built-in headwinds" impeding employment for minority groups.[13] In *Watson v. Fort Worth Bank and Trust*, Justice O'Connor described the positions argued by the parties as "stark and uninviting alternatives."[14] In his dissent in *Wards Cove Packing Company v. Atonio*, Justice Stevens described the living and working conditions at the defendant's canneries as "a plantation economy."[15]

These are examples of words and phrases used in distinctive ways. In each case, the author was especially effective in selecting the words to express the idea. In each case, the author's effective use of language merits recognition, and other writers who use these phrases should give credit to the original author by using quotation marks.

---

13. 401 U.S. 424, 432 (1971).
14. 487 U.S. 977, 989 (1988).
15. 490 U.S. 642, 662 n. 4 (1989).

Like the "reasonable person" standard or the "best interests of the child" standard, the "using the words of another" standard is open to interpretation. It is far better either to use quotation marks or to paraphrase the passage more thoroughly than to risk questions about whose writing the passage really reflects.

B. Choosing to Use Quotation Marks

Even if quotation marks are not required, a legal writer may choose to use them anyway—to communicate information important to the reader. The most common occasions for this kind of quoting are when the analysis must apply a particular legal test or when the analysis must construe particular words of a statute. Here are examples of each:

PARTICULAR LEGAL TEST
A lawyer must use the degree of skill commonly exercised by a "reasonable, careful and prudent lawyer." *Cook, Flanagan & Berst v. Clausing*, 438 P.2d 865, 867 (Wash. 1968).

PARTICULAR WORDS OF STATUTE
Title VII makes it unlawful for a labor organization "to exclude or expel" an individual because of religion. 42 U.S.C. §2000-2(c)(1) (1994).

Even though quotation marks would not be required for these words, the writer should use them anyway to let the reader know that these are the words at issue in the analysis.

C. Overquoting

Chapter 7 warned against using too many quotations.[16] There, in the working draft stage, the reason for the warning was the danger of confusing copying the authorities with analyzing them. The editing stage raises two more reasons to minimize quotes. First, many readers are tempted to skip quoted material entirely. Perhaps they assume that the quoted material simply supports the points already asserted by the current writer. Perhaps they are discouraged by the single-spacing of a block quote. Whatever the reason, busy readers do tend to skim or skip quoted material.

Second, a quotation seldom communicates your point as clearly, directly, and succinctly as you could. After all, the original writer was not writing about *your* case. Your paraphrase can do what quotations cannot, that is, tie the substance of the precedential source directly to the issues of *your* case.

As a general rule, limit yourself to quoting only in the following circumstances:

1. Quote when the issue will turn on the interpretation of particular words of a statute, rule, or key case, as described above. Limit the

---

16. ALWD Rule 47.1 contains the same caution.

quotation to *those particular words* so your reader will understand the issue and your analysis of it. Here is an example of part of a discussion using quotation marks for this purpose:

> A lawyer must use great care in deciding whether to undertake representation of a new client when that representation might be directly adverse to an existing client. The existing client must consent to the lawyer's representation of the new client. ABA Model R. Prof. Conduct 1.7(a)(2) (1998). However, even if the client consents, the lawyer must not undertake the new representation unless the lawyer "reasonably believes" that the new representation will not "adversely affect the relationship" with the existing client. *Id.* at §1.7(a)(1).

2. Quote *key* language from an authority with a great deal of precedential value. This could be mandatory authority or highly respected persuasive authority such as an opinion of the United States Supreme Court, a provision of a Restatement of Law, or an opinion written by a respected judge.
3. Quote *key* language when the author has found a particularly effective way to express the idea you want to convey.

> Under Rule 60(b) the court possesses "a grand reservoir of equitable power" to accomplish justice. *Thompson v. Kerr-McGee Ref. Corp.*, 660 F.2d 1380, 1385 (10th Cir. 1981).

D. The Mechanics of Quoting

Here is an editing checklist to help you flag the most common quotation errors:

1. Quotations of fifty or more words, or four or more typed lines of text, should be indented from both side margins. The indentation indicates that the material is quoted, thus eliminating the need for quotation marks around the quoted material. Indented quotations should be single-spaced. *ALWD* R. 47.5(a); *Bluebook* R. 5.1(a).
2. Quotations shorter than fifty words or four typed lines of text should not be indented or single-spaced and should be enclosed within quotation marks. *ALWD* R. 47.4(a); *Bluebook* R. 5.1(b).
3. Place end punctuation within the quotation marks if it is part of the material you are quoting. For punctuation you add, place commas and periods inside the quotation marks, but place other added punctuation outside the quotation marks. *ALWD* R. 47.4(d); *Bluebook* R. 5.1(b).

> "Discriminatory employment practices are prohibited."
> [The period is part of the quoted material.]
>
> The statute prohibits "discriminatory employment practices".
> [The period is not part of the quoted material.]
>
> Does the statute prohibit "discriminatory employment practices"?
> [The question mark is not part of the quoted material.]

4. Show changes in the quotation by using brackets and ellipses. Use brackets when you replace letters or words or when you add material to the quotation:

> "[R]egulations [of employee appearance] making distinctions on the basis of sex will not support allegations of discrimination unless [the regulations] are unreasonable or unevenly enforced."

In the first bracket, the uppercase *R* replaces a lowercase *r* because in the original the quoted language did not constitute the beginning of a sentence. The second and third brackets identify material added or substituted to clarify, simplify, or shorten the quoted material. *ALWD* R. 48.1-48.3; *Bluebook* R. 5.2 & 5.3.

5. To signal the omission of letters, use empty brackets. For instance, write "draft[]" when omitting the "ing" from "drafting." *ALWD* R. 48.2; *Bluebook* R. 5.2.

6. To signal the omission of one or more words within the quotation, use ellipses. An ellipsis is a series of three dots with a space before, between, and after. *ALWD* R. 49.2 & 49.3; *Bluebook* R. 5.3.

> "The evidence included a communication . . . suggesting that the employee should wear clothing of a more feminine style."

7. Do not use an ellipsis at the beginning of a quotation. A reader will assume that the original source may include material ahead of the quoted material. *ALWD* R. 49.3(b)(2); *Bluebook* R. 5.3(b)(i).

8. Similarly, do not use an ellipsis at the end of a quotation *to signal the omission of material beyond the end of a block quotation concluding with a complete sentence.* A reader will assume that the original source may contain material after the quoted sentence. *ALWD* R. 49.3(b)(3); *Bluebook* R. 5.3(b)(iv).

9. When you are using material that was a *part* of a sentence in the original but you are using it as a complete sentence in your text, indicate the omitted material at the end of the quotation by placing an ellipsis between the last quoted material and the punctuation at the end of the sentence.

> "The mere existence of a grievance procedure does not insulate an employer from liability . . . ."

The ellipsis will tell your reader that in the original the sentence contained additional material. *ALWD* R. 49.4(b); Bluebook R. 5.3(b)(iii).

10. Use a parenthetical clause after the citation to signal citations or footnotes you have omitted from inside the quotation or to signal emphasis you have added or deleted. *ALWD* R. 49.3(d); *Bluebook* R. 5.3. For example:

> The court observed that a partner's interest in partnership property "is a derivative interest subject to significant limitations. [A partner] has *no right to use this property for other than partnership purposes* without the consent of the other partners." *Bellis v. U.S.*, 417 U.S. 85, 98 (1974) (citations omitted, emphasis added).

The original material contained citations after "limitations" and before the next sentence. The italicized phrase was not italicized in the original.

11. If you find an error in the quoted material, either alter the quotation to correct the error or signal the error by following it with "sic" enclosed in brackets. *ALWD* R. 48.5; *Bluebook* R. 5.2. For example:

> "The party least anxious to settle was her [sic]."

E. Editing Quotations

Edit quotations down to the key words so your reader does not have to sift through the quoted material for your point. Editing must not change the meaning, but within that constraint you have great latitude to clear away the underbrush. Often the most effective quotation has been edited down to a short phrase or even a single word, perhaps with the key language italicized or underlined. Moderate use of italics and underlining in quoted material can help overcome the tendency of busy readers to skim quotations. They may still skim the rest of the quotation, but an italicized or underlined word may draw their attention at least to the most important part.

For instance, assume that you represent the defendant in a case in which the plaintiff alleges that she was sexually harassed when her supervisor pressured her into going to dinner with him and kissing him. You are writing a brief to the trial court on the issue of what the plaintiff must prove. Compare the following quotations:

Example 1

The Supreme Court has held that "the District Court in this case erroneously focused on the 'voluntariness' of respondent's participation in the claimed sexual episodes. The correct inquiry is whether respondent by her conduct indicated that the alleged sexual advances were unwelcome, not whether her actual participation in sexual intercourse was involuntary." *Meritor Sav. Bank v. Vinson*, 477 U.S. 57, 68 (1986).

Example 2

The Supreme Court has held that a plaintiff cannot prove a sexual harassment claim merely by showing that she participated in the sexual conduct involuntarily. She must prove that "by her conduct [she] *indicated* that the alleged sexual advances were unwelcome." *Meritor Sav. Bank v. Vinson*, 477 U.S. 57, 68 (1986) (emphasis added).

Which manner of quoting distills the key distinction and highlights it for your reader? Which states the legal principle as it would apply to the procedural posture of your case? Which states the legal principle in language that would be applicable to the facts of your case? Which is more readable?

Now that your citations and quotations are in proper form, turn your attention to editing the rest of the document.

CHAPTER 21

Paragraphs, Sentences, and Style

The final step in the writing process is editing. Good editing requires reading the document as if you have never seen it before. Try to arrive at the editing stage with enough time to put the document down for a day or at least for several hours. Then read as if you were a complete stranger to the document. Use the following suggestions as part of your editing process.

I. PARAGRAPHING

Each paragraph should have a topic or a thesis sentence, which generally appears as the first sentence of the paragraph. The paragraph should be limited to information about that topic or thesis, and it should fit smoothly and logically between its neighbors.

These paragraphing principles are crucial in legal writing. They are more than just principles of writing style; they are important to the substance of your analysis. Proper paragraphing will improve the substance of your analysis by helping you flesh out and order your thoughts, make appropriate decisions about the depth of your analysis for each point, and think of new points you want to include. Here are some important guidelines for paragraphing:

When possible, use a thesis sentence rather than a topic sentence. A topic sentence identifies the topic the paragraph will discuss, but that is all it does. A paragraph centered on a topic sentence is better than a paragraph without either kind of lead sentence, but it is apt to discuss the topic without ever making a point. A thesis sentence, however, asserts a position. A paragraph centered on a thesis sentence will support or explain this position. It will focus on the material that "proves" the assertion in the thesis sentence.[1] Often the thesis is the rule itself, a part of the rule, or a point about how the rule functions. Compare the following paragraphs. Which has the best thesis

---

1. A paragraph or even several paragraphs can refer to the thesis sentence of the prior paragraph by using a clear relational word or phrase (for example, "similarly") or when the context otherwise clearly communicates that the point of the subsequent paragraph is to provide additional evidence for the prior paragraph's thesis.

sentence? Notice how the thesis sentence articulates a point that advances the analysis. Notice how its discipline has led the writer to analyze rather than merely report on the authorities.

Cantwell v. Denton [citation] dealt with the issue of when a choice is sufficiently voluntary to constitute assumption of the risk. In that case, the defendant negligently caused a fire in an apartment building, and a father entered the burning building to save his child. The court held that the father's action was not sufficiently voluntary to constitute assumption of the risk. [citation]	A choice is not sufficiently voluntary to constitute assumption of the risk if the defendant's negligence has forced the plaintiff to choose between the threatened harm and another equal or greater harm. *Cantwell v. Denton* [citation]. In *Cantwell,* the defendant had negligently caused a fire in an apartment building. A father had to choose between entering the burning building and standing by while his child's life was in danger. The court held that standing by while the child was in danger would have been an equal or greater harm. [citation] Under such circumstances, the court held, the choice to subject one's self to danger is not "voluntary" in the sense necessary to constitute assumption of the risk. [citation]

    As you clarify for yourself the point of the paragraph, often you will realize that the *topic* contains several different *theses,* each deserving its own supporting material from the authorities. Thus, the discipline of using thesis sentences leads you to a more thorough and complete analysis because it helps you notice additional points you had not yet seen.

    Keep the paragraph's content within its thesis. Limiting the paragraph's content to information about the paragraph's thesis will help you find the gaps in your reasoning and in the "proof" you have found in the authorities. If you limit the paragraph to material that supports the thesis, you will notice if you have little or no support for that thesis. You will know when you need to go back to the authorities in search of stronger support.

    Keep your paragraphs moderately short. Limit paragraphs to one-third to one-half of a double-spaced page. Keeping your paragraph short will keep you focused on the thesis. A long paragraph often has one of these two problems: (1) it has wandered from its thesis, or (2) the thesis is too big to be covered without dividing it into subpoints. A large thesis generally produces a large paragraph that mixes information about the subpoints more or less randomly. It also results in a discussion that is not sufficiently fleshed out. The best way to avoid these two problems is to keep your paragraph lengths at or below a half-page, double-spaced.

Use a transitional word, phrase, or sentence each time you move on to a new point. Being explicit about the relationships between the theses of succeeding paragraphs will help you insure that your reasoning is logical. Here is a list of commonly used transitions:

TRANSITIONS[2]

Addition

also	in addition	not only
and	in fact	then
furthermore	moreover	

Sequence

first	next	finally
second		

Comparison

both	likewise	in comparison

Contrast

but	despite	nevertheless
while	still	however
instead	even though	notwithstanding
on the other hand	even so	
in contrast	though	

Concession

although	even though	though

Illustration

for instance	in particular	specifically
to illustrate	for example	

Result

accordingly	consequently	as a result
therefore	for	since
because	thus	

Summary

accordingly	thus	therefore
in summary		

Emphasis

above all	more important	chiefly

---

2. Adapted from David Angell & Brent Heslop, *The Elements of E-Mail Style* 62-64 (Addison-Wesley Publ. 1994).

Thesis sentences and proper paragraphing can make a major substantive difference in your analysis. If you implement those principles in your first draft, you will save yourself several revisions. However, if you cannot concentrate on the material and on paragraphing at the same time, simply write your initial draft in your normal way and then, in your first revision, edit your paragraphs and add thesis sentences where necessary.

STRATEGIES FOR USING PARAGRAPHING TO IMPROVE YOUR ANALYSIS

1. *Check your thesis sentences and paragraphs.* For each paragraph, first ask yourself what your point is. Identify your thesis sentence, and underline it on your draft. Then identify the paragraph(s) that support that thesis, and be sure you know how all of the other material in that paragraph pertains to that point. Now evaluate the strength of your analysis of that point by evaluating the strength of the supporting paragraph(s). This kind of point-by-point evaluation of the building blocks can dramatically improve your analysis. It helps you identify weak spots, leaps of logic, and misuse of sources.

2. *Check paragraph length.* Use the yardstick of a maximum length of about one-half of a double-spaced page. For those paragraphs that run longer, ask yourself whether the paragraph's thesis has subpoints you should separate. Often, as you separate these subpoints of the analysis and treat them in separate paragraphs, you will find that the subpoints deserve more analysis than you had originally thought. As a matter of fact, sometimes you will find whole new issues you had overlooked.

3. *Check your transitions.* Identify each transition to a new point, and ask yourself how the new point is connected to the former point. Be sure that each transition is clearly communicated.

4. *Read all of the underlined thesis sentences in order.* They should provide a logically ordered summary of your reasoning, point by point.

II. CHOOSE STRONG SUBJECTS AND VERBS

One of the characteristics of good style is the predominance of strong subjects and verbs. Here are some of the most effective techniques for finding and using stronger subjects and verbs.

A. Active Voice

Much legal writing is filled with unnecessary passive verbs. Learn to spot them, evaluate whether they serve a purpose, and get rid of them if they do not. You can recognize passive verbs by checking the subject of the sentence. Ask yourself whether the subject performed the action described by the verb.

If it did, then you have used a verb in the active voice. If it did not, but instead was acted *upon,* you have found a passive-voiced verb.

Active   Ms. Watson signed a covenant-not-to compete.
Passive   A covenant-not-to-compete was signed by Ms. Watson.

The subject of the first sentence is Ms. Watson. Did she do what the verb describes? Did she "sign"? Yes she did, and therefore you know that the first sentence uses the active voice. However, the subject of the second sentence is the covenant. Did the covenant sign? Of course not. The covenant was acted upon; the signing happened *to* the covenant. Therefore, you know that the second sentence uses the passive voice.

Why are sentences overloaded with passive verbs undesirable? First, writing in the passive voice requires more words. You can see this on a small scale in the example above, and the effect can compound in a sentence with more than one passive verb.

Passive   It was insisted by Carrolton that the covenant had been breached by Ms. Watson.

Active   Carrolton insisted that Ms. Watson had breached the covenant.

Locate the passive verbs in the first sentence, which contains fourteen words. Notice that the second sentence contains only nine words, a reduction of 36 percent.

Second, writing in the passive voice causes lack of clarity. Sentences in the passive voice often omit altogether the identity of the actor; yet the actor's identity is usually important. These versions of our earlier examples reflect this problem of ambiguity:

A covenant-not-to-compete was   [Who signed?]
    signed.
It was insisted that the covenant had   [Who insisted? Who breached?]
    been breached.

Finally, writing in the passive voice is less forceful. A sentence in the active voice drives forward in a straight line; the subject "does" the action to the object. But a sentence in the passive voice moves in reverse, backing in stops and starts toward the subject. Like a car, a sentence driving ahead moves more smoothly and forcefully than a sentence in reverse.

While writing in the active voice is generally preferable, an occasional passive-voiced verb can serve a particular function. For instance, a passive verb can sometimes eliminate the need for using a masculine noun or pronoun, as section V explains. In persuasive writing, a number of strategic considerations may call for a passive verb. Also, sometimes the identity of the actor is not important, and a passive verb can appropriately focus the attention on the object of the action. In court documents, a passive verb may allow you to avoid references to yourself or your firm. And sometimes using a passive verb can allow you to begin the sentence with a smooth transition from earlier material.

However, most legal writing, including the case law you spend so much time reading, relies far too much on verbs in the passive voice. Because so much of what you are reading everyday is infected with passivitis, you will have to struggle against developing the habit yourself.

EXERCISE 21-1
Active Voice

Underline each passive-voiced verb and edit the sentence to eliminate those verbs. If editing would require knowing the name of a person or organization, simply create a name.

1. After a notice of appeal was filed by the defendant, the assessment of attorneys' fees was entered and payment was made a condition of probation.
2. The appropriate time to decide a motion for defense fees and costs is not set out by the statute.
3. The motion to dismiss was made by the defendant and was heard by the court on May 15.
4. Disparaging reports about Carter's performance had been made by the hospital's Credentials Committee.
5. The initial discussions by the Executive Committee of Green's abilities were prompted by Carter's testimony against Green.

B. Nominalizations

The second technique for focusing on strong subjects and verbs is avoiding nominalizations. Nominalizations are nouns that began life as a verb and should have been content with their lot in life. When such a verb aspires to upward social mobility, it finds that it needs a crowd around it. Suddenly, your sentence has several more words than it used to.

No nominalization	The sellers decided to accept the buyer's offer.
One nominalization	The sellers *made a decision* to accept the buyer's offer.

If your sentence contains several nominalizations, the party can get really out of hand.

No nominalizations	The sellers decided to accept the buyer's offer, so they authorized their broker to announce their decision.
Three nominalizations	The sellers *made a decision* to accept the buyer's offer, so they *issued an authorization to* their broker to *make an announcement of* their decision.

Wordiness is not the only problem nominalizations cause. Sentences using nominalizations are both weaker and less clear than sentences in which the verbs stay where they belong. Since nominalizations are still verbs at heart, they do a poor job of being nouns; they are by nature more vague than "real" nouns. Worse yet, when the hole left by the departed verb is filled, the substitute verb is usually weaker than the departed verb.[3] These consequences combine to weaken the sentence and obscure the meaning.

---

3. Verbs like "make," "issue," "is," and "had" are much weaker than action verbs like "agree," "announce," "object," "collide," and "revise."

Here are examples of common nominalizations and the verb forms to which they should return.

Change	To
enter into an agreement	agree
contains a provision	provides
have a collision	collide
file a motion	move
give consideration to	consider
had knowledge that	knew
effect a termination	terminate
make an assumption	assume
make a decision	decide
places emphasis on	emphasizes
it is a requirement of the contract that	the contract requires that
commencement of discovery will occur	discovery will commence

EXERCISE 21-2
Nominalizations

Underline the nominalizations, and edit the sentences to eliminate them.

1. New York law is very protective of medical peer review procedures, so a challenge to the procedures would not be beneficial to our client.
2. The Executive Committee members made a statement to the effect that the Vice President had given them assurance that the Personnel Office had made an announcement of its decision.
3. The County Tax Assessor's Office made a number of new assessments to properties with locations in Midtown.
4. This letter serves as confirmation of our meeting last week, during which our firm agreed to provide representation to First National Bank.
5. The arbitrator made a determination that the claim for damages was reasonable.

C. Throat-Clearing

Another major obstacle to focusing on strong subjects and verbs is the habit of "throat-clearing"—using introductory phrases that communicate little more than "I'm getting ready to say something here." In judicial opinions and practitioner-writing, you will notice an abundance of throat-clearing. Here are some examples:

> It is interesting to note that . . .
> It is important to remember that . . .
> It seems that . . .

> It is clear (or obvious) that . . .
> It is widely understood that . . .
> As noted above . . .
> As to . . .
> With respect (or regard) to . . .

Other examples introduce an assertion by claiming responsibility for it, such as "The defendant submits (or believes, argues, or contends) that. . . . "

One can speculate about why these phrases slip into our writing. They may reflect a natural human insecurity about the material that is to follow; they may reflect an inaccurate perception that these phrases elevate the tone or convey an objective perspective; they may simply be habits born of reading the legal writing of others. Whatever the reason, throat-clearing phrases impede rather than advance good writing. If some of these phrases slip into your writing in the working-draft stage, edit them out in revision. Let your sentences proceed directly to your point without working into that point with a throat-clearing phrase.

EXERCISE 21-3
Throat-clearing

Edit each sentence to eliminate the throat-clearing structures.

1. ~~The Court should note that~~ the *Harmon* case was decided prior to the statute's adoption.
2. ~~It could be argued that~~ the plaintiff was not injured as a result of the other car's excessive speed but rather as a result of the plaintiff's malfunctioning breaks.
3. ~~It appears that~~ the defendant left the jurisdiction in order to avoid testifying, so ~~it should be clear that~~ the sanctions would apply.
4. ~~The court's language makes it clear~~ that the court considered whether to make the payment of fees a condition of probation.

D. Sentences Beginning with Forms of "It Is" or "There Is"

Sentence constructions beginning with forms of "it is" or "there is" always lack force and often lack clarity. Like the constructions described above, they obscure the subject and verb. Try to reword these constructions to put the "real" subject and action up front in their usual spots.

Change	It is unethical to contact a party represented by another lawyer.
To	Contacting a party represented by another lawyer is unethical.
Change	There are four defendants seeking dismissal on jurisdictional grounds.
To	Four defendants are seeking dismissal on jurisdictional grounds.

EXERCISE 21-4
"It Is" or "There Is" Structures

Edit each sentence to eliminate the "it is" or "there is" structure.

1. The cases are distinguishable because there was no notice of appeal filed in *Finkelstein*.
2. It is irrelevant in determining whether *Roberts* should control this case that the underlying trial was a criminal proceeding as opposed to a civil proceeding.
3. On September 9, 2006, Matthews filed a notice of appeal asserting that there was insufficient evidence to show that he had the requisite intent.
4. It is worth noting that the Second District has chosen not to follow the Fourth District's ruling on this issue.
5. The Florida Supreme Court recognized that there must be a line drawn to establish a clear standard for deciding which court has jurisdiction.
6. In *Finkelstein*, there was no appeal by the defendant.
7. It is irrelevant that Matthews filed a notice of appeal because the motion for a fee assessment was independent of the appeal.
8. There is a parallel between fee assessments and restitution requirements. Fee assessments and restitution requirements are parallel orders.
9. It is important for the stability of the legal system to ensure consistent decisions from the courts.
10. Furthermore, there are not enough significant differences between restitution orders and fee awards to support different results.
11. There is no claim that may be entertained by the trial court because the entire case falls within the jurisdiction of the appellate court.
12. Fees and costs cannot be assessed until there has been a determination of guilt.
13. Failure to pay the assessed fees and costs would result in incarceration even though there was no order for imprisonment as part of the sentence.
14. The Florida cases demonstrate that there is no exception in the criminal context to the rule that the filing of a notice of appeal divests a trial court of jurisdiction to assess fees.

III. AVOIDING WORDINESS

A. Revise Phrases That Can Be Replaced by a Single Word

Unnecessary phrases abound in poor legal writing. Phrases beginning with "the fact that" are nearly always culprits, but many other phrases create clutter as well. Here are examples of common unnecessary phrases and their single-word synonyms.

Change	To
at the time when	when
at the point in time when	when
as a result of	because
by reason of the fact that	because
due to the fact that	because
for a period of one week	for one week
for the purpose of	to
for these reasons	therefore
inasmuch as	since
in many cases	often
in order to	to
it was formerly the case that	formerly or previously
previous to	before
that was a case where	there

Also watch for phrases that can be replaced by adjectives.

Change   the contract between Wigby and Matthews
To   the Wigby-Matthews contract

Change   The buyer discovered six violations of code requirements. All of the violations dealt with plumbing.
To   The buyer discovered six plumbing code violations.

Change   . . . for the purpose for which it was intended . . .
To   . . . for the intended purpose . . .

B. Avoid Legalese

For the same reasons, purge your writing of unnecessary legalese. When writing to a law-trained reader, you may choose to use some legal terms unfamiliar to laypersons because those terms communicate legal concepts more clearly and concisely than nonlegal terms would. But do not resort to the jargon of law unless it is necessary to convey your point clearly and concisely. Here are examples of unnecessary legalese:

assuming *arguendo*
the *instant* case
the *above-captioned* case
the *said* defendant
the *aforementioned* contract
the items *hereinafter* described
to remove *therefrom*
to wit
whereas

the party of the first part
supra (except when properly used in a legal citation)
all Latin words except those few that have become true terms of art, such
   as "pro se," "res ipsa," "pro bono," "prima facie"

C. Avoid Redundancies

Redundancies can slip into language easily. Here are examples:

advance planning
final outcome
first and foremost
honest truth
old adage
past experience
point in time
reason is because
whether or not

D. Avoid Intensifiers

Because generations of writers have overused words like "clearly" or "very," these and other common intensifiers have become virtually meaningless. As a matter of fact, they have begun to develop a connotation exactly opposite their original meaning. So many writers (lawyers and judges alike) have used those labels in place of well-reasoned analysis that some readers see these intensifiers as signaling a weak analysis. Rid your writing of these words:

clearly
extremely
obviously
quite
very

IV. OTHER CHARACTERISTICS OF GOOD STYLE

A. Keeping the Subject and Verb Close Together

The basic components of a sentence are the subject, the verb, and the object. A reader tackles a sentence by searching for those components. First, a reader looks for the subject. Once the subject is found, the reader's urge to find the verb is strong. The primary meaning of a sentence is communicated by the combination of the subject and the verb. A reader who can't find and mentally combine them quickly will be frustrated and confused.

The primary impediment to finding and mentally combining the subject and verb is the placement of long modifying phrases between them. Legal writers are especially prone to this weakness. Usually the problem is caused by trying to say too much in one sentence. For instance, consider this example:

> In the first month of his marriage, the defendant, who was only nineteen at the time and who had not completed high school or developed a trade and who had just lost his part-time job, was charged with robbing a convenience store at the corner of Bayside and Tenth Avenue.

This writer has a lot to say about the defendant — probably more than one sentence can bear. The result is the placement of several modifying phrases or clauses between the subject and the verb. The solution is to remove those interrupting modifying phrases and clauses. Since the sentence really has no other place for them, another sentence is necessary. Notice that the information about the defendant falls into two categories: general information about the defendant and specific information about a particular event. The solution is to use separate sentences, one or more for each category of information.

> In the first month of his marriage, the defendant was charged with robbing a convenience store at the corner of Bayside and Tenth Avenue. He was only nineteen at the time. He had not completed high school or developed a trade, and he had just lost his part-time job.

Not only is the second version easier to read, it helps the reader organize the information as well.

Use these guidelines to manage long modifying phrases:

- Where clarity is not a problem, move the long phrase to one end of the sentence. This placement allows the reader to read quickly. It places the primary emphasis on the main clause, and it maximizes clarity.
- If clarity is a problem, place the modifying phrase close to the word it modifies. If the resulting sentence separates the subject and verb by too great a distance, separate the material into two or more sentences.

EXERCISE 21-5
Keeping the Subject and Verb Close Together

Edit to keep the subjects and verbs closer together.

1. The applicable rule the Florida courts have fashioned in relation to this issue states that a trial court does retain jurisdiction to assess attorney's fees and costs during the pendency of an appeal.
2. A potential counter-argument to established Florida law that the assessment of fees and costs is a collateral and independent issue from the underlying trial or appeal and should be excepted from the general rule transferring jurisdiction to the appellate court upon the filing of an appeal can be found in the case of *Woods v. State*.

B. Avoiding Long Sentences

The more complex the message, the simpler the medium must be. Long sentences bury the subject and verb and tax a reader's patience. Use 25 words as a benchmark for gauging maximum length.

EXERCISE 21-6
Avoiding Long Sentences

Edit to eliminate excessively long sentences.

1. The court followed the *Wyatt* ruling in *Lee v. State*, when it affirmed the trial court's imposition of § 938 fees and costs upon the defendant, who argued unsuccessfully that his notice appealing a first degree murder conviction divested the trial court of its jurisdiction to assess fees and costs.
2. On September 16, 2006, after Defendant had filed the Notice of Appeal, the Public Defender filed a Motion for Fees and Costs, asking the trial court to assess fees and costs against Defendant, pursuant to § 938, consisting of attorney's fees and investigative costs totaling $1,040.

C. Unnecessary Variations

Clear legal writing requires consistency in terms. Once you pick a term, use the same term for each reference. Otherwise your reader will have to decide, with each new term, whether you mean something different from the prior term. Professor Wydick uses this example:

> The first case was settled for $20,000, and the second piece of litigation was disposed of out of court for $30,000, while the price of the amicable accord reached in the third suit was $50,000.

The readers are left to ponder the difference between a *case,* a *piece of litigation,* and a *suit.* By the time they conclude that there is no difference, they have no patience left for *settled, disposed of out of court,* and *amicable accord,* much less for what the writer was trying to tell them in the first place.[4]

In legal writing, consistency is important. Do not worry about seeming repetitious; it is far more important to be understood.

D. Parallelism

Sentences with repeated elements should maintain a parallel structure. A sentence has a repeated structure when it contains a list or when it contains more than one of the same kind of element. For instance, the following sentence has two dependent clauses:

> Acme Pest Control selected the plaintiff for lay-off because she had the least seniority and because she was consistently late to work.

Notice that the dependent clauses use a parallel structure. They each begin with "because she" followed by a verb. Here is a version of this sentence that does not maintain a parallel structure:

> Acme Pest Control selected the plaintiff for lay-off because she had the least seniority and because of her tardiness.

---

4. Richard C. Wydick, *Plain English for Lawyers* 66 (4th ed., Carolina Academic Press 1998).

In this version of the sentence, the first "because" is followed by a subject and verb, but the second is followed by a prepositional phrase.

To maintain parallelism, be sure that all items in a list and all repeated structures use the same grammatical elements. If the list is complex, you can repeat the last common word so your reader will have no difficulty understanding how each item of the list relates to the rest of the sentence. If a reader will have no difficulty, you do not need to repeat the common word.

Not parallel   Problems occur when the parties conceal relevant documents or by deluging the opponent with irrelevant documents.

Parallel   Problems occur when the parties conceal relevant documents or when they deluge the opponent with irrelevant documents.

Now that the structure is parallel, extra words can go:

Problems occur when the parties conceal relevant documents or deluge the opponent with irrelevant documents.

EXERCISE 21-7
Parallelism

Edit to achieve parallelism.

1. When Officers Dale and Hathaway found the victims, they were bruised, hungry, and suffered from exhaustion.
2. To prevail in a claim for employment discrimination, the plaintiff must prove that (1) his employer is covered by the act; (2) that he was terminated because of his age; and (3) a causal link between his termination and his damages.

V. GENDER-NEUTRAL WRITING

Gender-neutral language is language that avoids masculine nouns and pronouns for *general* reference. While the use of masculine nouns and pronouns for general reference is technically permissible, most of today's good writers avoid or minimize it. For example:

Change   A person cannot recover damages for injuries sustained primarily as a result of *his* own negligence.

To   A person cannot recover damages for injuries sustained primarily as a result of *that person's* own negligence.

Using gender-neutral language smoothly is not always easy. Here are some helpful strategies:

A. Techniques for Nouns: Elimination or Substitution

1. Where possible without loss of clarity, eliminate the noun entirely. For instance, you could probably eliminate the term "bat boys" from the following sentence without altering the meaning.

   > . . . to all players, coaches, [bat boys,] ticket takers, concession workers, or other employees whose jobs are related to the sport of baseball.

2. Substitute gender-neutral synonyms where the noun is needed.

Use	*Rather than*
worker	workman
mail carrier	mailman
chairperson	chairman
supervisor	foreman
server	waitress
reporter	newsman
housekeeper	maid
firefighter	fireman
police officer	policeman
flight attendant	stewardess
persons, individuals	men, mankind
staffing	manning

B. Techniques for Pronouns

1. Where showing possession is not necessary to the meaning, substitute "the" or "an" for "his" or "her."

   > . . . a plaintiff may petition the court for relief, attaching to *the* [rather than "his"] complaint a copy of . . .

2. Repeat the antecedent. The antecedent is the noun to which the pronoun refers. In the following sentence, "doctor" is the antecedent:

   > . . . to a doctor and the nurses, secretaries, and receptionists in *the doctor's* [rather than "his"] office . . .

3. Make the antecedent plural so you can use the plural (nongendered) pronoun "their."

   > The license fee applies to *taxi drivers* [rather than "a taxi driver"] driving *their* [rather than "his"] own taxi*s*.

   Do not use the plural pronoun without pluralizing the antecedent. Here is an example of this error:

   > Anyone who rides a roller coaster must assume the risk, and cannot recover for *their* injuries.

4. Rephrase to use a clause beginning with "who."

> *Change*   A person must assume the risk of injury if he rides a roller coaster.
>
> *To*   A person who rides a roller coaster must assume the risk of injury.

5. Eliminate the pronoun by using a passive-voiced verb.

> If the examining physician knows that the person *being examined* [rather than "he is examining"] has been under treatment . . .

> *Warning:* Use this technique sparingly. As section IIA explained, overusing the passive voice produces poor style.

6. Substitute "one." This technique can seem stilted, but it may suffice from time to time.

> *Change*   A person should always tell the truth in order to preserve his reputation.
>
> *To*   One should always tell the truth in order to preserve one's reputation.

The less formal "you" or "your" may work in less formal documents but *not* in court documents.

> You should always tell the truth in order to preserve *your* reputation.

7. Rephrase the clause entirely.

> *Change*   For each speaker, enclosed is an outline of his presentation, a copy of the exercise he has prepared, and a memorandum explaining his exercise.
>
> *To*   Each speaker has prepared a presentation outline, an exercise, and an explanatory memorandum. Copies are enclosed.

8. Where elimination, substitution, and rephrasing fail, use both pronouns separated by a conjunction, such as "or."

> A parent may enroll his or her child . . .

9. Slash constructions (his/her, he/she, s/he) are not recommended for formal professional writing.

C. Techniques for Proper Names and Titles

Unless strategic considerations intervene, use the following guidelines for referring to people:

Be consistent in the use of courtesy titles. If you do not use "Mr." for men, do not use "Miss," "Mrs.," or "Ms." for women.

Unless you have a good reason, use "Ms." rather than "Mrs." or "Miss." The object is to treat men and women the same. Since the courtesy title for men ("Mr.") does not indicate a marital status, the title for women should not do so either. You can decide to use "Mrs." or "Miss" when a reader prefers it, when the legal issue makes marital status relevant, when using the title will eliminate confusion, or when you have a particular strategic reason.

Be consistent in the use of first names and last names. You can use last names only, first and last names together, or (rarely) first names only. However, unless you have a good strategic reason, apply your decision equally to both genders.

PART SEVEN

Oral Advocacy

CHAPTER 22

Oral Argument

This chapter and your first law school oral argument provide only a glimpse of appellate practice. Appellate lawyers must know much more than this introduction can provide. Consider taking a course in appellate practice and procedure. The first time you handle a case on appeal, you will be glad to have had that important training.

These next sections present material designed for a law school oral argument. In actual law practice, some of the details of presentation and formality expected in a particular court may differ from those expected in a law school setting. However, the fundamental concepts presented here will be equally applicable. In actual law practice, you can adjust your presentation to that expected in a particular court by observing a few oral arguments before you present your own. You will not find these small differences to be a problem.

This chapter describes an appellate argument rather than a trial-level argument. Again, the fundamental principles of delivering a trial-level argument and an appellate argument are the same, and you will be able to adapt your presentation by observing arguments by other lawyers in a trial-court setting.

I. THE PURPOSE OF ORAL ARGUMENT

Before you plunge into preparing your oral argument, consider its purpose. An oral argument is not simply an opportunity to say orally what you have already said in writing. If that were the purpose of oral argument, the judges would not waste your time or theirs. They would simply read your brief and issue a ruling.

Rather, an oral argument is *an opportunity for the judges to ask you questions.* They want to clarify their understanding of your arguments. They want to give you a chance to alleviate their concerns about adopting the position you advocate. They want to have a conversation. As your only chance to speak directly with those who will decide your case, oral argument is an important opportunity.

Oral argument also provides you a chance to return the judges' deliberation to the big picture and to emphasize the narrative themes and policy rationales that underlie your legal argument—the themes that show not just how the law *does* support your position, but also why it *should*. Direct, eye-to-eye contact often is the best way to bring home the importance of those fundamental aspects of your argument.

II. FORMALITIES AND ORGANIZATION OF ORAL ARGUMENT

The first step in preparing for oral argument is to understand the formalities you will encounter and the overall organization your argument should follow. Here is an overview of the oral argument:

A. Preliminary Formalities

Usually you will be seated at counsel table, waiting for the judges to enter and call your case. A bailiff will announce the entry of the judges by saying something like this:

> Oyez, oyez, oyez. All rise. The First Circuit Court of . . . is now in session. All those with business before this Honorable Court may now draw near.

As soon as the bailiff begins this speech, stand up and remain standing until the judges are seated and the Chief Judge tells you to be seated. The Chief Judge will then call your case and ask if the lawyers are ready, saying something like this:

> The Court calls the case of *Jones v. Brown*. Is counsel for the appellant ready? . . . Is counsel for the appellee ready?

When the judge asks you if you are ready, stand up and say "Ready, Your Honor." The Chief Judge will then instruct counsel for the appellant to proceed.

B. The Appellant's Argument

As the lawyer for the moving party, counsel for the appellant goes first. You may be the only lawyer for the appellant, or you may have co-counsel arguing one of the issues. Use the following structure, leaving out the mention of co-counsel if you are arguing alone:

> May it please the Court. My name is Russell Stege, and along with my co-counsel, Susan Marks, I represent the Appellant, Paul Giray. I would ask the Court for permission to reserve two minutes for rebuttal. [Pause to allow the Chief Justice to respond.]
>
> Thank you, your Honor. Mr. Giray respectfully asks this Court to . . . [state in one or two phrases the ruling you seek, for example, "reverse the trial court's entry of summary judgment and remand the case for trial"].

> The issue(s) before the Court is/are whether ... [state each issue in one sentence, phrased favorably to your side[1]]. Ms. Marks will argue the damages issue, and I will argue the adverse possession issue.

Then give the Court a short overview of the arguments you will make.

> Your Honors, Mr. Giray will show that the undisputed facts in this case simply are not adequate to establish the elements of adverse possession. [In two or three sentences, state a summary of your argument so the judges will have a sense of the arguments you will make and the order in which you will present them. This is also a good spot to introduce your narrative theme, as described in section III below.]
>
> Your Honors, the facts are these: ... [Inform the Court of the relevant facts, and then begin the main section of your argument, as described in section III.]

C. Argument of Co-Counsel for the Appellant

If you are co-counsel arguing a second issue for the Appellant, you will argue next. Go to the podium as soon as your co-counsel leaves it without waiting for an invitation from the judges. If the judges are still writing or conversing when you arrive at the podium, wait a moment until they are ready or until one of them tells you that you may begin. Then introduce yourself and identify your client, as the first lawyer did. You do not need to introduce your co-counsel from whom the Court has already heard. Nor do you need to repeat the request to reserve time for rebuttal. Proceed to a short overview of the arguments you will make:

> May it please the Court, my name is Susan Marks, and I also represent Paul Giray. I will argue the issue of the adequacy of money damages in this case. Your Honors, even if the undisputed facts were sufficient to establish a claim for adverse possession, an award of money damages would be more than sufficient in this case. [In two or three sentences, state a summary of your argument.]

Your co-counsel has already stated the facts, so you do not need to repeat them. Simply begin your legal argument, perhaps starting with your narrative theme. The rest of your argument should proceed just as described above for the first advocate.

D. The Appellee's Argument

Go to the podium as soon as counsel for the Appellant leaves it. If the judges are still writing or conversing, wait a moment until they are ready or until one of them tells you that you may begin. Then introduce yourself, your co-counsel, if any, and your client, just as the first lawyer did. As counsel for the appellee, you do not have a rebuttal, so you do not need to reserve any time. Then give the Court a short overview of the arguments you will make:

> May it please the Court, my name is Elizabeth Tunnesen, and along with Jason Kennedy, I represent Carol Cole. Ms. Cole requests the Court to affirm

---

1. Use the same techniques you used to phrase favorably the Questions Presented in your brief. See Chapter 15, section I.

the trial court's order granting summary judgment. Mr. Kennedy will argue the damages issue, and I will argue the adverse possession issue. I will show that the undisputed facts are more than sufficient to establish each element of adverse possession.

Give the Court a short overview of the arguments you will make, perhaps introducing your narrative theme. Counsel for the appellant has already provided the facts of the case, so you need only add or clarify any *important* fact omitted from the appellant's fact statement.

> Ms. Cole agrees with the facts as stated by the Appellant. However, the Court should also be aware that ...

If you do not need to clarify or add an important fact, simply proceed to the rest of your argument, following the format described above.

E. Argument of Co-Counsel for the Appellee

Your argument should follow the format described for the second lawyer for the appellant.

F. Concluding the Argument

No matter whether you argue for the appellant or the appellee, you will have to reach a graceful and persuasive ending while negotiating the constraints of the time cards. Prepare a conclusion consisting of a short summary (three to five sentences) of your best points, phrased compellingly, and a request for the relief you seek:

> [A summary of your strongest arguments] .... Therefore, the appellant requests that the Court reverse the trial court's entry of summary judgment and remand the case for trial on the adverse possession claim. Thank you, Your Honors.

Try to be ready to begin your conclusion when the one-minute card goes up. When the "zero" card is raised, you may finish your sentence, but then you must stop. Simply say, "Thank you, Your Honors," and sit down. If you are in the middle of answering a judge's question when the zero card goes up, stop and say to the Chief Judge:

> Your Honor, I see that my time is up. May I finish answering Judge Nottingham's question and have a moment to conclude?

The Chief Judge will probably say "yes." If so, finish your answer and take *no more than forty-five seconds* to deliver your conclusion. If the Chief Judge declines your request, simply say "Thank you, Your Honors," and sit down.

G. Rebuttal

After counsel for the appellee has finished arguing, one of the lawyers for the appellant will deliver the rebuttal. If you will be delivering the rebuttal, listen carefully during the appellee's argument to identify a weak point or a point on which opposing counsel has damaged your case but which you can remedy with a strong, extremely brief rebuttal. When counsel for the appellee concludes, go to the podium and deliver your rebuttal in one to two minutes, say, "Thank you, Your Honors," and sit down. The goal is to make your point in a compelling way and to sit down without prompting further questioning from the bench. Have one rebuttal prepared in advance, and use this prepared rebuttal in case you panic and cannot put together a compelling rebuttal based on what you have heard in the appellant's argument.

III. THE CONTENT OF ARGUMENT

The following procedural facets of your case will be crucial to the success of your oral argument. You must know how these procedural concepts apply to your case, and you must be able to phrase your arguments accurately in light of those effects.

A. The Standard of Review

The standard of review governs how much deference the appellate court must give to the decision of the judge or jury at the trial level. Review the material on the standard of review in Chapter 17. If the standard of review is favorable to your side, be especially sure to phrase your argument in its terms. No matter how much you choose to emphasize the standard, be ready to respond clearly and succinctly to a judge's question regarding the appropriate standard.

B. The Burden of Proof

Be sure you know the relevant burden of proof on the issue you are arguing. The burden of proof identifies the party who has the responsibility of proving the necessary facts and persuading the trial court. Usually, the plaintiff bears the burden of proving the elements of the cause of action, and the defendant bears the burden of proving an affirmative defense. On a procedural issue, the moving party often bears the burden. For instance, on a motion to compel discovery, the moving party would bear the burden of proof. Check the authorities on your legal issue to be sure you know which party bears the burden of proving each aspect of the case.

C. The Trial-Level Procedural Posture

Finally, your argument may be affected by the trial-level procedural posture of the ruling from which the appeal arose. The trial-level procedural posture defined the appropriate legal question in the trial court, and it is the decision on that legal question that is now on appeal. For instance, if the appeal is from a ruling granting summary judgment, the question before the trial court judge was whether the undisputed facts entitled the moving party to judgment without the necessity of a trial. Therefore, the role of the appellate court is to decide whether the trial judge ruled correctly *on that legal question*. If the appeal is from a judge's decision after a bench trial, the question is whether the facts in the trial record are sufficient to sustain the ruling (in other words, whether a reasonable judge, reviewing that trial record, could have decided the case in the way this judge did). Therefore, the role of the appellate court is to decide whether the trial judge ruled correctly *on that legal question*. Check the authorities to be sure of the implications of your case's trial-level procedural posture, and frame your arguments and your answers with that posture in mind.

D. Themes

Your case needs a theme, an overriding point to which you repeatedly return. Your theme should be the most persuasive big-picture point you have. Commonly, themes are based in the case's narrative (narrative reasoning), in the policies implicated by the case (policy-based reasoning), in the strength of the doctrinal law (rule-based and analogical reasoning), or in the case's procedural posture. Select a narrative theme if the most powerful part of your argument is based on your client's compelling facts:

> Your Honors, this is a case about a record title-holder who sat by and watched his neighbor build a garage, knowing that the neighbor believed the garage to be properly located on his own land. Then, just as the garage was completed, the record title-holder told his neighbor that the garage was six inches over the property line and demanded that the neighbor tear it down.

If the most compelling point of your argument is a policy implication, select a theme based on that policy:

> Even if a minor is less than completely candid about his age, the law should still require a merchant to take the remarkably simple precaution of asking to see the minor's driver's license. Such a requirement does not burden the merchant at all, and it protects against the very real danger that a merchant might find it profitable to be too easily convinced of an eager young customer's age.

If the most compelling part of your argument is the strength of the law on your side, select a theme that capitalizes on this strength:

> Despite the plaintiff's admittedly sympathetic facts, the law in this jurisdiction could not be more clear. A wrongful death action simply cannot be sustained for the death of a nonviable fetus. The legislature of this state has expressly declared this to be the law, and no fewer than five rulings of the Supreme Court have agreed.

If the most compelling part of your argument is the procedural posture of the trial court decision on which the appeal is based, select a theme that keeps bringing the discussion back to that procedural posture:

> The defendant strenuously disagrees with the inferences the plaintiff asks the Court to draw from the affidavits. However, even if the affidavits did support the plaintiff's inferences, the fact remains that this case comes before the Court on appeal from a summary judgment ruling. The question is not whether the plaintiff's inferences are possible, or even whether they are the

most likely, but rather whether they are the *only* possible inferences. Clearly they are not.

IV. PREPARATION

A. The Record

Thoroughly know the facts in the Record. For the important facts, be able to cite the page on which they appear. Do not overstate the facts, and do not state as facts the inferences you ask the court to draw from the facts. If you misstate facts, you will have lost credibility with the court, and if you misstate facts intentionally, you will have acted unethically.[2]

B. Outline Your Argument

Usually the outline of your argument should mirror the large-scale organization of your brief, as described in Chapter 7. The first level of headings should articulate your position on each relevant element of the governing rule. Under each heading, place as subheadings each argument you will make on that element, and under that subheading, place each point you will make in that part of the argument.

C. Prepare Your Folder

Prepare a folder with your notes for oral argument. You can use a file folder and small index cards. Open the folder and use both sides for your opening and closing language (in case you panic), for important factual information to which you might need to refer (for example, dates and relevant numbers you might not remember), and for the outline of your argument.

Consider including two outlines, one for a cold bench (a bench that asks few questions) and one for a hot bench (a bench that leaves you little time for your scripted material). The outline for the cold bench is your expanded outline—the one you will use if the judges are quiet and you have time to present most of your prepared material. The outline for the hot bench is compressed into just the main points you want to make in case you have only a few minutes. You can start with the expanded outline but shift to the compressed outline as necessary during the argument.

Reserve one area of the folder for the index cards. For each important case, statute or regulation, summarize on a card the important information from that source and quote any key language. Tape the cards on top of each other with the bottom of each card protruding a quarter of an inch from beneath the card on top of it. Tape the cards to the folder along the card's top edge, so the cards can be

---

2. *See* Chapter 14, section I.

flipped up like an address file. In the visible space on the bottom of each card, write the name or the case, statute, or regulation. Practice finding the information on the cards and in the other parts of the folder quickly and easily.

D. Script the Entire Opening, the Conclusion, and Your Prepared Rebuttal

While you cannot and should not try to script the body of the argument, the opening and closing should be scripted, essentially memorized, delivered with full eye contact, and spoken as if they were not memorized. This preparation will guarantee that you say what you want to say and that you say it smoothly and effectively. While your extemporaneous responses may not always be smooth, your beginnings and endings can and should achieve a high level of poise and persuasion.

E. Practice

Practice delivering your argument to friends. Have the friends question you just as they would if they were the judges before whom you will argue. Practice at least five or six times, and more if possible. Go through the whole argument each time, and then ask for feedback. Use these practice benches to improve both your knowledge of the case and the smoothness of your delivery.

F. Visit the Courtroom

Familiarize yourself with the room where you will argue. Imagine yourself delivering your argument there, and remind yourself that you belong there, advocating for your client. Psychologically claim the space.

V. HANDLING QUESTIONS FROM THE BENCH

Since a primary purpose of oral argument is to answer the judges' questions, a big part of your preparation should consist of getting ready to provide those answers. Here are some important points to guide your preparation.

A. Anticipate Questions

Ask yourself what you would want to know if you were a judge hearing the case. What parts of the argument would be hard to accept and why? What will your opponent argue? What key cases or statutes will the court be most concerned about? Also, pay close attention to the questions you receive in your practice rounds. Prepare answers for all of these questions.

B. Attitude

The judges will ask you questions, and they will often interrupt you to do it. This is part of the role of a judge. It is efficient and it saves you precious time. When a judge interrupts you, stop talking *immediately* and listen to what the judge is saying. Then answer the judge's question as best you can. Treat the question for what it is — a valuable opportunity to clarify a point about which the judge is concerned. Do not appear to be rushing through the answer so you can get back into your prepared argument. The judge's question is more important than your prepared argument.

The right to interrupt belongs only to the judge, however. Never interrupt a judge. No matter how badly you want to speak, wait patiently until the judge has finished speaking before you utter a sound.

C. Recognize Types of Questions

You will encounter three basic kinds of questions: friendly questions; questions genuinely seeking clarification of information; and adversarial questions.

A friendly question is designed to help you present your argument or make an additional point. A judge may want you to make a certain point primarily for the benefit of another judge, or a judge may simply be pleased to have thought of another point and may want to share it. Be sure to recognize a friendly question and to make use of the opportunity it gives you to agree with a judge and to articulate and validate the judge's point.

A question genuinely seeking information is an opportunity to be helpful to a judge who needs a point clarified. Do so willingly. Then, if you have a point to make about the subject of the inquiry, you can use this chance to make it, but only after you have answered the judge's question.

You may find that most of the questions you receive are adversarial, designed to test your arguments. Despite their threatening nature, these are the questions you should welcome most because these are the questions that allow you to resolve the concerns that may stand in the way of achieving the result you seek. Often these questions will be politely phrased, but sometimes a judge will deliver the question in an intimidating, angry, or even rude manner. Your job is to answer politely but firmly, ignoring the packaging of the question and responding only to its content. Do not respond in anger, even if you are feeling angry. Remain calm, at least outwardly, and answer the question as best you can.

> Your Honor, I must respectfully disagree. In the *Jones* case, the Supreme Court did not hold that .... Rather, ... And this is precisely why ....

D. Listen Carefully to the Question

You may find that your nervousness impedes your ability to listen carefully to the question. After you hear the first part of the question, you may assume that you know what the judge will be asking, and your nervousness may cause you to begin scrambling to formulate an answer. Yet you cannot answer a question that you have misunderstood. When a judge begins to speak, remember to listen carefully to the whole question before you answer.

E. Clarify the Question

Sometimes you will not understand a question even when you have listened carefully. This may happen because you are nervous or because the judge has not articulated the question clearly. Simply admit that you did not understand the question, apologize, and ask the judge to repeat it. If you think that you may have understood it but you are not sure, you can clarify your understanding: "Is Your Honor asking whether ...?"

F. Begin with a Clear, Direct Answer

Usually you will want to say a number of things in response to a question. However, you should always begin with a very short, direct answer to the question in the form in which the judge posed it: "Yes, Your Honor," or "No, Your Honor, I must respectfully disagree," or "Your Honor, that has sometimes been the case, but not always." After you have responded directly, you can go on to explain your answer, but the judge should know within roughly your first ten words what your answer to the question will be.

G. Returning to Your Prepared Presentation

When you have finished answering a question, return immediately to your prepared presentation. Do not wait for the judge to respond or to give you permission to return to your prepared material. Try to find a way to connect the ending of your answer to an entry point into your argument so that the answer seamlessly weaves you right back into your prepared material. However, if you cannot think of a connection on the spot, simply return to your argument.

H. Handling Questions on Your Co-Counsel's Issue

Sometimes a judge will ask you a question about the issue your co-counsel has already argued or will shortly argue. Try to answer it if you can, but qualify your answer by admitting that your co-counsel may be able to provide a better answer. This should minimize the chance that the judge will pursue the matter further.

> Your Honor, since *Home Finders* dealt with the issue of sufficiency of money damages, my co-counsel may be the best person to assist the Court on this question. However, I believe that the court there held that....

I. Handling a Question for Which You Do Not Have an Answer

While your hard work should prepare you for most questions, you may be asked a question for which you do not have an answer. A judge might ask you about a case or a statute with which you are not familiar, about how your issue compares to the comparable issue in some other area of law, or about how some particular procedural practice would affect your position. Even experienced appellate attorneys do not know all aspects of the law. If you do not know the answer to a judge's question, admit it. You can offer to find the answer and provide it to the court promptly after the argument concludes:

> Your Honor, I regret that I am not familiar with *Hatcher v. Norman*. However, if the Court allows, I will provide the Court with an answer to this question within twenty-four hours after today's argument concludes.

J. Agreeing When You Can

Remember that you will probably receive a friendly question here and there, so do not automatically disagree each time the judge engages you. You can even agree partially with the concerns underlying some adversary questions as well, but go on to show why that valid concern does not defeat your position:

> Yes, Your Honor, I agree that this is a legitimate concern. However, ...

K. Referring to Earlier Questions or Comments from the Bench

Remember the questions directed to you or to your opponent; you can refer to them when appropriate in your argument. If a judge has asked you a friendly question or made a friendly comment, you can refer to it later in the argument. You can refer also to the adversarial questions or comments directed to opposing counsel.

> As Justice Bailey pointed out, ...

Use this technique sparingly, however. Some judges may be irritated to hear their own words used in this manner more than once or, at most, twice during an argument.

VI. PRESENTATION

A. Dress

Wear a conservative suit.

B. Body, Hands, and Eyes

Stand straight, with your weight equally placed on both feet, and remain behind the podium. Maintain eye contact with the judges, and include the whole bench in that eye contact. Do not read your argument. Rather, speak to the judges conversationally, looking down at your notes now and then. Lay your hands on the podium, and use them only moderately for occasional small gestures. Do not grip the podium. Do not put your hands in your pockets or clasp them behind your back.

C. Voice

Speak at a moderate pace. Do not allow your nervousness to cause you to speak too quickly, but do speak with a degree of energy appropriate for discussion of an important matter about which you and your client care deeply. Speak firmly and loudly enough to be heard.

D. References

Refer to the bench as "Your Honors" or "the Court." Refer to individual judges as "Your Honor" or "Justice [last name]." Refer to clients by their last name preceded by "Mr." or "Ms." or by other appropriate titles, such as "Dr." Refer to other lawyers as "counsel for Appellant/Appellee" or as "opposing counsel."

E. Nervousness

Oral argument will probably make you a little nervous, but remember that judges are human beings. Like you, they are trying to do a hard job well, and they will sometimes fall short. While they have more experience than you do at this point in your legal career, they probably remember when they did not. All they ask of you, and all you need ask of yourself, is to do your best.

APPENDICES

Sample Office Memorandum

To: Requesting Attorney
From: Summer Clerk
Date: November 9, 2002
Re: Beth Buckley; file # 756385; stolen car; whether Buckley can disaffirm purchase of car based on her minority

QUESTION PRESENTED

Can Buckley, a minor, disaffirm the purchase of a car when she misunderstood the sales agent's question and therefore accidentally misrepresented her age as eighteen?

BRIEF ANSWER

Probably yes. A minor can disaffirm a contract unless the minor's fraudulent misrepresentation induced the other party to rely justifiably on the representation. On Buckley's facts, a court would probably rule that an innocent misrepresentation such as Buckley's is not fraudulent and therefore would not prevent a minor from disaffirming a contract. A court might also rule that the seller did not justifiably rely on Buckley's representation.

FACTS

Our client, Beth Buckley, is seventeen and a high school senior. She will turn eighteen on December 15. Two months ago she bought a used car for $3,000 from Willis Chevrolet. She paid cash, using the money she had saved from her summer job. Buckley purchased collision insurance for the car, but she did not insure against theft. Last week the car was stolen, and Buckley has asked what she can do about her loss.

When Buckley first looked at cars on the lot, the sales agent asked if she was old enough to buy a car. Buckley did not realize that she had to be eighteen to enter into a contract, even when paying cash. She thought the sales agent was asking whether she was old enough to drive, so she

-1-

said "yes." The agent did not ask to see any identification and did not raise the subject of age again.

The next day Buckley returned to the lot, selected the car she wanted to purchase, and completed the transaction. She recalls "signing a bunch of papers," but she did not read them and does not know what they said. She says that the sales agent did not attempt to explain the documents. He simply showed her where to sign, and she signed on those lines. She does not know if she still has copies of the documents, but she will look among her papers and let us know.

DISCUSSION

I. Can Beth Buckley disaffirm the contract?

A minor does not have the capacity to make a binding contract, but a contract made by a minor is not automatically void. *Hood v. Duren,* 125 S.E. 787 (Ga. Ct. App. 1924). Generally, one who is a minor at the time of making a contract can disaffirm the contract within a reasonable time after reaching the age of majority. O.C.G.A. § 13-3-20 (1982); *Merritt v. Jowers,* 193 S.E. 238 (Ga. 1937). The rationale for the rule is the recognition that minors have not yet attained sufficient maturity to be responsible for the decisions they make, so the rule protects them from at least some of the consequences of bad decisions. *See generally White v. Sikes,* 59 S.E. 228 (Ga. 1907).

However, a minor is estopped from disaffirming a contract if (a) the minor made a false and fraudulent representation of his or her age; (b) the contracting party justifiably relied on the minor's representation; and (c) the minor has reached the age of discretion. *Carney v. Southland Loan Co.,* 88 S.E.2d 805 (Ga. 1955). Because the first element is the most problematic in Buckley's case, the memo will discuss it first.

  A. Buckley's unintentional misrepresentation of her age probably is
     insufficient to establish fraudulent misrepresentation.

The first element necessary for estoppel is a false and fraudulent representation. A minor makes a false and fraudulent representation when the minor affirmatively and intentionally states a false age, intending that the seller rely on the information. For instance, in *Carney* the minor told the car sales agent that he was twenty-two, the agent recorded that information on the loan application, and the minor signed the application and purchased the car. The court affirmed the trial court's holding that the minor had fraudulently misrepresented his age and was estopped from disaffirming the contract. *Id.* at 807-808.

Similarly, in *Clemons v. Olshine,* 187 S.E. 711 (Ga. Ct. App. 1936), the minor told the clothing sales agent that he was twenty-one and signed a contract confirming the representation. The court held that his fraudulent misrepresentation estopped him from disaffirming. In *Watters v. Arrington,* 146 S.E. 773 (Ga. Ct. App. 1929), another car purchase case, several agents of the seller testified that the minor had twice affirmatively stated his age to be twenty-one. The court affirmed the jury's verdict for the seller, holding that a minor's fraudulent misrepresentation of age estops the minor from disaffirming the contract.

The courts distinguish this kind of intentional, knowing misrepresentation from unintentional, even negligent misrepresentations of age. For instance, in *Woodall v. Grant & Co.*, 9 S.E.2d 95 (Ga. Ct. App. 1940), the minor had simply signed without reading a form contract that contained a representation that he was of age. There the court held that the representation in the contract did not estop the minor because the minor had not read the contract. The court reasoned that minors are not required to read contracts. *Id.* at 95. The *Carney* decision distinguished *Woodall* by pointing out that in *Woodall* "the minor's only sin, if any, was his failure to read a contract which . . . stated that he was of age, while in [*Carney*] the minor falsely gave the information put into the contract." *Carney*, 88 S.E.2d at 808.

The most recent relevant case, *Siegelstein v. Fenner & Beane*, 17 S.E.2d 907 (Ga. Ct. App. 1941), reaffirmed the *Carney/Woodall* distinction. In *Siegelstein*, the jury returned a verdict for the defendant, and the appellate court reversed on other grounds. However, the appellate court affirmed the trial court's jury instruction, stating that a minor's false representation of age "will not affect his power to disaffirm a contract unless [the representation] was made *fraudulently*." *Id.* at 910 (emphasis supplied).

The rule holding minors responsible only for intentional affirmative misrepresentations is consistent with the policy behind allowing minors to disaffirm their contracts. Minors, by definition, are more likely than adults to make errors and other innocent misrepresentations. Given this symmetry of rationale, the courts are likely to continue allowing minors to disaffirm despite innocent, even negligent, misrepresentations.

Here, the sales agent simply asked Buckley whether she was old enough to buy a car. Buckley misunderstood the question, thinking that the agent was asking whether she was old enough to drive. Thus she innocently answered "yes." She did not affirmatively state an age at all. This kind of misunderstanding is exactly the sort of confusion a minor is likely to experience.

Buckley's representation that she was old enough to buy a car is significantly different from the representations in the cases holding that the minor cannot disaffirm. Unlike the minors in *Carney*, *Clemons*, and *Watters*, Buckley never stated her age at all. Also unlike the facts in those cases, Buckley's assertion, taken to mean what she intended it to mean (that she was old enough to drive), was not even false. Further, Buckley made only this single, ambiguous statement, in comparison to the several oral and written assertions of a specific age, as in the facts of the earlier cases.

Buckley's statement is much closer to the situation in *Woodall*, in which the minor made the representation unknowingly. In *Woodall*, the minor did not know that he was making the representation because he did not read the form contract he was signing. Buckley did not know that she might be making a representation that she was eighteen because she misunderstood the agent's question. In both cases, the requisite intent to deceive is absent. Since Buckley did not intend to deceive Willis Chevrolet, a court would probably allow her to disaffirm the contract.

However, Buckley must realize that the sales agent's testimony describing their conversation may differ from hers. The agent may remember the conversation differently or may testify falsely. Others may claim to have overheard the conversation. One way or another, Buckley's testimony may be controverted. Further, the documents Buckley signed may have contained representations of age, and other witnesses may testify that Buckley read them. If we decide to proceed with Buckley's case, we will need to learn what testimony Willis Chevrolet will offer and what the documents contain. On the facts we now have, however, a court would probably conclude that Buckley did not fraudulently misrepresent her age.

B. Willis Chevrolet's reliance on Buckley's representation was probably reasonable.

The next element requires the injured party to have justifiably relied on the representation. *Carney*, 88 S.E.2d at 808. The cases that describe this element allude to the minor's physical appearance, the minor's life circumstances known to the injured party, the lack of any reason to cause the party to suspect the representation, and the lack of a ready means of confirming the representation. *Clemons*, 187 S.E. at 712-713; *Hood*, 125 S.E. at 788; *Carney*, 88 S.E.2d at 808; *Watters*, 146 S.E. at 773-774.

For instance, in *Carney*, the court points out that the minor was married, was a father, and appeared to be of the age of majority. 88 S.E.2d at 808. In *Hood*, the court points to the minor's physical appearance and to the seller's knowledge that the minor had been married and living independently with his wife for about four years. 125 S.E. at 788. While the decisions sometimes articulate the standard as whether the defendant "failed to use all ready means" to ascertain the truth, *see, e.g., Carney*, 88 S.E.2d at 808, none of the reported decisions have found circumstances requiring the defendant to go further than the minor's representation. In fact, *Clemons* specifically held that a contracting party need not undertake an affirmative investigation beyond the representation of age when the contracting party has no reason to doubt the assertion. 187 S.E. at 713-714.

Buckley's facts do not indicate whether the sales agent knew anything about Buckley's life circumstances that would lead the agent to suspect that Buckley might not be eighteen. The facts also do not include a physical description of Buckley, although we can infer that she looks young, since the agent questioned her about her age. Although this issue would be a question of fact at trial, the facts seem similar to the facts in the reported cases. Contrary to the facts in *Hood*, Buckley is close enough to eighteen that an agent probably would not be expected to suspect her minority simply from her appearance. Also unlike the *Hood* facts, we have no reason to believe that the agent knew anything about Buckley's life, nor that he had any reason other than her appearance to suspect that she was a minor. Therefore, the facts may not be sufficient to require the agent to go further than questioning Buckley.

However, one might argue that the agent had at least one "ready means" to verify Buckley's answer, namely asking to see her driver's license. There is no discussion of requiring this simple verification in any of the prior cases, but at least for some of them, that may be because drivers licenses were not required at the time those cases were decided. Not only would this solution have been simple, but requiring it would facilitate an important policy rationale for the rule. The rule is designed to discourage sellers from being too ready to contract with minors, despite the inherent pressure to make sales. Requiring sellers to verify the ages of buyers who appear young would counteract the possible tendency of sellers to be too easily convinced of a buyer's majority.

The court's ruling on the second element probably would be a close one. However, based on the applicable case law, a court probably would find the agent's reliance reasonable.

C. Buckley had almost certainly reached the age of discretion when she made the representation of her age.

A minor cannot be held responsible for a misrepresentation unless the minor had reached the age of discretion when he or she made the misrepresentation. *Carney,* 88 S.E.2d at 808; *Clemons,* 187 S.E. at 713. A minor reaches the age of discretion when the minor has developed the capacity to conceive a fraudulent intent. *Clemons* points out that most minors have reached the age of discretion for criminal prosecution for fraud at least by the age of fourteen, though probably not by the age of ten. *Clemons* concludes that the eighteen-year-old minor in that case was well within the age of discretion. *Id.* at 713.

Buckley was seventeen when she bought the car, just a few months away from the age of majority. She is three years older than the presumptive age of discretion for criminal prosecution, and criminal prosecution probably requires more assurance of sufficient age than simple estoppel in a contract action. A court almost certainly would conclude that Buckley had reached the age of discretion.

CONCLUSION

Buckley can disaffirm unless (1) she fraudulently misrepresented her age, (2) Willis Chevrolet justifiably relied upon the misrepresentation, and (3) Buckley had reached the age of discretion. On the facts as we presently understand them, a court would probably rule that Buckley did not misrepresent her age. A court might also rule that Willis Chevrolet was not justified in relying on Buckley's representation. Given the probable absence of one required element and the possible absence of another, Buckley can probably disaffirm the contract.

Sample Trial-Level Brief

IN THE UNITED STATES DISTRICT COURT
FOR THE DISTRICT OF COLORADO

RANDALL BROWNLEY,
    Plaintiff

  v.

                                  Civ. No. 95-14867

SCOTT DUNN, d/b/a DUNN CREDIT
BUREAU,
        Defendant

BRIEF IN SUPPORT OF DEFENDANT'S MOTION
TO SET ASIDE DEFAULT JUDGMENT

INTRODUCTION

This is an action alleging a violation of Section 607(b) of the Fair Credit Reporting Act (FCRA), 15 U.S.C.A. § 1681e(b) (West 1995). The Complaint was filed and served upon Scott Dunn on October 27, 1995. Default judgment was entered six days ago, on November 17, 1995, just one day after the expiration of Mr. Dunn's time to answer the Complaint. Mr. Dunn now files a Motion to Set Aside this Default Judgment, along with a supporting affidavit and a proposed Answer to the Complaint. This brief is filed in support of Mr. Dunn's Motion.

STATEMENT OF FACTS

In September 1995, a potential lender contacted Dunn Credit Bureau requesting a credit report on the Plaintiff. Aff. Scott Dunn ¶ 10 (Nov. 26, 1995). The Credit Bureau prepared the report, and it contained a reference to an unpaid department store account. Aff. Scott Dunn ¶ 11. Upon the discovery of this item on his credit report, the Plaintiff contacted Mr. Dunn to demand that the item be removed, arguing that the charged merchandise had been defective and that the defect was the reason for his nonpayment. Aff. Scott Dunn ¶ 12. Mr. Dunn asked the Plaintiff to provide this explanation in writing and promised to include it along with the store's version of the account. Aff. Scott Dunn ¶ 13.

The Plaintiff refused to provide the written explanation, but again demanded that the item be entirely removed. Aff. Scott Dunn ¶ 14. Mr. Dunn replied by letter, declining to delete the item entirely but repeating the offer to include the Plaintiff's defense to the item. Aff. Scott Dunn ¶ 14. The Plaintiff did not respond to Mr. Dunn's letter, and Mr. Dunn did not hear from the Plaintiff again. Aff. Scott Dunn ¶ 15.

On October 27, 1995, copies of the Summons and Complaint in this action were served at Mr. Dunn's home by leaving them with Mr. Dunn's sixteen-year-old son, Gregory. (Ret. of Serv. Oct. 30, 1995.) On that day, Mr. Dunn and his wife had traveled to Denver, planning to return the next day. Aff. Scott Dunn ¶ 3.

However, on the evening of October 27, Mrs. Dunn suffered a serious heart attack and was hospitalized. Aff. Scott Dunn ¶ 4. Gregory left immediately for Denver. In the midst of the crisis surrounding his mother's heart attack, Gregory did not think to tell his father about the delivery of an envelope to the family home. Aff. Scott Dunn ¶ 6.

Mr. Dunn remained in Denver with his wife for two weeks until Mrs. Dunn was released from the hospital to return home. Aff. Scott Dunn ¶ 5. Upon his return, Mr. Dunn began going in to his office part-time, while continuing to care for his wife. Aff. Scott Dunn ¶ 7. Mr. Dunn did not find the envelope until November 20, 1995. On that day, Mr. Dunn moved a stack of papers on the table in the family room and found the envelope there. Aff. Scott Dunn ¶ 8.

Mr. Dunn immediately called his attorney and began the preparations to file an Answer to the Complaint. Aff. Scott Dunn ¶ 9. Shortly after the initial telephone conversation with his attorney, Mr. Dunn learned that a default judgment had been entered three days earlier. Aff. Scott Dunn ¶ 9. Mr. Dunn now seeks an order, pursuant to Fed. R. Civ. P. 60(b), setting aside this default judgment.

ARGUMENT

I. THE DEFAULT JUDGMENT SHOULD BE SET ASIDE BECAUSE IT WAS ENTERED AS A RESULT OF INADVERTENCE OR EXCUSABLE NEGLECT AND BECAUSE THE DEFENDANT HAS A MERITORIOUS DEFENSE TO THE PLAINTIFF'S ALLEGATIONS.

Fed. R. Civ. P. 60(b) grants the Court the discretion to relieve a party from a final judgment entered as a result of inadvertence or excusable neglect. When the judgment was entered upon the moving party's default, the moving party must also demonstrate the existence of a potentially meritorious defense. *In re Stone*, 588 F.2d 1316, 1319 (10th Cir. 1978). Any doubts are to be resolved in favor of adjudication on the merits. *In re Roxford Foods, Inc.*, 12 F.3d 875, 879 (9th Cir. 1993). Mr. Dunn's facts easily establish both Rule 60(b) requirements.

A. The Defendant's Default Resulted from Excusable Neglect Because Service Was Effected upon the Defendant's Minor Son and the Crisis of His Mother's Heart Attack Caused the Son to Forget to Inform the Defendant of the Service.

Mr. Dunn meets the first requirement for Rule 60(b) relief because the default resulted from excusable neglect.

The United States Supreme Court has defined the term "excusable neglect," in the context of bankruptcy filings, to include giving "little attention or respect" or "leav[ing] undone or unattended . . . esp[ecially] through carelessness." *Pioneer Inv. Servs. Co. v. Brunswick Assocs. Ltd. Partnership*, 507 U.S. 380 (1993). Last year the Tenth Circuit adopted this definition of excusable neglect in the context of a Rule 60(b) motion. *City of Chanute, Kansas v. Williams Nat. Gas Co.*, 31 F.3d 1041 (10th Cir. 1994). The Tenth Circuit specifically held that Rule 60(b) relief is not limited to circumstances beyond the moving party's control. *Id.* at 1046.

The Tenth Circuit's analysis of excusable neglect considers four factors: (1) the potential prejudice to the nonmoving party; (2) the length of delay; (3) the reason for the delay; and (4) the degree of good faith of the moving party. *Id.* at 1046-1047.

The first factor, the prejudice to the nonmoving party, must amount to more than simply delaying enforcement of the judgment. *Feliciano v. Reliant Tooling Co.*, 691 F.2d 653, 656-657 (3d Cir. 1982). Usually cognizable prejudice involves some change of position in reliance on the judgment. The second factor, the length of delay, measures both the time since the entry of judgment and the time since the party became aware of the judgment. *See Lasky v. International Union,* 27 Fed. R. Serv. 2d 473, 477 (E.D. Mich. 1978), *aff'd,* 638 F.2d 954 (6th Cir. 1981).

The third factor examines the validity of the reason for the delay and whether the delay was willful. The Tenth Circuit has consistently affirmed orders setting aside default judgments entered as a result of understandable error or inadvertence as opposed to willful action by the defendant. For example, the court affirmed a decision to set aside a default judgment entered while the plaintiff believed that his new attorney was negotiating a settlement that would resolve the litigation. *Thompson v. Kerr-McGee Ref. Corp.,* 660 F.2d 1380 (10th Cir. 1981). The Tenth Circuit also affirmed an order granting Rule 60(b) relief from a judgment caused by confusion about filing a notice of appeal. *Romero v. Peterson,* 930 F.2d 1502 (10th Cir. 1991).

The excusable reasons for delay in these cases contrast with cases in which the default resulted from a willful decision by the defendant. For example, in *Cessna Fin. Corp. v. Bielenberg Masonry Contracting, Inc.,* 715 F.2d 1442 (10th Cir. 1983), the court affirmed the trial court's decision denying relief to a corporate defendant whose representatives had decided not to answer the complaint because they believed that the corporate defendant would escape liability in bankruptcy. In *United States v. Theodorovich,* 102 F.R.D. 587 (D.D.C. 1984), the court denied relief because the default judgment had resulted from defendant's willful decisions not to attend his own properly scheduled depositions.

The final factor asks whether the defendant has acted in good faith. This factor invites the court to consider the broad equitable question of whether the moving party has dealt in good faith with the court and with the other parties to the litigation.

Applying these four factors to the present case demonstrates that Rule 60(b) relief is certainly appropriate here. First, granting the Defendant's Motion would not cause the Plaintiff to suffer any cognizable prejudice. The default judgment was entered less than one week ago. The only cognizable prejudice that would result from setting aside the judgment stems from the costs the Plaintiff incurred in seeking the entry of the judgment. The Defendant has offered to pay those reasonable costs Aff. Scott Dunn ¶ 16, and an order to that effect would sufficiently relieve the Plaintiff of even this small prejudice. *Littlefield v. Walt Flanagan and Co.,* 498 F.2d 1133 (10th Cir. 1974).

The "length of delay" factor also weighs in favor of granting the motion. Only three days elapsed between the entry of the default judgment and the Defendant's discovery of the litigation. Only three days elapsed between the Defendant's discovery and the filing of the Motion and supporting documents. By comparison, the Tenth Circuit found a delay of thirty-one days "short." *City of Chanute,* 31 F.3d at 1047. A six-day delay is well within permissible bounds.

The third factor, the validity of the reason for delay, is often the most important factor. In the present case, this critical factor is the most compelling of all. Here, the delay was caused by the sudden and serious heart attack of Mr. Dunn's wife and Gregory's mother Aff. Scott Dunn ¶¶ 4-9. That a teenager should forget to tell his father about the Summons and Complaint under such circumstances is certainly understandable. This is precisely the sort of omission that Rule 60(b) is designed to forgive.

Mr. Dunn's good faith also argues for relieving the Defendant from judgment. Mr. Dunn has dealt with both the Court and the Plaintiff entirely in good faith. The delay was not caused by any stratagem or artifice. Mr. Dunn was entirely unaware of the litigation. Immediately upon learning of the Complaint, Mr. Dunn hurriedly contacted his attorney and began the process of responding to the litigation Aff. Scott Dunn ¶ 9. Mr. Dunn's offer to bear the Plaintiff's costs is further evidence of his good faith.

Thus all four factors of the Rule 60(b) analysis place the Defendant's situation squarely within the parameters for Rule 60(b) relief and establish that Mr. Dunn meets the first requirement for setting aside the default judgment.

> B. The Defendant Has a Meritorious Defense to the Complaint Because the Credit Report Accurately Reflects the Plaintiff's Admitted Failure to Pay the Account.

Mr. Dunn also meets the second requirement for Rule 60(b) relief, the existence of a meritorious defense. A plaintiff alleging a violation of 15 U.S.C. § 1681e(b) must establish two elements: (1) that the credit report is inaccurate; and (2) that the inaccuracy flows from the reporting agency's failure to follow reasonable procedures. *Cahlin v. General Motors Corp.*, 936 F.2d 1151, 1156 (11th Cir. 1991). Establishing inaccuracy is a threshold requirement for a Section 1681e(b) claim. *Id.* at 1156.

The accuracy requirement of the FCRA does not require the credit reporting agency to delete all reference to an unpaid account merely because it is disputed. This is true even if the consumer ultimately pays the account. *Id.* In *Cahlin*, the plaintiff's credit report included reference to a disputed account. Initially the account was unpaid, but after it appeared on the credit report, the consumer settled the account for partial payment. The consumer then demanded that the credit agency delete all reference to the account. *Id.* at 1155.

The Eleventh Circuit held that Section 607(b) does not require a credit reporting agency to report only favorable information. The court specifically held that the agency did not have to delete the reference to the disputed account even though the dispute was settled, explaining that such an interpretation would gut the very purpose of a credit report. *Id.* at 1158.

Here the Plaintiff's credit report accurately reflects his failure to pay the balance owed on a department store charge account Aff. Scott Dunn

¶11. Further, unlike the account in *Cahlin,* the Plaintiff's account remains unpaid. The Credit Bureau offered to include the consumer's written statement describing the dispute, as required by 15 U.S.C.A. § 1681*i*(b) (West 1995). The Plaintiff refused. This refusal is the only impediment to a more complete description of the Plaintiff's dispute with the account holder. The Plaintiff's demand that the item be removed entirely would have decreased rather than increased the report's accuracy because it would have omitted all reference to an admittedly unpaid, though disputed, debt. The Act simply does not require this sort of concealment of a consumer's true credit history.

Thus, the Plaintiff's credit report is accurate, and the Credit Bureau did not violate FCRA. Mr. Dunn has a meritorious defense to the Plaintiff's Complaint.

CONCLUSION

Mr. Dunn meets both requirements for Rule 60(b) relief. All four factors for evaluating inadvertence or excusable neglect strongly argue in favor of granting Mr. Dunn relief under Rule 60(b). Further, the Plaintiff's credit report met the accuracy requirement under FCRA, and thus Mr. Dunn has a meritorious defense to the complaint. Mr. Dunn respectfully requests the Court to enter an order setting aside the judgment and allowing him to file his Answer and to otherwise defend this action.

DATED: _____

_____
Attorney for the Defendant

CERTIFICATE OF SERVICE

I, _____, attorney for the Defendant, do hereby certify that I have served upon the Plaintiff a complete and accurate copy of this Brief in Support of the Defendant's Motion to Set Aside Default Judgment, by placing the copy in the United States Mail, sufficient postage affixed and addressed as follows:

[name and address of Plaintiff's attorney]

DATED: _____

_____
Attorney for the Defendant

Sample Appellate Brief

The issue addressed in this brief is essentially a pure question of law, requiring interpretation of a rule of evidence. Therefore, the rule explanation sections focus primarily on the language of the rule, the intent of the rule's drafters, and the policies served by adhering to the rule's plain language. The writer relies on case authorities as well, but since the cases are not mandatory authority for this court, the writer presents the cases as further support for the primary arguments of plain meaning, intent of the drafters, and policy.

In both the "plain language" section and the "intent of the drafters" section, notice how closely the writer focuses on the actual words of Rule 615. If the case authority had defined the Rule's terms more fully, the writer would have relied primarily on case authority for the definitions of the words used in the Rule. Even without strong case authority defining the terms, however, a writer can use legal and other dictionaries to parse each word of a rule or statute, as the writer has done here.

In the "intent of the drafters" section, the writer casts the Rule as primarily defining what restrictions a party can force on other parties as a matter of course, without justifying the need for the restrictions. This section expressly articulates the primary theme of the brief, contrasting the trial court's powers with the powers given to parties. The section relies on a canon of statutory construction to point out not only what is included in the Rule's plain language, but also what is omitted. The writer also discusses the Rule's silence on important questions that would arise routinely if the Rule had been intended to have the scope urged by the appellant. This section ends by pointing out that the trial court, which presumably knew what it meant by its own order, did not intend that the order apply in the manner the appellant has proposed, thus harkening back to the theme of reliance on the court's trial management powers.

Then, after the rule explanation sections, the writer applies the Rule to the facts of the case before the court. The way the Rule will apply to these facts is clear, but the writer uses the rule application section as an opportunity to reinforce the points made in the rule explanation sections and to reassure the court that justice will not be infringed by a ruling in the appellee's favor.

IN THE UNITED STATES COURT OF APPEALS
FOR THE FIFTEENTH[1] CIRCUIT

DENNIS IRVING,
    Appellant

v.

Docket No. 04-1234

THE UNITED STATES
    OF AMERICA,
      Appellee.

BRIEF OF THE APPELLEE[2]

---

1. This is a hypothetical circuit.

2. This brief is based on briefs written by students in the Spring 2005 Advanced Writing Groups at Mercer University School of Law. Professor Beth Cook of the Pennsylvania State University Dickinson School of Law graciously allowed the use of the problem that was adapted for that class.

TABLE OF CONTENTS

TABLE OF AUTHORITIES

QUESTION PRESENTED

Whether Rule 615 of the Federal Rules of Evidence should be expanded to apply to communications outside the courtroom where (1) the trial court did not intend that its routine Rule 615 order should limit outside conversation; (2) the defendant never requested a broad sequestration order; (3) the court did not instruct witnesses to refrain from discussing their testimony; (4) a police officer spoke about his testimony to his co-worker; and (5) during the co-worker's subsequent testimony, the defendant was able to cross-examine the co-worker about the conversation.

RULE OF EVIDENCE INVOLVED

Federal Rule of Evidence 615 provides:

At the request of a party the court shall order witnesses excluded so that they cannot hear the testimony of other witnesses, and it may make the order of its own motion. This rule does not authorize exclusion of (1) a party who is a natural person, or (2) an officer or employee of a party which is not a natural person designated as its representative by its attorney, or (3) a person whose presence is shown by a party to be essential to the presentation of the party's cause, or (4) a person authorized by statute to be present.

STANDARD OF REVIEW

Because rulings on motions to exclude testimony raise predominately legal questions regarding the interpretation of the Federal Rules of Evidence, the appellate court reviews those evidentiary rulings de novo. *U.S. v. Angwin*, 271 F.3d 786, 798 (9th Cir. 2001).

STATEMENT OF THE CASE

On May 8, 2004, the Defendant, Dennis Irving, sold to Nathan Roberts more than 50 grams of methamphetamine, a Schedule II controlled substance. (R. 1.) Officers Miller and Nelson witnessed the transaction and immediately arrested both men. (R. 1.) Subsequently, a grand jury indicted the Defendant for offenses involving the possession and distribution of methamphetamine. (R. 2.)

In pretrial proceedings, the district court granted the Defendant's Motion to Exclude Witnesses Pursuant to Rule 615 of the Federal Rules of Evidence and specifically ordered all prospective witnesses to leave the courtroom. (R. 4.) The court, however, did not instruct the witnesses or counsel that witnesses were prohibited from discussing their testimony with each other. (R. 4.)

On September 22, 2004, the trial began. That day, during the government's case-in-chief, Officer Nelson testified that he had seen the Defendant hand to Roberts the envelope containing the drugs. (R. 5.) Later that evening, Officer Nelson had dinner with Officer Miller, who was scheduled to testify the following day. (R. 6.) A research assistant for the Defendant's attorney was seated nearby. (R. 7.) According to the research assistant, as the officers ate dinner, Officer Nelson described the testimony he had given at trial that morning. (R. 7.) In pre-trial statements, Officer Miller had described first seeing the two men at the point where the envelope was already in Roberts's hand. (R. 7.) Allegedly, after hearing a description of Officer Nelson's testimony, Officer Miller stated that he now remembered seeing the Defendant hand the envelope to Roberts. (R. 7.)

The next day, the Defendant moved to exclude Officer Miller's testimony, arguing that the dinner conversation between Officers Nelson and Miller the previous evening violated the court's Rule 615 order to exclude witnesses from the courtroom. (R. 5.) The district court heard argument and denied Defendant's motion. (R. 6.) The court reasoned that a witness's refreshed recollection of events (1) was common when talking to another person involved in the same incident; (2) was not evidence that the witness planned to perjure himself; and (3) did not violate the court's Rule 615 order, which barred witnesses only from being physically present in the courtroom. (R. 6.)

Later that day, Officer Miller testified at trial. (R. 7.) The Defendant's attorney cross-examined Officer Miller, confronting him with his previous statements and questioning him about his conversation with Officer Nelson the previous evening. (R. 6.) After hearing this cross-examination and all of the other evidence in the case, the jury convicted the Defendant on all counts. (R. 7.) The District Judge sentenced the Defendant to serve 56 months in a federal prison (R. 7.), and the Defendant has now filed this appeal.

SUMMARY OF THE ARGUMENT

Federal Rule of Evidence 615 provides that upon the request of a party, the trial court "shall order witnesses excluded so that they cannot hear the testimony of other witnesses." Fed. R. Evid. 615. The Appellant asks this Court to hold that a routine Rule 615 order also prohibits witnesses from discussing their testimony with each other. Neither the plain meaning of the Rule, the intent of its drafters, nor sound public policy support the Appellant's argument.

First, the plain meaning of Rule 615 is limited to physical presence in the courtroom. The Rule provides that witnesses shall be "excluded," meaning "expelled" or "barred"—a reference to physical presence, not to communication. The Rule sets out the reason for the exclusion, "so that" they do not "hear testimony." The word "testimony" means sworn statements of a competent witness in a trial, affidavit, or deposition. Therefore, by definition, witnesses cannot "hear testimony" unless they are present when the testimony is being given. Several courts, including the First and Eighth Circuits, have so held.

Further, the plain language of the Rule indicates the drafter's intention to limit only presence in the courtroom. Since a trial court already has the power to restrict witness communication as part of its inherent authority to manage proceedings before it, the Rule's primary purpose is to define the restrictions a *party* can impose unilaterally upon other parties. By expressly delineating the power to exclude witnesses from the courtroom, the Rule impliedly withholds from parties other, broader powers. Also, the drafters did not address several key questions that would arise regularly if Rule 615 had been intended to apply beyond the courtroom, such as exactly what witnesses are prohibited from saying and whether the prohibition precludes attorneys from preparing witnesses for their testimony.

Finally, application of Rule 615 beyond its express terms would disrupt the Rule's carefully crafted balance of the rights of parties and the efficient administration of trials. Broad witness sequestration is available outside Rule 615 in those cases where restrictions on witness communication are appropriate. Blanket restrictions, however, would be burdensome to witnesses and unworkable for the trial court. Enforcement proceedings would interrupt trials and squander judicial resources. Without guidance about what sorts of communications are prohibited, outcomes of these hearings would be unpredictable. Witnesses unwilling to risk charges of contempt of court would be inclined not to testify at all.

According to its express terms, the drafter's intent, and sound policy rationales, a routine Rule 615 order is limited to excluding witnesses from physical presence in the courtroom and does not apply to conversations between witnesses. Therefore, the Rule 615 order below did not prohibit the conversation between Officers Nelson and Miller. The Government respectfully requests this Court to affirm the trial court's denial of the Defendant's motion to exclude testimony.

ARGUMENT

I. THE COURT SHOULD AFFIRM THE TRIAL COURT'S DECISION BECAUSE RULE 615 PROHIBITS ONLY PHYSICAL PRESENCE IN THE COURTROOM AND THEREFORE DOES NOT APPLY TO OUTSIDE COMMUNICATIONS SUCH AS THE DINNER CONVERSATION BETWEEN OFFICERS NELSON AND MILLER.

Rule 615 provides that, upon a party's request, the trial court "shall order witnesses *excluded* so that they cannot hear the *testimony* of other witnesses." Fed. R. Evid. 615 (emphasis added). According to the Rule's plain language, a Rule 615 order bans prospective witnesses from the courtroom, but does not restrict communication outside the courtroom. The Defendant seeks to extend the scope of Rule 615 beyond its plain language, in contravention of the intent of the Rule's drafters and in derogation of the trial court's inherent discretionary authority to manage its courtroom. The district court rejected such an interpretation of the rule, and this Court should affirm the district court's ruling.

A.   The Plain Language of Rule 615 Applies Only to a Witness's Physical Presence in the Courtroom.

The first step in interpreting a rule is to examine the language itself. If the language is plain and unambiguous, a court should not look past this plain meaning. *Shotz v. City of Plantation*, 344 F.3d 1161, 1167 (11th Cir. 2003); *Thompson v. Goeztmann*, 337 F.3d 489 (5th Cir. 2003). Dictionaries often are used to confirm the plain meaning of statutory text.

The issue before the Court concerns only one sentence of Rule 615: "At the request of a party the court shall order witnesses excluded so that they cannot hear the testimony of other witnesses, and it may make the order of its own motion." Fed. R. Evid. 615. The phrase at issue is "*exclude* [] so that they cannot *hear . . . testimony.*" *Id.* (emphasis added). "Exclude" means to "expel or ban." *Merriam-Webster's Collegiate Dictionary* (11th ed. 2003). "Testimony" means "evidence that a competent witness under oath or affirmation gives at trial or in an affidavit or deposition." *Black's Law Dictionary* 1485 (Bryan A. Garner ed., 7th ed., West 2000). The plain, ordinary, straightforward language of the rule, therefore, provides only that witnesses are banned from the courtroom so they do not hear other witnesses *as they testify.*

The Rule goes on to identify the reason for exclusion from the courtroom: "so that they cannot hear the testimony of other witnesses." This phrase does not define a broad category of situations to which the Rule will apply. Rather, the phrase expressly uses the language of purpose ("so that") to set out the reason for the exclusion from the courtroom. The plain language of Rule 615, therefore, says nothing at all about what a witness may say or do outside the courtroom. *See U.S. v. Scharstein*, 531 F. Supp. 460, 462-63 (E.D. Ky. 1982).

Even if the word "exclude" could be redefined to refer to something other than banning an individual from the courtroom, Rule 615, by its own terms, would apply only to hearing *testimony*. A participant in a restaurant conversation over dinner is not "hearing testimony." In that setting, no one is under oath, no one is being questioned by an attorney, and no rules of evidence apply. The express language of Rule 615 does not apply to communications of that sort. *See* 29 Charles Alan Wright & Victor James Gold, *Federal Practice and Procedure* § 6243, at 57 ("Testimony is given only in a formal legal context such as a deposition, hearing, or trial. Thus witness communication outside that context does not enable witnesses to 'hear testimony.'").

Several courts have held that the language of Rule 615 limits only physical presence of witnesses in the courtroom. For instance, in *Sepulveda v. U.S.*, 15 F.3d 1161, 1176 (1st Cir. 1993), the First Circuit held the Rule inapplicable to extra-courtroom communication. In that case, the defendants had been charged with offenses relating to the distribution of cocaine, and the trial court had issued a Rule 615 order before trial began. *Id.* at 1176. Later in the trial, the defendants alleged that extra-courtroom witness contact had violated the Rule 615 order. The court held that a Rule 615 order does not prohibit witness communication, stating that the Rule 615 order had "plowed a straight furrow in line with Rule 615 itself [and therefore] did not extend beyond the courtroom." *Id.* at 1176.

The Eighth Circuit also has held Rule 615 inapplicable to extra-courtroom communications. *U.S. v. Smith*, 578 F.2d 1227, 1235 (8th Cir. 1978). In *Smith*, defendants were on trial for offences associated with the distribution of heroin. *Id.* at 1229. Early in the trial, the court had issued a Rule 615 order excluding witnesses from the courtroom. As trial progressed, a police officer took notes and relayed information to government witnesses waiting to testify. *Id.* at 1234. The trial court held that this conduct did not violate the Rule 615 order because Rule 615 only excludes witnesses from the courtroom. *Id.* The Eighth Circuit affirmed the trial court's holding, noting that the defendants had not requested additional restrictions beyond Rule 615. *Id.* at 1235. The appellate court stated that the question of whether to instruct witnesses not to communicate with other witnesses is within a trial court's discretion. *Id.* at 1235. Such a discretionary instruction is not, therefore, mandated by the plain language of Rule 615.

Similarly, the court in *Scharstein* held that the plain language of Rule 615 limits only physical presence in the courtroom. 531 F. Supp. at 463-64. In *Scharstein*, defendants had been charged with illegally manufacturing, storing, and transporting explosives. *Id.* at 461. The court declined to expand the application of Rule 615 to prohibit witnesses from conferring with each other outside the courtroom. The court stated, "[T]his court believes that there is no reason to go beyond the plain language of the Rule," observing that the question of whether to instruct witnesses not to discuss their testimony is within the court's discretion and not required by Rule 615. Id. at 463; *see also Lapenna v. Upjohn Co.*, 665 F. Supp. 412, 413 (E.D. Pa. 1987) (declining to apply Rule 615 "beyond the literal meaning of the rule").

B. The Drafters Did Not Intend Rule 615 to Apply Broadly to Communication Outside the Courtroom

Not only does the plain language of Rule 615 call for affirmance here, but indications of the drafters' intent support that result as well. Since a trial court already has inherent power to limit witness communication outside the courtroom, *Sepulveda*, 15 F.3d at 1176, the primary purpose of Rule 615 is to identify the restrictions *a party* can impose unilaterally on other trial participants. Therefore, the key inquiry is what unilateral and unrestrained powers the Rule's drafters intended to give to parties.

The drafters of the Rule rightly limited the unrestrained power the Rule would give to parties. At common law, when a court ordered sequestration, the order could include (1) preventing witnesses from hearing other witnesses testify; and (2) preventing prospective witnesses from consulting other witnesses. *Sepulveda*, 15 F.3d at 1176 (citing 6 John Wigmore, *Evidence* § 1840). When the drafters expressly included in Rule 615 the power to "exclude" witnesses, they impliedly excluded the right to impose other more intrusive limitations. According to the canon of statutory construction *expressio unius est exclusio alterius*, the expression of one thing implies the exclusion of another. *Thompson*, 337 F.3d at 499. Rule 615, therefore, does not give parties the unilateral power to prohibit communication outside the courtroom. That power remains within the discretion of the trial court.

In fact, Rule 615 does not use the term "sequester" at all. *Black's Law Dictionary* defines "sequester" to mean "to segregate or isolate [a witness] during trial." *Black's Law Dictionary* 1370 (Bryan A. Garner, ed., 7th ed., West 2000). Tellingly, the drafters did not use the term "sequester" in Rule 615. Rather, they selected only the first aspect of common law sequestration (the aspect that does not "segregate or isolate a witness") and refrained from using the term "sequester" to describe the scope of Rule 615. These drafting decisions provide further indication of an intent to withhold broad sequestration powers from the scope of Rule 615. *Scharstein*, 531 F. Supp. at 464.

Further, the drafters did not define categories of communication allegedly prohibited by the Rule—as they surely would have done had they intended to restrict communication. Violation of a trial court's order constitutes contempt of court, rendering the offending person at risk of fine or imprisonment. *U.S. v. Johnston*, 578 F.2d 1352 (10th Cir. 1978). A reading of Rule 615 to prohibit certain kinds of communication outside the courtroom would mean that witnesses who spoke outside the courtroom would be subject to contempt proceedings. If the drafters had intended to impose such serious individual liability for trial witnesses, they surely would have set out the prohibition clearly and defined its parameters unambiguously. The Appellant's proposed construction would render trial witnesses vulnerable to contempt proceedings without fair notice of what they must not do or what the penalties might be. The drafters cannot have intended such a result.

If the drafters had intended the construction urged by the Appellant, they also would have had to address the question of whether trial attorneys could continue preparing witnesses for their testimony. To prepare a witness to testify, any competent attorney confers with the witness about the status of the trial proceedings and about the testimony to come. *See generally U.S. v. DeJongh*, 937 F.2d 1, 3 (1st Cir. 1991) (A lawyer "would be foolhardy to call an important witness without attempting, first, to debrief the witness."). Because parties adjust their strategies as the trial progresses, these witness conferences are an essential part of trying a case. *Scharstein*, 531 F. Supp. at 463. In fact, the right to prepare a witness for his or her testimony is so fundamental that deprivation of this right may raise Due Process concerns. *Scharstein*, 531 F. Supp. at 463-64 (citing *Potashnic v. Port City Construction Company*, 609 F.2d 1001 (5th Cir. 1980)).

Had the drafters intended Rule 615 to limit extra-courtroom communication, they could have chosen either to prohibit trial attorneys from preparing witnesses or to exempt trial attorneys. Exempting trial attorneys would have rendered the proposed construction of Rule 615 pointless, however. Witnesses who have already testified would be precluded from speaking to prospective witnesses, but trial counsel could still describe prior testimony freely. In fact, since attorneys know precisely what will be most relevant in future testimony, allowing attorneys to describe prior testimony would be far more problematic than allowing other witnesses to describe their own testimony. To hold that Rule 615 prohibits witnesses from talking to each other but allows attorneys to prepare prospective witnesses for their testimony "would be an exercise in futility." *Scharstein*, 531 F. Supp. at 464.

Prohibiting trial attorneys from preparing witnesses, on the other hand, would have resulted in a sea change in standard trial preparation. Again, like the question of individual witness liability, such a drastic result would have called for express language in the Rule itself, language clearly applying the Rule to attorney conduct and identifying what attorneys could and could not say during witness preparation. Since the drafters did not address the question of whether and how Rule 615 would apply to communication with attorneys, it is most likely that the drafters did not intend to apply Rule 615 to extra-courtroom communication.

Finally, the intent of the Rule's drafters is not the only intent relevant to the question before this Court. The trial court issued its order under the authority of Rule 615, but an order limiting outside communication could have been issued as part of the court's inherent powers of trial management. *Sepulveda*, 15 F.3d at 1176. Therefore, the more important inquiry may be what the *trial court intended* by its order. A court's interpretation of its own order is given great weight. *Sepulveda*, 15 F.3d at 1177; *U.S. v. Smith*, 578 F.2d at 1235 ("holding that it is within the discretion of the trial court to determine whether or not a sequestration order has been violated"). If, as here, the *trial court* did not intend it's order to constrain conversation outside the courtroom, that order should not be redefined on appeal.

Both the intent of the drafters and the intent of the trial court issuing the order demonstrate that the conversation at issue did not violate the court's order. Neither the provisions of Rule 615 nor the court's own language reflect an intent to reach beyond the courtroom doors.

C. Expanding Rule 615 Beyond Its Express Terms Would Disrupt the Rule's Balance Between Providing Truth-Testing Strategies and Minimizing Unnecessary Litigation Costs.

The purposes of the Federal Rules of Evidence are to secure fairness in administration, eliminate unjustifiable expense and delay, ascertain the truth, and determine proceedings fairly. Fed. R. Evid. 102. The Rules aim to balance the need for legitimate truth-testing strategies with the need to minimize unnecessary expense. Expanding the scope of Rule 615 would unnecessarily disrupt the delicate balance Rule 615 has achieved.

Applying Rule 615 to out-of-court conduct is not necessary to obtain truthful testimony. Barring witnesses from the courtroom prevents them from hearing testimony directly, so their only knowledge of prior testimony will be by the general recollection of others. In most cases, this limitation will be sufficient. *Sepulveda*, 15 F.3d at 1176. Further, a party suspecting that witness contact may have influenced testimony is free to cross-examine a witness about that contact and its content, as occurred in the case before the Court. For cases in which greater protection is appropriate, the trial court can, *sua sponte* or on proper motion, impose greater limitations, including ordering witnesses not to disclose their testimony. In fact, this reliance on the discretion of the trial court is fundamental to the federal trial process. *Scharstein*, 531 F. Supp. at 464 ("The general approach of the Federal Rules of Evidence is to place heavy reliance on the discretion of the trial court in conducting a fair trial."). Thus, the very protection the Appellant seeks is already available without stretching Rule 615 beyond its intended application.

Not only is expansion of the Rule's scope unnecessary, but application to out-of-court communications would result in significant and often unnecessary administrative costs. First, enforcement would be extremely difficult. A court can easily enforce an order banning witnesses from the courtroom, but violations outside the judge's presence are difficult to discover. 29 Charles Alan Wright & Victor James Gold, *Federal Practice and Procedure*, § 6243, at 63 (West 1997). Further, enforcing routine orders prohibiting witness contact would require the court to undertake "an undue amount of supervision" over witnesses, distracting the court from its primary function. *Scharstein*, 531 F. Supp. at 464 n.7.

Second, extension of the Rule would result in long delays during trials. Each time two witnesses talked, there could be grounds for a motion alleging a violation of Rule 615 and a resulting evidentiary hearing to learn the content of the conversation. Witnesses would be called upon to disclose publically everything they had said to each other. These hearings would occur frequently, especially in long trials with many witnesses. *Id.* at 464. Constant interruptions would impede trial management, increase litigation costs, and absorb significant judicial resources. Courts would be "bogged down in numerous inquiries . . . when there is no genuine need to do so." *Id.*

Third, the outcome of these hearings would be uncertain at best. The Rule does not define what kinds of communication would be prohibited. Neither parties nor witnesses nor the district court itself would know whether a violation had occurred if a witness stated that she had testified; that her testimony was over; that the cross-examination had been brief; that she had been nervous; that she had testified about a particular topic; or that a particular question had been asked. With no clear standard of what could and could not be said, hearings would be numerous and issues would be difficult to resolve. *Id.*; 29 Wright, *Federal Practice* at § 6243.

Fourth, extension of the Rule would place unrealistic hardships on witnesses. An order limiting out-of-court communication between witnesses places far greater burdens on witnesses than does mere exclusion from the courtroom. Wright, *Federal Practice* at § 6243. Witnesses testifying in the same case often are spouses or co-workers. Communication between spouses or other close associates should be restricted only when absolutely necessary, not any time a party decides to invoke Rule 615.

Fifth, extending the Rule to out-of-court statements would render witnesses vulnerable to contempt proceedings. The combination of this vulnerability and the lack of clarity about what kinds of communication are prohibited would discourage witnesses from testifying. Discouraging testimony would impede the goal of obtaining truthful testimony to a far greater degree than would a decision to keep Rule 615 within its intended bounds.

Sixth, to apply Rule 615 to out-of-court conversations would be to give any party, as a matter of right, the ability to impose significant limitations on all witnesses in the case, including spouses and co-workers who must continue to have close daily contact with each other as the trial progresses. A party could use Rule 615 as another way to make the trial experience as unpleasant as possible for opposing parties and witnesses. This approach to trial management does not assist in achieving just and fair results at trial.

Only one circumstance—the reading of transcripts of actual testimony—justifies the application of Rule 615 beyond its express terms. In *Miller v. U.S.*, 650 F.2d 1365, 1367 (5th Cir. 1981), the trial court had entered an order excluding witnesses under Rule 615. *Id.* at 1372. During the trial, however, the defendant's expert witness was provided with daily transcripts of the trial testimony. The district court held that providing transcripts of testimony violated the Rule 615 order, and the appellate court affirmed, explaining that the harm of *reading* testimony is potentially greater than the harm of *hearing* testimony. *Id.* Accordingly, the court held that a Rule 615 order prohibits witnesses from reading trial transcripts prior to testifying. *Id.* at 1373.

The *Miller* exception does not apply to conversation outside the courtroom, however. The court in *Miller* compared hearing actual testimony with reading a transcript and found the key difference to be that a listener would have to rely on his or her memory of the testimony while a reader would not. *Id.* at 1372. This key distinction does not apply to conversation outside the courtroom. Unlike the reader of a transcript, who can thoroughly study the actual testimony, a participant in a conversation must rely on his or her memory of the conversation. Perhaps more significantly, the *speaker* must rely on memories of the testimony as well. By the very rationale explained in *Miller*, therefore, the danger of casual conversation outside the courtroom is considerably smaller than the danger Rule 615 is designed to prevent. Thus, the *Miller* exception does not apply to extra-courtroom conversation. In fact, *Miller's* very rationale demonstrates a key reason for limiting Rule 615 to "testimony" rather than to mere recollections of testimony.

Further, the narrow *Miller* exception is consistent with the rationales on which Rule 615 is based. The *Miller* exception does not impose the administrative costs and personal impositions on witnesses that the Appellant's construction would impose. Prohibiting the reading of transcripts creates a bright-line test, easily applied in enforcement proceedings. Witnesses need not wonder what they may and may not say. Parties need not wonder what conduct may violate the Rule 615 order. Also, a witness has access to trial transcripts only through trial attorneys, who are officers of the court and therefore more easily and effectively governed by trial court orders. Further, the prohibition on reading transcripts does not interfere with normal daily interactions between witnesses who live or work together or who encounter each other in casual interactions in the hallway.

In all other circumstances, trial judges have broad discretion to limit contact between witnesses when appropriate. *Sepulveda*, 15 F.3d at 1176. In those few cases in which a small nuance in testimony may determine the outcome, a Rule 615 exclusion of witnesses may be insufficient. *Scharstein*, 531 F. Supp. at 464. In such cases, the trial court can use its broad case management powers to determine whether "extra-courtroom prophylaxis" is necessary and what means best accomplishes the goal in that case. *Sepulveda*, 15 F.3d at 1176 (citing *U.S. v. Arias-Santana*, 964 F.2d 1262, 1266 (1st Cir. 1992)). Since trial courts already have the power to restrict communication when appropriate, the only effect of broadening Rule 615 to include such restrictions would be to shift the power from the trial court's discretion and place it instead in the unrestrained hands of a party. Nothing in the language or history of Rule 615 indicates that the drafters intended such a result.

D. The Casual Dinner Conversation of Officers Nelson, and Miller Did Not Violate the Rule 615 order.

On September 22, 2004, Officers Nelson and Miller had dinner together. (R. 6.) During their meal, the conversation ranged over topics of common interest. Officer Nelson had testified in the Irving trial that day. (R. 7.) He related to his dinner companion his recollection of his testimony, including his testimony of having seen Irving hand the drug-filled envelope to Roberts. Officer Nelson's description prompted Officer Miller to recall that he had seen the transfer as well. (R. 7.)

This dinner conversation between the officers did not violate the Rule 615 order. The trial court's order made reference only to whether and when witnesses could be in the courtroom, exactly as the plain language of Rule 615 provides. At no time during the trial did the court instruct witnesses not to speak to each other. This was no mere inadvertent omission by the court. As demonstrated by the court's denial of defendant's motion to exclude, the trial court did not *intend* that its order should apply to communication outside the courtroom.

Nor does this case fall within the narrow *Miller* exception. In *Miller*, the reading of daily transcripts was held to violate Rule 615. 650 F.2d at 1374. The court concluded that reading transcripts eliminated the need to rely on memory and was thus more dangerous than actual witness presence in the courtroom. Here, however, Officer Nelson had to rely on his recollection of his testimony. Then, Officer Miller had to rely on *his* recollection of what Officer Nelson had recalled. These key differences render the officers' conversation far less problematic than either physical presence in the courtroom or the reading of trial transcripts.

In fact, this double reliance on memory is even less problematic than the situation the Eighth Circuit permitted in *U.S. v. Smith*, 578 F.2d 1227, where an officer in the courtroom was taking notes and relaying information to prospective witnesses. Here, no one was planted in the courtroom taking notes. There was no plot to circumvent the prohibition on access to actual testimony. Two co-workers simply had dinner together and spoke of their day's events, as friends and co-workers often do.

Additionally, prohibiting these officers from speaking to each other likely would have made no difference here. Officers Nelson and Miller had worked together on this case for months. Together, they had arrested the Defendant and worked with the prosecutor to prepare the case for trial. During that process, they would have seen each other daily. Undoubtedly, they had discussed the case on countless occasions. They may well have discussed the case immediately before trial began. Whether or not the officers communicated on September 22, no doubt the prosecutor would have carefully prepared Officer Miller for his testimony the next day. The prosecutor would have highlighted the factual question of the drug transfer and would have told Officer Miller about the status of the testimony on that point. Officer Miller's recollection would have been just as refreshed by that description as it was by the description of his co-worker the night before. In such a circumstance, there is little point in prohibiting a discussion on September 22nd that normally could have happened both on September 21st and on September 23rd.

Further, whether the conversation occurred before or after trial began, the Defendant would have been able to confront Officer Miller with his prior statements and question him about conversations with others—just as the Defendant did. Thus, in either case, the jury would have been fully informed of the circumstances surrounding Officer Miller's testimony. In neither case would there be reason to second-guess the jury's ability to gauge the officer's credibility and the accuracy of his recollection.

Finally, reading Rule 615 beyond its express terms is not necessary to preserve the availability of broad sequestration in appropriate cases. As part of its inherent authority, the court below had the power to impose, *sua sponte*, extra-courtroom restrictions on witnesses. The court did not find those restrictions necessary here. If the Defendant disagreed, the Defendant had the opportunity to request those restrictions, but the Defendant did not make the request. Had counsel sought such an order, and had the trial court issued it, Officers Nelson and Miller certainly would have complied. The Defendant did not seek the order, however, and cannot now bootstrap a routine Rule 615 order into the order Defendant wishes he had sought.

CONCLUSION

Both the plain language of Rule 615 and all available indicators of the drafters' intent show that the Rule governs only physical presence in the courtroom and not conversations such as that between Officers Nelson and Miller. Further, application of Rule 615 according to its express terms preserves the Rule's carefully crafted balance of the rights of parties and the efficient administration of trials. Therefore, the Government respectfully requests this Court to affirm the trial court's denial of the Defendant's motion to exclude testimony.

_____

Counsel for the United States

Sample Letters

Retainer Letter

[date]

Ms. Elizabeth S. Bradenton
Pinnellas Landscaping, Inc.
8537 South Washington St.
Newton, TX 65432

Dear Ms. Bradenton:

It was a pleasure meeting with you in our office this week. We appreciate your selection of Harris, Felton, and Cox to represent Pinnellas Landscaping, Inc. in a breach of contract action against Charles and Dorothy Cott. This letter confirms my understanding of the legal matter and the terms on which we agreed.

I understand that the Cotts contracted with Pinnellas Landscaping to landscape their commercial properties. After the work was completed, the Cotts refused to pay for the work, claiming that both the plants and the labor were inferior. You have attempted to resolve the matter informally, but the Cotts continue to refuse any payment. You would like our firm to represent Pinnellas Landscaping and, if necessary, to file a complaint against the Cotts to collect the contract price as well as any other damages to which Pinnellas may be entitled.

Our fee will be based on the amount of time we devote to the case. An hourly fee arrangement insures that Pinnellas Landscaping will not be required to pay for any more services than are actually required for its case. My hourly rate is $200, and the hourly rate for my paralegal is $80.00. It is impossible to determine in advance how much time will be needed, but we will do our best to minimize the time required while still providing Pinnellas Landscaping with diligent and competent representation. In addition, Pinnellas Landscaping will be responsible for costs our firm incurs on its behalf. These costs may include such charges as filing fees, service-of-process fees, telephone and travel costs, and costs for depositions. By this agreement, you are appointing us as agents for Pinnellas Landscaping and authorizing us to make expenditures on its behalf. I will obtain your advance specific authorization for any expenditures in excess of $1,000.

As I explained, it is our custom to charge a retainer in commercial litigation. For this case, a retainer of $3,000 will be sufficient to commence the representation. We will apply the retainer to fees and costs as they accrue, and we will ask Pinnellas Landscaping to renew the retainer when its balance falls below $500. Each month, I will send a statement itemizing the fees and costs incurred that month so you can monitor both the expenses of the litigation and the substantive developments on the case. Any credit balance remaining at the conclusion of the matter will be refunded promptly.

I am enclosing a copy of this retainer letter and a pre-addressed envelope. If these arrangements are satisfactory, please sign the copy in the space provided and return the signed copy along with the retainer. Upon receipt of the signed retainer letter and the retainer fee, the representation will commence. We will first attempt to settle the claim without the need for litigation, and we will relay any settlement offers to you for your consideration. Sometimes parties who have been unwilling to settle a dispute previously will change their minds once an attorney is retained. However, if the Cotts remain unwilling to settle the matter fairly, we will file suit on Pinnellas Landscaping's behalf and seek all remedies allowed by law.

I look forward to working with you to resolve this matter as quickly and favorably as possible. Should you at any time have questions about these arrangements, please feel free to call me.

Very truly yours,

Keith Salter
Attorney at Law

_____

Elizabeth S. Bradenton

Informal Advice Letter

[date]

Mr. Joseph S. Crimshaw
Crimshaw Plumbing Supply
1245 Glenwood Dr.
Gooding, New State 55832

RE: Crimshaw Plumbing Supply; personnel matter

Dear Joe:

Last week, I said that I would research the question of whether you can require an existing sales employee to sign a covenant not to compete in order to retain his employment. My research indicates that you can require the employee to sign a non-competition covenant as long as the employee is an "at will" employee and as long as the terms of the covenant are reasonable. I will explain that conclusion more fully below, but first let me summarize my understanding of the facts that have raised this question for you.

Facts: I understand that about a year ago, you hired Steven Lewis to call on potential customers and take orders for plumbing supply products. Lewis told you that he had been selling plumbing supply products for ten years for another company but was recently laid off when that company reduced its work force. He told you orally that he wished to go to work for another established company and stay there until he retires in ten years. I understand that you did not offer him any particular term of employment and that he did not make any promises to you about how long he would stay or whether he would leave and compete against Crimshaw Plumbing Supply. You have now heard a rumor indicating that Lewis is planning to open his own plumbing supply business in about a year and that he will be directly competing against Crimshaw Plumbing. You would like to require Crimshaw to sign a covenant not to compete with Crimshaw for three years after he leaves Crimshaw's employment.

Issues: These facts raise two issues: (1) whether a current employee can be required to sign a covenant not to compete; and (2) what covenant terms are enforceable.

Research and Legal Conclusions: On the first issue, no statute or reported case in our state has addressed the question of whether continuation of employment can be conditioned on the signing of a covenant not to compete. However, all employment contracts are treated as "at will" employment unless the contract specifies otherwise. Assuming that you did not offer Lewis employment for any particular period of time, he is an "at will" employee. You can terminate an "at will" employee at any time as long as the termination is not for a particular prohibited reason, such as the employee's race, religion, or sex.

While no reported cases in our jurisdiction have dealt with requiring an employee to sign a non-competition covenant, several cases did deal with requiring a current "at will" employee to abide by other kinds of newly instituted rules of employment such as new attendance or dress requirements or new rules requiring particular training or certifications. These cases have uniformly upheld an employer's right to institute new employment rules or requirements and to condition continued employment on compliance with those rules.

Further, I was able to find several cases in other jurisdictions that dealt specifically with requiring a current employee to sign a covenant not to compete, and those cases all permitted the requirement. In those cases, the courts stated that there was no significant difference between requiring the signing of a non-competition covenant and requiring the employee to abide by other newly-instituted rules. While a court in our state would not be required to follow the ruling of a case from another state, these cases do provide additional support for our position.

On the second issue, the cases in our state uniformly hold that a signed covenant not to compete is enforceable if its terms are reasonable. Customary terms set out the geographic area of the restriction, the duration of the restriction, and a description of the restricted activities. The opinions all recite that the restrictions should not be broader than necessary to protect the employer's business. Commonly, durational terms do not exceed one year, and geographic restrictions do not exceed the area of the employer's primary market. The restricted activities are limited to the activities the employee performed for the former employer plus any additional activities for which the employee could profitably use confidential information obtained from the former employer (such as a customer list). Consequently, if you are going to require Lewis to sign a covenant, we should carefully discuss its terms, and I would recommend that you allow our firm to draft the agreement for you so we can help you create terms a court would enforce.

Advice: First, if competition from former sales employees is a concern, as I suspect it is, I suggest that you ask all new sales employees to sign a non-competition agreement with carefully drafted terms. This will prevent future occasions in which the current delicate situation arises.

Second, it appears that legally you can condition Lewis's continued employment on the signing of a covenant not to compete. However, you may want to think carefully about whether to bring the issue to a head in this way. If Lewis has not yet decided whether to start his own business, presenting him with a covenant at this point may push him to decide to leave and begin to compete immediately. Further, presenting him with a legal document and requiring him to either sign it or be fired may cause him to react emotionally. He may feel both strong-armed and suspected of wrong-doing, in which case he may react by doing exactly what you are trying to prevent. Therefore, you will need to assess carefully the risks of acting as compared to the risks of waiting.

If you decide to ask for the non-competition agreement, I suggest that you consider two possible strategies. If Lewis is a valuable employee you would like to keep, consider whether you can devise a promotion or some other increase in status or benefits and present the covenant as part of that new position. If a promotion or increase in benefits is not feasible, you might present the covenant as a new policy applying to a whole category of employees so Lewis does not feel singled out and personally offended.

I hope this information is helpful. I would be happy to discuss this matter with you further. Let me know if you would like us to assist in any other way.

Very truly yours,

Keith Salter
Attorney at Law

Status Letter

[date]

Ms. Elizabeth S. Bradenton
Pinnellas Landscaping, Inc.
8537 South Washington St.
Newton, TX 65432

RE: Pinnellas Landscaping, Inc. v. Charles and Dorothy Cott

Dear Beth:

As you know, we have filed a set of interrogatories and scheduled the defendants' depositions for June 12th. Yesterday we received word that the Cotts' attorney plans to set your deposition for June 12th immediately following the defendants' depositions. Since you had already planned to attend the Cotts' depositions on that day, I presume you are available for your own deposition that day as well. Let me know right away if that is not the case.

We should meet prior to the 12th to discuss all three depositions. Your help will be important in preparing me to depose the Cotts, and I will help you prepare for your own deposition as well. In case you have not ever been deposed, let me tell you that you need not worry about the experience. I will be with you throughout the process, and I will handle any objections to the questions you are asked. In our meeting, I'll explain what to expect and help you anticipate the questions and think through your answers. Please call my secretary in the next several days to schedule a time for us to prepare for the depositions, and don't hesitate to call me if you have questions or concerns we should address before that meeting.

Very truly yours,

Keith Salter
Attorney at Law

Demand Letter

March 20, 2003

CERTIFIED MAIL
RETURN RECEIPT REQUESTED

Harold M. Lawler
Susan S. Lawler
9754 West 14th St.
Newton, TX 65432

RE: State Bank Loan Account 12345

Dear Mr. and Mrs. Lawler:

Your loan with State Bank, account number 12345, is delinquent in the amount of $1,489.78. Since this delinquency represents four months of missed payments, State Bank is exercising its right under the contract to declare the entire balance of the loan due. Our firm has been retained to collect the balance of your loan plus all late fees and accrued interest. As of today, that amount is $17,225.51.

State Bank has authorized us to file suit against you and to seek all lawful remedies for your breach as well as your payment of our attorneys' fees for collecting the loan balance. If you wish to avoid a lawsuit and liability for our fees, you must pay the sum of $17,225.51 to this office on or before April 2, 2003. You must pay this amount by certified check or money order made out to State Bank. If you do not pay this amount on or before April 2, we will have no recourse other than to file suit against you. You are hereby instructed to direct all further communication about this matter to our firm and not to State Bank or any of its employees.

Very truly yours,

Keith Salter
Attorney at Law

cc: Charles A. Miller
    State Bank Credit Dept.

Cases

Lucy v. Zehmer

196 Va. 493, 84 S.E.2d 516 (1954)

Supreme Court of Appeals of Virginia

Buchanan, Justice.

This suit was instituted by W.O. Lucy and J.C. Lucy, complainants, against A.H. Zehmer and Ida S. Zehmer, his wife, defendants, to have specific performance of a contract by which it was alleged the Zehmers had sold to W.O. Lucy a tract of land owned by A.H. Zehmer in Dinwiddie county containing 471.6 acres, more or less, known as the Ferguson farm, for $50,000. J.C. Lucy, the other complainant, is a brother of W.O. Lucy, to whom W.O. Lucy transferred a half interest in his alleged purchase.

The instrument sought to be enforced was written by A.H. Zehmer on [Saturday,] December 20, 1952, in these words: "We hereby agree to sell to W.O. Lucy the Ferguson Farm complete for $50,000.00, title satisfactory to buyer," and signed by the defendants, A.H. Zehmer and Ida S. Zehmer.

The answer of A.H. Zehmer admitted that at the time mentioned W.O. Lucy offered him $50,000 cash for the farm, but that he, Zehmer, considered that the offer was made in jest; that so thinking, and both he and Lucy having had several drinks, he wrote out "the memorandum" quoted above and induced his wife to sign it; that he did not deliver the memorandum to Lucy, but that Lucy picked it up, read it, put it in his pocket, attempted to offer Zehmer $5 to bind the bargain, which Zehmer refused to accept, and realizing for the first time that Lucy was serious, Zehmer assured him that he had no intention of selling the farm and that the whole matter was a joke. Lucy left the premises insisting that he had purchased the farm.

Depositions were taken and the decree appealed from was entered holding that the complainants had failed to establish their right to specific performance, and dismissing their bill. The assignment of error is to this action of the court. . . .

The defendants insist that the evidence was ample to support their contention that the writing sought to be enforced was prepared as a bluff or dare to force Lucy to admit that he did not have $50,000; that the whole matter was a joke; that the writing was not delivered to Lucy and no binding contract was ever made between the parties.

It is an unusual, if not bizarre, defense. When made to the writing admittedly prepared by one of the defendants and signed by both, clear evidence is required to sustain it.

In his testimony Zehmer claimed that he "was high as a Georgia pine," and that the transaction "was just a bunch of two doggoned drunks bluffing to see who could talk the biggest and say the most." That claim is inconsistent with his attempt to testify in great detail as to what was said and what was done. It is contradicted by other evidence as to the condition of both parties, and rendered of no weight by the testimony of his wife that when Lucy left the restaurant she suggested that Zehmer drive him home. The record is convincing that Zehmer was not intoxicated to the extent of being unable to comprehend the nature and consequences of the instrument he executed, and hence that instrument is not to be invalidated on that ground. It was in fact conceded by defendants' counsel in oral argument that under the evidence Zehmer was not too drunk to make a valid contact.

The evidence is convincing also that Zehmer wrote two agreements, the first one beginning "I hereby agree to sell." Zehmer first said he could not remember about that, then that "I don't think I wrote but one out." Mrs. Zehmer said that what he wrote was "I hereby agree," but that "I" was changed to "We" after that night. The agreement that was written and signed is in the record and indicates no such change. Neither are the mistakes in spelling that Zehmer sought to point out readily apparent.

The appearance of the contract, the fact that it was under discussion for forty minutes or more before it was signed; Lucy's objection to the first draft because it was written in the singular, and he wanted Mrs. Zehmer to sign it also; the rewriting to meet that objection and the signing by Mrs. Zehmer; the discussion of what was to be included in the sale, the provision for the examination of the title, the completeness of the instrument that was executed, the taking possession of it by Lucy with no request or suggestion by either of the defendants that he give it back, are facts which furnish persuasive evidence that the execution of the contract was a serious business transaction rather than a casual, jesting matter as defendants now contend. . . .

If it be assumed, contrary to what we think the evidence shows, that Zehmer was jesting about selling his farm to Lucy and that the transaction was intended by him to be a joke, nevertheless the evidence shows that Lucy did not so understand it but considered it to be a serious business transaction and the contract to be binding on the Zehmers as well as on himself. The very next day he arranged with his brother to put up half the money and take a half interest in the land. The day after that he employed an attorney to examine the title. The next night, Tuesday, he was back at Zehmer's place and there Zehmer told him for the first time, Lucy said, that he wasn't going to sell and he told Zehmer, "You know you sold that place fair and square." After receiving the report from his attorney that the title was good he wrote to Zehmer that he was ready to close the deal.

Not only did Lucy actually believe, but the evidence shows he was warranted in believing that the contract represented a serious business transaction and a good faith sale and purchase of the farm.

In the field of contracts, as generally elsewhere, "We must look to the outward expression of a person as manifesting his intention rather than to his secret and unexpressed intention. 'The law imputes to a person an intention corresponding to the reasonable meaning of his words and acts.' "

At no time prior to the execution of the contract had Zehmer indicated to Lucy by word or act that he was not in earnest about selling the farm. They had argued about it and discussed its terms, as Zehmer admitted, for a long time. Lucy testified that if there was any jesting it was about paying $50,000 that night. The contract and the evidence show that he was not expected to pay the money that night. Zehmer said that after the writing was signed he laid it down on the counter in front of Lucy. Lucy said Zehmer handed it to him. In any event there had been what appeared to be a good faith offer and a good faith acceptance, followed by the execution and apparent delivery of a written contract. Both said that Lucy put the writing in his pocket and then offered Zehmer $5 to seal the bargain. Not until then, even under the defendants' evidence, was anything said or done to indicate that the matter was a joke. Both of the Zehmers testified that when Zehmer asked his wife to sign he whispered that it was a joke so Lucy wouldn't hear and that it was not intended that he should hear.

The mental assent of the parties is not requisite for the formation of a contract. If the words or other acts of one of the parties have but one reasonable meaning, his undisclosed intention is immaterial except when an unreasonable meaning which he attaches to his manifestations is known to the other party. " . . . The law, therefore, judges of an agreement between two persons exclusively from those expressions of their intentions which are communicated between them. . . . "

An agreement or mutual assent is of course essential to a valid contract, but the law imputes to a person an intention corresponding to the reasonable meaning of his words and acts. If his words and acts, judged by a reasonable standard, manifest an intention to agree, it is immaterial what may be the real but unexpressed state of his mind.

So a person cannot set up that he was merely jesting when his conduct and words would warrant a reasonable person in believing that he intended a real agreement.

Whether the writing signed by the defendants and now sought to be enforced by the complainants was the result of a serious offer by Lucy and a serious acceptance by the defendants, or was a serious offer by Lucy and an acceptance in secret jest by the defendants, in either event it constituted a binding contract of sale between the parties. . . .

The complainants are entitled to have specific performance of the contract sued on. The decree appealed from is therefore reversed and the cause is remanded for the entry of a proper decree requiring the defendants to perform the contract in accordance with the prayer of the bill.

Reversed and remanded.

BARTON V. MITCHELL COMPANY

507 So. 2d 148 (Fla. Dist. Ct. App. 1987)

Fourth District Court of Appeal of Florida

WALDEN, Judge.

This is a landlord tenant action. Ms. Barton leased [the] premises for five years from the Mitchell Company for the purpose of operating a retail store selling patio furniture. The lease began on November 1, 1982. On August 3,

1985, Ms. Barton vacated the property. The landlord sued Ms. Barton, and following the non-jury trial, received judgment for $18,929.57, plus interest, basically representing rent to the date of the judgment and rent thereafter for the unexpired term. Ms. Barton appeals. We reverse based upon our view that the landlord breached a material provision of the lease to the end that Ms. Barton was constructively evicted from the premises.

The pertinent facts are not disputed.

In October or November of 1984, the landlord leased an adjacent space to Body Electric, which space adjoined Ms. Barton's space on two sides. Body Electric operated an exercise studio. Loud music, screams, shouts and yells accompanied the operation of Body Electric during business hours. The intensity and volume of such noise manifestly impacted upon the operation of Ms. Barton's business. It caused the walls to vibrate, and a painting to fall off the wall. It made it difficult, if not impossible, for Ms. Barton to conduct her business. She lost customers and salespersons because of the noise.

Ms. Barton complained over and over to the landlord. The landlord promised repeatedly to remedy the problem to include insulating the uninsulated party walls. The landlord did nothing in the period from October or November 1984 till August 3, 1985 when Ms. Barton vacated. On the same day and immediately following Ms. Barton's departure, the landlord undertook some measures to alleviate the noise problem. . . .

As we view it, the dispositive lease proviso is paragraph 40 entitled Quiet Enjoyment:

> Tenant, upon paying the rents and performing all of the terms on its part to be performed, shall peaceably and quietly enjoy the Demised Premises subject nevertheless, to the terms of this lease and to any mortgage, ground lease or agreements to which this lease is subordinated or specifically not subordinated as provided in Article 29(b) hereof.

When there is a constructive eviction such constitutes a breach of the covenant of quiet enjoyment. *Richards v. Dodge*, 150 So. 2d 477 (Fla. 2d DCA 1963). A constructive eviction occurs when a tenant is essentially *deprived of the beneficial enjoyment of the leased premises where they are rendered unsuitable for occupancy for the purposes for which they are leased* (emphasis added). Hankins v. Smith, 103 Fla. 892, 138 So. 494 (1931).

Since this was a large shopping center, we assume, we hope correctly, that all leases were similar. In paragraph 11 of the printed lease, it was stated that, "nor shall tenant maintain any loud speaker device or any noise making device in such manner as to be audible to anyone not within the premises."

Thus, from our overview, we hold, according to the mentioned authorities, that Ms. Barton was constructively evicted from the premises at the time of her departure and, therefore, has no responsibility for rent thereafter. Here, the landlord was advised of the difficulty. The landlord acknowledged responsibility and agreed to remedy the situation and had the means to do so. The terms of the lease with reference to noise could have been enforced against Body Electric. The walls could have been insulated. Yet the landlord did nothing. Despite the damage to her business, Ms. Barton waited a reasonable time for the landlord to act.

The judgment on appeal is REVERSED.

ANSTEAD and DELL, JJ., concur.

SAMPLE CASE BRIEF

1. *Barton v. Mitchell Co.*
   507 So. 2d 148 (Fla. Dist. Ct. App. 1987)
   4th Dist. Court of Appeal—Fla.

2. *Facts:* (The facts are undisputed.)
   Tenant (Barton) signed a 5 year lease of commercial space for a patio furniture store. The lease included a term promising that tenant "shall peaceably and quietly enjoy the Demised Premises. . . . "

   Subsequently, landlord (Mitchell Co.) leased adjacent space to Body Electric (an exercise studio). Loud music, screams, shouts and yells regularly came from the exercise studio. The noise vibrated the walls and made conducting tenant's business difficult or impossible. Tenant lost customers and employees as a result. Tenant complained to landlord repeatedly. Landlord promised to remedy the problem, including by insulating the walls if necessary, but landlord did nothing. Tenant vacated with a little over two years remaining on the lease. That day, the landlord took some action. The case doesn't say what the landlord did.

3. *Procedural History:*
   Landlord sued Tenant for rent due for the rest of the lease term.
   Trial Court: Landlord won $18,929.57 plus interest, representing past and future rent for rest of lease term (non-jury trial). Tenant appealed.

4. *Issue(s):*
   Does a landlord's failure to control vibration and noise made by other tenants constitute constructive eviction?

5. *Rule(s) of Law:*
   - "A constructive eviction occurs when a tenant is essentially deprived of the beneficial enjoyment of the leased premises where they are rendered unsuitable for occupancy for the purposes for which they are leased."
   - A constructive eviction breaches the covenant of quiet enjoyment.

6. *Holding(s):*
   Excessive vibration and noise caused by another tenant constitutes constructive eviction when it interferes with a commercial tenant's business and when the landlord had notice of the problem and had the ability to remedy the problem but did not act within a reasonable time.

7. *The Court's Order:*
   Trial court's judgment was reversed.

8. *Reasoning:*
   The court did not expressly explain its reasoning except by pointing to these key facts: (1) the tenant notified the landlord and waited a reasonable time; (2) the landlord had the ability to stop the problem (by requiring the other tenant to stop the noise and vibration or by insulating

the walls); and (3) the landlord did not take any action. The result would seem, however, to protect the ability of commercial tenants to conduct their businesses without unreasonable interference (a positive economic benefit).

9. *New Information:*
   Here the problem was caused by actions of another tenant, not the landlord. The court held the landlord responsible anyway, since the landlord could have corrected the problem but did not.

10. *Questions, Comments, and Speculations:*
   - Interesting that the court speculated that the lease for Body Electric was the same as the lease for the tenant and based its holding on the assumption that the Body Electric lease permitted the landlord to regulate Body Electric's noise ("nor shall tenant maintain any loud speaker device or any noise making device in such manner as to be audible to anyone not within the premises"). Tenant's lawyer must not have made this argument or provided the court with Body Electric's lease. Why not?
   - Would the result have been the same if tenant's lease had not included a provision promising quiet enjoyment? Would the court have held that a covenant of quiet enjoyment is implied in commercial leases? Maybe not since the court calls the lease provision "the dispositive lease proviso" and since the court does not mention an implied covenant.

GOLDMAN V. KANE

3 Mass. App. Ct. 336, 329 N.E.2d 770 (1975)

Massachusetts Appeals Court

HALE, Chief Justice.

[Barry Kane represented Lawrence Hill, a law school graduate but not a lawyer. Kane had represented Hill for several years on various matters. In April 1971, Hill signed an agreement to purchase a boat for $31,500 and paid a deposit of $3,150. Hill agreed to pay the balance on May 17. Kane advised Hill about miscellaneous legal matters pertaining to the purchase and registration of the boat. Hill also asked Kane to arrange for the financing of the balance of the purchase price. When Kane could not arrange a loan through a bank, Hill told Kane to sell a piece of real property Hill owned. Kane put the property on the market, but the property did not sell. With one day to go before losing the deposit, Hill told Kane that he was in dire need of the money to complete the sale. Kane told Hill that the timing and Hill's financial circumstances made it "virtually impossible" to get a loan. After several telephone conversations, Kane offered to arrange for Kane's corporation to lend Hill $30,000. However, Hill would have to transfer to Kane's corporation absolute title to the unsold real property, to all of the personal property located on the real property, and to a smaller boat Hill owned. In addition, Hill would have to secure the loan with a mortgage on the new boat. Kane urged Hill not to accept these terms, but Hill insisted. In July 1971, Kane's corporation sold the real property and the personal property located on it for $86,000. Subsequently, Hill defaulted on the loan. Kane seized the boat and sold it. Hill's estate thereafter sued Kane and his corporation, alleging that Kane had breached his fiduciary duty as Hill's attorney. Judgment for the plaintiff; defendants appealed.]

The defendants argue that even if an attorney-client relationship existed the record does not support the conclusion that there was a breach of that relationship. We disagree. The relationship of attorney and client is highly fiduciary in nature. "Unflinching fidelity to their genuine interests is the duty of every attorney to his clients. Public policy hardly can touch matters of more general concern than the maintenance of an untarnished standard of conduct by the attorney at law toward his client."

The law looks with great disfavor upon an attorney who has business dealings with his client which result in gains to the attorney at the expense of the client. "The attorney is not permitted by the law to take any advantage of his client. The principles holding the attorney to a conspicuous degree of faithfulness and forbidding him to take personal advantage of his client are thoroughly established." When an attorney bargains with his client in a business transaction in a manner which is advantageous to himself, and if that transaction is later called into question, the court will subject it to close scrutiny. In such a case, the attorney has the burden of showing that the transaction "was in all respects fairly and equitably conducted; that he fully and faithfully discharged all his duties to his client, not only by refraining from any misrepresentation or concealment of any material fact, but by active diligence to see that his client was fully informed of the nature and effect of the transaction proposed and of his own rights and interests in the subject matter involved, and by seeing to it that his client either has independent advice in the matter or else receives from the attorney such advice as the latter would have been expected to give had the transaction been one between his client and a stranger."

Applying these principles to the case at bar, it is clear that the judge was correct in concluding that Kane, by entering into the transaction, breached his fiduciary duty to Hill. While the defendants contend that Kane's conduct did not constitute a breach of his fiduciary duty because Hill fully understood the nature and effect of the transaction and because Kane advised Hill against it, in the circumstances of this case, Kane's full disclosure and his advice were not sufficient to immunize him from liability. The fundamental unfairness of the transaction and the egregious overreaching by Kane in his dealings with Hill are self-evident. In light of the nature of the transaction, Kane, at a bare minimum, was under a duty not to proceed with the loan until he was satisfied that Hill had obtained independent advice on the matter. The purpose of such requirement is to be certain that in a situation where an attorney deals with a client in a business relationship to the attorney's advantage, the "presumed influence resulting from the relationship has been neutralized." . . .

Judgment affirmed.

JACOBSON V. KAMERINSKY[1]

Karen Jacobson had gallbladder surgery on June 30, 1984. Her doctor negligently left a surgical sponge in the surgery site when he closed the incision. The sponge caused Jacobson considerable physical difficulty and subsequently resulted in a second surgery to remove it. After the second surgery Jacobson decided to seek legal representation for a medical malpractice claim against her first surgeon. She saw Kamerinsky's office sign, sought his advice, and agreed to retain him to bring her claim. Kamerinsky had been admitted to practice law only ten weeks when he accepted Jacobson's case.

Kamerinsky correctly realized that the surgeon was clearly liable for Jacobson's damages. He tried to negotiate a settlement of the claim with the surgeon and the surgeon's insurance carrier so that litigation would not be necessary. As the weeks and months went by, Jacobson contacted Kamerinsky periodically to learn whether there was any progress on her claim. He would tell her that negotiations were proceeding well and that he should have a settlement for her soon. Several times he told her that he had obtained an expert opinion that leaving a surgical sponge inside the body was clearly medical malpractice. He explained that he had not yet filed suit because, since liability was so clear, he hoped to negotiate a settlement without the necessity of filing suit.

Shortly before the statute of limitations expired, when negotiations had not been successful, Kamerinsky filed suit in the appropriate state trial court. However, he had failed to research the requirements for bringing a medical malpractice action. State law requires that prior to filing suit a medical malpractice plaintiff must first file a charge before the medical Malpractice Screening Panel, complete the Panel's discovery and hearing process, and obtain a decision from the Panel. [citation omitted] Failure to go through these steps results in the dismissal of the plaintiff's court action. [citation omitted] The lawyer for the doctor successfully moved for the dismissal of the plaintiff's claim, and the plaintiff was precluded from completing the Screening Panel process and refiling the suit because by then the statute of limitations had expired and the medical malpractice claim was barred.

Ms. Jacobson brought this legal malpractice claim against Kamerinsky, arguing that Kamerinsky's failure to file a charge before the Screening Panel constituted legal malpractice and resulted in $500,000 damage to Jacobson. A jury found in favor of Jacobson and awarded her $425,000 in damages. Kamerinsky appeals, arguing that his error did not constitute malpractice.

A lawyer is held to a standard of competency that meets or exceeds the professional skill and diligence commonly exercised by reasonable and prudent lawyers in this state [citation to state's highest court]. Lawyers are not guarantors of a successful result; nor are they required to surpass human limitations. Lawyers are often called upon to exercise professional judgment in representing and advising clients. A good faith error in judgment is not legal malpractice as long as the lawyer's judgment was reasonable under the circumstances.

Kamerinsky's failure was more than an error in judgment, however. The failure to comply with the filing requirements was readily preventable by proper legal research. The Medical Malpractice Act creates the Screening

---

1. [This is a hypothetical case based on several real cases.]

Panel and the requirement of completing the Panel's hearing process before suit is filed. The debate and ultimate passage of the Act had been covered by the press extensively, the Screening Panel requirement being the most controversial provision of the Act. Even if Kamerinsky was not aware of the Act from the public press coverage, he certainly should have been aware of the Act and its requirements as a result of the prominent coverage of the new requirements by the State Bar Journal and the several Continuing Legal Education programs that explained the Act's provisions.

However, no lawyer should rely on press or state bar journalists to keep apace with statutory changes. Kamerinsky had a duty to conduct thorough legal research concerning statutory requirements for filing a lawsuit. Filing lawsuits is something general practitioners are familiar with doing, and it is well within the area of competence required of all lawyers.

Kamerinsky argues that medical malpractice litigation is a complex and difficult area of the law and that he, as a novice lawyer, should not be held to the standard of an experienced litigator. As we established above, researching and complying with statutory requirements for filing a lawsuit are tasks well within the standard of practice expected of all lawyers. However, even if they were not, Kamerinsky cannot undertake representation on a case without being held to the standard expected of all lawyers practicing in this state. A lawyer must either decline the representation or meet the appropriate standard of competence required for the representation. If bringing a medical malpractice claim requires knowledge or experience that Kamerinsky did not already have or could not obtain, he had no business accepting the case. All clients are entitled to at least the minimum standard of knowledge, skill, and diligence. Further, allowing lawyers to meet a lower standard if they can demonstrate a lower level of skill or knowledge would not encourage lawyers to develop their levels of skill, knowledge, and experience.

Judgment affirmed.

Index

Singapore MATH

LEVEL 2 A&B

Thinking Kids®
An imprint of Carson-Dellosa Publishing LLC
Greensboro, North Carolina

Table of Contents

Table of Contents

INTRODUCTION TO SINGAPORE MATH

Welcome to Singapore Math! The math curriculum in Singapore has been recognized worldwide for its excellence in producing students highly skilled in mathematics. Students in Singapore have ranked at the top in the world in mathematics on the *Trends in International Mathematics and Science Study* (TIMSS) in 1993, 1995, 2003, and 2008. Because of this, Singapore Math has gained in interest and popularity in the United States.

Singapore Math curriculum aims to help students develop the necessary math concepts and process skills for everyday life and to provide students with the ability to formulate, apply, and solve problems. Mathematics in the Singapore Primary (Elementary) Curriculum cover fewer topics but in greater depth. Key math concepts are introduced and built on to reinforce various mathematical ideas and thinking. Students in Singapore are typically one grade level ahead of students in the United States.

The following pages provide examples of the various math problem types and skill sets taught in Singapore.

At an elementary level, some simple mathematical skills can help students understand mathematical principles. These skills are the counting-on, counting-back, and crossing-out methods. Note that these methods are most useful when the numbers are small.

1. The Counting-On Method

Used for addition of two numbers. Count on in 1s with the help of a picture or number line.

$$7 + 4 = \textbf{11}$$

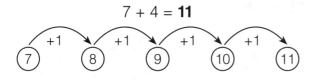

2. The Counting-Back Method

Used for subtraction of two numbers. Count back in 1s with the help of a picture or number line.

$$16 - 3 = \textbf{13}$$

3. The Crossing-Out Method

Used for subtraction of two numbers. Cross out the number of items to be taken away. Count the remaining ones to find the answer.

$$20 - 12 = \textbf{8}$$

A **number bond** shows the relationship in a simple addition or subtraction problem. The number bond is based on the concept "part-part-whole." This concept is useful in teaching simple addition and subtraction to young children.

To find a whole, students must add the two parts.

To find a part, students must subtract the other part from the whole.

The different types of number bonds are illustrated on the next page.

1. Number Bond (single digits)

3 (part) + 6 (part) = **9** (whole)

9 (whole) − 3 (part) = **6** (part)

9 (whole) − 6 (part) = **3** (part)

2. Addition Number Bond (single digits)

= 9 + 1 + 4   `Make a ten first.`

= 10 + 4

= **14**

3. Addition Number Bond (double and single digits)

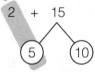

= 2 + 5 + 10   `Regroup 15 into 5 and 10.`

= 7 + 10

= **17**

4. Subtraction Number Bond (double and single digits)

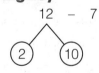

10 − 7 = 3

3 + 2 = **5**

5. Subtraction Number Bond (double digits)

10 − 5 = 5

10 − 10 = 0

5 + 0 = **5**

Students should understand that multiplication is repeated addition and that division is the grouping of all items into equal sets.

1. Repeated Addition (Multiplication)

Mackenzie eats 2 rolls a day. How many rolls does she eat in 5 days?

$$2 + 2 + 2 + 2 + 2 = 10$$
$$5 \times 2 = 10$$

She eats **10** rolls in 5 days.

2. The Grouping Method (Division)

Mrs. Lee makes 14 sandwiches. She gives all the sandwiches equally to 7 friends. How many sandwiches does each friend receive?

$$14 \div 7 = 2$$

Each friend receives **2** sandwiches.

One of the basic but essential math skills students should acquire is to perform the 4 operations of whole numbers and fractions. Each of these methods is illustrated below.

1. The Adding-Without-Regrouping Method

```
  H T O
  3 2 1     O: Ones
+ 5 6 8     T: Tens
─────────
  8 8 9     H: Hundreds
```

Since no regrouping is required, add the digits in each place value accordingly.

2. The Adding-by-Regrouping Method

```
  H T O
 ¹4 9 2     O: Ones
+ 1 5 3     T: Tens
─────────
  6 4 5     H: Hundreds
```

In this example, regroup 14 tens into 1 hundred 4 tens.

3. The Adding-by-Regrouping-Twice Method

```
   H  T  O
   ¹2 ¹8 6        O: Ones
 +  3  6  5       T: Tens
   6  5  1        H: Hundreds
```

Regroup twice in this example.
First, regroup 11 ones into 1 ten 1 one.
Second, regroup 15 tens into 1 hundred 5 tens.

4. The Subtracting-Without-Regrouping Method

```
   H  T  O
   7  3  9        O: Ones
 -  3  2  5       T: Tens
   4  1  4        H: Hundreds
```

Since no regrouping is required, subtract the digits in each place value accordingly.

5. The Subtracting-by-Regrouping Method

```
   H  T  O
   5  ⁷8 ¹¹1      O: Ones
 -  2  4  7       T: Tens
   3  3  4        H: Hundreds
```

In this example, students cannot subtract 7 ones from 1 one. So, regroup the tens and ones. Regroup 8 tens 1 one into 7 tens 11 ones.

6. The Subtracting-by-Regrouping-Twice Method

```
   H  T  O
   ⁷8 ⁹0 ¹⁰0     O: Ones
 -  5  9  3       T: Tens
   2  0  7        H: Hundreds
```

In this example, students cannot subtract 3 ones from 0 ones and 9 tens from 0 tens. So, regroup the hundreds, tens, and ones. Regroup 8 hundreds into 7 hundreds 9 tens 10 ones.

7. The Multiplying-Without-Regrouping Method

```
      T  O
      2  4        O: Ones
 ×       2        T: Tens
      4  8
```

Since no regrouping is required, multiply the digit in each place value by the multiplier accordingly.

8. The Multiplying-With-Regrouping Method

```
    H  T  O
    ¹3 ²4 9       O: Ones
 ×        3       T: Tens
  1, 0  4  7      H: Hundreds
```

In this example, regroup 27 ones into 2 tens 7 ones, and 14 tens into 1 hundred 4 tens.

9. The Dividing-Without-Regrouping Method

```
       2 4 1
     ┌───────
   2 │ 4 8 2
     - 4
     ─────
       8
     - 8
     ─────
         2
       - 2
       ─────
         0
```

Since no regrouping is required, divide the digit in each place value by the divisor accordingly.

10. The Dividing-With-Regrouping Method

```
       1 6 6
     ┌───────
   5 │ 8 3 0
     - 5
     ─────
       3 3
     - 3 0
     ─────
         3 0
       - 3 0
       ─────
         0
```

In this example, regroup 3 hundreds into 30 tens and add 3 tens to make 33 tens. Regroup 3 tens into 30 ones.

11. The Addition-of-Fractions Method

$$\frac{1}{6} \times \frac{2}{2} + \frac{1}{4} \times \frac{3}{3} = \frac{2}{12} + \frac{3}{12} = \frac{5}{12}$$

Always remember to make the denominators common before adding the fractions.

12. The Subtraction-of-Fractions Method

$$\frac{1}{2} \times \frac{5}{5} - \frac{1}{5} \times \frac{2}{2} = \frac{5}{10} - \frac{2}{10} = \frac{3}{10}$$

Always remember to make the denominators common before subtracting the fractions.

13. The Multiplication-of-Fractions Method

$$\frac{\cancel{3}^{1}}{5} \times \frac{1}{\cancel{9}_{3}} = \frac{1}{15}$$

When the numerator and the denominator have a common multiple, reduce them to their lowest fractions.

14. The Division-of-Fractions Method

$$\frac{7}{9} \div \frac{1}{6} = \frac{7}{\cancel{9}_{3}} \times \frac{\cancel{6}^{2}}{1} = \frac{14}{3} = 4\frac{2}{3}$$

When dividing fractions, first change the division sign ($\div$) to the multiplication sign ($\times$). Then, switch the numerator and denominator of the fraction on the right hand side. Multiply the fractions in the usual way.

Model drawing is an effective strategy used to solve math word problems. It is a visual representation of the information in word problems using bar units. By drawing the models, students will know of the variables given in the problem, the variables to find, and even the methods used to solve the problem.

Drawing models is also a versatile strategy. It can be applied to simple word problems involving addition, subtraction, multiplication, and division. It can also be applied to word problems related to fractions, decimals, percentage, and ratio.

The use of models also trains students to think in an algebraic manner, which uses symbols for representation.

The different types of bar models used to solve word problems are illustrated below.

1. The model that involves addition

Melissa has 50 blue beads and 20 red beads. How many beads does she have altogether?

$$50 + 20 = \mathbf{70}$$

2. The model that involves subtraction

Ben and Andy have 90 toy cars. Andy has 60 toy cars. How many toy cars does Ben have?

$$90 - 60 = \mathbf{30}$$

3. The model that involves comparison

Mr. Simons has 150 magazines and 110 books in his study. How many more magazines than books does he have?

$$150 - 110 = \mathbf{40}$$

4. The model that involves two items with a difference

A pair of shoes costs $109. A leather bag costs $241 more than the pair of shoes. How much is the leather bag?

$$\$109 + \$241 = \mathbf{\$350}$$

5. The model that involves multiples

Mrs. Drew buys 12 apples. She buys 3 times as many oranges as apples. She also buys 3 times as many cherries as oranges. How many pieces of fruit does she buy altogether?

$$13 \times 12 = \mathbf{156}$$

6. The model that involves multiples and difference

There are 15 students in Class A. There are 5 more students in Class B than in Class A. There are 3 times as many students in Class C than in Class A. How many students are there altogether in the three classes?

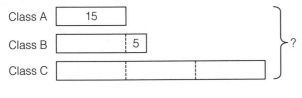

$$(5 \times 15) + 5 = \mathbf{80}$$

7. The model that involves creating a whole

Ellen, Giselle, and Brenda bake 111 muffins. Giselle bakes twice as many muffins as Brenda. Ellen bakes 9 fewer muffins than Giselle. How many muffins does Ellen bake?

$$(111 + 9) \div 5 = 24$$
$$(2 \times 24) - 9 = \mathbf{39}$$

8. The model that involves sharing

There are 183 tennis balls in Basket A and 97 tennis balls in Basket B. How many tennis balls must be transferred from Basket A to Basket B so that both baskets contain the same number of tennis balls?

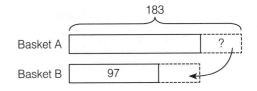

$$183 - 97 = 86$$
$$86 \div 2 = \mathbf{43}$$

9. The model that involves fractions

George had 355 marbles. He lost $\frac{1}{5}$ of the marbles and gave $\frac{1}{4}$ of the remaining marbles to his brother. How many marbles did he have left?

L: Lost
B: Brother
R: Remaining

$$5 \text{ parts} \rightarrow 355 \text{ marbles}$$
$$1 \text{ part} \rightarrow 355 \div 5 = 71 \text{ marbles}$$
$$3 \text{ parts} \rightarrow 3 \times 71 = \mathbf{213} \text{ marbles}$$

10. The model that involves ratio

Aaron buys a tie and a belt. The prices of the tie and belt are in the ratio 2 : 5. If both items cost $539,

(a) what is the price of the tie?

(b) what is the price of the belt?

$539 ÷ 7 = $77

Tie (2 units) → 2 x $77 = **$154**

Belt (5 units) → 5 x $77 = **$385**

11. The model that involves comparison of fractions

Jack's height is $\frac{2}{3}$ of Leslie's height. Leslie's height is $\frac{3}{4}$ of Lindsay's height. If Lindsay is 160 cm tall, find Jack's height and Leslie's height.

1 unit → 160 ÷ 4 = 40 cm

Leslie's height (3 units) → 3 × 40 = **120 cm**

Jack's height (2 units) → 2 × 40 = **80 cm**

Thinking skills and strategies are important in mathematical problem solving. These skills are applied when students think through the math problems to solve them. The following are some commonly used thinking skills and strategies applied in mathematical problem solving.

1. Comparing

Comparing is a form of thinking skill that students can apply to identify similarities and differences.

When comparing numbers, look carefully at each digit before deciding if a number is greater or less than the other. Students might also use a number line for comparison when there are more numbers.

Example:

3 is greater than 2 but smaller than 7.

2. Sequencing

A sequence shows the order of a series of numbers. *Sequencing* is a form of thinking skill that requires students to place numbers in a particular order. There are many terms in a sequence. The terms refer to the numbers in a sequence.

To place numbers in a correct order, students must first find a rule that generates the sequence. In a simple math sequence, students can either add or subtract to find the unknown terms in the sequence.

Example: Find the 7th term in the sequence below.

1,	4,	7,	10,	13,	16	?
1st	2nd	3rd	4th	5th	6th	7th
term	term	term	term	term	term	term

Step 1: This sequence is in an increasing order.

Step 2: 4 – 1 = 3   7 – 4 = 3

The difference between two consecutive terms is 3.

Step 3: 16 + 3 = 19

The 7th term is **19**.

3. Visualization

Visualization is a problem solving strategy that can help students visualize a problem through the use of physical objects. Students will play a more active role in solving the problem by manipulating these objects.

The main advantage of using this strategy is the mobility of information in the process of solving the problem. When students make a wrong step in the process, they can retrace the step without erasing or canceling it.

The other advantage is that this strategy helps develop a better understanding of the problem or solution through visual objects or images. In this way, students will be better able to remember how to solve these types of problems.

Some of the commonly used objects for this strategy are toothpicks, straws, cards, strings, water, sand, pencils, paper, and dice.

4. Look for a Pattern

This strategy requires the use of observational and analytical skills. Students have to observe the given data to find a pattern in order to solve the problem. Math word problems that involve the use of this strategy usually have repeated numbers or patterns.

Example: Find the sum of all the numbers from 1 to 100.

Step 1: <u>Simplify the problem.</u>
Find the sum of 1, 2, 3, 4, 5, 6, 7, 8, 9, and 10.

Step 2: <u>Look for a pattern.</u>
$1 + 10 = 11$ $2 + 9 = 11$
$3 + 8 = 11$ $4 + 7 = 11$
$5 + 6 = 11$

Step 3: <u>Describe the pattern.</u>
When finding the sum of 1 to 10,

add the first and last numbers to get a result of 11. Then, add the second and second last numbers to get the same result. The pattern continues until all the numbers from 1 to 10 are added. There will be 5 pairs of such results. Since each addition equals 11, the answer is then $5 \times 11 = 55$.

Step 4: <u>Use the pattern to find the answer.</u>
Since there are 5 pairs in the sum of 1 to 10, there should be ($10 \times 5 = 50$ pairs) in the sum of 1 to 100.
Note that the addition for each pair is not equal to 11 now. The addition for each pair is now ($1 + 100 = 101$).
$50 \times 101 = 5050$
The sum of all the numbers from 1 to 100 is **5,050**.

5. Working Backward

The strategy of working backward applies only to a specific type of math word problem. These word problems state the end result, and students are required to find the total number. In order to solve these word problems, students have to work backward by thinking through the correct sequence of events. The strategy of working backward allows students to use their logical reasoning and sequencing to find the answers.

Example: Sarah has a piece of ribbon. She cuts the ribbon into 4 equal parts. Each part is then cut into 3 smaller equal parts. If the length of each small part is 35 cm, how long is the piece of ribbon?
$3 \times 35 = 105$ cm
$4 \times 105 = 420$ cm
The piece of ribbon is **420 cm**.

6. The Before-After Concept

The *Before-After* concept lists all the relevant data before and after an event. Students can then compare the differences and eventually solve the problems. Usually, the Before-After concept and the mathematical model go hand in hand to solve math word problems. Note that the Before-After concept can be applied only to a certain type of math word problem, which trains students to think sequentially.

Example: Kelly has 4 times as much money as Joey. After Kelly uses some money to buy a tennis racquet, and Joey uses $30 to buy a pair of pants, Kelly has twice as much money as Joey. If Joey has $98 in the beginning,
(a) how much money does Kelly have in the end?
(b) how much money does Kelly spend on the tennis racquet?

Before

After

(a) $98 - $30 = $68
2 × $68 = $136
Kelly has **$136** in the end.

(b) 4 × $98 = $392
$392 − $136 = $256
Kelly spends **$256** on the tennis racquet.

7. Making Supposition

Making supposition is commonly known as

"making an assumption." Students can use this strategy to solve certain types of math word problems. Making assumptions will eliminate some possibilities and simplifies the word problems by providing a boundary of values to work within.

Example: Mrs. Jackson bought 100 pieces of candy for all the students in her class. How many pieces of candy would each student receive if there were 25 students in her class?

In the above word problem, assume that each student received the same number of pieces. This eliminates the possibilities that some students would receive more than others due to good behavior, better results, or any other reason.

8. Representation of Problem

In problem solving, students often use representations in the solutions to show their understanding of the problems. Using representations also allow students to understand the mathematical concepts and relationships as well as to manipulate the information presented in the problems. Examples of representations are diagrams and lists or tables.

Diagrams allow students to consolidate or organize the information given in the problems. By drawing a diagram, students can see the problem clearly and solve it effectively.

A list or table can help students organize information that is useful for analysis. After analyzing, students can then see a pattern, which can be used to solve the problem.

9. Guess and Check

One of the most important and effective problem-solving techniques is *Guess and Check*. It is also known as *Trial and Error*. As the name suggests, students have to guess the answer to a problem and check if that guess is correct. If the guess is wrong, students will make another guess. This will continue until the guess is correct.

It is beneficial to keep a record of all the guesses and checks in a table. In addition, a *Comments* column can be included. This will enable students to analyze their guess (if it is too high or too low) and improve on the next guess. Be careful; this problem-solving technique can be tiresome without systematic or logical guesses.

Example: Jessica had 15 coins. Some of them were 10-cent coins and the rest were 5-cent coins. The total amount added up to $1.25. How many coins of each kind were there?

Use the guess-and-check method.

Number of 10¢ Coins	Value	Number of 5¢ Coins	Value	Total Number of Coins	Total Value
7	7 × 10¢ = 70¢	8	8 × 5¢ = 40¢	7 + 8 = 15	70¢ + 40¢ = 110¢ = $1.10
8	8 × 10¢ = 80¢	7	7 × 5¢ = 35¢	8 + 7 = 15	80¢ + 35¢ = 115¢ = $1.15
10	10 × 10¢ = 100¢	5	5 × 5¢ = 25¢	10 + 5 = 15	100¢ + 25¢ = 125¢ = $1.25

There were **ten** 10-cent coins and **five** 5-cent coins.

10. Restate the Problem

When solving challenging math problems, conventional methods may not be workable. Instead, restating the problem will enable students to see some challenging problems in a different light so that they can better understand them.

The strategy of restating the problem is to "say" the problem in a different and clearer way. However, students have to ensure that the main idea of the problem is not altered.

How do students restate a math problem?

First, read and understand the problem. Gather the given facts and unknowns. Note any condition(s) that have to be satisfied.

Next, restate the problem. Imagine narrating this problem to a friend. Present the given facts, unknown(s), and condition(s). Students may want to write the "revised" problem. Once the "revised" problem is analyzed, students should be able to think of an appropriate strategy to solve it.

11. Simplify the Problem

One of the commonly used strategies in mathematical problem solving is simplification of the problem. When a problem is simplified, it can be "broken down" into two or more smaller parts. Students can then solve the parts systematically to get to the final answer.

2A LEARNING OUTCOMES

Unit 1 Numbers 1-1,000
Students should be able to
- recognize and write numbers up to 1,000 in numerals and words.
- identify the place value of numbers up to 1,000.
- compare and arrange numbers up to 1,000.
- complete number patterns.

Unit 2 Adding and Subtracting Numbers 1-1,000
Students should be able to
- add and subtract numbers up to 1,000 by regrouping ones, tens, or hundreds.
- solve 1-step story problems related to addition and subtraction.

Review 1
This review tests students' understanding of Units 1 & 2.

Unit 3 Fun With Models (Adding and Subtracting)
Students should be able to
- draw models involving addition and subtraction of 2 numbers.
- draw models involving addition of 3 numbers.

Unit 4 Multiplying and Dividing
Students should be able to
- multiply numbers by 2, 3, 4, 5, and 10.
- divide numbers by 2, 3, 4, 5, and 10.

Review 2
This review tests students' understanding of Units 3 & 4.

Unit 5 Multiplying and Dividing Numbers by 2 and 3
Students should be able to
- multiply and divide numbers by 2 and 3.

Unit 6 Multiplying and Dividing Numbers by 4, 5, and 10
Students should be able to
- multiply numbers by 4, 5, and 10.
- divide numbers by 4, 5, and 10.
- solve 1-step multiplication and division story problems.

Unit 7 Fun With Models (Multiplying and Dividing)
Students should be able to
- draw models involving multiplication and division.

Review 3
This review tests students' understanding of Units 5, 6, & 7.

Unit 8 Length
Students should be able to
- measure objects in meters, centimeters, inches, feet, and yards.
- compare items of different lengths.
- add, subtract, multiply, and divide different lengths.
- solve 1-step story problems related to length.

Unit 9 Mass
Students should be able to
- measure items in kilograms, grams, ounces, and pounds.
- compare items of different masses.
- add, subtract, multiply, and divide different masses.
- solve 1-step story problems related to mass.

Review 4
This review tests students' understanding of Units 8 & 9.

Mid-Review
This review is an excellent assessment of students' understanding of all the topics in the first half of this book.

Singapore Math Level 2A & 2B

FORMULA SHEET

Unit 1 Numbers 1-1,000

Numbers can be written as words.

Example: 549 **five hundred and forty-nine**

Place value

The value of a digit is based on its place value in the number.

Examples: In 637,

        the digit **7** is in the **ones** place,

        the digit **3** is in the **tens** place, and

        the digit **6** is in the **hundreds** place.

Comparing numbers

Use the place value starting with hundreds to compare 2 numbers.

- When one number is bigger than the other, use the words *greater than* to describe it.
- When one number is less than the other, use the words *smaller than* to describe it.

Order and Pattern

When arranging a set of numbers in order,

- determine if the series must begin with the largest or the smallest,
- compare the place value of the numbers,
- arrange the numbers in the correct order.

For number pattern problems,

- determine if the number pattern is in an increasing or a decreasing order,
- find the difference between 2 consecutive numbers,
- apply the difference to find the unknown number.

Unit 2 Adding and Subtracting Numbers 1-1,000

Adding without regrouping

- Add the digits in the ones place first.
- Add the digits in the tens place.
- Add the digits in the hundreds place.

Adding with regrouping

- Add the digits in the ones place first. Regroup the ones if there are more than 10 ones.
- Add the digits in the tens place. Add another ten if there is a regrouping of ones. Regroup the tens if there are more than 10 tens.
- Add the digits in the hundreds place. Add another hundred if there is a regrouping of tens.

Subtracting without regrouping

- Subtract the digits in the ones place first.
- Subtract the digits in the tens place.
- Subtract the digits in the hundreds place.

Subtracting with regrouping

- Subtract the digits in the ones place first. If this is not possible, regroup the tens and ones.
- Subtract the digits in the tens place. If this is not possible, regroup the hundreds and tens.
- Subtract the digits in the hundreds place.

Unit 3 Fun With Models (Adding and Subtracting)

Models are pictorial representations of mathematical problems. Models make the problems easier to understand and solve.

The following is an example of a model involving simple addition.

The following is an example of a model involving addition of 3 items.

The following is an example of a model involving simple subtraction.

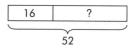

The following is an example of a model involving comparing.

The following is an example of a model in a 2-part story problem.

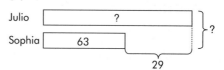

Singapore Math Level 2A & 2B

Unit 4 Multiplying and Dividing

Multiplication is also known as repeated addition.

Keywords: *times*, *multiply*, or *product*

For example, 4 × 5 = 4 + 4 + 4 + 4 + 4

4	×	5	=	20
(number)		(number of times)		(result)

Division is the opposite of multiplication.

Keywords: *equal*, *equally*, or *divide*

The ÷ sign is used to represent division in a number sentence.

Examples: 20 ÷ 4 = 5   or   20 ÷ 5 = 4

Unit 5 Multiplying and Dividing Numbers by 2 and 3

Below are the multiplication tables of 2 and 3.

×	2	3
1	2	3
2	4	6
3	6	9
4	8	12
5	10	15
6	12	18
7	14	21
8	16	24
9	18	27
10	20	30
11	22	33
12	24	36

Unit 6 Multiplying and Dividing Numbers by 4, 5, and 10

Below are the multiplication tables of 4, 5, and 10.

×	4	5	10
1	4	5	10
2	8	10	20
3	12	15	30
4	16	20	40
5	20	25	50
6	24	30	60
7	28	35	70
8	32	40	80
9	36	45	90
10	40	50	100
11	44	55	110
12	48	60	120

Unit 7 Fun With Models (Multiplying and Dividing)

The following is an example of a model involving simple multiplication.

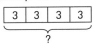

The following are examples of a model involving simple division.

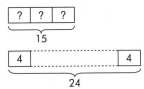

Unit 8 Length

Length is how long an object is.
Height is how tall an object is.

Units of measurement are meters (m), centimeters (cm), inches (in.), feet (ft.), and yards (yd.).

When measuring the length of an object with a ruler, always place the object starting at the 0 on the ruler. If the starting point of the object is not at 0, subtract the markings on both ends of the object to find the actual length of the object.

<u>4 operations of length</u>
When adding, subtracting, multiplying, and dividing lengths, make sure that they are in the same unit of measurement.

Unit 9 Mass

Mass is how heavy an object is.

Units of measurement are kilograms (kg), grams (g), ounces (oz.), and pounds (lb.).

<u>Comparing the mass of 2 objects</u>
When 2 objects have the same mass, use the words *as heavy as*.
When the mass of one object is heavier than that of the other object, use the words *more than*.
When the mass of one object is lighter than that of the other object, use the words *less than*.

<u>Reading the mass of an object using a scale</u>
When the object is placed on a scale, the needle will move and point to a number. That number is the mass of the object. Note the unit of measurement on the scale.

<u>4 operations of mass</u>
When adding, subtracting, multiplying, and dividing masses, make sure that they are in the same unit of measurement.

Unit 1: NUMBERS 1–1,000

Examples:

1. Write 909 in words.   <u>nine hundred and nine</u>

2. In 285, which digit is in the tens place?   <u>8</u>

3. In 704, in which place is the digit 4?   <u>ones</u>

4. Fill in the blank with *greater* or *smaller*.

    530 is _____ than 503.   <u>greater</u>

5. 50 less than 955 is _____.   <u>905</u>

6. Fill in the missing numbers in the number pattern.

    410, 430, _____, _____, 490, 510   <u>450, 470</u>

Count the squares, and write the correct numbers on the lines.

1.

    _____

2.

    _____

Singapore Math Level 2A & 2B

3. _____

4. _____

5. _____

Write the following numbers as words on the lines.

6. 760 _____

7. 378 _____

8. 456 _____

9. 202 _____

10. 1,000 _____

Write the numbers on the lines.

11. five hundred and sixty-two _____

12. seven hundred and seventy-nine _____

13. one hundred and ten _____

Singapore Math Level 2A & 2B

14. three hundred and fifty-eight   _____

15. nine hundred and seven   _____

Fill in each blank with the correct answer.

16. 825 = _____ hundreds _____ tens _____ ones

17. 630 = _____ hundreds _____ tens _____ ones

18. 705 = _____ hundreds _____ tens _____ ones

19. 459 = _____ hundreds _____ tens _____ ones

20. 1,000 = _____ hundreds _____ tens _____ ones

21. In 671, the digit 7 is in the _____ place.

22. In 415, the digit 4 is in the _____ place.

23. In 567, the digit 5 is in the _____ place.

24. In 928, the digit _____ is in the hundreds place.

25. In 873, the digit _____ is in the ones place.

26. In 609, the digit _____ is in the tens place.

Fill in each blank with *smaller* **or** *greater*.

27. 400 is _____ than 40.

28. 926 is _____ than 962.

29. 370 is _____ than 730.

30. 805 is _____ than 580.

31. 235 is _____ than 352.

Singapore Math Level 2A & 2B

Arrange these numbers in order. Begin with the smallest.

32. | 397 | | 379 | | 973 | | 937 |

_____

33. | 192 | | 129 | | 319 | | 219 |

_____

34. | 715 | | 571 | | 751 | | 511 |

_____

35. | 163 | | 116 | | 316 | | 313 |

_____

36. | 404 | | 434 | | 443 | | 344 |

_____

Arrange these numbers in order. Begin with the largest.

37. | 570 | | 705 | | 507 | | 750 |

_____

38. | 314 | | 413 | | 134 | | 341 |

_____

39. | 289 | 960 | 187 | 517 | 608 |

_____

40. | 320 | 190 | 857 | 220 | 456 |

_____

41. | 927 | 279 | 727 | 970 | 290 |

_____

Fill in each blank with the correct answer.

42. 10 more than 560 is _____.

43. 20 less than 680 is _____.

44. _____ is 100 more than 778.

45. _____ is 200 less than 695.

46. _____ is 5 less than 279.

Complete the number patterns.

47. 280, 290, _____, _____, 320

48. 970, 870, 770, _____, _____

49. 760, _____, 800, 820, _____

50. 430, 460, _____, _____, 550

51. _____, _____, 650, 750, 850

Singapore Math Level 2A & 2B

Unit 2: ADDING AND SUBTRACTING NUMBERS 1–1,000

Examples:

1.
```
  3 1 6
+ 1 2 1
-------
  4 3 7
```

2.
```
  6 2 5
- 3 1 3
-------
  3 1 2
```

3.
```
  ¹  ¹
  4 8 3
+ 3 9 8
-------
  8 8 1
```

4.
```
    6 9 10
  X̶ 0̶ 0̶
- 2 9 3
-------
  4 0 7
```

Solve the addition problems below.

1.
```
  1 4 3
+ 2 1 4
```

2.
```
  3 1 2
+ 4 8 1
```

3.
```
  7 3 2
+ 1 4 5
```

4.
```
  2 0 1
+ 2 8 3
```

5.
```
  8 2 1
+ 1 6 3
```

Solve the subtraction problems below.

6.
```
  5 6 9
- 2 3 4
```

7.
```
  9 3 2
- 1 2 1
```

8. 736
  − 204

10. 859
  − 607

9. 375
  − 152

Solve the following addition problems by regrouping.

11. 135
  + 109

14. 256
  + 380

12. 505
  + 295

15. 462
  + 208

13. 737
  + 129

16. 397
  + 546

Solve the following subtraction problems by regrouping.

17. 353
  − 174

20. 632
  − 171

18. 971
  − 369

21. 412
  − 124

19. 400
  − 205

22. 500
  − 178

Singapore Math Level 2A & 2B

23.
```
   8 0 0
 - 2 8 0
```

24.
```
   9 8 0
 - 5 5 5
```

25. Match each balloon to the correct tag.

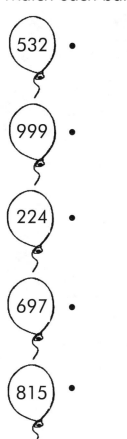

532 •

999 •

224 •

697 •

815 •

• 🎀 592 – 368

• 🎀 446 + 369

• 🎀 1,000 – 468

• 🎀 319 + 680

• 🎀 856 – 159

Fill in each empty box with a +, – or = sign.

26.

73		42		115
70		30		40
3		72		75

27.

231		124		355
115		96		19
116		220		336

27

Solve the following story problems. Show your work in the space below.

28. Lena collects 389 stickers. Anne collects 317 more stickers than Lena. How many stickers does Anne collect?

Anne collects _____ stickers.

29. Tom has 416 bottle caps. John has 29 bottle caps fewer than Tom. How many bottle caps does John have?

John has _____ bottle caps.

30. Mr. Abdul sold 586 roses on Monday. He sold 237 roses on Tuesday. How many roses did he sell altogether?

He sold _____ roses altogether.

Singapore Math Level 2A & 2B

31. There were 416 visitors to a museum on Saturday. There were 555 visitors to the museum on Sunday. How many visitors were at the museum on both days?

_____ visitors were at the museum on both days.

32. Marcus and Jack spent $837 at a computer fair. If Jack spent $469, how much did Marcus spend?

Marcus spent $_____.

REVIEW 1

Write the following numbers as words on the lines.

1. 375 _____

2. 919 _____

Write the numbers on the lines.

3. two hundred and twelve   _____

4. three hundred and three   _____

5. Arrange these numbers in order. Begin with the largest.

313	420	179	402	917

   _____, _____, _____, _____, _____

6. Arrange these numbers in order. Begin with the smallest.

812	128	182	281	218

   _____, _____, _____, _____, _____

Fill in each blank with the correct answer.

7. 10 more than 360 is _____.

8. 50 less than 876 is _____.

9. 536, _____, 496, 476, _____

Solve the problems below. Show your work.

10. $\begin{array}{r} 608 \\ +129 \\ \hline \end{array}$

14. $\begin{array}{r} 700 \\ -435 \\ \hline \end{array}$

11. $\begin{array}{r} 576 \\ +188 \\ \hline \end{array}$

15. $\begin{array}{r} 328 \\ -109 \\ \hline \end{array}$

12. $\begin{array}{r} 154 \\ +365 \\ \hline \end{array}$

16. $\begin{array}{r} 860 \\ -389 \\ \hline \end{array}$

13. $\begin{array}{r} 312 \\ +498 \\ \hline \end{array}$

17. $\begin{array}{r} 542 \\ -379 \\ \hline \end{array}$

Solve the following story problems. Show your work in the space below.

18. The table below shows the number of people who went to the zoo on 3 different days.

Monday	Tuesday	Wednesday
379	686	575

(a) How many more people went to the zoo on Wednesday than on Monday?

_____ more people went to the zoo on Wednesday than on Monday.

(b) How many fewer people went to the zoo on Monday than on Tuesday?

_____ fewer people went to the zoo on Monday than on Tuesday.

19. Aaron has collected 494 stamps. He wants to collect 1,000 stamps. How many more stamps does Aaron need to collect?

Aaron needs to collect _____ more stamps.

20. Jazmin sold 360 flowers on Friday. She sold 265 flowers on Saturday. How many flowers did Jazmin sell on both days?

Jazmin sold _____ flowers on both days.

Unit 3: FUN WITH MODELS (ADDING AND SUBTRACTING)

Examples:

1. James has 93 postcards.

   Anya has 62 postcards.

   How many postcards do they have altogether?

   $$93 + 62 = 155$$

   They have **155** postcards altogether.

2. Aunt Lily had $59.

   She spent $17 on a book.

   How much did she have left?

   $$\$59 - \$17 = \$42$$

   She had **$42** left.

Draw the models, and solve the following story problems.

1. Danny has 576 bookmarks. Emilio has 186 bookmarks. How many bookmarks do they have altogether?

They have _____ bookmarks altogether.

2. Eddy has 280 chickens. He sells 168 chickens. How many chickens does he have left?

He has _____ chickens left.

3. A shopkeeper sold 360 oranges on Monday. He sold 275 oranges on Tuesday and another 150 oranges on Wednesday. How many oranges did he sell altogether?

He sold _____ oranges altogether.

Singapore Math Level 2A & 2B

4. Samantha had 96 seashells. She gave some to her best friend. She had 78 seashells left. How many did she give to her best friend?

$$\square \bigcirc \square = \square$$

She gave _____ seashells to her best friend.

5. Andy received 131 stamps from his father. His sister gave him 280 stamps. How many stamps did he have altogether?

$$\square \bigcirc \square = \square$$

He had _____ stamps altogether.

6. There are 216 chickens, 137 ducks, and 97 rabbits on a farm. How many animals are there on the farm?

$$\square \bigcirc \square \bigcirc \square = \square$$

There are _____ animals on the farm.

Singapore Math Level 2A & 2B

7. Malik had 720 trading cards. He gave some to his brother. He had 465 trading cards left. How many trading cards did he give to his brother?

He gave _____ trading cards to his brother.

8. Hitomi saves $310. Her brother saves $280 more than Hitomi.

(a) How much does her brother save?

Her brother saves $_____.

(b) How much do they save altogether?

They save $_____ altogether.

Singapore Math Level 2A & 2B

Unit 4: MULTIPLYING AND DIVIDING

Examples:

1.

There are 5 plates on a table.

There are 2 crackers on each plate.

How many crackers are there altogether?

$$5 \times 2 = 10$$

There are **10** crackers altogether.

2.

Natalie bought 16 ears of sweet corn.

She put an equal number of ears of corn into 4 bags.

How many ears of corn are there in each bag?

$$16 \div 4 = 4$$

There are **4** ears of sweet corn in each bag.

Look at the pictures carefully, and fill in each blank with the correct answer.

1.

6 twos = _____

6 × 2 = _____

2.

5 fours = _____

5 × 4 = _____

3.

7 threes = _____

7 × 3 = _____

Singapore Math Level 2A & 2B

4.

5 fives = _____

5 × 5 = _____

5.

3 nines = _____

3 × 9 = _____

Study the pictures below. Fill in each blank with the correct answer.

6.

_____ + _____ + _____ + _____ + _____ + _____ = _____

7.

_____ + _____ + _____ + _____ + _____ = _____

Singapore Math Level 2A & 2B

8.

_____ + _____ + _____ = _____

9.

____ + ___ + ___ + ___ + ___ + ___ + ___ + ___ = _____

10.

_____ + _____ + _____ + _____ = _____

Look at the pictures carefully, and fill in each blank with the correct answer.

11.

7 × _____ = _____

Singapore Math Level 2A & 2B

12.

_____ × 5 = _____

13.

2 × _____ = _____

14.

5 × _____ = _____

15.

_____ × 4 = _____

Singapore Math Level 2A & 2B

16. There are 3 kittens on each mat.

_____ × _____ = _____

There are _____ kittens altogether.

17. There are 10 eggs on each tray.

_____ × _____ = _____

There are _____ eggs altogether.

18. There are 4 teddy bears in each group.

_____ × _____ = _____

There are _____ teddy bears altogether.

44

19. There are 5 magazines on each shelf.

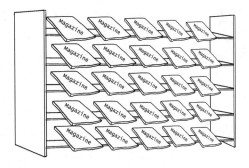

_____ × _____ = _____

There are _____ magazines altogether.

20. There are 7 pieces of candy in each box.

_____ × _____ = _____

There are _____ pieces of candy altogether.

21. Divide 12 balls into 3 equal groups.

12 ÷ _____ = _____

There are _____ balls in each group.

Singapore Math Level 2A & 2B

22. Divide 20 bottle caps into 2 equal groups.

$$20 \div \underline{\hspace{2cm}} = \underline{\hspace{2cm}}$$

There are _____ bottle caps in each group.

23. Divide 9 hats into groups of 3.

$$9 \div \underline{\hspace{2cm}} = \underline{\hspace{2cm}}$$

There are _____ groups of hats.

24. Divide 20 ice-cream cones into groups of 4.

$$20 \div \underline{\hspace{2cm}} = \underline{\hspace{2cm}}$$

There are _____ groups of ice-cream cones.

Singapore Math Level 2A & 2B

25. Divide 18 pens into groups of 3.

$$18 \div \underline{\hspace{1.5cm}} = \underline{\hspace{1.5cm}}$$

There are _____ groups of pens.

Write 2 multiplication and division sentences for each set of pictures.

26.

_____ × _____ = _____   _____ × _____ = _____

_____ ÷ _____ = _____   _____ ÷ _____ = _____

27.

_____ × _____ = _____   _____ × _____ = _____

_____ ÷ _____ = _____   _____ ÷ _____ = _____

Singapore Math Level 2A & 2B

28.

_____ × _____ = _____   _____ × _____ = _____

_____ ÷ _____ = _____   _____ ÷ _____ = _____

29.

_____ × _____ = _____   _____ × _____ = _____

_____ ÷ _____ = _____   _____ ÷ _____ = _____

30.

_____ × _____ = _____   _____ × _____ = _____

_____ ÷ _____ = _____   _____ ÷ _____ = _____

Singapore Math Level 2A & 2B

REVIEW 2

Look at the pictures carefully, and fill in each blank with the correct answer.

1.

7 twos = _____

7 × 2 = _____

2.

_____ + _____ + _____ + _____ + _____ +

_____ + _____ + _____ + _____ = _____

Write 2 multiplication and division sentences for each set of pictures.

3.

_____ × _____ = _____   _____ × _____ = _____

_____ ÷ _____ = _____   _____ ÷ _____ = _____

4.

_____ × _____ = _____   _____ × _____ = _____

_____ ÷ _____ = _____   _____ ÷ _____ = _____

Study the pictures carefully, and fill in each blank with the correct answer.

5.   Divide 15 spoons into 3 equal groups.

15 ÷ _____ = _____

There are _____ spoons in each group.

50

6. Divide 32 pieces of candy into groups of 4.

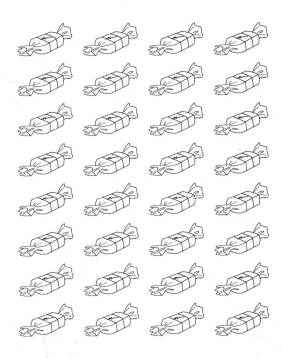

32 ÷ _____ = _____

There are _____ groups of candy.

7. Divide 14 socks into 2 equal groups.

14 ÷ _____ = _____

There are _____ socks in each group.

51

8. There are 6 flowers in each vase.

_____ × _____ = _____

There are _____ flowers altogether.

9. There are 5 buttons on each shirt.

_____ × _____ = _____

There are _____ buttons altogether.

10. There are 3 lollipops in each bowl.

_____ × _____ = _____

There are _____ lollipops altogether.

Singapore Math Level 2A & 2B

Draw the models, and solve the following story problems.

11. Abby has 796 stickers in her collection. Her sister gives her another 159 stickers. How many stickers does Abby have?

Abby has _____ stickers.

12. Jaya has 187 oranges. She uses 93 oranges to make some juice for a party. How many oranges does she have left?

She has _____ oranges left.

13. Benjamin scored 96 on his English test. He scored 82 on his math test. What was his combined score for both tests?

He scored _____ on both tests combined.

Singapore Math Level 2A & 2B

14. (a) Mrs. Anderson baked 455 cookies at her bakery on Saturday. She baked 380 cookies on Sunday. How many cookies did she bake during the weekend?

She baked _____ 835 _____ cookies during the weekend.

(b) She gave 172 cookies to her son's school. How many cookies did she have left?

She had _____ 663 _____ cookies left.

15. Katrina has 496 books. Isabel has 388 books. How many books do they have in all?

They have _____ 884 _____ books in all.

16. Cameron spent $285 on a trip to Florida. Antonio spent $62 less than Cameron. How much did Antonio spend?

Antonio spent $ _____ .

54

17. Dmitri has 9 marbles. Adrian has 8 marbles. Zackary has 6 marbles. How many marbles do the 3 boys have altogether?

    The 3 boys have _____ marbles altogether.

18. Mr. Simon had 245 oranges and 379 apples. 188 pieces of fruit were rotten. How many pieces of fruit did Mr. Simon have left?

    Mr. Simon had _____ pieces of fruit left.

19. Kaylee spent $503 in June. She spent $128 less in June than in July. How much did she spend in July?

    She spent $_____ in July.

20. 586 visitors went to the zoo in November. 253 fewer visitors went to the zoo in December. How many visitors went to the zoo in these 2 months?

    _____ visitors went to the zoo in these 2 months.

Unit 5: MULTIPLYING AND DIVIDING NUMBERS BY 2 AND 3

Examples:

1. Rick has 3 notebooks.
    There are 10 pages in each notebook.
    How many pages are there in all?

    $$3 \times 10 = 30$$

    There are **30** pages in all.

2. Mrs. Mendoza has 18 carrots.
    She gives each rabbit 2 carrots.
    How many rabbits does she give all her carrots to?

    $$18 \div 2 = 9$$

    She gives all her carrots to **9** rabbits.

1. Fill in each blank by counting in twos.

2. Fill in each blank by counting in threes.

Singapore Math Level 2A & 2B

Fill in each blank with the correct answer.

3. 4 × 2 = _____

4. 6 × 2 = _____

5. 5 × 3 = _____

6. 8 × 2 = _____

7. 9 × 3 = _____

8. 3 × 3 = _____

9. 7 × 3 = _____

10. 9 × 2 = _____

11. 6 × 3 = _____

12. 5 × 2 = _____

Fill in each blank with the correct answer.

13. _____ × 2 = 20

14. _____ × 3 = 15

15. 2 × _____ = 12

16. 3 × _____ = 9

17. 3 × _____ = 18

18. 3 × _____ = 27

19. 2 × _____ = 10

20. _____ × 3 = 12

21. _____ × 2 = 16

22. _____ × 2 = 18

Fill in each blank with the correct answer.

23. 30 ÷ 3 = _____

24. 21 ÷ 3 = _____

25. 16 ÷ 2 = _____

26. 18 ÷ 3 = _____

27. 14 ÷ 2 = _____

28. 8 ÷ 2 = _____

29. 12 ÷ 2 = _____

30. 15 ÷ 3 = _____

31. 10 ÷ 2 = _____

32. 24 ÷ 3 = _____

Singapore Math Level 2A & 2B

33. Match each car to the correct owner.

Singapore Math Level 2A & 2B

Solve the following story problems. Show your work in the space below.

34. Taylor bought 4 boxes of cake. There were 3 pieces of cake in each box. How many pieces of cake were there altogether?

There were _____ pieces of cake altogether.

35. There are 3 stars on a flag. There are 7 flags. How many stars are there altogether?

There are _____ stars altogether.

Singapore Math Level 2A & 2B

36. Each tricycle has 3 wheels. There are 15 wheels altogether. How many tricycles are there?

There are _____ tricycles.

37. Eliza baked 14 muffins. She gave 2 muffins to each of her friends. How many friends did she give the muffins to?

She gave the muffins to _____ friends.

38. Minh packs 3 tennis balls into each bag. If there are 27 tennis balls, how many bags will she need?

She will need _____ bags.

Singapore Math Level 2A & 2B

39. The picture below shows several items sold at a drugstore.

eraser $2 each

pencil 20¢ each

pen $3 each

(a) Jane buys 4 erasers. How much does she pay in all?

$_____

(b) Luke has $12. How many pens can he buy?

_____ pens

(c) Ken buys 3 pens. How much does he pay altogether?

$_____

(d) Jade has $16. How many erasers can she buy?

_____ erasers

(e) There are 4 students in a group. If Mrs. Moran gives 3 pencils to each student, how many pencils does she need to buy?

_____ pencils

40. Complete the crossword puzzle with the correct answers.

12	÷		=	6
÷				×
	÷		=	
=				=
	×	9	=	18

Singapore Math Level 2A & 2B

Unit 6: MULTIPLYING AND DIVIDING NUMBERS BY 4, 5, AND 10

Examples:

1. There are 10 SUVs in a parking lot.

    Each SUV has 4 wheels.

    How many wheels are there altogether?

    $$10 \times 4 = 40$$

    There are **40** wheels altogether.

2. Uncle Ron works 5 days each week.

    How many days does he work in 8 weeks?

    $$8 \times 5 = 40$$

    He works **40** days in 8 weeks.

3. There are 80 pens.

    Andre ties 10 pens in each bundle.

    How many bundles of pens does Andre tie?

    $$80 \div 10 = 8$$

    Andre ties **8** bundles of pens.

Singapore Math Level 2A & 2B

Complete the following tables.

1. Each car has 4 wheels.

Number of cars	1	2	4		9
Number of wheels	4	8		28	

2. Each hand has 5 fingers.

Number of hands	2		6		10
Number of fingers	10	20		45	

3. Each vase has 10 flowers.

Number of vases	3		7	8	
Number of flowers	30	50			100

64

Fill in each blank with the correct answer.

4. $6 \times 4 = $ _____

5. $3 \times 5 = $ _____

6. $6 \times 5 = $ _____

7. $9 \times 5 = $ _____

8. $3 \times 10 = $ _____

9. $8 \times 10 = $ _____

10. $9 \times 4 = $ _____

11. $7 \times 10 = $ _____

12. $2 \times 4 = $ _____

13. $7 \times 5 = $ _____

Fill in each blank with the correct answer.

14. $30 \div 5 = $ _____

15. $20 \div 10 = $ _____

16. $16 \div 4 = $ _____

17. $40 \div 5 = $ _____

18. $24 \div 4 = $ _____

19. $90 \div 10 = $ _____

20. $12 \div 4 = $ _____

21. $100 \div 10 = $ _____

22. $10 \div 5 = $ _____

23. $40 \div 10 = $ _____

Write 2 multiplication and division sentences for each set of pictures.

24.

_____ $\times$ _____ = _____   _____ $\div$ _____ = _____

_____ $\times$ _____ = _____   _____ $\div$ _____ = _____

Singapore Math Level 2A & 2B

25.

_____ × _____ = _____   _____ ÷ _____ = _____

_____ × _____ = _____   _____ ÷ _____ = _____

26.

_____ × _____ = _____   _____ ÷ _____ = _____

_____ × _____ = _____   _____ ÷ _____ = _____

Singapore Math Level 2A & 2B

27.

_____ × _____ = _____   _____ ÷ _____ = _____

_____ × _____ = _____   _____ ÷ _____ = _____

28.

_____ × _____ = _____   _____ ÷ _____ = _____

_____ × _____ = _____   _____ ÷ _____ = _____

Solve the following story problems. Show your work in the space below.

29. Mom buys 6 bags of apples. There are 5 apples in each bag. How many apples are there altogether?

There are _____ apples altogether.

30. Sam spends $10 every week. How much does he spend in 8 weeks?

Sam spends $_____ in 8 weeks.

31. Leyla bought 4 meters of fabric. Each meter cost $7. How much did Leyla spend altogether?

Leyla spent $_____ altogether.

Singapore Math Level 2A & 2B

32. Dad sews 15 buttons on 3 shirts. How many buttons are there on each shirt?

There are _____ buttons on each shirt.

33. Alicia packs 10 packages of crackers into each bag. If there are 100 packages of crackers, how many bags does Alicia need?

Alicia needs _____ bags.

34. Maggy saves $5 every month. How much will she save in 10 months?

Maggy will save $_____ in 10 months.

Singapore Math Level 2A & 2B

Unit 7: FUN WITH MODELS (MULTIPLYING AND DIVIDING)

Examples:

1. Gigi uses 5 oranges to make a glass of juice.

    She makes 7 glasses of juice.

    How many oranges does she use altogether?

    $7 \times 5 = 35$

    She uses **35** oranges altogether.

2. Yumi spent $24 on some T-shirts.

    Each T-shirt cost $6.

    How many T-shirts did she buy?

    $\$24 \div \$6 = 4$

    She bought **4** T-shirts.

Singapore Math Level 2A & 2B

Draw the models, and solve the following story problems.

1. There are 5 albums. Each album contains 10 stamps. How many stamps are there in all?

   There are _____ stamps in all.

2. There are 3 eggs in a bag. How many eggs are there in 6 bags?

   There are _____ eggs in 6 bags.

3. Grace and 4 friends share 30 oranges equally. How many oranges does each of them have?

   Each of them has _____ oranges.

Singapore Math Level 2A & 2B

4. Hakeem buys 4 packets of stickers. There are 9 stickers in each packet. How many stickers does he buy?

He buys _____ stickers.

5. Kelly bought 18 sunflowers. She placed on equal number into 2 vases. How many sunflowers were there in each vase?

There were _____ sunflowers in each vase.

6. Ms. Drew gave 36 markers to some children. Each child received 4 markers. How many children did Ms. Drew give the markers to?

Ms. Drew gave the markers to _____ children.

Singapore Math Level 2A & 2B

7. Each child has 7 library books. How many books do 5 children have?

5 children have _____ library books.

8. Mom bought 21 rolls. She placed 3 rolls on each plate. How many plates did she use?

She used _____ plates.

Singapore Math Level 2A & 2B

REVIEW 3

Match each kite to the correct girl.

1.

 •

•
24

2.

 •

•
15

3.

 •

•
18

4.

 •

•
8

5.

 •

•
14

Singapore Math Level 2A & 2B

Fill in each blank with the correct answer.

6. 80 ÷ 10 = _____

7. 45 ÷ 5 = _____

8. 12 ÷ 2 = _____

9. 24 ÷ 3 = _____

10. 28 ÷ 4 = _____

11. _____ × 4 = 16

12. 10 × _____ = 20

13. 6 × _____ = 18

14. _____ × 5 = 25

15. _____ × 10 = 100

Draw the models, and solve the following story problems.

16. There are 6 pencils in a box. How many pencils are there in 4 boxes?

   There are _____ pencils in 4 boxes.

17. Zoe and 3 cousins shared a sum of $36. How much did each of them receive?

   Each of them received $_____.

18. Dad makes 50 muffins. He gives all the muffins to some friends. Each friend receives 5 muffins. How many friends does Dad give the muffins to?

Dad gives the muffins to _____ friends.

19. There are 30 pieces of colored paper in a package. There are 6 different colors. How many pieces of each color are there if the package contains an equal number of pieces for each color?

There are _____ pieces of each color.

20. Mrs. Yamamoto has 4 children. She buys a pair of gloves for each child. How many gloves does she buy?

She buys _____ gloves.

Unit 8: LENGTH

Examples:

1.

   What is the length of the card shown above?

   $$12 - 3 = 9$$

   The length of the card is **9 cm**.

2. Charlotte walked 345 yd. to a café.
   She walked another 150 yd. to the park.
   How far did she walk in all?

345 yd.	150 yd.

   ?

   $$345 + 150 = 495$$

   She walked **495 yd.** in all.

3. Fanny sews 4 pieces of ribbon to each side of a square cushion.
   If she uses 36 cm of ribbon altogether, what is the length of each piece of ribbon?

?	?	?	?

   36 cm

   $$36 \div 4 = 9$$

   The length of each piece of ribbon is **9 cm**.

79

Write *more* or *less* on the lines.

1. The height of a flagpole is _____ than 1 m.

2. The length of a box of tissues is _____ than 1 m.

3. The length of a pencil is _____ than 1 m.

4. The height of a four-story school is _____ than 1 m.

5. The length of a workbook is _____ than 1 m.

Fill in each blank with the correct answer.

6. Ribbon A ⬡ 2 yd.

   Ribbon B ⬡ 6 yd.

   Ribbon C ⬡ 4 yd.

   (a) Ribbon _____ is the shortest.

   (b) Ribbon _____ is the longest.

   (c) Ribbon A is _____ yd. shorter than Ribbon C.

   (d) Ribbon C is _____ yd. shorter than Ribbon B.

   (e) Ribbon B is _____ yd. longer than Ribbon C.

   (f) Ribbon B is _____ yd. longer than Ribbon A.

7.

3 m | Window A

1 m | Window B

5 m | Window C

Singapore Math Level 2A & 2B

(a) Window _____ is the tallest.

(b) Window _____ is the shortest.

(c) Window A is _____ m shorter than Window C.

(d) Window B is _____ m shorter than Window A.

(e) Window C is _____ m taller than Window B.

(f) Window C is _____ m taller than Window A.

8. Use a ruler to draw a line 4 in. long. Label it XY.

9. Use a ruler to draw a line 6 in. long. Label it WX.

10. Use a ruler to draw a line 5 in. long. Label it YZ.

Measure the following items with a ruler, and answer questions 11 to 14.

11.

The pen is _____ cm long.

Singapore Math Level 2A & 2B

12.

The envelope is _____ cm long.

13.

The notebook is _____ cm wide.

14.

The calculator is _____ cm wide.

Fill in each blank with *longer than* **or** *shorter than*.

15. A _____   B _____

Line B is _____ Line A.

Singapore Math Level 2A & 2B

16. A _____   B _____

     Line A is _____ Line B.

17. A _____   B _____

     Line A is _____ Line B.

18. Study the picture carefully. Fill in each blank with the correct answer.

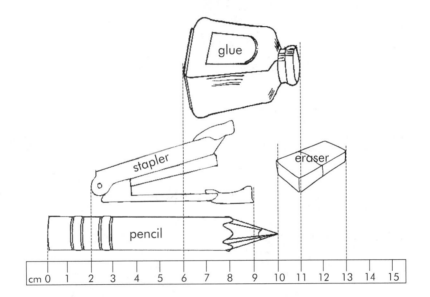

(a)   The stapler is _____ cm long.

(b)   The eraser is _____ cm long.

(c)   The bottle of glue is _____ cm long.

(d)   The pencil is _____ cm long.

(e)   The eraser is _____ cm shorter than the pencil.

(f)   The stapler is _____ cm longer than the bottle of glue.

(g)   The longest item is the _____.

(h)   The shortest item is the _____.

Singapore Math Level 2A & 2B

19.

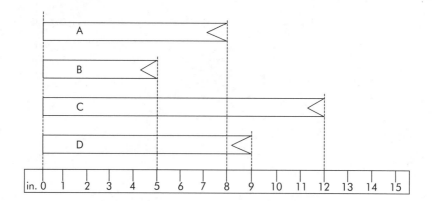

(a)   Ribbon A is _____ in. long.

(b)   Ribbon B is _____ in. long.

(c)   Ribbon C is _____ in. long.

(d)   Ribbon D is _____ in. long.

(e)   Ribbon _____ is the longest.

(f)   Ribbon _____ is the shortest.

(g)   Ribbon C is _____ in. longer than Ribbon A.

(h)   Ribbon D is 3 in. shorter than Ribbon _____.

Fill in each blank with the correct answer.

20. 38 in. + 78 in.   = _____ in.

21. 125 cm – 89 cm   = _____ cm

22. 236 yd. + 279 yd.   = _____ yd.

23. 468 cm – 318 cm   = _____ cm

24. 200 yd. – 65 yd.   = _____ yd.

25. 399 m + 121 m   = _____ m

Singapore Math Level 2A & 2B

Solve the following story problems. Show your work in the space below. Draw the appropriate models.

26. Miles sewed 278 in. of curtains on Monday. He sewed 516 in. of curtains on Tuesday. Find the total length of curtains Miles sewed on both days.

The total length of curtains Miles sewed on both days was _____ in.

27.

After school, Rosie goes to the grocery store to buy some milk before going home. How far does she travel?

She travels _____ m.

28. The stadium is 350 yd. away from Samir's house. Samir jogs to the stadium and back to his house. How far does he jog?

He jogs _____ yd.

29. Kate has a piece of ribbon 26 cm long. June has a piece of ribbon that is 13 cm shorter than Kate's ribbon.

(a)   What is the length of June's ribbon?

June's ribbon is _____ cm long.

(b)   Find the total length of the 2 ribbons.

The total length of the 2 ribbons is _____ cm long.

Singapore Math Level 2A & 2B

30. Nicholas placed 3 boxes side by side. The length of each box was 10 in. What was the length of the 3 boxes?

The length of the 3 boxes was _____ in.

31. Juan placed 8 toothpicks along a straight line. The length of each toothpick was 5 cm. What was the length of 8 toothpicks?

The length of 8 toothpicks was _____ cm.

32. Mr. Oliver cuts a rope that is 6 ft. long into 2 equal pieces. What is the length of each piece of rope?

The length of each piece of rope is _____ ft.

Singapore Math Level 2A & 2B

33. Leo tears a strip of paper that is 27 cm long into equal pieces. Each piece of paper measures 3 cm. How many pieces of paper does Leo have?

Leo has _____ pieces of paper.

34. The length of a piece of string is 32 in. Gabrielle cuts the string into equal pieces. Each piece of string measures 4 in. How many pieces of string does Gabrielle have?

Gabrielle has _____ pieces of string.

Unit 9: MASS

Examples:

1. What is the mass of the bag of sugar below?

    4 oz.

2. The mass of a bag of fruit is 12 kg. The mass of a bag of raisins is 7 kg lighter than the bag of fruit. What is the mass of the bag of raisins?

    Fruit | 12 kg |

    Raisins | ? | 7 kg

    $12 - 7 = 5$

    The mass of the bag of raisins is **5 kg**.

3. Mrs. Giggs has 5 identical packages. Each package has a mass of 3 lb. What is the mass of all 5 packages?

    | 3 | 3 | 3 | 3 | 3 |
    ?

    $5 \times 3 = 15$

    The mass of all 5 packages is **15 lb**.

Fill in each blank with *more than* **or** *less than*.

1.

The mass of the toy ship is _____ 1 kg.

2.

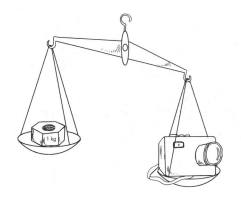

The mass of the camera is _____ 1 kg.

3.

The mass of the toy car is _____ 4 oz.

4.

The mass of the oranges is _____ 2 kg.

5.

The mass of the boy is _____ 50 lb.

Look at each picture carefully. Write the correct mass on the lines provided.

6.

_____ oz.

7.

_____ lb.

8.

_____ oz.

9.

_____ kg

10.

_____ kg

Singapore Math Level 2A & 2B

11. Study the pictures below, and fill in each blank with the correct answer.

(a)   The mass of the watermelon is _____ kg.

(b)   The mass of the bunch of bananas is _____ kg.

(c)   The mass of the pineapple is _____ kg.

(d)   The _____ is the heaviest.

(e)   The _____ is the lightest.

(f)   Arrange the fruit in order. Begin with the heaviest fruit.

_____

12. Study the pictures below, and fill in each blank with the correct answer.

Alan   Susan   Anne

(a)   Alan has a mass of _____ lb.

(b)   Susan has a mass of _____ lb.

(c)   Anne has a mass of _____ lb.

(d)   _____ is the lightest.

(e)   _____ is the heaviest.

(f)   Arrange them in order. Begin with the lightest mass.

_____

Look at each picture carefully. Fill in each blank with the correct answer.

13.

The mass of each ⬜ is 1 g.

The stapler is _____ g.

14.

The mass of each ⬜ is 1 oz.

The bottle is _____ oz.

15.

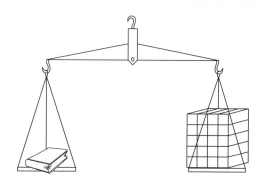

The mass of each ⬜ is 1 g.

The dictionary is _____ g.

Singapore Math Level 2A & 2B

16.

The mass of each ▭ is 1 oz.

The toy vase is _____ oz.

17.

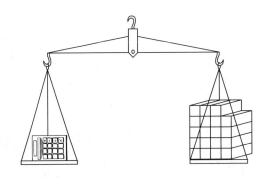

The mass of each ▭ is 1 g.

The calculator is _____ g.

Look at the following kitchen scales. Fill in each blank with the correct answer. Include the unit in your answer.

18.

_____

19.

_____

96

20.

_____

21.

_____

Fill in each blank with the correct answer. Include the unit in your answer.

22.

The umbrella has a mass of _____.

23.

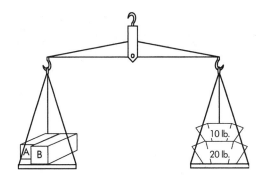

Box B has a mass of _____.

24.

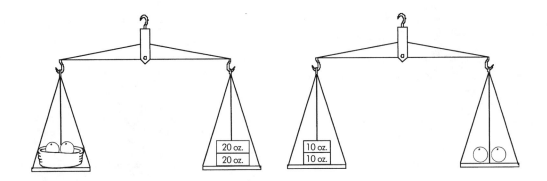

(a) The basket of oranges has a mass of _____.

(b) The oranges have a mass of _____.

(c) The basket has a mass of _____.

25.

(a) The teddy bear has a mass of _____.

(b) The teddy bear and the doll have a mass of _____.

(c) The doll has a mass of _____.

Singapore Math Level 2A & 2B

26. Sam has a pet at home. Fill in each blank with the correct answer, and match the letters to the numbers in the boxes below. The first one has been done for you. Find out what pet Sam has at home.

(a)   14 kg + 15 kg   = | 29 kg | M |

(b)   20 oz. + 15 oz.   = | | R |

(c)   360 g + 250 g   = | | A |

(d)   170 lb. + 360 lb.   = | | S |

(e)   415 g + 235 g   = | | E |

(f)   509 lb. + 137 lb.   = | | T |

(g)   816 g + 45 g   = | | H |

		M				
861	610	29	530	646	650	35

27. Adam's birthday is coming soon. Fill in each blank with the correct answer, and match the letters to the numbers to find out what Adam wants for his birthday.

(a)   585 oz. – 232 oz. = [   ] S

(b)   616 kg – 307 kg = [   ] Z

(c)   900 lb. – 450 lb. = [   ] U

(d)   369 kg – 180 kg = [   ] L

(e)   838 lb. – 639 lb. = [   ] E

(f)   620 g – 505 g   = [   ] P

(g)   246 oz. – 97 oz. = [   ] Z

115   450   309   149   189   199   353

Singapore Math Level 2A & 2B

Solve the following story problems. Show your work in the space below. Draw the appropriate models.

28. Aliyah uses 50 kg of flour, 14 kg of sugar, and 13 kg of butter to bake 10 cakes. How many kilograms of ingredients does she use altogether?

   She uses _____ kg of ingredients altogether.

29. Aidan has a mass of 43 lb. Tom is 10 lb. heavier than Aidan. What is Tom's mass?

   Tom's mass is _____ lb.

30. A contractor uses 83 kg of cement and sand to build a wall. If he uses 27 kg of sand, how much cement does he use?

   He uses _____ kg of cement.

Singapore Math Level 2A & 2B

31. Angelo's family eats 13 oz. of rice every week. Noah's family eats 4 oz. less of rice. How much rice does Noah's family eat every week?

Noah's family eats _____ oz. of rice every week.

32. Kelly bought 380 g of meat. She then bought some fish. If the total mass of these 2 items was 945 g, how many grams of fish did she buy?

She bought _____ g of fish.

33. Aunt Rebecca bought 3 bags of tomatoes. Each bag had a mass of 2 lb. What was the total mass of the 3 bags of tomatoes?

The total mass of the 3 bags of tomatoes was _____ lb.

Singapore Math Level 2A & 2B

34. Colin bought 20 kg of flour. Each bag of flour had a mass of 5 kg. How many bags of flour did Colin buy?

Colin bought _____ bags of flour.

35. Priscilla has 10 plums. Each plum has a mass of 4 oz. What is the total mass of the 10 plums?

The total mass of the 10 plums is _____ oz.

36. Mom bought 12 kg of strawberries. She divided the strawberries equally into 4 bags. What was the mass of each bag?

The mass of each bag of strawberries was _____ kg.

Singapore Math Level 2A & 2B

REVIEW 4

Fill in each blank with the correct answer.

1.

(a)   The hair clip is _____ cm long.

(b)   The ribbon is _____ cm long.

(c)   The comb is _____ cm long.

(d)   The rubber band is _____ cm long.

(e)   The ribbon is shorter than the comb by _____ cm.

(f)   The hair clip is longer than the rubber band by _____ cm.

(g)   The total length of the hair clip and the comb is _____ cm.

(h)   Arrange the items in order. Begin with the shortest.

_____

2.

The mass of the watermelon is _____ oz.

3.   Which line is the shortest?

A ———

B ——————

C ————————————

Line _____ is the shortest.

4.

The mass of the toy robot is _____ g.

Singapore Math Level 2A & 2B

5.

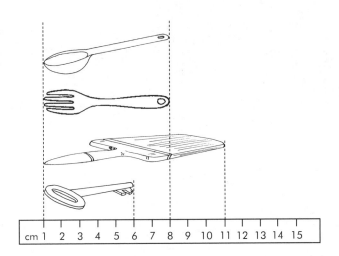

(a) The key is _____ cm long.

(b) The paintbrush is _____ cm long.

(c) The spoon is _____ cm long.

(d) The fork is _____ cm long.

(e) The key is shorter than the fork by _____ cm.

(f) The paintbrush is longer than the spoon by _____ cm.

(g) The _____ and _____ have the same length.

(h) Arrange the items in order. Begin with the longest.

6.

The mass of the cat is _____ lb.

Singapore Math Level 2A & 2B

7.

(a)   The mass of the toy car is _____.

(b)   The mass of the toy plane is _____.

(c)   The mass of the toy ship is _____.

(d)   The _____ is the heaviest.

(e)   The _____ is the lightest.

8.   Which line is the longest?

A ——————

B ————————————

C ——————————————————

Line _____ is the longest.

Singapore Math Level 2A & 2B

Fill in each blank with *more than* or *less than*.

9.

The bag of rice is _____ 3 lb.

10.

The purse is _____ 2 lb.

Fill in each blank with the correct answer.

11. 40 yd. + 68 yd. = _____ yd.

12. 435 in. – 79 in. = _____ in.

13. 616 in. – 327 in. = _____ in.

14. 125 ft. + 225 ft. = _____ ft.

15. 609 yd. + 163 yd. = _____ yd.

Singapore Math Level 2A & 2B

Solve the following story problems. Show your work in the space below. Draw the appropriate models.

16.

supermarket   360 m   David's house   525 m   shopping center

How much farther is David's house from the shopping center than from the supermarket?

David's house is _____ m farther from the shopping center than from the supermarket.

17. Amanda jogs from her house to the stadium every day. Her jogging route is shown below.

Amanda's house   375 yd.   school   425 yd.   stadium

How far does Amanda jog from her house to the stadium?

Amanda jogs _____ yd. from her house to the stadium.

Singapore Math Level 2A & 2B

18. Kenya came back from a trip. She brought along 2 pieces of luggage that weighed 8 lb. each. Find the total mass of her luggage.

The total mass of her luggage was _____ lb.

19. Jonathan bought some cherries. Each cherry had a mass of 3 g. The total mass of the cherries was 15 g. How many cherries did he buy?

He bought _____ cherries.

20. Su-Lin placed 5 rulers side by side. Each ruler had a length of 10 cm. What was the length of the 5 rulers?

The length of the 5 rulers was _____ cm.

Singapore Math Level 2A & 2B

MID-REVIEW

Fill in each blank with the correct answer.

1.

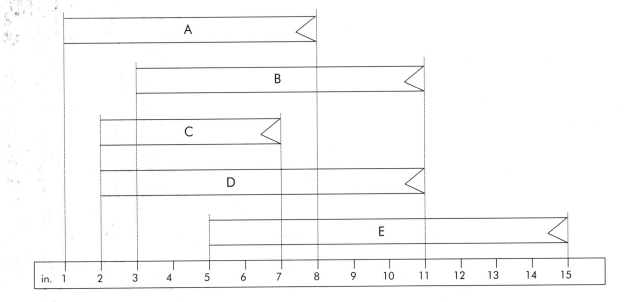

(a) Ribbon B is _____ in. long.

(b) Ribbon C is _____ in. long.

(c) Ribbon D is _____ in. long.

(d) Ribbon E is _____ in. long.

(e) The total length of ribbons A and C is _____ in.

(f) Arrange the ribbons in order. Begin with the longest.

_____

2.

The mass of the rabbit is _____ kg.

3. Write the number in words on the line.

647 _____

4. Arrange the following numbers in order. Begin with the smallest.

415	303	540	405	330

_____, _____, _____, _____, _____

5. The product of 3 and 9 is _____.

6. The sum of 237 and 508 is _____.

7. The difference between 717 and 169 is _____.

8. 10 more than 590 is _____.

9. 120 is 10 less than _____.

Singapore Math Level 2A & 2B

10. Write 2 multiplication and division sentences using the pictures below.

_____ × _____ = _____   _____ × _____ = _____

_____ ÷ _____ = _____   _____ ÷ _____ = _____

11. Complete the number pattern.

660, _____, 700, 720, _____

12. Divide 24 bees into 4 equal groups.

24 ÷ _____ = _____

There are _____ bees in each group.

Fill in each blank with the correct answer.

13. (a)   105 cm + 68 cm = _____

    (b)   32 lb. – 16 lb. = _____

    (c)   _____ × 3 = 24

    (d)   612 + 258 = _____

    (e)   300 – 125 = _____

Write the correct answers on the lines.

14.   The table below shows the different colors of roses sold by a florist in a week.

red	315
yellow	197
white	280

(a)   How many fewer yellow roses were sold than white ones?

(b)   How many red and white roses were sold altogether?

15.   Omar wants to buy a remote-controlled airplane. It costs $65, but he has only $49. How much more money does he need?

116

16. Emily used 185 cm of cloth to sew some cushion covers. She used 275 cm of cloth to sew blankets. How much cloth did she use altogether?

460

$$\begin{array}{r} 185 \\ +\ 275 \\ \hline 460 \end{array}$$

17. Michael has 35 baseball cards. He gives an equal number of cards to 5 friends. How many cards does each friend get?

7

18. Mei baked 460 dog biscuits on Friday. She baked 150 fewer biscuits on Saturday.

    (a) How many dog biscuits did she bake on Saturday?

    ✓

    310

    460 | 150

    (b) How many dog biscuits did she bake altogether?

    S=310
    F=460

    $$\begin{array}{r} +310 \\ 460 \\ \hline 770 \end{array}$$

    $$\begin{array}{r} -460 \\ 150 \\ \hline 310 \end{array}$$

    770

19. Imani plants 3 rows of cacti in her garden. There are 7 cacti in each row. How many cacti does she plant altogether?

21

20. Vivian walks 150 yd. from her house to a store. She then walks another 180 yd. to a playground. How far does Vivian walk in all?

330

$$\begin{array}{r} +180 \\ 150 \\ \hline 530 \end{array}$$

House   150 yar Store   180   PlayGround

Singapore Math Level 2A & 2B

Solve the following story problems. Show your work in the space below. Draw the appropriate models.

21. Dakota has 5 kiwi fruits. Each kiwi has a mass of 10 g. What is the total mass of the 5 kiwis?

22. Mrs. Coleman collected 32 pages of homework from a group of students. Each student turned in 4 pages. How many students did Mrs. Coleman collect the pages from?

Singapore Math Level 2A & 2B

23. Hannah receives a daily allowance of $2. How much money does she receive from Monday to Friday?

10$ Mo tas wen tur Fri
       2   2   2   2   2

24. 3 girls shared a piece of cloth equally. The total length of the piece of cloth was 9 yd. What was the length of cloth received by each girl?

3   3   3

9

25. A carpenter needs 4 days to build a bookshelf. How many days does he need to make 3 bookshelves?

12

4   4   4

CHALLENGE QUESTIONS

Solve the following problems on another sheet of paper.

1. Guess the 3-digit number based on the hints below.

    - The first digit is greater than 7 and is an even number.

    - The second digit is smaller than 7 and is the smallest odd number.

    - The third digit is the difference between the first and the second digits.

2. Parker bought a skateboard for $126. He paid the cashier the exact amount with 10 bills. Identify the bills he used to pay for the skateboard.

3. Jessica has twice as many apples as Deepak. Deepak has 3 times as many apples as Gina. Gina has 2 apples. Draw a model, and find the number of apples Jessica has.

4. Mr. Schneider's mass is 2 digits. The first digit is 3 times the second digit. Both digits are odd numbers, and his mass is greater than 35 kg. What is Mr. Schneider's mass?

5. The sum of 2 facing pages of an opened dictionary can be divided by 3. The result of the division is 3. What are the 2 facing pages?

6. Carlos, Tyler, and Danny each have a ruler. Tyler's ruler is longer than Carlos's ruler but shorter than Danny's ruler. Who has the shortest ruler?

7. Jenna had a box of marbles. Her mother gave her twice the number of marbles Jenna already had. Her father gave her 3 times the number of marbles her mother gave her. Jenna had 27 marbles in the end. How many marbles did she have in the beginning?

Singapore Math Level 2A & 2B

8. Simon had a bill. He used it to buy a shirt for $20 and received the change in four bills of the same amount. What was the bill that Simon had in the beginning?

9. The sum of 3 consecutive numbers, or 3 numbers in a row, is 9. What are the 3 numbers?

10. The sum of 2 facing pages of an opened comic book can be divided by 3. The result is 7. What are the 2 facing pages?

11. Mia is heavier than Dante but lighter than Sierra. Who is the heaviest among the 3 children?

Singapore Math Level 2A & 2B

2B LEARNING OUTCOMES

Unit 10 Mental Calculations
Students should be able to
- add 2 numbers mentally.
- subtract 2 numbers mentally.

Unit 11 Money
Students should be able to
- count and write money in dollars and cents.
- convert dollars to cents or cents to dollars.
- compare money.
- solve story problems related to money.

Review 5
This review tests students' understanding of Units 10 & 11.

Unit 12 Fractions
Students should be able to
- understand that fractions are equal parts.
- identify fractions from $\frac{1}{2}$ to $\frac{1}{12}$.
- compare and arrange fractions.
- add and subtract like fractions.
- solve story problems related to fractions.

Unit 13 Time
Students should be able to
- read and write the correct time.
- use *A.M.*, *P.M.*, *hr.,* and *min.* correctly.
- draw hour and minute hands correctly.
- find the time half an hour or one hour before/after a certain time.

Review 6
This review tests students' understanding of Units 12 & 13.

Unit 14 Volume
Students should be able to

- compare volumes of liquid.
- read and measure volumes of liquid in liters and gallons.
- add, subtract, multiply, and divide volume.
- solve story problems related to volume.

Unit 15 Graphs
Students should be able to
- read and understand picture graphs with scales.
- create picture graphs with scales.
- use picture graphs to solve problems.

Review 7
This review tests students' understanding of Units 14 & 15.

Unit 16 Lines and Surfaces
Students should be able to
- recognize straight lines and curves.
- recognize objects with only flat surfaces.
- count the number of flat surfaces an object has.

Unit 17 Shapes and Patterns
Students should be able to
- recognize squares, rectangles, circles, semicircles, quarter circles, and triangles in 2-D objects.
- recognize cubes, cuboids, cones, and cylinders in 3-D objects.
- draw 2-D shapes on dot or square grids.
- complete a pattern.

Review 8
This review tests students' understanding of Units 16 & 17.

Final Review
This review is an excellent assessment of students' understanding of all the topics in this book.

FORMULA SHEET

Unit 10 Mental Calculations

Addition and subtraction can be done mentally by rounding numbers and breaking up numbers.

Mental addition by rounding numbers
① Round one of the addends, A, to the nearest ten.
② Mentally add the rounded number to the other addend, B.
③ Subtract the difference between the rounded number and addend A from the sum.

Mental addition by breaking up numbers
When one of the addends, A, is less than 10,
① break up the other addend, B, into ones and tens/ hundreds.
Example: Break up 364 into 4 and 360.
② Add the ones to get a sum.
③ Add the sum to the remaining tens/hundreds to get the final answer.
Apply the same method to an addend that is less than 100 or 1,000.

Mental subtraction by rounding numbers
① Round one of the subtrahends, A, to the nearest ten.
② Mentally subtract the rounded number from the other subtrahend, B.
③ Add the difference between the rounded number and subtrahend A to the result in ②.

Mental subtraction by breaking up numbers
When one of the subtrahends, A, is less than 10,
① break up the other subtrahend, B, into ones and tens/ hundreds.
Example: Break up 526 into 6 and 520.
② Subtract the ones to get a result.
③ Add the result in ② to the remaining tens/hundreds.
Apply the same method to a subtrahend that is less than 100 or 1,000.

Unit 11 Money

Writing dollars and cents
$1 = 100¢
When writing dollars and cents, place a dollar sign ($) in the front and a decimal point (.) to separate them.
Example: $8.95
When writing dollars without any cents, add 2 zeros after the decimal point.
Example: $8.00
When writing cents without any dollars, add a zero before the decimal point.
Example: $0.95

Converting dollars to cents
• Remove the dollar sign ($) and the decimal point (.).

• Place the cent symbol (¢) after the number.
Example: $20.50 = 2,050¢

Converting cents to dollars
• Remove the cent symbol (¢).
• Place the dollar sign ($) before the number.
• Place the decimal point (.) just before the last 2 digits.
Example: 3,000¢ = $30.00

Comparing money
• Compare the dollars of the 2 amounts first.
• If the dollars are the same, compare the cents.

Unit 12 Fractions

In a fraction, each part must be equal.
Examples of a fraction: $\frac{1}{2}$, $\frac{2}{5}$, and $\frac{8}{8}$.
To make a whole, make sure all denominators are common. All numerators add up to equal the denominator.
Example: $\frac{2}{8}$ and $\frac{6}{8}$ make a whole.

Comparing and arranging fractions in order
• When denominators of all fractions are the same, compare their numerators.
  The largest fraction has the highest value in the numerator.
  Example: $\frac{4}{5}$, $\frac{2}{5}$, $\frac{1}{5}$
  largest

• When numerators of all fractions are the same, compare their denominators.
  The largest fraction has the smallest value in the denominator.
  Example: $\frac{1}{4}$, $\frac{1}{8}$, $\frac{1}{12}$
  largest

This table can be useful when comparing fractions.

$\frac{1}{2}$		$\frac{1}{8}$	
$\frac{1}{3}$		$\frac{1}{9}$	
$\frac{1}{4}$		$\frac{1}{10}$	
$\frac{1}{5}$		$\frac{1}{11}$	
$\frac{1}{6}$		$\frac{1}{12}$	
$\frac{1}{7}$			

Singapore Math Level 2A & 2B

Adding and subtracting fractions
- Make sure denominators of all fractions are the same.
- Add and subtract the numerators accordingly.

When one of the subtrahends is a whole, convert the whole into a fraction before subtracting.

Unit 13 Time

There are 24 hours in a day.

1 hour = 60 minutes

Numbers 1 to 12 can be seen on the face of a clock, as well as the hour hand and minute hand.

The minute hand is longer than the hour hand.

When the minute hand moves from one number to another, 5 minutes has passed.

When the hour hand moves from one number to another, 1 hour has passed.

The units of measurement for time are hour (hr.) and minute (min.).

Writing and reading time

We read the time on the clock as three twenty-five.
We write it as 3:25.

The abbreviation *A.M.* means before noon and *P.M.* means after noon.

Hence *A.M.* is used to talk about time between 12 midnight and 11:59 in the morning.

P.M. is used to talk about time between 12 noon and 11:59 at night.

We can find the time before/after a certain time if the duration is given.

Examples: 10:00 A.M. is 1 hr. before 11:00 A.M.

7:00 P.M. is 1 hr. after 6:00 P.M.

9:30 A.M. is 30 min. before 10:00 A.M.

5:30 P.M. is 30 min. after 5:00 P.M.

Unit 14 Volume

The volume of water in a container is the amount of water the container holds.

Comparing volume

- When the water level in 2 identical containers is the same, use the words *as much as*.
- When the water level in one container is higher than that of the other container, use the words *more than*.
- When the water level in one container is lower than that of the other container, use the words *less than*.

The unit of measurement for volume is liter (L) or gallon (gal.).

Unit 15 Graphs

Symbols represent the items in picture graphs.

Note the scales used in picture graphs. The symbol can stand for 1 item, 2 items, or even more.

Picture graphs help organize information for easy interpretation and problem solving.

Unit 16 Lines and Surfaces

Examples of straight lines:

Examples of curves:

Examples of items with only flat surfaces:

Unit 17 Shapes and Patterns

2-dimensional shapes and objects

Examples of different shapes:

square rectangle triangle circle semicircle quarter circle

These shapes can be used to create a 2-dimensional figure.

An example of a 2-dimensional figure that is made of 2 quarter circles, a square, and a triangle.

3-dimensional objects

Examples of 3-dimensional objects:

cube   cuboid   cylinder   cone

These shapes can be used to create a 3-dimensional figure.

An example of a 3-dimensional figure that is made of 2 cubes and a cylinder.

Patterns

Shapes can be used to create a repeated pattern.

An example of a repeated pattern using different shapes:

An example of a repeated pattern using different sizes:

An example of a repeated pattern using different colors:

Unit 10: MENTAL CALCULATIONS

Examples:

1. What is 69 + 7?

    69 + 10 = 79

    79 − 3 = 76

    69 + 7 = **76**

2. What is 364 + 5?

    364 = 360 + 4

    4 + 5 = 9

    360 + 9 = 369

    364 + 5 = **369**

3. What is 158 + 30?

    158 = 108 + 50

    50 + 30 = 80

    108 + 80 = 188

    158 + 30 = **188**

4. What is 592 + 400?

    592 = 500 + 92

    500 + 400 = 900

    900 + 92 = 992

    592 + 400 = **992**

5. What is 95 − 9?

    95 − 10 = 85

    85 + 1 = 86

    95 − 9 = **86**

6. What is 438 − 60?

    438 − 100 = 338

    338 + 40 = 378

    438 − 60 = **378**

7. What is 247 − 40?

    247 = 207 + 40

    40 − 40 = 0

    207 + 0 = 207

    247 − 40 = **207**

8. What is 689 − 300?

    689 = 600 + 89

    600 − 300 = 300

    300 + 89 = 389

    689 − 300 = **389**

Singapore Math Level 2A & 2B

Solve the following addition problems mentally.

1. 64 + 8 = _____

2. 89 + 7 = _____

3. 26 + 5 = _____

4. 18 + 9 = _____

5. 57 + 6 = _____

6. 45 + 8 = _____

7. 37 + 5 = _____

8. 78 + 8 = _____

9. 94 + 9 = _____

10. 56 + 7 = _____

11. 127 + 5 = _____

12. 764 + 9 = _____

13. 262 + 6 = _____

14. 948 + 8 = _____

15. 435 + 7 = _____

16. 584 + 6 = _____

17. 623 + 9 = _____

18. 806 + 9 = _____

19. 366 + 5 = _____

20. 119 + 6 = _____

Singapore Math Level 2A & 2B

21. 513 + 6 = _____

22. 836 + 20 = _____

23. 723 + 80 = _____

24. 190 + 70 = _____

25. 428 + 40 = _____

26. 762 + 70 = _____

27. 503 + 90 = _____

28. 869 + 80 = _____

29. 623 + 60 = _____

30. 770 + 200 = _____

31. 323 + 600 = _____

32. 165 + 800 = _____

33. 248 + 500 = _____

34. 657 + 300 = _____

35. 195 + 700 = _____

36. 108 + 200 = _____

37. 588 + 400 = _____

38. 645 + 100 = _____

39. 199 + 600 = _____

40. 756 + 200 = _____

Singapore Math Level 2A & 2B

Solve the following subtraction problems mentally.

41. 52 – 5 = _____

42. 46 – 9 = _____

43. 81 – 8 = _____

44. 30 – 7 = _____

45. 88 – 3 = _____

46. 79 – 5 = _____

47. 64 – 4 = _____

48. 28 – 9 = _____

49. 93 – 1 = _____

50. 59 – 7 = _____

51. 620 – 5 = _____

52. 404 – 6 = _____

53. 875 – 4 = _____

54. 740 – 2 = _____

55. 519 – 9 = _____

56. 264 – 7 = _____

57. 329 – 6 = _____

58. 183 – 5 = _____

59. 916 – 3 = _____

60. 534 – 8 = _____

Singapore Math Level 2A & 2B

61. 415 − 30 = _____

62. 338 − 90 = _____

63. 587 − 60 = _____

64. 860 − 50 = _____

65. 609 − 10 = _____

66. 281 − 20 = _____

67. 758 − 40 = _____

68. 495 − 70 = _____

69. 164 − 80 = _____

70. 626 − 60 = _____

71. 758 − 300 = _____

72. 834 − 600 = _____

73. 905 − 800 = _____

74. 631 − 500 = _____

75. 978 − 900 = _____

76. 505 − 100 = _____

77. 784 − 400 = _____

78. 435 − 200 = _____

79. 876 − 700 = _____

80. 980 − 800 = _____

Singapore Math Level 2A & 2B

Unit 11: MONEY

Examples:

1. Andy receives a sum of money from his parents.
    How much does Andy receive?

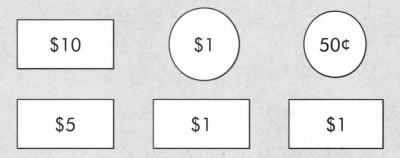

    Andy receives **$18.50**.

2. Change $3.95 to cents.

    $3.95 = **395¢**

3. Change 1,000¢ to dollars.

    1,000¢ = **$10.00**

4. Natalie spent $12.60 on food.
    Sammi spent $15.60, and Omar spent $20.90.
    Who spent the most money?

          Among the 3 amounts, $20.90 is the greatest.

    Omar spent the most money.

1. Write the correct amount of money in numerals.

   (a) ten dollars _____

   (b) two dollars and fifty cents _____

   (c) forty-four dollars and forty cents _____

   (d) thirty-nine dollars and eighty-five cents _____

   (e) sixty-seven dollars and ninety cents _____

   (f) fifty dollars and five cents _____

   (g) nineteen dollars and seventy cents _____

   (h) eighty-seven cents _____

   (i) twelve dollars and fifteen cents _____

   (j) twenty dollars and twenty-five cents _____

2. Write the amount of money in words.

   (a) $12.30 = _____ dollars and _____ cents

   (b) $45.45 = _____ dollars and _____ cents

   (c) $67.05 = _____ dollars and _____ cents

   (d) $15.55 = _____ dollars and _____ cents

   (e) $ 7.90 = _____ dollars and _____ cents

   (f) $11.80 = _____ dollars and _____ cents

   (g) $36.60 = _____ dollars and _____ cents

   (h) $20.15 = _____ dollars and _____ cents

   (i) $59.95 = _____ dollars and _____ cents

   (j) $70.70 = _____ dollars and _____ cents

Singapore Math Level 2A & 2B

Write the correct amount of money on the lines provided.

3.

                                                    _____¢

4.

                                                    $_____

5.

                                                    $_____

6.

                                                    $_____

7.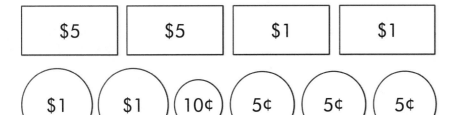

                                                    $_____

The amount of money each item costs is shown below. Write the correct amount of money on the lines provided.

8.

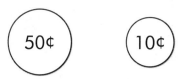

An eraser costs _____.

9.

A book costs _____.

10.

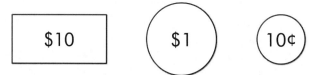

A bag of birdseed costs _____.

11.

A set of colored pencils costs _____.

12.

A notebook costs _____.

Singapore Math Level 2A & 2B

13. Write the following amounts in cents.

(a) $2.25 = _____ ¢

(b) $10.50 = _____ ¢

(c) $35.75 = _____ ¢

(d) $50.05 = _____ ¢

(e) $27.35 = _____ ¢

(f) $89.05 = _____ ¢

(g) $100.30 = _____ ¢

(h) $40.40 = _____ ¢

(i) $15.95 = _____ ¢

(j) $20.55 = _____ ¢

14. Write the following amounts in dollars.

(a) 416¢ = $_____

(b) 1,875¢ = $_____

(c) 3,005¢ = $_____

(d) 805¢ = $_____

(e) 1,750¢ = $_____

(f) 960¢ = $_____

(g) 1,005¢ = $_____

(h) 7,600¢ = $_____

(i) 18¢ = $_____

(j) 59¢ = $_____

Fill in each blank with the correct answer.

15. Christopher spends $26.50 in a week.
George spends $32.50 in a week.

(a) $_____ is more than $_____.

(b) _____ spends more money.

16. Marcos saves $55.85 in a month.
Noelle saves $45.90 in a month.

(a) $_____ is less than $_____.

(b) _____ saves more money.

17. Mrs. Adams has $67.80.
    Mrs. Morales has $65.90.

    (a) $_____ is more than $_____.

    (b) $_____ is less than $_____.

    (c)   _____ has less money.

18. Samira's weekly allowance is $26.50.
    Kate's weekly allowance is $19.60.
    Lucy's weekly allowance is $23.25.

    (a) $_____ is the smallest amount of money.

    (b) $_____ is the largest amount of money.

    (c)   _____ has the most weekly allowance.

    (d)   _____ has the least weekly allowance.

Solve the following story problems. Show your work in the space below.

19. A book costs $3. Malia bought 6 books. How much did she pay for the books?

    She paid _____ for the books.

Singapore Math Level 2A & 2B

20. A peach costs 55¢. A banana costs 25¢ less than the peach. What is the total cost of the peach and the banana?

The total cost of the peach and the banana is _____.

21. Aunt Rose earns $350 in a week. Uncle James earns $190 more per week than Aunt Rose. How much money do both of them earn in a week?

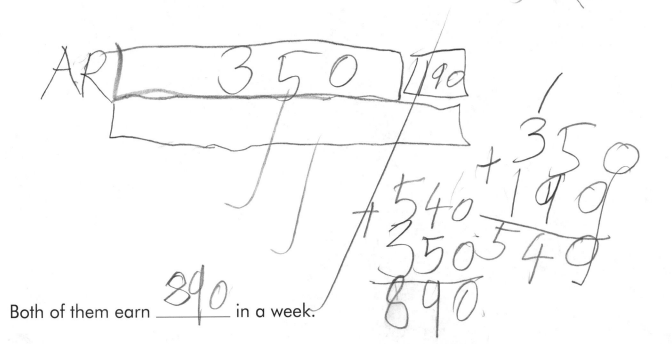

Both of them earn __890__ in a week.

Singapore Math Level 2A & 2B

22. Gina bought a doll for $29. She gave the cashier $100. How much change did she receive?

She received ___71___ in change.

23. Mr. Singh gives his son $40 every 10 days. If his son spends an equal amount of money every day, how much money does he spend per day?

He spends ___4___ per day.

Singapore Math Level 2A & 2B

REVIEW 5

Fill in each blank with the correct answer.

1. Write ninety-nine dollars and nine cents in numerals. _____

2. Add 814 and 90 mentally. _____

3. $55.15 = _____ dollars and _____ cents

4. How much money is shown below?

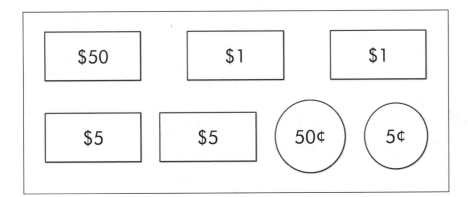

    $50 $1 $1

    $5 $5   50¢   5¢

    _____

5. Write $62.85 in cents. _____

6. Add 604 and 200 mentally. _____

7. Grace has $30.05. Jerome has $35.55.

    (a) $_____ is more than $_____.

    (b) _____ has more money.

8. Subtract 9 from 546 mentally. _____

Singapore Math Level 2A & 2B

9. Write 3,840¢ in dollars.   _____

10. Subtract 60 from 743 mentally.   _____

11.

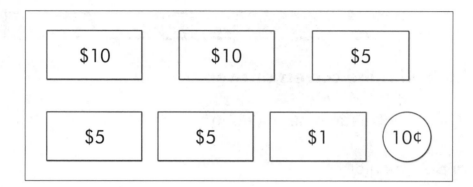

    A purse costs _____.

12. Uncle Sam pays $45 for a bouquet of roses.
    Uncle Rafael pays $42 for a bouquet of sunflowers.

    (a) $_____ is less than $_____.

    (b)   _____ pays more for the flowers.

13. $100.10 = _____ dollars and _____ cents

14. Add 5 and 686 mentally.   _____

15. Subtract 400 from 712 mentally.   _____

Singapore Math Level 2A & 2B

Solve the following story problems. Show your work in the space below.

16. Emma saves $2 each day. How much money does she save in a week?

Emma saves _____14_____ in a week.

17. Samantha bought a calculator. She gave the cashier $50 and received $2 in change. How much did the calculator cost?

The calculator cost _____$48_____.

Singapore Math Level 2A & 2B

18. Vera bought a dress for $49. She bought a shirt for $35. How much money did she spend in all?

She spent _____ in all.

19. Uncle Ronald gives some money to his 3 children. Each child receives $7. How much money does Uncle Ronald give to his children in all?

Uncle Ronald gives _____ to his children in all.

20. Natasha pays $60 for 6 identical towels. How much does each towel cost?

Each towel costs _____.

144

Singapore Math Level 2A & 2B

Unit 12: FRACTIONS

Examples:

1. Arrange $\frac{3}{7}$, $\frac{1}{7}$, and $\frac{5}{7}$ in order, beginning with the smallest.

    $$\underbrace{\frac{1}{7}, \qquad \frac{3}{7}, \qquad \frac{5}{7}}_{\text{smallest}}$$

2. Add $\frac{2}{9}$ and $\frac{5}{9}$.

    $$\frac{2}{9} + \frac{5}{9} = \frac{7}{9}$$

3. What is $1 - \frac{5}{6}$?

    $$1 - \frac{5}{6} = \frac{6}{6} - \frac{5}{6} = \frac{1}{6}$$

4. Lexi used $\frac{3}{8}$ of the butter in the morning. She used $\frac{4}{8}$ of the butter in the afternoon. What fraction of the butter did Lexi use altogether?

    | M | M | M | A | A | A | A | |

    M: Morning
    A: Afternoon

    $$\frac{3}{8} + \frac{4}{8} = \frac{7}{8}$$

    Lexi used $\frac{7}{8}$ of the butter altogether.

Put a check mark (✓) in the box if the shape is divided into equal parts.

1.

3.

2.

4.

What fraction of each figure is shaded? Write the correct answer on the line.

5.   _____

8.   _____

6.   _____

9.   _____

7.   _____

Singapore Math Level 2A & 2B

Shade the parts of each figure to show the correct fractions.

10. $\dfrac{2}{3}$

11. $\dfrac{4}{9}$

12. $\dfrac{5}{11}$

13. $\dfrac{6}{8}$

14. $\dfrac{5}{6}$

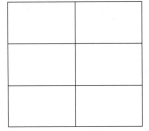

Singapore Math Level 2A & 2B

Fill in each blank with the correct answer.

15.

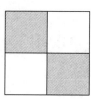

(a) _____ parts of the figure are shaded.

(b) There are _____ equal parts altogether.

(c) _____ of the figure is shaded.

(d) _____ of the figure is not shaded.

16.

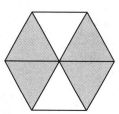

(a) _____ parts of the figure are shaded.

(b) There are _____ equal parts altogether.

(c) The fraction of the figure that is shaded is _____.

(d) The fraction of the figure that is not shaded is _____.

17.

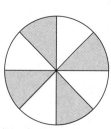

(a) _____ out of _____ equal parts are shaded.

(b) _____ of the figure is shaded.

Singapore Math Level 2A & 2B

18.

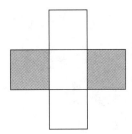

(a) _____ out of _____ equal parts are shaded.

(b) _____ of the figure is shaded.

19.

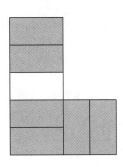

(a) _____ out of _____ equal parts are shaded.

(b) _____ of the figure is shaded.

20. Lisa cuts a cake into 8 equal parts. Her brother eats 2 parts.

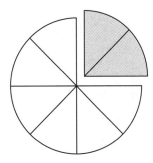

(a) _____ parts of the cake are left.

(b) The fraction of the cake that her brother eats is _____.

(c) The fraction of the cake left is _____.

(d) _____ and _____ make a whole.

Singapore Math Level 2A & 2B

21. Hiroshi cuts a loaf of bread into 5 equal parts. He eats 3 parts.

(a) _____ parts of the bread are left.

(b) The fraction of the bread that Hiroshi eats is _____.

(c) The fraction of the bread left is _____.

(d) _____ and _____ make a whole.

Fill in each blank with the correct answer.

22. _____ and $\frac{1}{3}$ make a whole.

23. _____ and $\frac{1}{2}$ make a whole.

24. $\frac{3}{7}$ and _____ make a whole.

25. _____ and $\frac{4}{11}$ make a whole.

26. _____ and $\frac{9}{12}$ make a whole.

27. $\frac{2}{5}$ and _____ make a whole.

28. $\frac{6}{8}$ and _____ make a whole.

29. $\frac{3}{9}$ and _____ make a whole.

30. _____ and $\frac{1}{4}$ make a whole.

31. _____ and $\frac{1}{6}$ make a whole.

Singapore Math Level 2A & 2B

Circle the larger fraction in each pair.

32.

$$\frac{1}{2}$$ $$\frac{1}{4}$$

33.

$$\frac{3}{8}$$ $$\frac{3}{6}$$

34.

$$\frac{5}{7}$$ $$\frac{5}{9}$$

Circle the smaller fraction in each pair.

35.

$$\frac{2}{6}$$ $$\frac{2}{4}$$

36.

$$\frac{1}{3}$$ $$\frac{1}{5}$$

151

Singapore Math Level 2A & 2B

37.

$\frac{6}{10}$

$\frac{6}{12}$

Color the correct part(s) of each figure to show the fractions. Then, circle the largest fraction in each set.

38.

$\frac{1}{8}$

$\frac{3}{8}$

$\frac{5}{8}$

39.

$\frac{2}{6}$

$\frac{2}{8}$

$\frac{2}{10}$
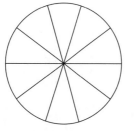

Singapore Math Level 2A & 2B

40.

$\dfrac{1}{4}$

$\dfrac{2}{4}$

$\dfrac{3}{4}$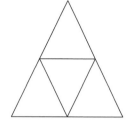

Color the part(s) of each figure to show the fractions. Then, circle the smaller fraction in each pair.

41.

$\dfrac{3}{9}$

$\dfrac{2}{9}$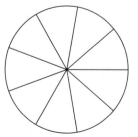

Singapore Math Level 2A & 2B

42. $\dfrac{4}{5}$

$\dfrac{4}{8}$

43. $\dfrac{8}{10}$

$\dfrac{6}{10}$

Circle the smaller fraction in each pair.

44. $\dfrac{1}{5}$ $\dfrac{1}{3}$

45. $\dfrac{2}{6}$ $\dfrac{2}{8}$

46. $\dfrac{4}{8}$ $\dfrac{3}{8}$

Singapore Math Level 2A & 2B

Circle the larger fraction in each pair.

47. $\frac{2}{3}$ $\frac{1}{3}$

48. $\frac{4}{8}$ $\frac{4}{5}$

49. $\frac{7}{10}$ $\frac{7}{11}$

Circle the largest fraction in each set.

50. $\frac{3}{5}$ $\frac{4}{5}$ $\frac{5}{5}$

51. $\frac{1}{10}$ $\frac{1}{11}$ $\frac{1}{12}$

52. $\frac{5}{7}$ $\frac{5}{8}$ $\frac{5}{9}$

Circle the smallest fraction in each set.

53. $\frac{1}{3}$ $\frac{1}{4}$ $\frac{1}{5}$

54. $\frac{7}{7}$ $\frac{4}{7}$ $\frac{5}{7}$

55. $\frac{5}{9}$ $\frac{6}{9}$ $\frac{3}{9}$

Singapore Math Level 2A & 2B

Arrange the fractions in each set. Begin with the largest.

56.

————— , ————— , —————
largest

57.

————— , ————— , —————
largest

58.

————— , ————— , —————
largest

Arrange the fractions in each set. Begin with the smallest.

59.

————— , ————— , —————
smallest

60.

————— , ————— , —————
smallest

61.

$$\dfrac{5}{10} \qquad \dfrac{5}{9} \qquad \dfrac{5}{12}$$

————, ————, ————
smallest

Add these fractions.

62. $\dfrac{1}{8} + \dfrac{2}{8} \quad = \dfrac{3}{8}$

63. $\dfrac{1}{10} + \dfrac{6}{10} = \dfrac{7}{10}$

64. $\dfrac{3}{12} + \dfrac{7}{12} = \dfrac{10}{12}$

65. $\dfrac{2}{7} + \dfrac{4}{7} \quad = \dfrac{6}{7}$

66. $\dfrac{1}{9} + \dfrac{5}{9} + \dfrac{2}{9} \quad = \dfrac{8}{9}$

67. $\dfrac{1}{5} + \dfrac{2}{5} + \dfrac{1}{5} \quad = \dfrac{4}{5}$

68. $\dfrac{2}{6} + \dfrac{1}{6} + \dfrac{1}{6} \quad = \dfrac{4}{6}$

69. $\dfrac{2}{11} + \dfrac{1}{11} + \dfrac{3}{11} = \dfrac{6}{11}$

Subtract these fractions.

70. $\dfrac{3}{4} - \dfrac{1}{4} \quad = \dfrac{2}{4}$

71. $\dfrac{5}{9} - \dfrac{3}{9} \quad = \dfrac{2}{9}$

72. $\dfrac{6}{7} - \dfrac{1}{7} \quad = \dfrac{5}{7}$

73. $1 - \dfrac{1}{10} \quad = \dfrac{9}{10}$

74. $\dfrac{5}{6} - \dfrac{1}{6} - \dfrac{2}{6} \quad = \dfrac{2}{6}$

75. $\dfrac{10}{11} - \dfrac{3}{11} - \dfrac{4}{11} = \dfrac{3}{11}$

76. $\dfrac{6}{8} - \dfrac{1}{8} - \dfrac{2}{8} \quad = \dfrac{3}{8}$

77. $\dfrac{10}{12} - \dfrac{2}{12} - \dfrac{5}{12} = \dfrac{3}{12}$

Solve the following story problems. Show your work in the space below.

78. Benny cuts a loaf of bread into 5 parts. His sister eats 2 pieces of the bread. What fraction of the bread is left?

$\dfrac{3}{5}$ of the bread is left.

79. Mom eats $\dfrac{1}{10}$ of a pizza. Dad eats $\dfrac{3}{10}$ of the pizza. Kaylee eats $\dfrac{1}{10}$ of the pizza. What fraction of the pizza have they eaten?

$$\dfrac{1}{10} + \dfrac{3}{10} + \dfrac{1}{10} = \dfrac{5}{10}$$

They have eaten _____ of the pizza.

Singapore Math Level 2A & 2B

80. Ileana used $\frac{1}{7}$ of her weekly allowance to buy a pencil case. She used another $\frac{3}{7}$ of it to buy some drawing materials. What fraction of her weekly allowance did she use?

$$\frac{1}{7} + \frac{3}{7} = \frac{4}{7}$$

She used $\frac{2}{7}$ of her weekly allowance.

81. Aunt Carol made a pitcher of orange juice. Her children drank $\frac{3}{8}$ of the orange juice. What fraction of the pitcher of orange juice was left?

$$1 - \frac{3}{8} = \frac{2}{8}$$

$\frac{2}{8}$ of the pitcher of orange juice was left.

82. $\frac{1}{6}$ of the people at a party are children. $\frac{3}{6}$ of the people are women. The remaining people are men. What fraction of the people at the party are children and women?

$$\frac{1}{6} + \frac{3}{6} = \frac{4}{6}$$

$\frac{4}{6}$ of the people at the party are children and women.

Singapore Math Level 2A & 2B

Unit 13: TIME

Examples:

1. Write the time shown on the clock.

    The time is **6:20**.

2. Kelly eats her lunch 1 hour after noon. Write <u>A.M.</u> or <u>P.M.</u> in the blank.

    She eats her lunch at 1:00 **P.M.**

3. Henry took a bus to the zoo at 11:00 A.M. He reached the zoo 30 minutes later. At what time did he reach the zoo?

    He reached the zoo at **11:30 A.M.**

---

1. Look at the clock below. Fill in each box with the correct answer.

The time shown on the clock is _____ A.M.

Singapore Math Level 2A & 2B

What time is it? Write the correct minutes on the lines below.

2.

_____ minutes after 8 o'clock

4.

_____ minutes after 6 o'clock

3.

_____ minutes after 4 o'clock

5.

_____ minutes after 7 o'clock

Write the correct time on the lines below.

6.

The time is _____.

8.

The time is _____.

7.

The time is _____.

9.

The time is _____.

Singapore Math Level 2A & 2B

Match each clock to the correct time.

10.

• 3:10

11.

• 5:20

12.

• 9:35

13.

• 11:05

14.

• 7:55

Draw the minute hand on each clock.

15.

The time is 4:15.

16.

The time is 6:00.

17.

The time is 11:30.

18.

The time is 1:45.

19.

The time is 2:10.

20.

The time is 8:55.

21.

The time is 9:05.

22.

The time is 3:50.

Singapore Math Level 2A & 2B

Read the time, and draw the hour and minute hands on each clock.

23.

The time is 1:20.

24.

The time is 10:30.

25.

The time is 11:15.

26.

The time is 3:55.

27.

The time is 5:00.

28.

The time is 9:25.

29.

The time is 6:45.

30.

The time is 7:10.

Singapore Math Level 2A & 2B

Fill in each blank with *A.M.* or *P.M.*

31. Pilar eats her breakfast
    at 8:00 _____ .

32. The class will end at 12:50 _____ .

33. Claire likes to take her dog for
    a walk after dinner. She usually
    gets home at 9:00 _____ .

34. Mrs. Thomas goes to the grocery store
    after preparing breakfast. She leaves
    her house at 10:00 _____ .

35. Braden and his family enjoy watching
    the evening news. The news will
    start at 9:30 _____ .

Singapore Math Level 2A & 2B

Fill in each blank with the correct answer.

36.

_____ is 30 min. after _____

37.

_____ is 30 min. after _____

38.

_____ is 1 hr. after _____

39.

_____ is 3 hr. before _____

40.

_____ is 4 hr. before _____

Singapore Math Level 2A & 2B

Draw the time on each clock. Fill in each blank with the correct answer.

41.

10:30 A.M. is 30 min. before _____.

42.

8:00 P.M. is 1 hr. after _____.

43.

5:30 A.M. is 30 min. after _____.

44.

3:30 P.M. is 30 min. before _____.

45.

1:00 P.M. is 1 hr. after _____.

Singapore Math Level 2A & 2B

REVIEW 6

 1. Which of the following are fractions? Put a check mark (✓) in the correct boxes.

(a)

(c)

(b)

Shade the parts of each figure to show the fractions.

2. $\frac{5}{6}$

3. $\frac{6}{10}$

169

Singapore Math Level 2A & 2B

Write the correct times on the lines below.

4.

10:25

6.

9:55

5.

5:00

7.

7:30

Draw the minute hand on each clock to show the correct time.

8.

3:45

10.

9:00

9.

2:15

11.

6:50

Singapore Math Level 2A & 2B

Arrange the fractions in each set. Begin with the largest.

12.

$$\frac{5}{7} \quad \frac{1}{7} \quad \frac{6}{7}$$

$$\underline{\frac{1}{7}}_{\text{largest}} , \quad \underline{\frac{5}{7}} , \quad \frac{6}{7}$$

Arrange the fractions in each set. Begin with the smallest.

13.

$$\frac{4}{8} \quad \frac{7}{8} \quad \frac{5}{8}$$

$$\underline{\frac{4}{8}}_{\text{smallest}} , \quad \underline{\frac{7}{8}} , \quad \underline{\frac{5}{8}}$$

Draw the time on each clock. Fill in each blank with the correct answer.

14. Mary left her house at 10:30 A.M. 30 minutes later, she reached her school. At what time did Mary reach her school?

30 minutes later

Mary reached her school at ____11:00____.

Singapore Math Level 2A & 2B

15. Leo has a guitar lesson every Saturday. His lesson lasts 1 hour. If his guitar lesson ends at 2:30 P.M., at what time does it start?

His guitar lesson starts at __1:30__.

16. All the Grade 1 and 2 students have recess at 9:45 A.M. Recess ends 30 minutes later. At what time does recess end?

Recess ends at __10:15__.

Do the following story problems. Show your work in the space below.

17. Anton and Jack shared a dish of nachos. If Anton ate $\frac{1}{2}$ of it, how much did Jack eat?

$$1 - \frac{1}{2} = \frac{1}{2}$$

Jack ate __$\frac{1}{2}$__ of the dish of nachos.

Singapore Math Level 2A & 2B

18. Deepak ate $\frac{2}{6}$ of a melon. John ate $\frac{3}{6}$ of the melon. What fraction of the melon did they eat?

$$\frac{2}{6} + \frac{3}{6} = \frac{5}{6}$$

They ate $\frac{5}{6}$ of the melon.

19. Harry poured a glass of milk. He drank $\frac{4}{7}$ of it. What fraction of the milk was left in the glass?

$$1 - \frac{4}{7} = \frac{3}{7}$$

$\frac{3}{7}$ of the milk was left in the glass.

20. Tariq borrows a book from the library. He reads $\frac{2}{5}$ of it. What fraction of the book does Tariq need to read in order to complete it?

$$1 - \frac{2}{5} = \frac{3}{5}$$

Tariq needs to read _____ of the book in order to complete it.

Singapore Math Level 2A & 2B

Unit 14: VOLUME

Examples:

1.

Cup A   Cup B   Cup C

(a) Which cup contains the most water?   **Cup A**

(b) Which cup contains the least water?   **Cup B**

2.

(a) Which jug contains the least water?   **Jug B**

(b) Which jug contains the most water?   **Jug C**

(c) How many fewer flasks of water can Jug A hold than Jug C? $9 - 5 = \underline{\mathbf{4}}$

(d) How many more flasks of water can Jug C hold than Jug B? $9 - 3 = \underline{\mathbf{6}}$

3.

 How many liters of water does the container hold?

The container holds **3** liters of water.

4. Uncle Norman filled 6 fish tanks with water. Each fish tank contained 4 gallons of water. How many gallons of water did Uncle Norman use to fill the fish tanks?

$6 \times 4 = 24$

Uncle Norman used **24** gallons of water to fill the fish tanks.

Fill in each blank with *more* or *less*.

1.

A   B

(a)   Bottle A contains _____ water than Bottle B.

(b)   Bottle B contains _____ water than Bottle A.

2.

A   B

(a)   Cup B contains _____ water than Cup A.

(b)   Cup A contains _____ water than Cup B.

Fill in each blank with the correct answer.

3.

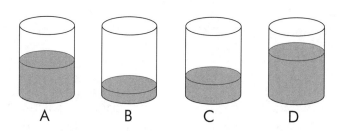

A   B   C   D

(a)   Container _____ has the greatest volume of water.

(b)   Container _____ has the least volume of water.

Singapore Math Level 2A & 2B

4.

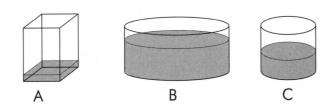

(a) Container _____ has the greatest volume of water.

(b) Container _____ has the least volume of water.

5.

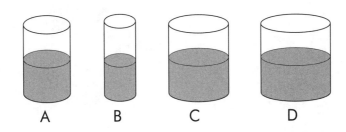

(a) Container _____ has the greatest volume of water.

(b) Container _____ has the least volume of water.

6. Study the pictures carefully. Fill in each blank with the correct answer.

(a) The _____ holds the greatest volume of water.

(b) The _____ holds the least volume of water.

(c)   The teapot holds _____ more glasses of water than the bowl.

(d)   The bowl holds _____ fewer glasses of water than the jug.

Write the volume of water in each container on the lines below.

7.

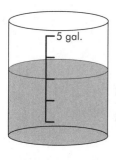

_____ gal. of water

9.

_____ oz. of water

8.

_____ L of water

10.

_____ L of water

Look at each picture carefully. Fill in the blanks with the correct answers.

11.

Thomas used _____ L of water to water his plants.

12.

Josefina used _____ gal. of water to wash laundry.

13.

Amy makes _____ L of iced tea.

14.

Mother makes _____ gal. of soup.

Solve the following story problems. Show your work in the space below.

15. Lily fills an empty fish tank with 2 buckets of water. Each bucket can hold 2 gal. of water. How many gallons of water are in the fish tank?

There are _____ gal. of water in the fish tank.

16. Mrs. Simon prepares 3 L of iced tea. Mrs. Suzuki prepares 5 L of lemonade. How many liters of drinks do they prepare altogether?

They prepare _____ L of drinks altogether.

17. Darius fills an empty tank with 4 gal. of water. Jack adds 3 gal. of water. Diego adds another 5 gal. of water. How much water can the tank hold?

The tank can hold _____ gal. of water.

18. Ayesha buys 8 L of orange juice. She gives 2 L of juice to Jane. How much orange juice does Ayesha have left?

Ayesha has _____ L of orange juice left.

19. Mr. Benson filled his car with 10 gal. of gas on Monday. He filled his car with 20 gal. of gas on Thursday. How many gallons of gas in all did Mr. Benson put in his car?

Mr. Benson put _____ gal. of gas in his car in all.

20. Maddy fills an empty container with 16 L of water. She then pours all the water equally into some jugs. Each jug holds 4 L of water. How many jugs does she use?

She uses _____ jugs.

Unit 15: GRAPHS

Examples:

The graph below shows the number of students in a class who went on different field trips throughout the year.

| Bird Park Field Trip | Botanical Garden Field Trip | Zoo Field Trip | Science Center Field Trip | Beach Field Trip |

Each ◇ stands for 10 students.

(a)   How many students went on the zoo field trip?   4 x 10 = **40**

(b)   How many students went on the beach field trip? 1 x 10 = **10**

(c)   How many more students went on the zoo field trip than the bird park field trip?
$$4 - 3 = 1$$
$$1 \times 10 = \underline{\textbf{10}}$$

(d)   How many fewer students went on the beach field trip than the botanical garden field trip?
$$2 - 1 = 1$$
$$1 \times 10 = \underline{\textbf{10}}$$

(e)   How many students went on all the field trips throughout the year?
$$3 + 2 + 4 + 4 + 1 = 14$$
$$14 \times 10 = \underline{\textbf{140}}$$

Singapore Math Level 2A & 2B

1. Angelo and Michael went to the zoo and saw these animals.
   They drew a picture graph to show the number of each animal.

Animals in the zoo

Monkeys	☆ ☆ ☆ ☆ ☆ ☆
Lions	☆ ☆
Giraffes	☆ ☆ ☆ ☆
Zebras	☆ ☆ ☆
Snakes	☆ ☆ ☆

Each ☆ stands for 4 animals.

(a) They saw _____ giraffes.

(b) They saw _____ monkeys.

(c) They saw _____ more giraffes than lions.

(d) They saw _____ fewer snakes than monkeys.

(e) They saw the most _____.

(f) They saw the fewest _____.

Singapore Math Level 2A & 2B

2. Study the picture graph carefully. Fill in each blank with the correct answer.

Cartons of milk sold in a week

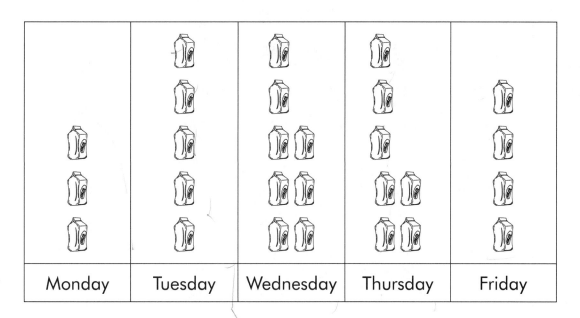

Monday	Tuesday	Wednesday	Thursday	Friday

(a) The most cartons of milk were sold on _____Wendnesday_____.

(b) 50 cartons of milk were sold on Tuesday.

Each 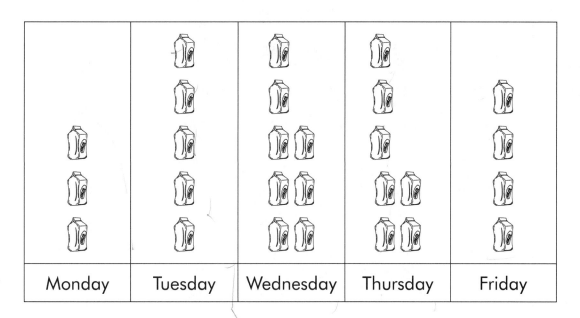 stands for ___10___ carton(s) of milk.

(c) ___40___ cartons of milk were sold on Friday.

(d) ___30___ more cartons of milk were sold on Thursday than on Friday.

(e) ___10___ fewer cartons of milk were sold on Monday than on Friday.

(f) ___20___ cartons of milk were sold on Tuesday and Thursday.

Singapore Math Level 2A & 2B

3. Below is a chart that shows the animals that Aiden's classmates keep as pets.

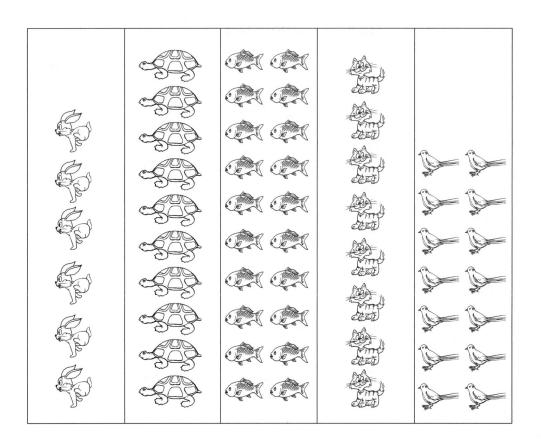

Help Aiden complete the picture graph below.

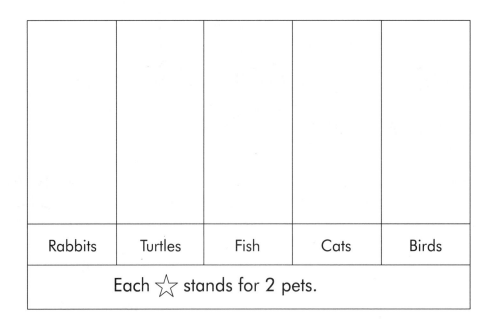

Rabbits	Turtles	Fish	Cats	Birds
Each ☆ stands for 2 pets.				

Singapore Math Level 2A & 2B

4. Study the picture graph below. Fill in each blank with the correct answer.

Number of books sold in a bookstore

Comic	
Fairytale	
Fiction	
Coloring	
	Each 📘 stands for 4 books.

(a) _____ books were the most popular.

(b) _____ books were the least popular.

(c) 4 fewer fairytale books were sold than _____ books.

(d) _____ more comic books were sold than fiction books.

(e) _____ fewer comic books were sold than coloring books.

5. Study the picture graph below. Fill in each blank with the correct answer.

Number of people at the movies

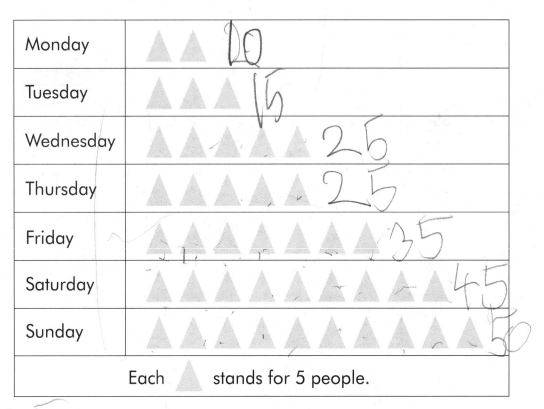

Monday	▲▲ 10
Tuesday	▲▲▲ 15
Wednesday	▲▲▲▲▲ 25
Thursday	▲▲▲▲▲ 25
Friday	▲▲▲▲▲▲▲ 35
Saturday	▲▲▲▲▲▲▲▲▲ 45
Sunday	▲▲▲▲▲▲▲▲▲▲ 50

Each ▲ stands for 5 people.

(a) _25_ people went to the movies on Wednesday.

(b) _5_ more people went to the movies on Friday than on Tuesday.

(c) 2 children went to the movies on Monday. There were _8_ adults at the movies on Monday.

(d) _95_ people went to the movies over the weekend.

(e) 16 adults went to the movies on Thursday. There were _9_ children at the movies on Thursday.

Singapore Math Level 2A & 2B

REVIEW 7

Write the volume of water in each container on the lines below.

1.

_____5_____ L of water

2.

_____2_____ gal. of water

3.

_____10_____ L of water

Fill in each blank with the correct answer.

4. **Favorite dinners of a group of children**

(handwritten annotations in table: 24, 12/9, 15, 18, 9; in Pizza column: 3, 6, 9, 12, 15, 18, 21, 24; in Meatloaf: 7)

Pizza	Meatloaf	Spaghetti	Tacos	Roast chicken

Each ⌣ represents 3 children.

(a) The number of children who like to eat tacos is ___18___.

(b) The number of children who like to eat spaghetti is ___15___.

(c) There are ___27___ fewer children who like to eat roast chicken than tacos.

(d) There are ___12___ more children who like to eat pizza than meatloaf.

(e) The total number of children who like to eat meatloaf and spaghetti is ___27___.

Singapore Math Level 2A & 2B

5.

(a) The container that holds the greatest volume of water is the _Jug_.

(b) The container that holds the least volume of water is the _Cup_.

(c) The jug holds _____ more ladles of water than the cup.

(d) The cup holds _____ fewer ladles of water than the teapot.

(e) The total number of ladles that the 3 containers can hold is _20_.

6. The pictures below show the types of seafood Mr. Kaufman sold at the fish market.

Complete the picture graph.

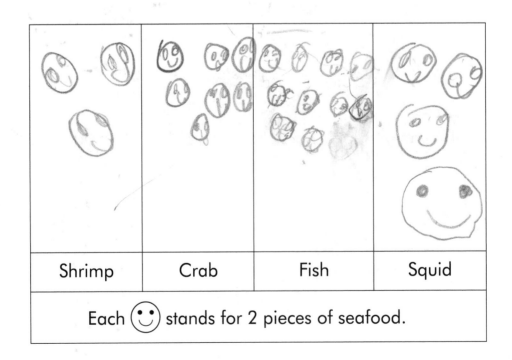

| Shrimp | Crab | Fish | Squid |

Each 😊 stands for 2 pieces of seafood.

Singapore Math Level 2A & 2B

Do the following story problems. Show your work in the space below.

7. Riley bought 2 bottles of fruit juice. Each bottle contained 8 oz. of fruit juice. How many ounces of fruit juice did Riley buy?

Riley bought _16_ oz. of fruit juice.

8. Li mixes 10 L of water with 8 L of frozen concentrate to make lemonade.

   (a) How many liters of lemonade does Li make?

   Li makes _18_ L of lemonade.

   (b) If Li gives 3 L of lemonade to her neighbor, how many liters of lemonade will she have left?

$$\begin{array}{r} 18 \\ -\ 3 \\ \hline 15 \end{array}$$

She will have _15_ L of lemonade left.

193

9. Isabelle collected 10 gal. of rainwater on Monday. She collected 15 gal. of rainwater on Wednesday. How much rainwater did she collect altogether?

She collected _**25**_ gal. of rainwater altogether.

10. Kate bought 5 L of milk over the weekend. She drank 2 L of milk on Monday and Tuesday. How much milk was left?

_**3**_ L of milk was left.

Singapore Math Level 2A & 2B

11. Andy needed to buy 20 gal. of drinks for his birthday party. He bought 10 gal. of drinks from Supermarket A and 5 gal. of drinks from Supermarket B.

(a) How many gallons of drinks did Andy buy?

Andy bought ___15___ gal. of drinks.

(b) How many more gallons did he need to buy?

He needed to buy ___5___ more gallons of drinks.

12. Eva bought 2 bottles of liquid detergent. Bottle A contained 8 L of liquid detergent. Bottle B contained 25 L of liquid detergent. How much liquid detergent did Eva buy altogether?

Eva bought ___33___ L of liquid detergent altogether.

Singapore Math Level 2A & 2B

13. Kenji removed some water from a tank using a bucket. The bucket could hold 2 gal. of water. He filled the bucket completely with water 6 times. How much water did he remove from the tank?

Kenji removed _____3_____ gal. of water from the tank.

14. Nick poured 24 L of orange juice into 4 containers equally. How much orange juice was there in each container?

There was _____6_____ L of orange juice in each container.

15. Mrs. Anderson recycles water by collecting used water from the washing machine. She collects 5 buckets of used water every week. Each bucket can hold 3 gal. of used water. How much used water does she collect every week?

She collects _____15_____ gal. of used water every week.

Singapore Math Level 2A & 2B

16. Jamie drinks 2 L of water daily. How much water does she drink in 10 days?

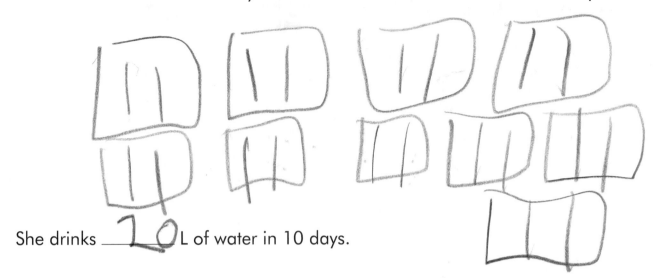

She drinks ___20___ L of water in 10 days.

17. Mr. Tomasek brews 17 gal. of coffee and 25 gal. of tea every day. How much coffee and tea does he brew every day?

He brews ___42___ gal. of coffee and tea every day.

18. Luisa pours 36 gal. of apple juice equally into some containers. Each container can hold 4 gal. of apple juice. How many containers does she need?

4 8 12 16 20
24 28 32
36

She needs ___9___ containers.

Singapore Math Level 2A & 2B

19. Alyssa bought 8 bottles of detergent. Each bottle of detergent was 2 L. How many liters of detergent did Alyssa buy?

Alyssa bought __16__ L of detergent.

20. George used 5 gal. of water to wash a car. How many cars did he wash if he used 35 gal. of water?

He washed __7__ cars if he used 35 gal. of water.

Singapore Math Level 2A & 2B

Unit 16: LINES AND SURFACES

Examples:

1. This picture is formed using straight lines and curves.

    (a) How many straight lines are there?   <u>**2**</u> straight lines

    (b) How many curves are there?   <u>**2**</u> curves

2. The object below is made from a tissue box and a toilet paper roll.

    How many flat surfaces does the object have?   <u>**5**</u> flat surfaces

Fill in each blank with the correct answer.

1.
2 3 4 5 7 8

Which of the above digits have

(a)   straight lines only?   _____

(b)   curves only?   _____

(c)   straight lines and curves?   _____

Singapore Math Level 2A & 2B

2.

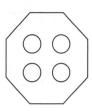

There are _____ straight lines and _____ curves in the above picture.

3.

There are _____ straight lines and _____ curves in the above picture.

4.

There are _____ straight lines and _____ curve in the above picture.

5.

There are _____ straight lines and _____ curves in the above picture.

6.

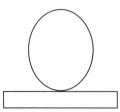

There are _____ straight lines and _____ curve in the above picture.

Singapore Math Level 2A & 2B

Look at these objects carefully. Fill in each blank with the correct answer.

7.

The candle has _____ flat surface(s).

8.

The box of tissues has _____ flat surface(s).

9.

The box of ice cream has _____ flat surface(s).

10.

The pot of flowers has _____ flat surface(s).

Singapore Math Level 2A & 2B

11.

The container has _____ flat surface(s).

For each object, count the number of flat surfaces. Write the correct answer on the lines below.

12.

_____ flat surfaces

13.

_____ flat surfaces

14.

_____ flat surfaces

15.

_____ flat surfaces

Singapore Math Level 2A & 2B

Unit 17: SHAPES AND PATTERNS

1. What shapes are used to form the figure below?

   The shapes are **quarter** **circle**, **square**, **rectangle**, and **triangle**.

2. Draw a figure using a cone, a cube, and a cylinder.

3. What comes next in the pattern below?

 ?

 comes next in the pattern.

Singapore Math Level 2A & 2B

Identify the shapes below.

1.

   _____

2.

   _____

3.

   _____

4.

   _____

5.

   _____

6.

   _____

7.

   _____

Singapore Math Level 2A & 2B

Each figure is made of 2 different shapes. Name the 2 shapes.

8.

This figure is made of a

_____ and

a _____ .

9.

This figure is made of a

_____ and

a _____ .

10.

This figure is made of a

_____ and

a _____ .

11.

This figure is made of a

_____ and

a _____ .

12.

This figure is made of a

_____ and

a _____ .

Singapore Math Level 2A & 2B

13. Look at the figure carefully, and fill in each blank with the correct answer.

The figure is formed by

(a) _____ rectangles,

(b) _____ triangles,

(c) _____ quarter circles,

(d) _____ circles,

(e) _____ squares, and

(f) _____ semicircles.

Draw lines to show the different shapes that make each figure.

14.

16.

15.

Singapore Math Level 2A & 2B

Fill in each blank with the name of the shaded part of each picture.

17.

_____

20.

_____

18.

_____

21.

_____

19.

_____

22.

_____

Carefully look at each shape on the left. Draw the same shape on the dot grid on the right.

23.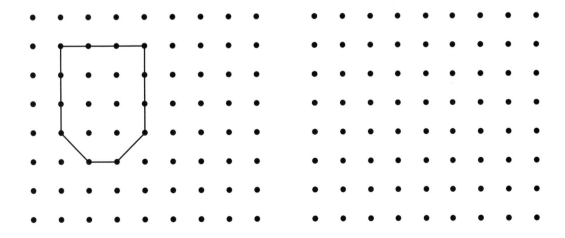

Singapore Math Level 2A & 2B

24.

25.

26.

27.

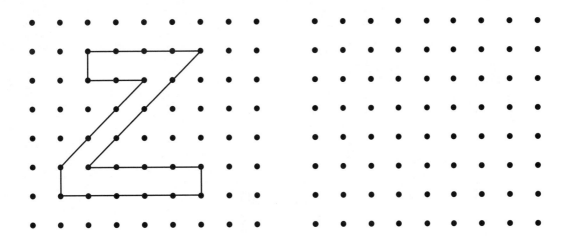

Carefully look at each shape on the left. Draw the same shape on the square grid on the right.

28.

29.

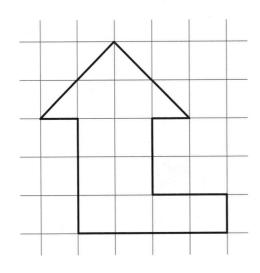

Singapore Math Level 2A & 2B

30.

31.

32.

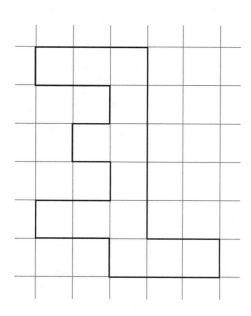

Singapore Math Level 2A & 2B

Put a check mark (✓) in the correct box to complete each pattern.

33.

34.

35.

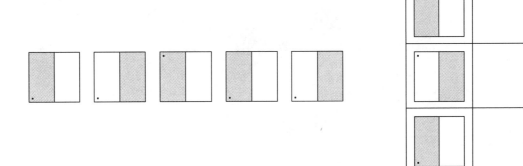

Singapore Math Level 2A & 2B

36.

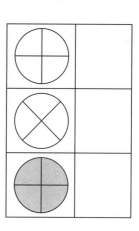

Complete the following patterns.

37.

 _____

38.

 _____

39.

 _____

Singapore Math Level 2A & 2B

REVIEW 8

Name the following shapes.

1.

_____

2.

_____

3.

_____

4.

_____

5.

_____

6.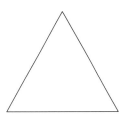

_____

Singapore Math Level 2A & 2B

7.

The figure above has _____ flat surface(s).

8.

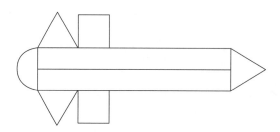

There are _____ triangles, _____ semicircles, _____ rectangles, and

_____ squares in the figure above.

Complete the following patterns.

9.

10.

11.

Singapore Math Level 2A & 2B

Draw dotted lines on each figure, and identify the shapes that form the figure on the lines below.

12.

13.

14.

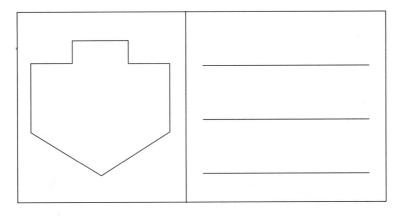

Singapore Math Level 2A & 2B

15.

There are _____ straight lines and _____ curves in the above picture.

16.

The battery has _____ flat surface(s).

Look at the shape on the left. Draw the same shape on the square grid on the right.

17.

 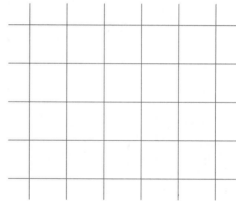

18. Color the objects that have only flat surfaces.

Singapore Math Level 2A & 2B

Carefully look at each shape on the left. Draw the same shape on the dot grid on the right.

19.

20.

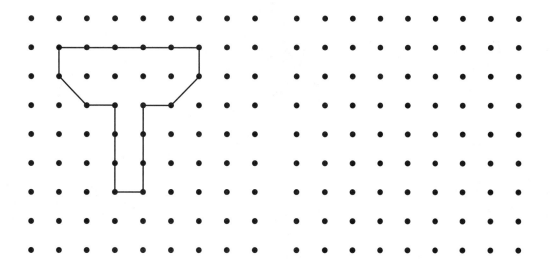

FINAL REVIEW

Fill in each blank with the correct answer.

1.

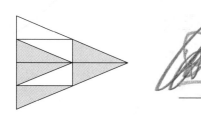

__5/8__ of the figure is shaded.

2. The picture graph below shows the number of eggs Jackson sold in a week.

Each ⬯ stands for 10 eggs.

(a) He sold __50__ eggs on Thursday.

(b) He sold __70__ eggs on Sunday.

(c) He sold __20__ more eggs on Friday than on Monday.

(d) He sold __50__ fewer eggs on Tuesday than on Saturday.

(e) He sold __60__ eggs altogether on Monday and Wednesday.

Singapore Math Level 2A & 2B

3. The time shown on the clock is 11:50 A.M.

30 minutes later, it will be __12:20__.

4. Shade $\frac{1}{4}$ of each figure.

(a)

50
+30
20

(b)

① → shade
4 → total

1×2   2
___   __
 8   8

5.

Container A can hold ___6___ L of water.

6. Complete the pattern.

860

7. Add 790 and 70 mentally. _____

1
+790
  70
____
 860

8. $\frac{2}{5}$ and ___$\frac{3}{5}$___ make one whole.

9. Draw the minute hand on the clock to show 6:40 P.M.

Singapore Math Level 2A & 2B

10. The figure on the right is made of a
    Cemi and a _rectangle_.

11. Look at the figures carefully.

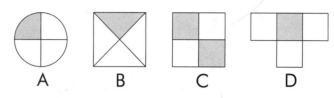

A   B   C   D

Figure _C_ does not belong in the group.

12. ⬜ × ⬜ = 100
    ⑤ × ⑤ = 25
    ⬜ × ⑤ = _50_

13. $\frac{1}{10} + \frac{4}{10} + \frac{2}{10} = \frac{7}{10}$

14. The figure below is made of 4 different shapes. Draw dotted lines to show the shapes.

15. Circle the largest fraction.

    $\frac{1}{12}$, $\frac{1}{9}$, $\frac{1}{11}$

16. $48.30 = _48_ dollars and _30_ cents

17. Subtract 90 from 345 mentally. _255_

18. Express 9,080¢ in dollars. _$90.80¢_

19. Subtract $\frac{2}{11}$ from $\frac{5}{11}$. _$\frac{3}{11}$_

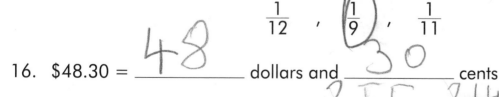

Solve the following story problems. Show your work in the space below.

20. Alice spent $30 at the supermarket. Sydney spent twice as much as Alice. How much did Sydney spend?

Sydney spent $60.

21. Patrick gave 5 cans of juice to each of his 7 friends. How many cans of juice did he give to his friends?

He gave 35 cans of juice to his friends.

Singapore Math Level 2A & 2B

22. 3 groups of students took part in an art competition. There were 129 students in Group A, 257 students in Group B, and 229 students in Group C. How many students took part in the art competition?

515 students took part in the art competition.

23. Terrell reads 4 books in a day. How many books will he read in a week?

He will read 28 books in a week.

24. Tyler and Jack make 600 L of fruit punch for an event. If Tyler makes 228 L of fruit punch, how many liters of fruit punch does Jack make?

Jack makes _372_ L of fruit punch.

25. Malak received $50 from his aunt and $30 from his uncle on his birthday. How much money did Malak receive in all?

Malak received $_80_ in all.

Singapore Math Level 2A & 2B

CHALLENGE QUESTIONS

Solve the following problems on another sheet of paper.

1. The chart below shows the number of pieces of clothing Mrs. Robinson sewed.

Number of days	1	3	6
Pieces of clothing	4	12	24

    How many pieces of clothing did Mrs. Robinson sew in 10 days?

2. Sam is 12 years old. His mother is 3 times his age. His father is 5 years older than his mother. How much older is Sam's father than Sam?

3. Use numbers from 10 to 18 to make each vertical and horizontal line equal to the numbers in the shaded boxes. Each number can be used only once.

4. Five minutes before recess, Carlos and Henry looked at their watches. Carlos's watch was 5 minutes faster than the classroom clock. Henry's watch was 5 minutes slower than the classroom clock. If Carlos's watch showed 9:50 A.M., what was the time shown on Henry's watch?

5. $\heartsuit + \triangle = 120$

    $\heartsuit + \heartsuit = 80$

    $\heartsuit + \triangle + \triangle + \triangle = $ _____

6. The product of 2 numbers is 50. The result of the division of the 2 numbers is 2. What are the 2 numbers?

Singapore Math Level 2A & 2B

7. Christopher had a bottle of orange juice. He gave some juice to his best friend. He then gave half of the remaining juice to his neighbor. He was left with $\frac{1}{4}$ of the bottle of orange juice. What fraction of the bottle of orange juice did Christopher give to his best friend?

8. Austin spent an hour watching cartoons followed by 2 hours of a nap, and 3 hours of homework. If Austin completed his homework at 10 P.M., what time did he start watching cartoons?

9. How many triangles are there in the figure shown below?
   (Hint: The triangles do not need to all be the same size.)

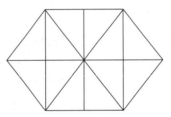

10. Fill in the blank with the correct answer.

11. Winnie uses some sticks to form 2 squares as shown below. How would you rearrange 4 matchsticks to form 3 rectangles?

12. It took Rico 30 minutes to wash his father's car and an hour to mow the lawn. Then, he took a 20-minute bath. By the time he stepped out of the bathroom, the hour hand pointed to 1 and the minute hand pointed to 4. On the clock, show the time Rico started to wash his father's car.

SOLUTIONS
Singapore Math Level 2A

Unit 1: Numbers up to 1,000

1. 4 hundreds 2 tens 5 ones = **425**
2. 3 hundreds 8 tens 7 ones = **387**
3. 5 hundreds 3 tens = **530**
4. 8 hundreds 7 ones = **807**
5. 10 hundreds = **1,000**
6. **seven hundred and sixty**
7. **three hundred and seventy-eight**
8. **four hundred and fifty-six**
9. **two hundred and two**
10. **one thousand**
11. **562**
12. **779**
13. **110**
14. **358**
15. **907**
16. **8, 2, 5**
17. **6, 3, 0**
18. **7, 0, 5**
19. **4, 5, 9**
20. **10, 0, 0**
21. **tens**
22. **hundreds**
23. **hundreds**
24. **9**
25. **3**
26. **0**
27. **greater**
28. **smaller**
29. **smaller**
30. **greater**
31. **smaller**
32. **379, 397, 937, 973**
33. **129, 192, 219, 319**
34. **511, 571, 715, 751**
35. **116, 163, 313, 316**
36. **344, 404, 434, 443**
37. **750, 705, 570, 507**
38. **413, 341, 314, 134**
39. **960, 608, 517, 289, 187**
40. **857, 456, 320, 220, 190**
41. **970, 927, 727, 290, 279**
42. 10 + 560 = **570**
43. 680 − 20 = **660**
44. 100 + 778 = **878**
45. 695 − 200 = **495**
46. 279 − 5 = **274**
47. **300, 310**
    290 − 280 = 10
    290 + 10 = 300
    300 + 10 = 310
48. **670, 570**
    970 − 870 = 100
    770 − 100 = 670
    670 − 100 = 570
49. **780, 840**
    820 − 800 = 20
    760 + 20 = 780
    820 + 20 = 840
50. **490, 520**
    460 − 430 = 30
    460 + 30 = 490
    490 + 30 = 520
51. **450, 550**
    750 − 650 = 100
    650 − 100 = 550
    550 − 100 = 450

Unit 2: Adding and Subtracting Numbers 1-1,000

1.
```
    1 4 3
  + 2 1 4
  -------
    3 5 7
```

2.
```
    3 1 2
  + 4 8 1
  -------
    7 9 3
```

3.
```
    7 3 2
  + 1 4 5
  -------
    8 7 7
```

4.
```
    2 0 1
  + 2 8 3
  -------
    4 8 4
```

5.
```
    8 2 1
  + 1 6 3
  -------
    9 8 4
```

6.
```
    5 6 9
  − 2 3 4
  -------
    3 3 5
```

7.
```
    9 3 2
  − 1 2 1
  -------
    8 1 1
```

8.
```
    7 3 6
  − 2 0 4
  -------
    5 3 2
```

9.
```
    3 7 5
  - 1 5 2
    2 2 3
```

10.
```
    8 5 9
  - 6 0 7
    2 5 2
```

11.
```
      1
    1 3 5
  + 1 0 9
    2 4 4
```

12.
```
    1 1
    5 0 5
  + 2 9 5
    8 0 0
```

13.
```
      1
    7 3 7
  + 1 2 9
    8 6 6
```

14.
```
    1
    2 5 6
  + 3 8 0
    6 3 6
```

15.
```
      1
    4 6 2
  + 2 0 8
    6 7 0
```

16.
```
    1 1
    3 9 7
  + 5 4 6
    9 4 3
```

17.
```
    2 14 13
    3̶ 5̶ 3̶
  - 1 7 4
    1 7 9
```

18.
```
      6 11
    9 7̶ 1̶
  - 3 6 9
    6 0 2
```

19.
```
    3 9 10
    4̶ 0̶ 0̶
  - 2 0 5
    1 9 5
```

20.
```
    5 13
    6̶ 3̶ 2
  - 1 7 1
    4 6 1
```

21.
```
    3 10 12
    4̶ 1̶ 2̶
  - 1 2 4
    2 8 8
```

22.
```
    4 9 10
    5̶ 0̶ 0̶
  - 1 7 8
    3 2 2
```

23.
```
    7 10
    8̶ 0̶ 0
  - 2 8 0
    5 2 0
```

24.
```
    7 10
    9 8̶ 0̶
  - 5 5 5
    4 2 5
```

25.

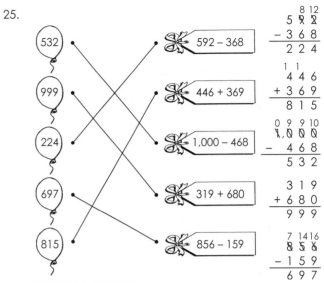

```
    8 12
    5 9̶ 2̶
  - 3 6 8
    2 2 4
```

```
    1 1
    4 4 6
  + 3 6 9
    8 1 5
```

```
    0 9 9 10
    1̶,0̶ 0̶ 0̶
  -   4 6 8
      5 3 2
```

```
    3 1 9
  + 6 8 0
    9 9 9
```

```
    7 14 16
    8̶ 5̶ 6̶
  - 1 5 9
    6 9 7
```

26.

73	+	42	=	115
−		+		−
70	−	30	=	40
=		=		=
3	+	72	=	75

27.

231	+	124	=	355
−		+		−
115	−	96	=	19
=		=		=
116	+	220	=	336

28.

389 + 317 = 706

Anne collects **706** stickers.

```
    1 1
    3 8 9
  + 3 1 7
    7 0 6
```

29.

416 − 29 = 387

John has **387** bottle caps.

```
    3 10 16
    4̶ 1̶ 6̶
  -   2 9
    3 8 7
```

30.

Monday	Tuesday
586	237

?

586 + 237 = 823

He sold **823** roses altogether.

```
    1 1
    5 8 6
  + 2 3 7
    8 2 3
```

31.

Saturday	Sunday
416	555

?

416 + 555 = 971

971 visitors were at the museum on both days.

32.

Marcus	Jack
?	$469

$837

```
  7 1217
  8 3 7
- 4 6 9
  3 6 8
```

$837 − $469 = $368
Marcus spent **$368**.

Review 1

1. **three hundred and seventy-five**
2. **nine hundred and nineteen**
3. **212**
4. **303**
5. **917**, **420**, **402**, **313**, **179**
6. **128**, **182**, **218**, **281**, **812**
7. 10 + 360 = **370**
8. 876 − 50 = **826**
9. **516**, **456**

   496 − 476 = 20
   536 − 20 = 516
   476 − 20 = 456

10.
```
    1
  6 0 8
+ 1 2 9
  7 3 7
```

11.
```
  1 1
  5 7 6
+ 1 8 8
  7 6 4
```

12.
```
  1
  1 5 4
+ 3 6 5
  5 1 9
```

13.
```
  1 1
  3 1 2
+ 4 9 8
  8 1 0
```

14.
```
  6 9 10
  7 0 0
- 4 3 5
  2 6 5
```

15.
```
    1 18
  3 2 8
- 1 0 9
  2 1 9
```

16.
```
  7 1510
  8 6 0
- 3 8 9
  4 7 1
```

17.
```
  4 1312
  5 4 2
- 3 7 9
  1 6 3
```

18. (a) 575 − 379 = 196

Wednesday	575
Monday	379 ?

```
  4 1615
  5 7 5
- 3 7 9
  1 9 6
```

196 more people went to the zoo on Wednesday than on Monday.

(b) 686 − 379 = 307

Tuesday	686
Monday	379 ?

```
    7 16
  6 8 6
- 3 7 9
  3 0 7
```

---

307 fewer people went to the zoo on Monday than on Tuesday.

19.

1,000 − 494 = 506
Aaron needs to collect **506** more stamps.

```
  0 9 910
  1 0 0 0
-   4 9 4
    5 0 6
```

20.

?	
360	265

360 + 265 = 625
Jazmin sold **625** flowers on both days.

```
    1
  3 6 0
+ 2 6 5
  6 2 5
```

Unit 3: Fun with Models (Adding and Subtracting)

1.

576	186

?

576 + 186 = 762
They have **762** bookmarks altogether.

```
  1 1
  5 7 6
+ 1 8 6
  7 6 2
```

2.

280

168	?

280 − 168 = 112
He has **112** chickens left.

```
  7 10
  2 8 0
- 1 6 8
  1 1 2
```

3.

?

360	275	150

360 + 275 + 150 = 785
He sold **785** oranges altogether.

```
    1
  3 6 0       6 3 5
+ 2 7 5     + 1 5 0
  6 3 5       7 8 5
```

4.

96

78	?

96 − 78 = 18
She gave **18** seashells to her best friend.

```
  8 16
  9 6
- 7 8
  1 8
```

5.

?

131	280

131 + 280 = 411
He had **411** stamps altogether.

```
    1
  1 3 1
+ 2 8 0
  4 1 1
```

6.

216	137	97

?

216 + 137 + 97 = 450
There are **450** animals on the farm.

```
    1           1 1
  2 1 6       3 5 3
+ 1 3 7     +   9 7
  3 5 3       4 5 0
```

7.

720

465	?

720 − 465 = 255
He gave **255** trading cards to his brother.

```
  6 1110
  7 2 0
- 4 6 5
  2 5 5
```

8. (a)

Hitomi	$310	
Brother		$280

?

$310 + $280 = $590
Her brother saves **$590**.

```
  3 1 0
+ 2 8 0
  5 9 0
```

(b) $310 + $590 = $900
They save **$900** altogether.

```
  1
  3 1 0
+ 5 9 0
  9 0 0
```

Unit 4: Multiplying and Dividing

1. **12, 12**
   2 + 2 + 2 + 2 + 2 + 2 = 12
2. **20, 20**
   4 + 4 + 4 + 4 + 4 = 20
3. **21, 21**
   3 + 3 + 3 + 3 + 3 + 3 + 3 = 21
4. **25, 25**
   5 + 5 + 5 + 5 + 5 = 25
5. **27, 27**
   9 + 9 + 9 = 27
6. 3 + 3 + 3 + 3 + 3 + 3 = **18**
7. 2 + 2 + 2 + 2 + 2 = **10**
8. 4 + 4 + 4 = **12**
9. 5 + 5 + 5 + 5 + 5 + 5 + 5 + 5 = **40**
10. 4 + 4 + 4 + 4 = **16**
11. **2, 14**
12. **4, 20**
13. **8, 16**
14. **3, 15**
15. **4, 16**
16. **6, 3, 18, 18**
17. **8, 10, 80, 80**
18. **3, 4, 12, 12**
19. **5, 5, 25, 25**
20. **5, 7, 35, 35**
21. **3, 4, 4**

22. **2, 10, 10**

23. **3, 3, 3**

24. **4, 5, 5**

25. **3, 6, 6**

26. **8 × 2 = 16**   **2 × 8 = 16**
    16 ÷ 8 = 2   **16 ÷ 2 = 8**
27. **3 × 7 = 21**   **7 × 3 = 21**

28. 21 ÷ 3 = 7   21 ÷ 7 = 3
    3 × 6 = 18   **6 × 3 = 18**
    18 ÷ 3 = 6   18 ÷ 6 = 3
29. **6 × 4 = 24**   **4 × 6 = 24**
    24 ÷ 6 = 4   **24 ÷ 4 = 6**
30. **4 × 3 = 12**   **3 × 4 = 12**
    12 ÷ 4 = 3   **12 ÷ 3 = 4**

Review 2

1. **14, 14**
   2 + 2 + 2 + 2 + 2 + 2 + 2 = 14
2. 3 + 3 + 3 + 3 + 3 + 3 + 3 + 3 + 3 = **27**
3. **4 × 3 = 12**   **3 × 4 = 12**
   12 ÷ 4 = 3   **12 ÷ 3 = 4**
4. **5 × 2 = 10**   **2 × 5 = 10**
   10 ÷ 5 = 2   **10 ÷ 2 = 5**
5. **3, 5, 5**

6. **4, 8, 8**

7. **2, 7, 7**

8. **3 × 6 = 18, 18**
9. **4 × 5 = 20, 20**
10. **7 × 3 = 21, 21**
11.
796 + 159 = 955
Abby has **955** stickers.

```
  1 1
  7 9 6
+ 1 5 9
  9 5 5
```

12.
187 − 93 = 94
She has **94** oranges left.

```
  0 18
  1 8 7
−   9 3
    9 4
```

13.
96 + 82 = 178
He scored **178** on both tests combined.

```
    9 6
+   8 2
  1 7 8
```

14. (a)
455 + 380 = 835
She baked **835** cookies during the weekend.

```
    1
    4 5 5
  + 3 8 0
    8 3 5
```

231

Singapore Math Level 2A & 2B

(b)

835 − 172 = 663
She had **663** cookies left.

```
  7 13
  8̶ 3̶ 5
− 1 7 2
  6 6 3
```

15.

496 + 388 = 884
They have **884** books in all.

```
  1 1
  4 9 6
+ 3 8 8
  8 8 4
```

16.
Cameron [$285]
Antonio [?] $62

```
  2 8 5
−   6 2
  2 2 3
```

$285 − $62 = $223
Antonio spent **$223**.

17.
[9 | 8 | 6]
     ?

9 + 8 + 6 = 23
The 3 boys have **23** marbles altogether.

18.
   245 + 379
[? | 188]

245 + 379 = 624

```
  1 1            5 11 14
  2 4 5          6̶ 2̶ 4̶
+ 3 7 9        − 1 8 8
  6 2 4          4 3 6
```

624 − 188 = 436
Mr. Simon had **436** pieces of fruit left.

19.
          ?
July [| $128]
June [$503]

```
    1
  5 0 3
+ 1 2 8
  6 3 1
```

$503 + $128 = $631
She spent **$631** in July.

20.
November [586]   }
December [? | 253]   } ?

586 − 253 = 333

586 + 333 = 919

```
  5 8 6        5 8 6
− 2 5 3      + 3 3 3
  3 3 3        9 1 9
                1
```

919 visitors went to the zoo in these 2 months.

Unit 5: Multiplying and Dividing Numbers by 2 and 3

1. **6, 8, 12**
2. **9, 12, 18**
3. **8**
4. **12**
5. **15**
6. **16**
7. **27**
8. **9**
9. **21**
10. **18**
11. **18**
12. **10**
13. **10**
14. **5**
15. **6**
16. **3**

17. **6**
18. **9**
19. **5**
20. **4**
21. **8**
22. **9**
23. **10**
24. **7**
25. **8**
26. **6**
27. **7**
28. **4**
29. **6**
30. **5**
31. **5**
32. **8**

33.

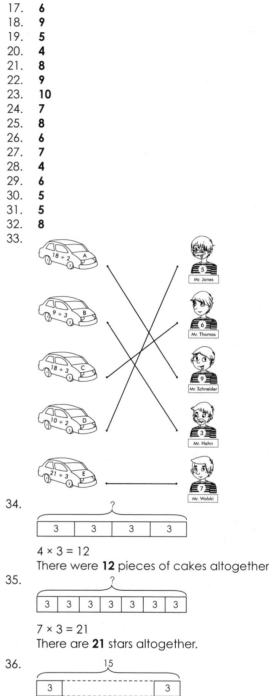

34.
        ?
[3 | 3 | 3 | 3]

4 × 3 = 12
There were **12** pieces of cakes altogether.

35.
              ?
[3 | 3 | 3 | 3 | 3 | 3 | 3]

7 × 3 = 21
There are **21** stars altogether.

36.
         15
[3 |----------| 3]

15 ÷ 3 = 5
There are **5** tricycles.

37.
         14
[2 |----------| 2]

14 ÷ 2 = 7
She gave the muffins to **7** friends.

38.
         27
[3 |----------| 3]

27 ÷ 3 = 9
She will need **9** bags.

39. (a) **8**

$4 \times \$2 = \$8$

(b) **4**

12

$\$12 \div \$3 = 4$

(c) **9**

?

$3 \times \$3 = \$9$

(d) **8**

16

$\$16 \div \$2 = 8$

(e) **12**

?

$4 \times 3 = 12$

40.

12	÷	**2**	=	6
÷				×
6	÷	**2**	=	**3**
=				=
2	×	9	=	18

Unit 6: Multiplying and Dividing Numbers by 4, 5, and 10

1.

Number of cars	1	2	4	**7**	9
Number of wheels	4	8	**16**	28	**36**

$4 \times 4 = 16$ $28 \div 4 = 7$ $9 \times 4 = 36$

2.

Number of hands	2	**4**	6	**9**	10
Number of fingers	10	20	**30**	45	**50**

$20 \div 5 = 4$ $6 \times 5 = 30$ $45 \div 5 = 9$ $10 \times 5 = 50$

3.

Number of vases	3	**5**	7	8	**10**
Number of flowers	30	50	**70**	**80**	100

$50 \div 10 = 5$ $7 \times 10 = 70$ $8 \times 10 = 80$ $100 \div 10 = 10$

4. **24**
5. **15**
6. **30**
7. **45**
8. **30**
9. **80**
10. **36**
11. **70**
12. **8**

13. **35**
14. **6**
15. **2**
16. **4**
17. **8**
18. **6**
19. **9**
20. **3**
21. **10**
22. **2**
23. **4**
24. $5 \times 4 = 20$ $20 \div 5 = 4$
    $4 \times 5 = 20$ $20 \div 4 = 5$
25. $6 \times 4 = 24$ $24 \div 6 = 4$
    $4 \times 6 = 24$ $24 \div 4 = 6$
26. $7 \times 10 = 70$ $70 \div 7 = 10$
    $10 \times 7 = 70$ $70 \div 10 = 7$
27. $8 \times 5 = 40$ $40 \div 8 = 5$
    $5 \times 8 = 40$ $40 \div 5 = 8$
28. $3 \times 4 = 12$ $12 \div 3 = 4$
    $4 \times 3 = 12$ $12 \div 4 = 3$
29.

$6 \times 5 = 30$
There are **30** apples altogether.

30.

?

$8 \times \$10 = \$80$
Sam spends **$80** in 8 weeks.

31.

?

$4 \times \$7 = \$28$
Leyla spent **$28** altogether.

32.

15

$15 \div 3 = 5$
There are **5** buttons on each shirt.

33.

100

$100 \div 10 = 10$
Alicia needs **10** bags.

34.

?

$10 \times \$5 = \$50$
Maggy will save **$50** in 10 months.

Unit 7: Fun With Models (Multiplying and Dividing)

1.

?

$5 \times 10 = 50$
There are **50** stamps in all.

2.

6 × 3 = 18
There are **18** eggs in 6 bags.

3.

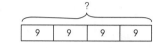

30 ÷ 5 = 6
Each of them has **6** oranges.

4.

4 × 9 = 36
He buys **36** stickers.

5.

18 ÷ 2 = 9
There were **9** sunflowers in each vase.

6.

36 ÷ 4 = 9
Ms. Drew gave the markers to **9** children.

7.

? (bar model with 7 7 7 7 7)

5 × 7 = 35
5 children have **35** library books.

8.

21 (bar model with 3 ... 3)

21 ÷ 3 = 7
She used **7** plates.

Review 3

1.

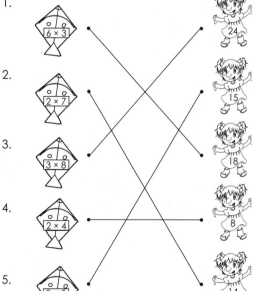

2.

3.

4.

5.

6. **8**
7. **9**
8. **6**
9. **8**
10. **7**
11. **4**
12. **2**
13. **3**
14. **5**
15. **10**
16.

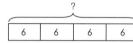

4 × 6 = 24
There are **24** pencils in 4 boxes.

17.

$36 (bar model with ? ? ? ?)

$36 ÷ 4 = $9
Each of them received **$9**.

18.

50 ÷ 5 = 10
Dad gives the muffins to **10** friends.

19.

30 ÷ 6 = 5
There are **5** pieces of each color.

20.

4 × 2 = 8
She buys **8** gloves.

Unit 8: Length

1. **more**
2. **less**
3. **less**
4. **more**
5. **less**
6. (a) **A**
   (b) **B**
   (c) 4 yd. – 2 yd. = **2** yd.
   (d) 6 yd. – 4 yd. = **2** yd.
   (e) 6 yd. – 4 yd. = **2** yd.
   (f) 6 yd. – 2 yd. = **4** yd.
7. (a) **C**
   (b) **B**
   (c) 5 m – 3 m = **2** m
   (d) 3 m – 1 m = **2** m
   (e) 5 m – 1 m = **4** m
   (f) 5 m – 3 m = **2** m
8. *Lines should be the appropiate lengths and labeled correctly.*
9. *Lines should be the appropiate lengths and labeled correctly.*

10. *Lines should be the appropiate lengths and labeled correctly.*
11. **5**
12. **3**
13. **4**
14. **2**
15. **longer than**
16. **longer than**
17. **shorter than**
18. (a) 9 cm – 2 cm = **7** cm
    (b) 13 cm – 10 cm = **3** cm
    (c) 11 cm – 6 cm = **5** cm
    (d) 10 cm – 0 cm = **10** cm
    (e) 10 cm – 3 cm = **7** cm
    (f) 7 cm – 5 cm = **2** cm
    (g) **pencil**
    (h) **eraser**
19. (a) 8 in. – 0 in. = **8** in.
    (b) 5 in. – 0 in. = **5** in.
    (c) 12 in. – 0 in. = **12** in.
    (d) 9 in. – 0 in. = **9** in.
    (e) **C**
    (f) **B**
    (g) 12 in. – 8 in. = **4** in.
    (h) **C**
       9 in. + 3 in. = 12 in.
20. **116**
```
    1
    3 8
  + 7 8
  1 1 6
```
21. **36**
```
  0 11 15
  Ⅹ Ⅻ Ⅹ
  -   8 9
      3 6
```
22. **515**
```
   1 1
   2 3 6
 + 2 7 9
   5 1 5
```
23. **150**
```
   4 6 8
 - 3 1 8
   1 5 0
```
24. **135**
```
  1 9 10
  Ⅹ Ⅹ Ⅹ
  -   6 5
    1 3 5
```
25. **520**
```
   1 1
   3 9 9
 + 1 2 1
   5 2 0
```
26.
```
     1
     2 7 8
   + 5 1 6
     7 9 4
```
278 + 516 = 794
The total length of curtains Miles sewed on both days was **794** in.

27.
```
        ?
  120 m   225 m
```
```
   1 2 0
 + 2 2 5
   3 4 5
```
120 + 225 = 345
She travels **345** m.

28.
```
        ?
  350 yd.   350 yd.
```
```
   1
   3 5 0
 + 3 5 0
   7 0 0
```
350 + 350 = 700
He jogs **700** yd.

29. (a)
```
  Kate   26 cm
  June   ?
           13 cm
```
```
   2 6
 - 1 3
   1 3
```
26 – 13 = 13
June's ribbon is **13** cm long.

(b)
```
        ?
  26 cm   13 cm
```
```
   2 6
 + 1 3
   3 9
```
26 + 13 = 39
The total length of the 2 ribbons is **39** cm long.

30.
```
             ?
  10 in.   10 in.   10 in.
```
3 × 10 = 30
The length of the 3 boxes was **30** in.

31.
```
                      ?
  5 cm 5 cm 5 cm 5 cm 5 cm 5 cm 5 cm 5 cm
```
8 × 5 = 40
The length of 8 toothpicks was **40** cm.

32.
```
         6 ft.
    ?        ?
```
6 ÷ 2 = 3
The length of each piece of rope is **3** ft.

33.
```
          27 cm
  3 cm -------------- 3 cm
```
27 ÷ 3 = 9
Leo has **9** pieces of paper.

34.
```
          32 in.
  4 in. -------------- 4 in.
```
32 ÷ 4 = 8
Gabrielle has **8** pieces of string.

Unit 9: Mass
1. **less than**
   The toy ship rises on the balance, so it is lighter.
2. **more than**
   The camera sinks on the balance, so it is heavier.
3. **less than**
4. **more than**
5. **more than**
6. **3**
7. **45**
8. **6**
9. **4**
10. **6**
11. (a) **4**
    (b) **5**
    (c) **2**

Singapore Math Level 2A & 2B

(d) **bunch of bananas**
(e) **pineapple**
(f) **bunch of bananas, watermelon, pineapple**
12. (a) **171**
(b) **135**
(c) **38**
(d) **Anne**
(e) **Alan**
(f) **Anne, Susan, Alan**
13. **4**
14. **6**
15. **20**
16. **9**
17. **19**
18. **200 g**
19. **450 g**
20. **50 g**
21. **380 g**
22. 500 g – 300 g = **200 g**
23. 30 lb. – 10 lb. = **20 lb.**
24. (a) 20 oz. + 20 oz. = **40 oz.**
(b) 10 oz. + 10 oz. = **20 oz.**
(c) 40 oz. – 20 oz. = **20 oz.**
25. (a) **200 g**
(b) **500 g**
(c) 500 – 200 = **300 g**
26. (b) **35 oz.**

```
    2 0
  + 1 5
    3 5
```

(c) **610 g**

```
    1
    3 6 0
  + 2 5 0
    6 1 0
```

(d) **530 lb.**

```
    1
    1 7 0
  + 3 6 0
    5 3 0
```

(e) **650 kg**

```
    1
    4 1 5
  + 2 3 5
    6 5 0
```

(f) **646 lb.**

```
    1
    5 0 9
  + 1 3 7
    6 4 6
```

(g) **861 g**

```
    1
    8 1 6
  +   4 5
    8 6 1
```

HAMSTER

27. (a) **353 oz.**

```
    5 8 5
  - 2 3 2
    3 5 3
```

(b) **309 g**

```
    0 16
    6 1̶ 6̶
  - 3 0 7
    3 0 9
```

(c) **450 lb.**

```
    8 10
    9̶ 0̶ 0
  - 4 5 0
    4 5 0
```

(d) **189 kg**

```
    2 16
    3̶ 6̶ 9
  - 1 8 0
    1 8 9
```

(e) **199 lb.**

```
    7 12 18
    8̶ 3̶ 8̶
  -  6 3 9
     1 9 9
```

(f) **115 g**

```
      1 10
    6 2̶ 0̶
  - 5 0 5
    1 1 5
```

(g) **149 oz.**

```
    1 13 16
    2̶ 4̶ 6̶
  -   9 7
    1 4 9
```

PUZZLES

28.

50 + 14 + 13 = 77
She uses **77** kg of ingredients altogether.

29.

43 + 10 = 53
Tom's mass is **53** lb.

30.

```
    7 13
    8̶ 3̶
  - 2 7
    5 6
```

83 – 27 = 56
He uses **56** kg of cement.

31.

13 – 4 = 9
Noah's family eats **9** oz. of rice every week.

32.

```
    8 14
    9̶ 4̶ 5
  - 3 8 0
    5 6 5
```

945 – 380 = 565
She bought **565** g of fish.

33.

3 × 2 lb. = 6 lb.
The total mass of the 3 bags of tomatoes was **6** lb.

34.

20 ÷ 5 = 4
Colin bought **4** bags of flour.

35.

10 × 4 = 40
The total mass of the 10 plums is **40** oz.

36.

12 ÷ 4 = 3
The mass of each bag of strawberries was **3** kg.

Singapore Math Level 2A & 2B

Review 4

1. (a) 6 cm – 1 cm = **5** cm
   (b) 10 cm – 1 cm = **9** cm
   (c) 12 cm – 1 cm = **11** cm
   (d) 3 cm – 1 cm = **2** cm
   (e) 11 cm – 9 cm = **2** cm
   (f) 5 cm – 2 cm = **3** cm
   (g) 5 cm + 11 cm = **16** cm
   (h) **rubber band, hair clip, ribbon, comb**
2. **2**
3. **A**
4. **400**
5. (a) 6 cm – 1 cm = **5** cm
   (b) 11 cm – 1 cm = **10** cm
   (c) 8 cm – 1 cm = **7** cm
   (d) 8 cm – 1 cm = **7** cm
   (e) 7 cm – 5 cm = **2** cm
   (f) 10 cm – 7 cm = **3** cm
   (g) **spoon, fork**
   (h) **paintbrush, spoon, fork, key /
       paintbrush, fork, spoon, key**
6. **17**
7. (a) **3**
   (b) **4**
   (c) **2**
   (d) **toy plane**
   (e) **toy ship**
8. **C**
9. **more than**
   The bag of rice sinks on the balance. This shows that the bag of rice is heavier.
10. **less than**
    The purse rises on the balance. This shows that the purse is lighter.
11. **108**
```
      4 0
    + 6 8
    1 0 8
```
12. **356**
```
    3 12 15
    4 3 5
    -   7 9
    3 5 6
```
13. **289**
```
    5 10 16
    6 1 6
    - 3 2 7
    2 8 9
```
14. **350**
```
      1
    1 2 5
    + 2 2 5
    3 5 0
```
15. **772**
```
      1
    6 0 9
    + 1 6 3
    7 7 2
```
16.
525 m

360 m
?

525 – 360 = 165
```
    4 12
    5 2 5
    - 3 6 0
    1 6 5
```
David's house is **165** m farther from the shopping complex than from the supermarket.

17.
?
375 yd.	425 yd.
```
    1 1
    3 7 5
    + 4 2 5
    8 0 0
```
375 + 425 = 800
Amanda jogs **800** yd. from her house to the stadium.

18.
?
8 lb.	8 lb.
2 × 8 = 16
The total mass of her luggage was **16** lb.

19.
15 g
3 g		3 g
15 ÷ 3 = 5
He bought **5** cherries.

20.
?
10 cm	10 cm	10 cm	10 cm	10 cm
5 × 10 = 50
The length of the 5 rulers was **50** cm.

Mid-Review

1. (a) 11 – 3 = **8** in.
   (b) 7 – 2 = **5** in.
   (c) 11 – 2 = **9** in.
   (d) 15 – 5 = **10** in.
   (e) A = 8 – 1 = **7** in.
       7 + 5 = **12** in.
   (f) **E, D, B, A, C**
2. **18**
3. **six hundred and forty-seven**
4. **303, 330, 405, 415, 540**
5. 3 × 9 = **27**
6. 237 + 508 = **745**
```
      1
    2 3 7
    + 5 0 8
    7 4 5
```
7. 717 – 169 = **548**
```
    6 10 17
    7 1 7
    - 1 6 9
    5 4 8
```
8. 10 + 590 = **600**
9. 120 + 10 = **130**
10. **6 × 2 = 12**   **12 ÷ 6 = 2**
    2 × 6 = 12   **12 ÷ 2 = 6**
11. **680, 740**
    720 – 700 = 20
    660 + 20 = 680
    720 + 20 = 740
12. **4, 6, 6**

13. (a) **173 cm**
```
      1
    1 0 5
    + 6 8
    1 7 3
```
   (b) **16 lb.**
```
    2 12
    3 2
    - 1 6
    1 6
```
   (c) **8 × 3 = 24**

(d) **870**

$$\begin{array}{r}{}^{1} \\ 6\ 1\ 2 \\ +\ 2\ 5\ 8 \\ \hline 8\ 7\ 0\end{array}$$

(e) **175**

$$\begin{array}{r}{}^{2\ 9\ 10} \\ \cancel{3}\ \cancel{0}\ \cancel{0} \\ -\ 1\ 2\ 5 \\ \hline 1\ 7\ 5\end{array}$$

14. (a) **83 fewer yellow roses**
    280 − 197 = 83

$$\begin{array}{r}{}^{1\ 17\ 10} \\ \cancel{2}\ \cancel{8}\ \cancel{0} \\ -\ 1\ 9\ 7 \\ \hline 8\ 3\end{array}$$

(b) **595 red and white roses**
315 + 280 = 595

$$\begin{array}{r}3\ 1\ 5 \\ +\ 2\ 8\ 0 \\ \hline 5\ 9\ 5\end{array}$$

15. **$16**

$65 − $49 = $16

$$\begin{array}{r}{}^{5\ 15} \\ \cancel{6}\ \cancel{5} \\ -\ 4\ 9 \\ \hline 1\ 6\end{array}$$

16. **460 cm of cloth**
185 + 275 = 460

$$\begin{array}{r}{}^{1\ \ 1} \\ 1\ 8\ 5 \\ +\ 2\ 7\ 5 \\ \hline 4\ 6\ 0\end{array}$$

17. **7 cards**
35 ÷ 5 = 7

18. (a) **310 dog biscuits**
    460 − 150 = 310

$$\begin{array}{r}4\ 6\ 0 \\ -\ 1\ 5\ 0 \\ \hline 3\ 1\ 0\end{array}$$

(b) **770 dog biscuits**
460 + 310 = 770

$$\begin{array}{r}4\ 6\ 0 \\ +\ 3\ 1\ 0 \\ \hline 7\ 7\ 0\end{array}$$

19. **21 cacti**
3 × 7 = 21

20. **330 yd.**
150 yd. + 180 yd. = 330 yd.

$$\begin{array}{r}{}^{1} \\ 1\ 5\ 0 \\ +\ 1\ 8\ 0 \\ \hline 3\ 3\ 0\end{array}$$

21.

5 × 10 = 50
The mass of the 5 kiwis is **50 g**.

22.

32 ÷ 4 = 8
Mrs. Coleman collected the pages from **8** students.

23. | $2 | $2 | $2 | $2 | $2 |

5 × $2 = $10
She receives **$10** from Monday to Friday.

24. 9 yd.

| ? | ? | ? |

9 ÷ 3 = 3
The length of cloth received by each girl was **3 yd.**

25. ?

| 4 | 4 | 4 |

3 × 4 = 12
He needs **12 days** to make 3 bookshelves.

Challenge Questions

1. first digit: ⑧ or 9
   second digit: 0, ①, 2, 3, 4, 5 or 6
   third digit: 8 − 1 = 7
   The 3-digit number is **817**.

2. Use the guess-and-check method.

Guess	$50	$10	$5	$1	Total
1	1	6	3	1	$126
2	1	7	1	1	$126

He used **one $50 bill, seven $10 bills, one $5 bill, and one $1 bill** to pay for the skateboard.

3.

2 × 6 = 12
Jessica has **12** apples.

4. 0 1 2 ③ 4 5 6 7 8 ⑨
   9 is 3 times 3.
   Both are odd numbers.
   Mr. Schneider's mass is **93 kg**.

5. 9 ÷ 3 = 3
   The sum of the 2 facing pages must be 9.
   page 4 + page 5 = 9
   The 2 facing pages are **4** and **5**.

6.

   Carlos has the shortest ruler.

7.

   27 ÷ 9 = 3
   She had **3** marbles in the beginning.

8. $100 − $20 = $80
   $80 ÷ 4 = $20
   He would receive four $20 bills.
   Simon had one **$100 bill** in the beginning.

9. 2 + 3 + 4 = 9
   The 3 numbers are **2**, **3**, and **4**.

10. 3 × 7 = 21
    The sum of the 2 facing pages is 21.
    page 10 + page 11 = 21
    The 2 facing pages are **10** and **11**.

11.

    Sierra is the heaviest among the 3 children.

Singapore Math Level 2A & 2B

SOLUTIONS
Singapore Math Level 2B

Unit 10: Mental Calculations

1. 64 + 10 = 74
   74 − 2 = **72**
2. 89 + 10 = 99
   99 − 3 = **96**
3. 26 + 10 = 36
   36 − 5 = **31**
4. 18 + 10 = 28
   28 − 1 = **27**
5. 57 + 10 = 67
   67 − 4 = **63**
6. 45 + 10 = 55
   55 − 2 = **53**
7. 37 + 10 = 47
   47 − 5 = **42**
8. 78 + 10 = 88
   88 − 2 = **86**
9. 94 + 10 = 104
   104 − 1 = **103**
10. 56 + 10 = 66
    66 − 3 = **63**
11. 127 + 10 = 137
    137 − 5 = **132**
12. 764 + 10 = 774
    774 − 1 = **773**
13. 2 + 6 = 8
    260 + 8 = **268**
14. 948 + 10 = 958
    958 − 2 = **956**
15. 435 + 10 = 445
    445 − 3 = **442**
16. 4 + 6 = 10
    580 + 10 = **590**
17. 623 + 10 = 633
    633 − 1 = **632**
18. 806 + 10 = 816
    816 − 1 = **815**
19. 366 + 10 = 376
    376 − 5 = **371**
20. 119 + 10 = 129
    129 − 4 = **125**
21. 3 + 6 = 9
    510 + 9 = **519**
22. 30 + 20 = 50
    806 + 50 = **856**
23. 20 + 80 = 100
    703 + 100 = **803**
24. 90 + 70 = 160
    100 + 160 = **260**
25. 20 + 40 = 60
    408 + 60 = **468**

26. 762 + 100 = 862
    862 − 30 = **832**
27. 503 + 100 = 603
    603 − 10 = **593**
28. 869 + 100 = 969
    969 − 20 = **949**
29. 20 + 60 = 80
    603 + 80 = **683**
30. 700 + 200 = 900
    900 + 70 = **970**
31. 300 + 600 = 900
    900 + 23 = **923**
32. 100 + 800 = 900
    900 + 65 = **965**
33. 200 + 500 = 700
    700 + 48 = **748**
34. 600 + 300 = 900
    900 + 57 = **957**
35. 100 + 700 = 800
    800 + 95 = **895**
36. 100 + 200 = 300
    300 + 8 = **308**
37. 500 + 400 = 900
    900 + 88 = **988**
38. 600 + 100 = 700
    700 + 45 = **745**
39. 100 + 600 = 700
    700 + 99 = **799**
40. 700 + 200 = 900
    900 + 56 = **956**
41. 52 − 10 = 42
    42 + 5 = **47**
42. 46 − 10 = 36
    36 + 1 = **37**
43. 81 − 10 = 71
    71 + 2 = **73**
44. 30 − 10 = 20
    20 + 3 = **23**
45. 8 − 3 = 5
    80 + 5 = **85**
46. 9 − 5 = 4
    70 + 4 = **74**
47. 4 − 4 = 0
    60 + 0 = **60**
48. 28 − 10 = 18
    18 + 1 = **19**
49. 3 − 1 = 2
    90 + 2 = **92**
50. 9 − 7 = 2
    50 + 2 = **52**

51. 620 – 10 = 610
    610 + 5 **615**
52. 404 – 10 = 394
    394 + 4 **398**
53. 5 – 4 = 1
    870 + 1 = **871**
54. 10 – 2 = 8
    730 + 8 = **738**
55. 9 – 9 = 0
    510 + 0 = **510**
56. 264 – 10 = 254
    254 + 3 = **257**
57. 9 – 6 = 3
    320 + 3 = **323**
58. 183 – 10 = 173
    173 + 5 = **178**
59. 6 – 3 = 3
    910 + 3 = **913**
60. 534 – 10 = 524
    524 + 2 = **526**
61. 415 – 100 = 315
    315 + 70 = **385**
62. 338 – 100 = 238
    238 + 10 = **248**
63. 80 – 60 = 20
    507 + 20 = **527**
64. 60 – 50 = 10
    800 + 10 = **810**
65. 100 – 10 = 90
    509 + 90 = **599**
66. 80 – 20 = 60
    201 + 60 = **261**
67. 50 – 40 = 10
    708 + 10 = **718**
68. 90 – 70 = 20
    405 + 20 = **425**
69. 164 – 100 = 64
    64 + 20 = **84**
70. 626 – 100 = 526
    526 + 40 = **566**
71. 700 – 300 = 400
    400 + 58 = **458**
72. 800 – 600 = 200
    200 + 34 = **234**
73. 900 – 800 = 100
    100 + 5 = **105**
74. 600 – 500 = 100
    100 + 31 = **131**
75. 900 – 900 = 0
    0 + 78 = **78**
76. 500 – 100 = 400
    400 + 5 = **405**
77. 700 – 400 = 300
    300 + 84 = **384**
78. 400 – 200 = 200
    200 + 35 = **235**
79. 800 – 700 = 100
    100 + 76 = **176**
80. 900 – 800 = 100
    100 + 80 = **180**

Unit 11: Money

1. (a) **$10.00**
   (b) **$2.50**
   (c) **$44.40**
   (d) **$39.85**
   (e) **$67.90**
   (f) **$50.05**
   (g) **$19.70**
   (h) **87¢**
   (i) **$12.15**
   (j) **$20.25**
2. (a) **twelve, thirty**
   (b) **forty-five, forty-five**
   (c) **sixty-seven, five**
   (d) **fifteen, fifty-five**
   (e) **seven, ninety**
   (f) **eleven, eighty**
   (g) **thirty-six, sixty**
   (h) **twenty, fifteen**
   (i) **fifty-nine, ninety-five**
   (j) **seventy, seventy**
3. 10¢ + 10¢ + 5¢ + 5¢ + 5¢ + 5¢ = **40¢**
4. $5 + $1 + $1 + $0.50 = **$7.50**
5. (3 × $10) + (4 × $5) + $0.25 + $0.25 + $0.10 + $0.10 + $0.05 + $0.05 + $0.05 = **$50.85**
6. $10 + $5 + $1 + (4 × $0.25) + $0.10 = **$17.10**
7. (2 × $5) + (4 × $1) + $0.10 + (3 × $0.05) = **$14.25**
8. 50¢ + 10¢ = **60¢**
9. $10.00 + $0.50 = **$10.50**
10. $11.00 + $0.10 = **$11.10**
11. $7.00 + $0.05 = **$7.05**
12. $2.00 + $0.40 = **$2.40**
13. (a) **225**
    (b) **1,050**
    (c) **3,575**
    (d) **5,005**
    (e) **2,735**
    (f) **8,905**
    (g) **10,030**
    (h) **4,040**
    (i) **1,595**
    (j) **2,055**
14. (a) **4.16**
    (b) **18.75**
    (c) **30.05**
    (d) **8.05**
    (e) **17.50**
    (f) **9.60**
    (g) **10.05**
    (h) **76.00**
    (i) **0.18**
    (j) **0.59**
15. (a) **32.50, 26.50**
    (b) **George**
16. (a) **45.90, 55.85**
    (b) **Marcos**
17. (a) **67.80, 65.90**
    (b) **65.90, 67.80**
    (c) **Mrs. Morales**
18. (a) **19.60**
    (b) **26.50**
    (c) **Samira**
    (d) **Kate**

Singapore Math Level 2A & 2B

19.

6 × $3 = $18
She paid **$18** for the books.

20.

peach   55¢
banana   ?   25¢

55¢ − 25¢ = 30¢
55¢ + 30¢ = 85¢
The total cost of the peach and the banana is **85¢**.

21.

Aunt Rose $350
Uncle James $190   }?

$350 + $190 = $540
Uncle James earns $540 in a week.
$350 + $540 = $890
Both of them earn **$890** in a week.

22.
$100
$29 | ?

$100 − $29 = $71
She received **$71** in change.

23.
$40
? ? ? ? ? ? ? ? ? ?

$40 ÷ 10 = $4
He spends **$4** per day.

Review 5

1. **$99.09**
2. 814 + 100 = 914
   914 − 10 = **904**
3. **fifty-five, fifteen**
4. $62.00 + $0.55 = **$62.55**
5. **6,285¢**
6. 600 + 200 = 800
   800 + 4 = **804**
7. (a) **35.55, 30.05**
   (b) **Jerome**
8. 546 − 10 = 536
   536 + 1 = **537**
9. **$38.40**
10. 743 − 100 = 643
    643 + 40 = **683**
11. $36.00 + $0.10 = **$36.10**
12. (a) **42, 45**
    (b) **Uncle Sam**
13. **one hundred, ten**
14. 686 + 10 = 696
    696 − 5 = **691**
15. 700 − 400 = 300
    300 + 12 = **312**
16.
?
$2 | $2 | $2 | $2 | $2 | $2 | $2

7 × $2 = $14
Emma saves **$14** in a week.

17.

$50 − $2 = $48
The calculator cost **$48**.

18.

$49 | $35
?

$49 + $35 = $84
She spent **$84** in all.

19.
?
$7 | $7 | $7

3 × $7 = $21
Uncle Ronald gives **$21** to his children in all.

20.
$60
? | ? | ? | ? | ? | ?

$60 ÷ 6 = $10
Each towel costs **$10**.

Unit 12: Fractions

1. ✓

2. ☐

3. ✓

4. ☐

5. $\frac{1}{4}$

6. $\frac{3}{8}$

7. $\frac{2}{6}$

8. $\frac{7}{12}$

9. $\frac{4}{7}$

Possible answers:

10.

11.

12.

13.

14.

241

Singapore Math Level 2A & 2B

15. (a) **2**

    (b) **4**

    (c) $\frac{2}{4}$

    (d) $\frac{2}{4}$

16. (a) **4**

    (b) **6**

    (c) $\frac{4}{6}$

    (d) $\frac{2}{6}$

17. (a) **4**, **8**

    (b) $\frac{4}{8}$

18. (a) **2**, **5**

    (b) $\frac{2}{5}$

19. (a) **6**, **7**

    (b) $\frac{6}{7}$

20. (a) **6**

    (b) $\frac{2}{8}$

    (c) $\frac{6}{8}$

    (d) $\frac{2}{8}$, $\frac{6}{8}$

21. (a) **2**

    (b) $\frac{3}{5}$

    (c) $\frac{2}{5}$

    (d) $\frac{3}{5}$, $\frac{2}{5}$

22. $\frac{2}{3}$

23. $\frac{1}{2}$

24. $\frac{4}{7}$

25. $\frac{7}{11}$

26. $\frac{3}{12}$

27. $\frac{3}{5}$

28. $\frac{2}{8}$

29. $\frac{6}{9}$

30. $\frac{3}{4}$

31. $\frac{5}{6}$

32. $\boxed{\frac{1}{2}}$

33. $\boxed{\frac{3}{6}}$

34. $\boxed{\frac{5}{7}}$

35. $\boxed{\frac{2}{6}}$

36. $\boxed{\frac{1}{5}}$

37. $\boxed{\frac{6}{12}}$

38. $\frac{1}{8}$

    $\frac{3}{8}$

    $\boxed{\frac{5}{8}}$

39. $\boxed{\frac{2}{6}}$

    $\frac{2}{8}$

    $\frac{2}{10}$

40. $\frac{1}{4}$

    $\frac{2}{4}$

    $\boxed{\frac{3}{4}}$

41. $\frac{3}{9}$

    $\boxed{\frac{2}{9}}$

42. $\frac{4}{5}$

    $\boxed{\frac{4}{8}}$

43. $\frac{8}{10}$

    $\boxed{\frac{6}{10}}$

44. $\boxed{\frac{1}{5}}$

45. $\boxed{\frac{2}{8}}$

46. $\boxed{\frac{3}{8}}$

47. $\boxed{\frac{2}{3}}$

48. $\boxed{\frac{4}{5}}$

49. $\boxed{\frac{7}{10}}$

50. $\boxed{\frac{5}{5}}$

51. $\boxed{\frac{1}{10}}$

Singapore Math Level 2A & 2B

52. $\left(\dfrac{5}{7}\right)$

53. $\left(\dfrac{1}{5}\right)$

54. $\left(\dfrac{4}{7}\right)$

55. $\left(\dfrac{3}{9}\right)$

56. $\dfrac{5}{6}, \dfrac{3}{6}, \dfrac{1}{6}$

57. $\dfrac{2}{3}, \dfrac{2}{8}, \dfrac{2}{9}$

58. $\dfrac{4}{10}, \dfrac{4}{11}, \dfrac{4}{12}$

59. $\dfrac{1}{12}, \dfrac{1}{11}, \dfrac{1}{10}$

60. $\dfrac{3}{9}, \dfrac{3}{6}, \dfrac{3}{5}$

61. $\dfrac{5}{12}, \dfrac{5}{10}, \dfrac{5}{9}$

62. $\dfrac{3}{8}$

63. $\dfrac{7}{10}$

64. $\dfrac{10}{12}$

65. $\dfrac{6}{7}$

66. $\dfrac{8}{9}$

67. $\dfrac{4}{5}$

68. $\dfrac{4}{6}$

69. $\dfrac{6}{11}$

70. $\dfrac{2}{4}$

71. $\dfrac{2}{9}$

72. $\dfrac{5}{7}$

73. $\dfrac{9}{10}$

74. $\dfrac{2}{6}$

75. $\dfrac{3}{11}$

76. $\dfrac{3}{8}$

77. $\dfrac{3}{12}$

78.

$\dfrac{5}{5} - \dfrac{2}{5} = \dfrac{3}{5}$

$\dfrac{3}{5}$ of the bread is left.

79.

M	F	F	F	K						M: Mom

M: Mom
F: Dad
K: Kaylee

$\dfrac{1}{10} + \dfrac{3}{10} + \dfrac{1}{10} = \dfrac{5}{10}$

They have eaten $\dfrac{5}{10}$ of the pizza.

80.

P: Pencil case
D: Drawing materials

$\dfrac{1}{7} + \dfrac{3}{7} = \dfrac{4}{7}$

She used $\dfrac{4}{7}$ of her weekly allowance.

81.

D: Drank

$\dfrac{8}{8} - \dfrac{3}{8} = \dfrac{5}{8}$

$\dfrac{5}{8}$ of the pitcher of orange juice was left.

82.

C: Children
W: Women

$\dfrac{1}{6} + \dfrac{3}{6} = \dfrac{4}{6}$

$\dfrac{4}{6}$ of the people at the party are children and women.

Unit 13: Time

1.

7:10

2. 4×5 minutes = **20**

3. 9×5 minutes = **45**

4. 1×5 minutes = **5**

5. 3×5 minutes = **15**

6. **ten o'clock / 10:00**

7. **five-fifteen / 5:15**

8. **one-thirty / 1:30**

9. **twelve o'clock / 12:00**

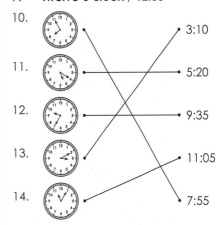

10. → 3:10

11. → 5:20

12. → 9:35

13. → 11:05

14. → 7:55

Singapore Math Level 2A & 2B

15.
16.
17.
18.
19.
20.
21.
22.
23.
24.
25.
26.
27.
28.
29.
30.

31. **A.M.**
32. **P.M.**
33. **P.M.**
34. **A.M.**
35. **P.M.**
36. **8:30,**
    8 o'clock / 8:00
37. **5 o'clock / 5:00,**
    4:30
38. **7:30, 6:30**
39. **9 o'clock / 9:00,**
    12 o'clock / 12:00
40. **6:15, 10:15**
41. **11:00 A.M.**

42. **7:00 P.M.**

43. **5:00 A.M.**

44. **4:00 P.M.**

45. **12:00 noon**

Review 6

1. (b)

(c)

2.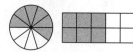

3.

244

4. **10:25**
5. **5:00 / 5 o'clock**
6. **8:55**
7. **7:30**
8.
9.
10.
11.
12. $\dfrac{6}{7}, \dfrac{5}{7}, \dfrac{1}{7}$
13. $\dfrac{4}{8}, \dfrac{5}{8}, \dfrac{7}{8}$
14.

    11 A.M.
15.

    1:30 P.M.
16.

    10:15 A.M.
17.

Anton	Jack
	?

    $1 - \dfrac{1}{2} = \dfrac{2}{2} - \dfrac{1}{2} = \dfrac{1}{2}$

    Jack ate $\dfrac{1}{2}$ of the dish of nachos.
18.

D	D	J	J	J

    D: Deepak
    J: John

    $\dfrac{2}{6} + \dfrac{3}{6} = \dfrac{5}{6}$

    They ate $\dfrac{5}{6}$ of the melon.
19.

D	D	D	D		

    D: Drank

$1 - \dfrac{4}{7} = \dfrac{7}{7} - \dfrac{4}{7} = \dfrac{3}{7}$

$\dfrac{3}{7}$ of the milk was left in the glass.

20.

R	R		

R: Read

$1 - \dfrac{2}{5} = \dfrac{5}{5} - \dfrac{2}{5} = \dfrac{3}{5}$

Tariq needs to read $\dfrac{3}{5}$ of the book in order to complete it.

Unit 14: Volume

1. (a) **more**
    (b) **less**
2. (a) **less**
    (b) **more**
3. (a) **D**
    (b) **B**
4. (a) **B**
    (b) **A**
5. (a) **D**
    (b) **B**
6. (a) **jug**
    (b) **bowl**
    (c) $5 - 2 = $ **3**
    (d) $8 - 2 = $ **6**
7. **3**
8. **5**
9. **15**
10. **2**
11. $1 + 1 + 1 = $ **3**
12. $2 + 2 + 2 + 2 = $ **8**
13. $2 + 2 = $ **4**
14. $1 + 1 + 1 = $ **3**
15.

2 gal.	2 gal.

    2×2 gal. = 4 gal.
    The fish tank is filled with **4 gal.** of water.
16.

3 L	5 L

    $3 L + 5 L = 8 L$
    They prepare **8 L** of drink altogether.
17.

4 gal.	3 gal.	5 gal.

    4 gal. + 3 gal. + 5 gal. = 12 gal.
    The tank can hold **12 gal.** of water.
18.

2 L	?

    8 L

    $8 L - 2 L = 6 L$
    Ayesha has **6 L** of orange juice left.
19.

10 gal.	20 gal.

    10 gal. + 20 gal. = 30 gal.
    Mr. Benson put **30 gal.** of gas in his car in all.

20.

16 L ÷ 4 L = 4
She used **4** jugs.

Unit 15: Graphs

1. (a) 4 × 4 = **16**
   (b) 6 × 4 = **24**
   (c) 2 × 4 = 8
       16 − 8 = **8**
   (d) 3 × 4 = 12
       24 − 12 = **12**
   (e) **monkeys**
   (f) **lions**
2. (a) **Wednesday**
   (b) 50 ÷ 5 = **10**
   (c) 4 × 10 = **40**
   (d) 7 × 10 = 70
       70 − 40 = **30**
   (e) 3 × 10 = 30
       40 − 30 = **10**
   (f) 50 + 70 = **120**
3. Rabbits → 6 ÷ 2 = 3☆
   Turtles → 10 ÷ 2 = 5☆
   Fish → 20 ÷ 2 = 10☆
   Cats → 8 ÷ 2 = 4☆
   Birds → 14 ÷ 2 = 7☆

4. (a) **Coloring**
       7 × 4 = 28
   (b) **Fiction**
       3 × 4 = 12
   (c) **Coloring**
       6 × 4 = 24
       28 − 24 = 4
   (d) **4**
       4 × 4 = 16
       16 − 12 = 4
   (e) **12**
       28 − 16 = 12
5. (a) **25**
       5 × 5 = 25
   (b) **20**
       Friday → 7 × 5 = 35
       Tuesday → 3 × 5 = 15
       35 − 15 = 20
   (c) **8**
       2 × 5 = 10
       10 − 2 = 8

(d) **95**
    Saturday → 9 × 5 = 45
    Sunday → 10 × 5 = 50
    45 + 50 = 95
(e) **9**
    5 × 5 = 25
    25 − 16 = 9

Review 7

1. **5**
2. **2**
3. **10**
4. (a) 6 × 3 = **18**
   (b) 5 × 3 = **15**
   (c) Roast chicken → 3 × 3 = 9
       Tacos → 6 × 3 = 18
       18 − 9 = **9**
   (d) Pizza → 8 × 3 = 24
       Meatloaf → 4 × 3 = 12
       24 − 12 = **12**
   (e) Spaghetti → 5 × 3 = 15
       12 + 15 = **27**
5. (a) **jug**
   (b) **cup**
   (c) 10 − 2 = **8**
   (d) 8 − 2 = **6**
   (e) 8 + 10 + 2 = **20**
6. Shrimp → 6 ÷ 2 = 3 ☺
   Crab → 14 ÷ 2 = 7 ☺
   Fish → 20 ÷ 2 = 10 ☺
   Squid → 8 ÷ 2 = 4 ☺

7.

2 × 8 oz. = 16 oz.
Riley bought **16 oz.** of fruit juice.

8. (a)

10 L + 8 L = 18 L
Li makes **18 L** of lemonade.

(b)

18 L − 3 L = 15 L
She will have **15 L** of lemonade left.

9.

10 gal. + 15 gal. = 25 gal.
She collected **25 gal.** of rainwater altogether.

10.

5 L – 2 L = 3 L
3 L of milk was left.

11. (a)

| 10 gal. | 5 gal. |

10 gal. + 5 gal. = 15 gal.
Andy bought **15 gal.** of drinks.

(b)

| 15 gal. | ? |
20 gal.

20 gal. – 15 gal. = 5 gal.
He needed to buy **5** more gallons of drinks.

12.

| 8 L | 25 L |
?

25 L + 8 L = 33 L
Eva bought **33 L** of liquid detergent altogether.

13.

| 2 gal. | 2 gal. | 2 gal. | 2 gal. | 2 gal. | 2 gal. |
?

6 × 2 gal. = 12 gal.
He removed **12 gal.** of water from the tank.

14.

| ? | ? | ? | ? |
24 L

24 L ÷ 4 = 6 L
There was **6 L** of orange juice in each container.

15.

| 3 gal. | 3 gal. | 3 gal. | 3 gal. | 3 gal. |
?

5 × 3 gal. = 15 gal.
She collects **15 gal.** of used water every week.

16.

| 2 L | 2 L | 2 L | 2 L | 2 L | 2 L | 2 L | 2 L | 2 L | 2 L |
?

10 × 2 L = 20 L
She drinks **20 L** of water in 10 days.

17.

| 17 gal. | 25 gal. |
?

17 gal. + 25 gal. = 42 gal.
He brews **42 gal.** of coffee and tea every day.

18.
36 gal.

| 4 gal. | - - - - - - - - | 4 gal. |

36 gal. ÷ 4 gal. = 9
She needs **9** containers.

19.

| 2 L | 2 L | 2 L | 2 L | 2 L | 2 L | 2 L | 2 L |
?

8 × 2 L = 16 L
Alyssa bought **16 L** of detergent.

20.
35 gal.

| 5 gal. | - - - - - - - - | 5 gal. |

35 gal. ÷ 5 gal. = 7
He washed **7** cars if he used 35 gal. of water.

Unit 16: Lines and Surfaces

1. (a) **4, 7**
   (b) **3, 8**
   (c) **2, 5**
2. **8, 4**
3. **5, 2**
4. **6, 1**
5. **6, 2**
6. **4, 1**
7. **1**
8. **6**
9. **6**
10. **1**
11. **2**
12. **6**
13. **5**
14. **0**
15. **5**

Unit 17: Shapes and Patterns

1. rectangle
2. triangle
3. square
4. quarter circle
5. circle
6. triangle
7. semicircle
8. triangle, semicircle
9. triangle, rectangle
10. circle, square
11. triangle, quarter circle
12. rectangle, circle
13. (a) **3**
    (b) **4**
    (c) **3**
    (d) **6**
    (e) **8**
    (f) **2**
14.
15.
16.
17. triangle
18. circle
19. semicircle
20. rectangle
21. quarter circle
22. square

Singapore Math Level 2A & 2B

23.

24.

25.

26.

27.

28.

29.

30.

31.

32.

33.

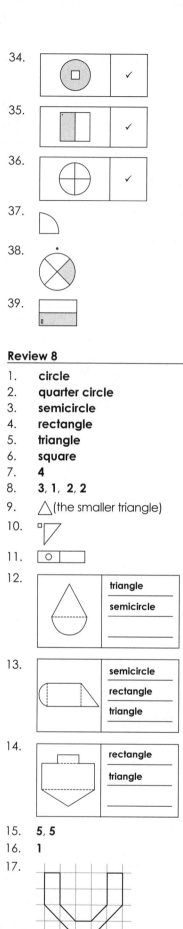

34. ✓

35. ✓

36. ✓

37.

38.

39.

Review 8

1. **circle**
2. **quarter circle**
3. **semicircle**
4. **rectangle**
5. **triangle**
6. **square**
7. **4**
8. **3, 1, 2, 2**
9. △ (the smaller triangle)
10.
11.
12. triangle
     semicircle
13. semicircle
     rectangle
     triangle
14. rectangle
     triangle
15. **5, 5**
16. **1**
17.

18. Color the **book**, **rectangle**, and **stamp**.

19.

20.

Final Review

1. $\frac{5}{8}$

2. (a) $5 \times 10 = $ **50**
   (b) $7 \times 10 = $ **70**
   (c) Monday $\rightarrow 4 \times 10 = 40$
       Friday $\rightarrow 6 \times 10 = 60$
       $60 - 40 = $ **20**
   (d) Tuesday $\rightarrow 3 \times 10 = 30$
       Saturday $\rightarrow 8 \times 10 = 80$
       $80 - 30 = $ **50**
   (e) Wednesday $\rightarrow 2 \times 10 = 20$
       $40 + 20 = $ **60**

3. **12:20 P.M.**

4. (a)
   (b)

5. $1\,L + 1\,L = 2\,L$
   1 jug can hold 2 L of water.
   $3 \times 2\,L = $ **6 L**

6.

7. $790 + 100 = 890$
   $890 - 30 = $ **860**

8. $\frac{5}{5} - \frac{2}{5} = \frac{3}{5}$

9.

10. **semicircle**, **rectangle**

11. **C**
    $\frac{2}{4}$ of Figure C is shaded, while $\frac{1}{4}$ of the rest of the figures are shaded.

12. $10 \times 10 = 100$
    $\triangle = 10$
    $5 \times 5 = 25$
    $\bigcirc = 5$
    $10 \times 5 = $ **50**

13. $\frac{7}{10}$

14.

15. $\left(\frac{1}{9}\right)$
    $\frac{1}{9}$ is the largest, and $\frac{1}{12}$ is the smallest.

16. **forty-eight**, **thirty**

17. $345 - 100 = 245$
    $245 + 10 = $ **255**

18. **$90.80**

19. $\frac{5}{11} - \frac{2}{11} = \frac{3}{11}$

20. Sydney | $30 | $30 | ?
    $30 + 30 = 60
    Sydney spent **$60**.

21. 5 5 5 5 5 5 5 | ?
    $7 \times 5 = 35$
    He gave **35** cans of juice to his friends.

22. 129 | 257 | 229 | ?
    $129 + 257 = 386$
    $386 + 229 = 615$
    615 students took part in the art competition.

23. 4 4 4 4 4 4 4 | ?
    $7 \times 4 = 28$
    He will read **28** books in a week.

24. 228 L | ? — 600 L
    $600\,L - 228\,L = 372\,L$
    Jack makes **372 L** of fruit punch.

25. $30 | $50 | ?
    $50 + 30 = 80
    Malak received **$80** in all.

Challenge Questions

1. 1 day $\rightarrow$ 4 pieces of clothing
   10 days $\rightarrow 10 \times 4 = 40$ pieces of clothing
   Mrs. Robinson sewed **40** pieces of clothing in 10 days.

2.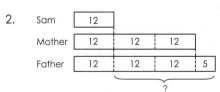

$2 \times 12 = 24$
$24 + 5 = 29$
Sam's father is **29** years older than Sam.

3.

18	10	13	41
11	15	16	42
14	17	12	43
43	42	41	

4.

5 min. slower   5 min. faster

Henry's watch   Classroom clock   Carlos's watch   9:50 A.M.

$5 + 5 = 10$
10 min. before 9:50 A.M. is 9:40 A.M.
The time shown on Henry's watch was **9:40 A.M.**

5. $2 \heartsuit \rightarrow 80$
$1 \heartsuit \rightarrow 80 \div 2 = 40$
$40 + \triangle = 120$
$\triangle = 120 - 40 = 80$
$\heartsuit + \triangle + \triangle + \triangle \rightarrow 40 + 80 + 80 + 80 = \textbf{280}$

6. Use the guess-and-check method.

	1st number	2nd number	1st number × 2nd number
Guess 1	1	50	
Guess 2	2	25	50
Guess 3	5	10	

The result of the division of the 2 numbers in Guess 1 and Guess 2 do not equal 2.
$10 \div 5 = 2$
The 2 numbers are **5** and **10**.

7.

B	N	L

B: Best friend
N: Neighbor
L: Left

Since $\frac{1}{4}$ of the bottle of orange juice was left, the amount of juice Christopher gave to his neighbor was also $\frac{1}{4}$.

$1 - \frac{1}{4} - \frac{1}{4} = \frac{4}{4} - \frac{1}{4} - \frac{1}{4} = \frac{2}{4} = \frac{1}{2}$

Christopher gave his best friend $\frac{2}{4}$ or $\frac{1}{2}$ of the bottle of orange juice.

8.

1 hr.   2 hr.   3 hr.

?   10 P.M.

$1 + 2 + 3 = 6$ hr.
6 hr. before 10 P.M. is 4 P.M.
He started watching cartoons at **4 P.M.**

9. **26**
The types of triangles in the figure are ◺, ◹, ▽, △,
◁, ▷, ◩ and ◪.

10. Use the guess-and-check method.
$8 \times 4 = 32$
$8 \div 4 = 2$
$8 + 4 = 12$
$(\!(\,- \diamondsuit = 8 - 4 = \textbf{4}$

11.

12. Rico stepped out of the bathroom at 1:20 P.M.

30 min.   1 hr.   20 min.

?   1:20 P.M.

30 min. + 1 hr. + 20 min. = 1 hr. 50 min.
1 hr. 50 min. before 1:20 P.M. is 11:30 A.M.

Singapore Math Level 2A & 2B

Notes

Notes

Notes

Notes

Singapore Math Level 2A & 2B

Notes

Notes

Singapore Math Level 2A & 2B